THE St. Thérèse of Lisieux

"Once again the vivid and penetrating biography of this luminous soul by Msgr. Laveille is made available. . . . Msgr. Laveille has drawn back the curtain and shown us the beauty of this soul as seen from without. Many details not mentioned by the Saint herself, either out of humility or not considered as coming under the scope of the work commanded by her superiors, are here seen for the first time. A detailed account of her early childhood and family life are given. It at once becomes evident where the seeds were planted which were to bloom forth so gloriously and thus illuminate the path for other little souls to follow."

Dominicana Journal (1952)

"This new edition of Msgr. Laveille's biography of St. Thérèse of Lisieux is a welcomed addition to the literature about her because it offers a window into how Thérèse was presented to the world at the time of her canonization."

Maureen O'Riordan

Curator of *Saint Therese of Lisieux: A Gateway*

"What is it that accounts for the perennial appeal of this gem of a biography, which is at once both timely and timeless? The author shows how simple, childlike souls, like that of Thérèse, bring superior intelligence to bear on the truths of faith."

From the foreword by **Susan Muto**

Author of *Twelve Little Ways to Transform Your Heart*

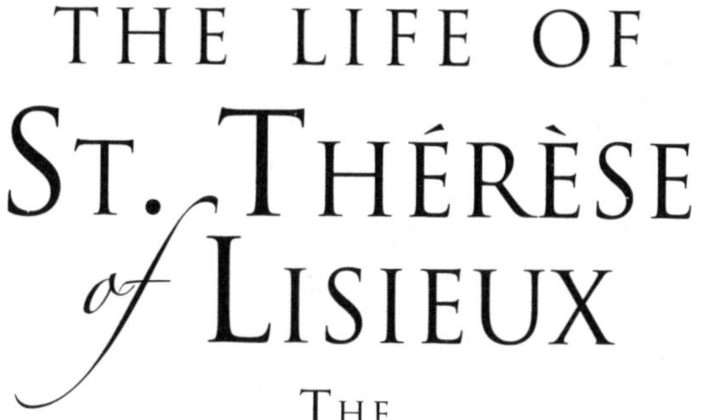

THE

ORIGINAL BIOGRAPHY

COMMISSIONED

by HER SISTER

AUGUST PIERRE LAVEILLE

Translated by Rev. M. Fitzsimons, O.M.I.
Foreword by Susan Muto

Christian Classics *Notre Dame, Indiana*

First published in English in 1929.
Nihil Obstat: Georgius D. Smith, *Censor deputatus.*
Imprimatur: Edm. Can. Surmont, *Vicarius generalis.*
Westmonasterii
Die 26a Novembris, 1928

Founded in 1865, Ave Maria Press is a ministry of the United States Province of Holy Cross.

www.christian-classics.com

Paperback: ISBN-13 978-0-87061-302-9

E-book: ISBN-13 978-0-87061-303-6

Cover images © Office Central de Lisieux and iStockphoto.com.

Cover and text design by Katherine Robinson.

Printed and bound in the United States of America.

Library of Congress Cataloging-in-Publication Data

Names: Laveille, August Pierre, 1856-1928, author. | Fitzsimons, M., 1896-1963, translator. | Muto, Susan, 1942- writer of foreword.

Title: The life of St. Thĕrĕse of Lisieux : the original biography commissioned by her sister / August Pierre Laveille ; translated by Rev. M. Fitzsimons, O.M.I. ; foreword by Susan Muto.

Other titles: Sainte Thĕrĕse de l'Enfant-Jĕsus. English

Description: Notre Dame, Indiana : Christian Classics, 2017. | "First published in English in 1929." | Includes bibliographical references and index.

Identifiers: LCCN 2016050670 (print) | LCCN 2016051735 (ebook) | ISBN 9780870613029 (pbk.) | ISBN 9780870613036

Subjects: LCSH: Thĕrĕse, de Lisieux, Saint, 1873-1897. | Christian saints--France--Lisieux--Biography.

Classification: LCC BX4700.T5 L3313 2017 (print) | LCC BX4700.T5 (ebook) |
DDC 282.092 [B] --dc23

LC record available at https://lccn.loc.gov/2016050670

Contents

Foreword to the New Edition

Story of a Soul, the story of St. Thérèse of Lisieux (1873–1897) as told in her own words, is a classic beloved by many readers. This unforgettable biography gives her legacy new life. As the "official biographer" commissioned by his subject's biological sister and religious superior, Mother Pauline, Monsignor Laveille's task was to create the definitive account of Thérèse's life. While Msgr. Laveille references in several notes earlier biographical works that may have been of interest to him,[1] his was the first complete biography composed according to the official documents of the Carmel of Lisieux and his own collected eyewitness accounts.

His love for the Little Flower allows him to go beyond mere history to the heart of her life of holiness. Msgr. Laveille has an uncanny ability to connect external events, such as the tragic death of her mother in 1877, to the growth of Thérèse's interior life. Each chapter embellishes the guiding motif of this work of love: Thérèse's discovery and practice of the "little way of confidence and abandonment."

What is it that accounts for the perennial appeal of this gem of a biography, which is at once both timely and timeless? The author reports the events of Thérèse's life with eyewitness accuracy. Unique as they are, they acquire universal significance. The author shows how simple, childlike souls, like that of Thérèse, bring superior intelligence to bear on the truths of faith. Under her loving gaze, a flower becomes a pointer to God's creative extravagance in creation. The dark nights associated with physical suffering are not dead ends; rather, they bolster one's spiritual strength and release supernatural graces beneficial to every member of Christ's Mystical Body. Similarly, the death of the young, seemingly before their time, serves to awaken in the faithful renewed confidence in the goodness of God.

Msgr. Laveille begins his book by walking us through Thérèse's ancestral origins dating to the sixteenth century, including references to military bravery ennobled by

Catholic faith that were part of her lineage. He also recounts the early lives of her saintly parents, Louis and Zélie Martin (canonized by the Church in October 2015).

Of Louis, a skilled clockmaker, the author writes: "At the sight of the flashing dawn or the waning sunset his handsome and clear-cut face reflected in turn his gladness in the beauty of the divine plan, or his sadness at parting with things which must pass with the day" (see p. 4).

In Zélie Guérin, a gifted manufacturer of point lace, Louis found his soul-mate. "The newly-married pair realized every day more and more the blessing of mutual charity" (see p. 8).

Both Louis and Zélie accepted in faith the sorrow of death, including that of their parents, sons, and even their grandchildren. Zélie wrote to her sister-in-law, who had carried a similar cross: "When I closed the eyes of my dear little children, when I laid them in the grave, my grief, though great, was always resigned. . . . I realize that my pain and anxiety cannot be compared to the eternal happiness of my dear children. They are not lost to me forever. Life is short and full of sorrow; we shall meet again in heaven" (see p. 17).

How prophetic these words were! While her four daughters (Léonie, Pauline, Céline, and Thérèse) would come to maturity and find their calling in the religious life, their beloved mother was destined to leave this world on August 28, 1877. With skill and compassion the author describes Thérèse's loss and the transformation she underwent after Mme. Martin's death.

By frequently citing her own words from *Story of a Soul* and through his interpretation of them as her biographer, Msgr. Laveille lets us see the source of Thérèse's ability to endure suffering and to discover its mystical meaning.

It was Divine Love. She saw it in action when she accompanied her father to Mass in the morning and went with him on pilgrimage to Paris and Rome. We trace every step of Thérèse's convent education and the lessons of love she learned there. During the family's move from Alençon to Lisieux, we witness the poignancy of her quest to grow beyond childishness to mature spiritual childhood, culminating in her father's loving gift of his daughter to the family of Carmel.

We see in these distinctions and deeds not only the guiding hand of Holy Providence but also the secret of Thérèse's sainthood: she does nothing on her own but everything in response to the beckoning of her Beloved.

The author wisely weaves the events of her life around a series of paradoxes. Bound by virtue of obedience to an obscure convent life, Thérèse becomes patroness of the missions. Countless suffering souls receive the benefits of the "rain of roses" she promised to send them after her death, making good on her promise to "spend my heaven doing good on earth." It was a promise, the author recollects, carved upon the wooden cross along with her name at the head of her grave: *"Jesus veux passer mon ciel a faire du bien sur la terre."*

What makes this book such a treasure are the small, personal details about the Little Flower. Because her announcement ("I will spend my heaven doing good on earth") was so promptly realized, it made "of this lowly mound crowned with lilies and roses a shrine of supplication and thanksgiving almost unparalleled in the whole world" (see p. 332).

Thérèse considered death a brief passage to eternal life, saying as the author records, "I feel that my mission is about to begin, my mission to make the good God loved as I love Him" (see p. 333).

This biography not only deserves to be read for its remarkable reporting; it ought also to be meditated upon for its everyday witness to the beauty of faith. We are at Thérèse's side when she fully converts to Christ, finds her vocation to love, and enters periods of great trial and greater triumph. We praise with the Lord the way in which she is able to discern the connection between the sacrifices asked of souls by God and the eternal reward awaiting them.

Under the steady gaze of his discerning eye, Msgr. Laveille lets us see how a soul on fire with the love of God finds a way to turn her multiple weaknesses into magnificent virtues. She transforms with the help of grace every selfish tendency into an act of charity.

Of the many accolades this Christian classic deserves, one of the most obvious concerns the author's ability to help us experience Thérèse's landscape as she experienced it. He follows with the precision of a master biographer every facet of her chronology. Impressive as well is the candid expression of his own love for the saint he chronicles. The book builds chapter after chapter to his final reflections on the gift of spiritual childhood that drew Thérèse to the heights of union with God: "To place oneself in the hands of God, and in confidence, love, and abandonment, allow oneself to be carried by Him to the highest pinnacle of charity by means of perfect correspondence with His grace—such is the 'little way'" (see p. 274).

To dwell on the descriptions of Thérèse's life offered in this classical biography yields great personal rewards. The truth is that feeble as our finite efforts to be a saint may be, they usher us into the loving embrace of the Infinite.

The author's filial gratitude to Thérèse becomes by the book's end our own. He takes us through the details of her canonization process and the many marvels attributed to her. In conclusion, he cites the discourse of His Holiness, Pope Pius XI on the occasion of the approbation of her miracles on February 11, 1923. The pope's words seem to me to characterize this classic itself: "This silent flower, these petals of resplendent hue, this perfume which fills the air, this beauty that displays itself only for the eyes of God, is not this the little Thérèse de l'Enfant Jésus?" (see p. 354).

Though her mystery, like that of any saint, may be impossible to penetrate, Msgr. Laveille succeeds in an extraordinary way in breathing new life into an already beautiful portrait.

Susan Muto, PhD
June 30, 2015

Preface to the Original French Edition

Letter to the Author from Monseigneur Baudrillart

Catholic Institute of Paris
74, Rue de Vaugirard

September 12, 1925

Monseigneur and dear Confrère,

You have graciously announced to me the publication in the near future of your *Life of St. Thérèse de l'Enfant Jésus.* The news has filled me with joy both on your account and hers, a sentiment which I had experienced the moment I learned that the Carmelites of Lisieux had chosen you to write a complete biography of their dear saint.

Assuredly, other biographies have already popularized this touching and holy life—biographies, too, of undeniable merit. Something more, however, remained to be done; it was fitting that a biography, definite as possible in facts, rich in document and doctrine, should be given to the clients of her in whose honour sanctuaries of prayer are being raised throughout the Christian world, and whom millions honour with tender devotion in the hidden sanctuary of the heart.

Who among spiritual biographers of our day is possessed of wider experience or surer doctrine than yours? How numerous the saints, both men and women, how many the Founders and Foundresses, whom you have already studied in their life and works. What a number of diverse figures have been delineated by your pen. How many minds and characters, differing widely, yet all one in a common sanctity, you have intimately known.

Has not your historian's pen therein acquired a singular suppleness, your judgement a more searching keenness?

In this special work, however, the ordinary qualities of the writer and historian, be they even possessed in an eminent degree, are not sufficient. The sense of the supernatural must be there, added to a profound knowledge of ascetic and mystical theology.

In all these respects nothing is wanting to you. Were you not formed in that grand school of spirituality of Bérulle and Condren which Abbé Brémond so justly calls the French school of the seventeenth century? Have you not for years taught in the Scholasticate and Novitiate of the Oratory, showing priestly souls the road to perfection? Have you not also found the Carmel closely associated with the beginnings of the Oratory in France?

Surely all these reasons point you out for the delicate task of depicting a life original in its extreme simplicity. You are indeed in a position to understand it completely.

That the word "original" will be disputed I have no doubt. In the opinion of many, original is but a polite word for eccentric. Original it is, however, amongst all the lives of the saints, because in it the development of the interior life is not supported by a chain of external events of notable importance or of actions capable of attracting attention. What could be more disconcerting than this to the historian who is merely an historian? "Where shall I begin—what facts are there to take hold of?" he anxiously asks himself.

Neither are there in evidence those extraordinary trials which call forth the special talent of the psychologist or theologian. A "little way of confidence and abandonment" lovingly followed for a few years under the guidance of a very holy rule; that is all.

All, yes; but how priceless that *all*! What consolation is to be found therein for the thousands whose lives are spent without events worthy of notice, but not without trial and suffering. What consolation, what example, and what comfort, too. What a blessing it is that the lessons of such a life should be brought to light by a master-hand.

Do not expect from me, dear Monseigneur, what is called a letter of approbation for your work. It would be of no advantage, and I would not presume to write thus to you. I have allowed my admiration for the author and for his undeniable talent to dictate these lines. This is not, however, the only motive which has determined me to write them, and to authorize their publication if you judge proper.

The Rector of the Catholic Institute of Paris knows that he owes a particular debt of recognition to St. Thérèse de l'Enfant Jésus. He would hold himself ungrateful if he did not seize every opportunity of proclaiming the singular blessings, "the shower of roses" which, in times of difficulty, the dear little saint has shed over the University he directs. He has experienced her immediate protection, and even at the risk of astonishing certain intellectuals, he will ever continue to proclaim the fact.

Likewise, he will meditate, and incite others to meditate, on the lessons which the life of St. Thérèse directly holds for "intellectuals."

The lesson of simplicity. I do not deny that there are men of superior intelligence, accustomed to the highest studies and most learned research, whose souls remain as simple as that of a child in presence of religious truths. In the measure that they remain simple before men, are they so before God. These, unfortunately, are exceptions. The greater number esteem themselves too great and too strong to submit their intelligence. Or, on the other hand, they require so many arguments, and place so many conditions, that they are never satisfied. Let them turn their eyes to this sweet child, white and straight as a lily, whose gaze is fixed peacefully on the highest truths, where candour of soul brings with it light to the understanding.

The lesson of faith amid trials to that faith. Whatever the candour and good will of a soul, it is almost impossible in a time like ours that a man who studies and thinks, who by force of circumstances and the necessities of his work finds himself confronted with many diverse systems, is not at some time or other tried in his faith. God, then, in His infinite wisdom ordained that this same child should experience in the midst of severe physical sufferings the anguish of this trial of faith, and that though living in the very heart of the supernatural, she should feel doubts about the reality of the supernatural. And withal her faith never wavered, any more than that of St. Vincent de Paul when severely tempted in faith regarding the Blessed Eucharist.

Lessons of confidence, too, in the ultimate effects, distant perhaps, yet certain, of all work done for God. How many times we have felt that we work in vain, that we speak and write without result. Our work remains obscure, or we appear to bear no fruit whatever. And still we labour for God and our neighbour. Why, then, such poor result? Listen to little Sœur Thérèse. When about to die at the age of twenty-four, she uttered these astonishing words: "I feel that my mission is now to begin." God will choose the moment when He will draw from our efforts the good He desires; nothing that has been done for Him will be definitely lost.

Sometimes even glory, the glory so dear to those who seek to influence the minds of men, will come abundantly. And I speak not only of the glory which in heaven is the fruit of grace, the crown of a saintly life. Is there, humanly speaking, in the world today a glory equal to that of our humble Carmelite? What name is more frequently on men's lips—what hero's portrait has been so rapidly multiplied, so widely scattered?

Her renown carries the name of the little town in which she lived to the ends of the earth. Beautiful town of Lisieux, long appreciated by those who know it, charmingly situated in the midst of rich and fragrant valleys and tree-studded plains, possessed of the most beautiful and artistic monuments in Normandy, its old houses jealously preserved; astir, too, with industrial activity, thus joining modern life to history without taking away any of its beauty—what more was wanting to this town? And yet, how few visited it, how few even mentioned its name!

The name became united with that of Thérèse, and behold, Lisieux has become a world-city equal to the most celebrated. As Teresa and Avila, Angela and Foligno, Francis and Assisi, so Thérèse and Lisieux have become inseparable names. Pilgrims come in crowds, and Lisieux takes its place for the centuries to come, among the holy cities of the world.

May your book, dear Monseigneur, maintain and even increase the glory of Thérèse de l'Enfant Jésus here below; may it multiply the number of souls eager for her powerful intercession, and at the same time increase our love of Him for whom she wished to live and die.

Alfred Baudrillart
Bishop of Himéria
Member of the French Academy

Introduction

On September 30, 1897, a young nun of twenty-four died at the Carmel of Lisieux. Her life had been so humble and so hidden that one of her companions, seeing that she was fading away, wondered what facts worthy of attention could be mentioned in the death notice.

And soon afterwards, her poor coffin was taken to the cemetery, accompanied by a few relatives.

Twenty-five years later, this almost unknown maiden was proclaimed a wonder-worker as renowned as she was bountiful, and her relics, raised to the altar, became the object of tenderest homage and veneration.

After another interval of two years, on May 17, 1925, in presence of more than 4,000 priests and 60,000 faithful, the Sovereign Pontiff, Pius XI, placed the crowning aureole on the forehead of the little nun of Lisieux. Almost a million spectators, gathered in Rome from every continent, standing there beneath the marvellous illuminations of St Peter's, hailed the young Carmelite in the splendour of her canonization, and Thérèse de l'Enfant Jésus became the most popular saint in the world.

In face of this wonderful enthusiasm, this "hurricane of glory"[1] which has raised the name of a lowly nun above all human renown, what can be said in her praise that has not been surpassed a thousandfold, that would not display miserable insufficiency?

Thus I will guard against undertaking the eulogy of the new saint after the solemn declarations of Pius X, Benedict XV, and Pius XI on the sublime quality of Thérèse's virtues, and the rare fruitfulness of her spiritual doctrine.

The task is, however, comparatively easy to a biographer who is solely desirous of following with exactitude the unobtrusive events of this brief life, spent entirely in the intimacy of her family and within the walls of an unknown cloister.

These events are, besides, the substance of this supernatural and resplendent life which the Church has just glorified. To appreciate all its splendour, it will not be out of place to show in their simplicity and in their original setting, the daily actions which were its partial source and habitual condition.

These have already been given with incomparable charm in the *Histoire d'une Ame*,[2] unequalled in its admirable simplicity, enlightening doctrine, sweet and impressive unction. Is not full satisfaction given in this book, multiplied as it is in thousands of copies, to the curiosity and devotion of all the admirers of "little Thérèse"?

I had thought so at first; but more attentive examination of the book has shown me that several traits in the saint's character have been omitted by her, probably through humility. These traits have been diligently noted by her companions in religion, more especially by those who were in a twofold manner her sisters here below. These testimonies, duly recorded in the acts of the different canonical processes, form two large volumes, the examination of which has revealed to me Thérèse's life, not only as seen by herself in the mirror of her modesty, but viewed from the outside with an unequalled keenness of perception and unerring judgment.

Certain it is that the young saint did not reveal everything. Yet how can one dare to undertake her biography, even with the aid of additional information, after her own heavenly-worded pages which in their numberless translations have already revealed to the world the exceptional beauty of her soul?

Two motives have conquered my fears: the confidence which the Rev. Mother Prioress of the Carmel of Lisieux, the saint's sister,[3] has reposed in me by charging me with a mission which will remain the great honour of my life, and the desire to show my gratitude to "little Thérèse" who has given to my family and to me undeniable marks of her protection.

Let me add that the fact of having been a member of the pilgrimage to Rome which, in 1887, allowed Thérèse Martin to submit the question of her vocation to Leo XIII, inspired in me a special attraction towards the young Carmelite who was so eager to give herself to God.

At all events, I have tried to find motives for undertaking a task which at first seemed rash.

Being incapable of producing anything to equal the graceful pages of the *Histoire d'une Ame*, I have borrowed Thérèse's own words whenever she has appeared to me to give the events of her life in their fullness. I have done this especially as regards her confidences and effusions on the mysteries of divine love, of which she speaks so familiarly with charming candour, but also with a supernatural wisdom under the impulse of the Holy Spirit.

Keeping to my rôle of biographer, I have avoided long dissertations on the diverse stages of Thérèse's spirituality, leaving this to other writers who, with more or less success, have undertaken to study her progress towards sanctity according to traditional classification.

For the details that are not in the *Histoire d'une Ame*, and which consequently form my own contribution to the work, I have scrupulously followed the testimony of the nuns at the Carmel and other well-known persons who were called to give evidence at the process of beatification.

Every page of my manuscript has been submitted to the careful revision of noted theologians and to the three Carmelite sisters of St. Thérèse de l'Enfant Jésus, so that the work appears with the explicit stamp and approbation of the most authoritative witnesses both as regards facts and doctrine.

With this book will close, so far as I can judge, an already long series of works consecrated to the glory of many saints. In revealing her admirable and engaging inner life, may it surround with new splendour the pleasing figure of the maiden of Lisieux.

May dear little Thérèse, on her part, shed around the last years of her biographer a little of that peace-giving joy which she has so frequently sown in earthly paths. May her angelic smile console the last hour of a priest devoted to the glory of her name; may her helping hand lead him to the arms of God!

Author's Note to the Third French Edition

Thirty thousand copies of this book have been sold in a few months. This shows that the dear saint has visibly blessed it, and that Providence has made use of it to benefit numberless souls.

Further information which I have received for the preparation of this third edition has enabled me to revise carefully the text. I have also been able to insert an appendix at the end of the book containing documents which fix certain family events regarding the saint's ancestors.

1

Ancestral Origin—Alençon— The Father and Mother of Thérèse Martin

The ancestors of St. Thérèse de l'Enfant Jésus on her father's side came originally from Athis-de-l'Orne, a borough of some importance situated in the Domfront district. As far back as the sixteenth century we find agriculturists here named Martin, but authentic record of "little Thérèse's" parentage dates from April 2, 1692. On this day was baptized in the church of Athis a child named John Martin. Of a lineal descendant of this John Martin was born a son, who was baptized in the same church, April 16, 1777, and received the name Pierre-François.

This child was later to be the grandfather of the glorious Carmelite whose life-story we are about to narrate. In him we recognize the head of that saintly family from which she has come; to his influence may be attributed in no small measure her eminent and highly developed virtues.

At the period of their son's baptism, the parents of Pierre-François Martin lived near the church of Athis[1] in the house at present occupied by registration officials and the sacristan. Afterwards they moved to a more completely rural dwelling, the "Quentinière." From here, as it would seem, Pierre-François set out for Alençon for his first military training.

The military expeditions of the Empire soon accustomed him to war, and he acquitted himself so well that we find him in 1823 captain in the 19th Light Infantry garrisoned at Bordeaux.[2] Here, in an old house in the rue Servandoni, on August 22, his wife, Marie-Anne-Fannie Boureau, gave him a son, who was baptized Louis-Joseph-Aloys-Stanislas, and was third of a family of five children.[3]

The brave officer was absent from home at this time, his company taking part, apparently, in the expedition to Spain led by the Duke of Angoulême with purpose of re-establishing the throne of Ferdinand VII.

The child was baptized privately, and weeks of waiting for the father's return followed. But he was not to return to Bordeaux until November. It was decided, therefore, that the solemn baptism should not be deferred so long, and on October 28, 1823, the ceremony was performed in the church of Saint Eulalie by the Abbé Martegoute, chaplain of the prisons in that city.

The saintly Archbishop of Bordeaux, Mgr. d'Aviau du Bois de Sanzay, attested in writing (January 14, 1824) to the authenticity of the certificate of baptism.[4] It was probably on this occasion that he said to the parents: "Rejoice, for this child is one of the predestined!" This prophetic vision vouchsafed to the virtuous Archbishop was truly to be fulfilled in the life then opening.

Captain Martin was himself one of the most powerful instruments of divine grace in the training of his son; from the beginning he set himself to infuse into this youthful mind his own deep faith and ardent piety. As far as his public duties permitted he watched over the education of Louis, took care to have him thoroughly instructed in religious truths, and made him also commence his classical studies.

At length the hour of retreat sounded for the brave soldier. Bearing with him the esteem of his superior officers, decorated with the Cross of Saint Louis, which he had obtained at the age of forty-seven during the Spanish campaign,[5] Captain Martin left Bordeaux for his native district, there to seek a well-earned repose and to provide for the future of his children.[6] With this end in view, instead of returning to the little house at Athis where his parents had lived, he went to Alençon, drawn thither by the more favourable resources of education offered in that town. From henceforth his life was to be one long series of charitable works and saintly example.

From Alençon the old soldier, accompanied by his children, went sometimes to Athis to visit the cousins and other relatives who remained in the old homes. Young Louis delighted in these visits to country homes where the service of God pre-dominated over every other thought. It was time, however, to consider his future career. The army was not without attraction for the son of Captain Martin, but what seemed to be a chance occurrence was to lead him to more peaceable occupations. In the town of Rennes Captain Martin had cousins, watchmakers by trade. During a visit there Louis discovered his taste for this profession, and began to learn it merely as an amateur. During his sojourn in Rennes he received from his parents letters which show the character of the people of Normandy ennobled by the ancient faith. From his mother, a daughter of this rural district so attached to Catholic practices, he received the following letter on August 25, 1842:

> What a joy it would be to me, my dear Louis, to offer you in person my heartiest and best wishes. Yet we must bear the crosses which God sends us, and thank him every day for the favours he has bestowed. I felt that he conferred a great blessing on me when I saw you for the first time in your Breton costume, your young heart filled with enthusiasm. . . . With what joy I pressed you to my heart, for you, dear son, are the dream of my nights and the constant subject of my thoughts.
>
> How many times do I not think of you when my soul, in prayer, follows the leading of my heart and darts up even to the foot of the divine throne. There, I pray with all the fervour of my soul that God may bestow on my children the interior happiness and calm which are so necessary in this turbulent world.

Then this true Christian, in her fear of the pernicious effects of youthful presumption in her son, adds: "Remain always humble, dear son."[7]

In Strasbourg dwelt another friend of the Martin family, also engaged in the clockmaker's business. Drawn to this city by the wish to be near one of his father's old comrades, Louis still continued the delicate work to which he had commenced his apprenticeship. This gave him an opportunity of closely examining the mechanism of the celebrated cathedral clock which aroused his admiration. Gradually he found growing within him an attraction for this work, which requires in addition to skilled hands so much application and taste. But Louis had higher aspirations than the study of an earthly career.

He had progressed in the practice of prayer and the frequent use of the Sacraments. Under this influence his thoughts no less than his love tended towards the joys of heaven. The beauty of creation, especially as shown in its varied aspects in the land of Normandy, filled him with delight, and was to him a mirror in which he contemplated the divine Creator. At the sight of the flashing dawn or the waning sunset his handsome and clear-cut face reflected in turn his gladness in the beauty of the divine plan, or his sadness at parting with things which must pass with the day.

He had reached his twentieth year when he reflected, with faith already supported by experience, that beyond all passing earthly splendour is the light of an eternal day which shines for those happy beings who contemplate the divine beauty. He realized that this great joy must be won by toil on earth, realized too that the surest way towards possession of the eternal reward of the invisible world is voluntary renunciation of the fleeting though alluring shadows which claim our attention here below. We find this youth, then, on a morning in September, 1843, slowly climbing up the slopes of Mount St. Bernard, gazing with wondering eyes at the majestic peaks above. He had travelled across France, partly on foot, partly by stage-coach, to seek at the Monastery hidden here amid the snows the secret of his vocation.

As he climbed upward, the wonderful stillness, the peaceful aspect of the wide spaces around, formed a powerful attraction towards this holy solitude, where he hoped to find, in familiar and daily communion with the Holy of Holies, that blessed peace for which his soul thirsted. On the threshold of life, with a realization of the storms that would beset him, he already said with the Prophet at sight of the city which was to shelter him: *"Haec requies mea in saeculum saeculi."*[8]

Louis Martin was received by the Superior of the Augustinian Monks with that kindliness and sweetness which instinctively opened all hearts. The Prior knew immediately that this clear-countenanced youth had not come merely for a night's shelter. His desire was to shield his innocence there till death, to devote his life, in accordance with the object for which the Monastery was founded, to the rescue of unfortunate travelers buried in the mountain gorges beneath the snow, or frozen by the glacial blast.

An attraction towards solitude, or the desire to be immolated in the service of others, is not always a sure mark of religious vocation. The postulant must have already received the remote preparation which would fit him for the functions of the Order to which he seeks admission. Thus the Prior set himself immediately to find out the capabilities of his young visitor.

"Have you finished your Latin studies, my son?"

Louis replied in the negative.

"I am sorry," said the Prior, "for it is an essential condition for admission to our brotherhood. But be not discouraged. Return to Normandy, work diligently, and when you have completed your humanities, we will gladly admit you to our Novitiate."[9]

Sad at heart, the pilgrim returned down the steeps of the glaciers, like a traveller who has been driven back into exile from the shores of his native land.

Would Captain Martin's means allow him to incur the expense of his son's classical studies? A loyal effort was made; Louis set himself earnestly to the study of Latin under the Curé of St. Leonard of Alençon. But illness soon compelled him to lay aside his books, and he decided finally to return to the watchmaker's workshop. After some time in Paris, where in all probability he completed his apprenticeship, he returned to the little town in Normandy made dear to him by family ties. Here he lived with his parents in the rue du Pont-Neuf, dividing his time between work, prayer, and some suitable distractions, in which he was joined by a few chosen friends, devoted like himself to works of charity.

In this way he lived until his thirty-fifth year, thinking still perhaps of the monastic life; at all events manifesting no desire to enter the married state, although his mother wished him to marry.

About this time a young daughter of Normandy, Zélie Guérin, born at Saint Denis-sur-Sarthon (Orne), presented herself at the Hôtel-Dieu of Alençon, directed by the Sisters of Saint Vincent de Paul. She belonged to one of the most religious families of the district. Her forefathers had given asylum to the clergy during the Revolution, and her own father was familiar in his childhood days with the ruses employed to evade the enraged pursuers of his uncle, a priest whom they had concealed in their house. Later, this child, having come to man's estate, was to take his part, like Pierre-François Martin, in the military campaigns of the Empire, was afterwards to serve as a *gendarme,* and then to retire to Alençon after forty years of military service.[10]

He had three children: an elder daughter, Marie Louise, who died, a Visitation nun, at Le Mans; Zélie, with whom we shall be largely concerned in the course of our narrative; and a son, Isidore, who early gave signs of his attraction to the medical profession.

As pupil of the *Dames de l' Adoration* at Alençon, Zélie Guérin had received a careful education, as attested by her numerous successes in study; she had also been formed there to true piety, and desired to serve God in the person of His poor. She confided her wishes to the Superioress of the Hôtel-Dieu, who declared unhesitatingly that God had other designs for Zélie than the religious life.

Disappointed, but sustained by faith, the young girl remained with her brother, sister, and parents, to await the decision of Providence regarding her future.

Her father, in 1843, had purchased a comfortable house, No. 42, rue Saint Blaise, where later he lived with his children. But the expenses consequent on the education of his son and daughters had made considerable inroads on the pension of the old soldier. Zélie, understanding that she was destined for the married state, felt that she must increase her dowry in order to meet the calls of her future life. She was in considerable anxiety as to the means of so doing, when, on December 8, 1851, Feast of the Immaculate Conception, she was suddenly interrupted in the midst of an absorbing work which excluded all freaks of the imagination. An interior voice seemed to give her this command: "Have Alençon point lace made."[11] This was the reply given by the Blessed Virgin to the anxious doubts which Zélie had confided to her.

The world-wide appreciation of this beautiful lace, the one kind in France worked entirely with the needle, is well known. Zélie Guérin studied the different processes of the manufacture, specialized in the assemblage of the pieces already prepared, and finally placed herself at the head of one of these enterprises for the production of that light and delicate lace destined to complete the richest attire in the land. Her employées worked in their own homes, whilst she took charge of the orders, supplied the designs, and carefully watched over the execution of the work. Soon the lace which she produced was classed amongst the most beautiful; 500 francs a metre was a not unusual price for her work, so that the profits soon grew into a capital of some importance.

Isidore Guérin, Zélie's father, lived at a short distance from the Church of Notre-Dame, and Captain Martin with his wife and son had at this time, as we know, a house in rue du Pont Neuf in the parish of Saint Pierre de Montsort.

Active, industrious, with a skilful hand, and a finely developed artistic taste, Louis Martin promised fair to become an expert in his profession; he had thoughts also of joining the lucrative business of jeweller to his trade of watchmaker. No acquaintanceship had as yet sprung up between the two families. Immersed in her daily task, Zélie Guérin satisfied herself with a petition to Providence to give her a worthy husband. Catholic not only in name, but in practice. She had asked God too, with profound faith, to bless her future union with many children, who might all be some in way consecrated to His service.

One day as she was crossing the bridge of Saint Leonard she met a young man, whose dignified and distinguished demeanour claimed her attention in a remarkable manner. She did not know him, but an interior voice made manifest to her once more the Providence of God watching over her life: "This is he whom I have prepared for thee." Those words led to the two lives being drawn together; and they were indissolubly united on July 13, 1858, in the Church of Notre-Dame at Alençon.

According to family records, the young husband, thinking, as many saints had done, to join to the blessing of Christian marriage the honour of continence, expressed this wish to his wife on the evening of their marriage. He was, without knowing it, going against what she felt to be God's design for her. Having learned this after a year, Louis renounced his plan of special perfection, and the young couple lived in conjugal fidelity, in perfect union of heart and will.

They had established themselves in the rue du Pont Neuf. The watchmaking, to which Louis had now joined the sale of jewellery, added to the Alençon point lace manufacture, proved a considerable source of income to the family. They set earnestly to work; reliable customers came in numbers; the future seemed assured.

The newly-married pair realized every day more and more the blessing of mutual charity. Endowed with a practical mind, with rare gifts of energy and untiring activity, Mme Martin was above all remarkable for her wonderful spirit of faith. One sole object dominated and directed her life. She could in all truth make this maxim of St. Françoise d'Amboise her own: "So act that in all things God be loved above all."

Louis, with perhaps a calmer disposition, his taste for religious communion with nature, his love for the poetry of light and shade ever varying with the mists of his homeland, was a model of that patient and active charity which lends so much charm and happiness to life in common. On one occasion he was seen to raise up a drunken man from the thronged street where he had fallen, then, without the slightest regard for human respect, take his box of tools, give him the support of his arm, and with gentle but firm admonition conduct him to his home. Again, one day at a railway station, having come across a poor victim of epilepsy dying with hunger and without sufficient money to take him back to his own village, the young man took off his hat, and, placing therein the first alms himself, went round to all the passengers for money to enable the poor sufferer to reach his home.

In the service of God, more especially in devotion to Jesus in the Tabernacle, did the intimate union of the newly-married couple find its full expression. M. and Mme Martin attended Mass every morning at half-past five; they knelt together at the Holy Table; and although very frequent communion was not yet in vogue in the French parishes, they endeavoured to receive the Holy Eucharist more frequently than every Sunday.

Despite the fatiguing duties of the household and the absorbing labour of the husband's daily business, at a time too when the spirit of mortification was growing weak in the better class families, they observed to the letter the fasts and abstinence of the Church. Another practice of renunciation must have proved very meritorious for them. It was customary at that time amongst the young country folk to come to Alençon every Sunday to make their purchases or on pleasure bent. The jewellers' windows formed the chief attraction for the gentler sex. When a marriage was in view their fiancés were liberal in the purchase of rings, trinkets, ear-rings, and the other ornaments so much appreciated, especially by village folk. But when the intending purchasers came to Louis Martin's establishment on Sunday they found the door closed; all business was suspended here out of respect for the Lord's day. This line of action entailed considerable loss for the young man. Some of his friends counselled a less rigorous practice which would not at the same time militate against the day of rest:

"Leave the side-door at least open; in this way your shop will to all appearances remain closed, while purchasers can come in quietly and you will not lose good sales."

"I prefer," replied Louis, "to draw down on my house the blessing of God."

This spirit of faith so openly manifested showed itself in a still more touching way in the quiet of the home. They prayed in common, endeavouring to put into the prayer addressed to God the Father the fervour of Captain Martin, whose accents as he recited the *Our Father* moved others to tears.

A habitual practice in the household was the study of the Lives of the Saints, in whom they recognized a spiritual brotherhood.

One day, as the young wife read the life of Madame Acarie, who after giving all her daughters to Carmel, consecrated herself also to God in the religious life, she exclaimed: "All her daughters Carmelites! Is it possible that a mother may have so great an honour?"[12]

With these thoughts in her heart she was glad to see her husband take his place each succeeding month at the nocturnal Adoration of the Blessed Sacrament. Whenever she accompanied him on a walk into the country, her greatest joy was to turn with him into some quiet church, where, in his devotion, he would kneel before a tabernacle too often abandoned.

Absorbed in his business, Louis Martin allowed himself from time to time one little recreation. He loved fishing, and often plied the hook along the Sarthe, whiling away a few hours in the charm of horizons veiled in blue mists. In this, as in other things, he wished that honest recreation should be seasoned with charity; eel and trout were sent for the most part to the Monastery of the Poor Clares at Alençon.

Following the example of her husband, Mme Martin was always ready to relieve misery and suffering. A servant in the household fell ill with a very painful attack of articular rheumatism. Her parents were poor and could not procure for her the proper treatment. The mistress devoted herself to the servant night and day until she was completely cured. At another time, Mme Martin was compelled to appear before a magistrate in consequence of her endeavours to rescue a child from the maltreatment of two evil old women, who had taken charge of her education, but who were exploiting her in a shameful manner.[13]

What, then, was wanting to these true Christians save to be enabled to transmit their own virtues to a numerous posterity? God gave a grand answer to the prayer of His servants; in a few years nine children were born to them.

They wished that each child from its entrance into the world should be consecrated to the Queen of heaven by receiving the name of Marie, and in time Marie-Louise, Marie-Pauline, Marie-Léonie, and Marie-Hélène, came to increase the joy of the home.

The parents, in their desire to multiply here below the noble works of their family, sought from God, by the intercession of St. Joseph, "a little missionary."

They believed that their prayer was heard when to the little daughters who filled the house with laughter and song was added a baby brother, who received the names of Marie-Joseph-Louis. Alas! scarce had he learned to smile at his mother, when, five months after his birth, he departed from this earth to intercede amid the angels for his parents and sisters.

Supplications and novenas were renewed with redoubled fervour; a priest, a child who would be a "great saint," was the goal of all their desires. Another little cherub seemed sent as an answer from above, but eight months later he too, Marie-Joseph-Jean-Baptiste, departed, to fulfil in heaven the mission that God saw fit to deny him in this world.

With this second cross, they understand that "the thoughts of the Lord are not our thoughts, His ways are not our ways."[14] And they ceased their supplications for a missionary. But who, considering the lives of the remaining children of Louis Martin, would have the hardihood to say that God had rejected his petition?

The two elder daughters were now old enough for school. Mme Martin considered that she could not do better than confide them to the care of her saintly sister, the Visitation nun, so Marie-Louise and Marie-Pauline were sent as boarders to the convent at Le Mans.

In order to meet the additional expense of educating her children and provide generally for her growing family, the courageous mother resolved to apply herself with renewed energy to the development of her lace industry. She accepted large orders, devoted long hours to the training of her workers, attended personally to the extensive commercial correspondence entailed, and brought to her artistic work so much activity and good taste that in a short time the renown and extent of her enterprise had greatly increased.

Such a life of activity left little time for recreation or rest. Mme Martin made a virtue of necessity. "Truth to tell," she wrote, "I seek no other recreation than to sit at my window putting together the pieces of my 'Point d'Alençon.'"[15]

In spite of all preoccupations her greatest joy was in her family life; it was, in fact, her one joy on earth, and she endeavoured to fulfil every duty to her children with characteristic simplicity, devotion, and good-will.

She had, as we know, one brother, Isidore Guérin, who, before he became the exemplary Catholic that we find him later, had been, as a young medical student, drawn to the dissipations of Paris life. We find his sister addressing to him at the time letters such as these:

> I am, my dear brother, greatly disquieted on your account, My husband constantly speaks to me with apprehension concerning you. He is well acquainted with Paris, and says that you will be surrounded by temptations which you will not resist because you are not sufficiently grounded in piety. He has given me an account of some of his own experiences, and shown me what courage is required to come out victorious. If you but knew through what trials he has passed! I beseech you, my dear Isidore, to act as he acted, be fervent in prayer, and you will not be carried away by the torrent. If you go under once you are lost. It is but the first step that counts on the road to evil as on the path to virtue; afterwards you will be carried on by the current.
>
> If you agree to do one thing which I am going to ask of you, and which you might well be willing to give me as a New Year's gift, I shall be happier than if you gave me all Paris. You live quite near

> Notre-Dame-des-Victoires. Well! make a little visit there even once a day to say a *Hail Mary* to the Blessed Virgin. You will find that she will protect you in a special manner, she will give you success in this world and eternal happiness in the world beyond. Think not that my words to you come from exaggerated piety without solid foundation; I have reason for confidence in Mary; I have received from her favours known only to myself. . . . You know well that life is very short. In a few brief years you and I will have reached the end; how happy we shall then be if our life has not tended to make our last hours bitter.[16]

The youth profited so much by this advice that he became soon afterwards one of the most practical and devoted Catholics of his time. He set up in business as a chemist in the town of Lisieux, and married a pious young girl, Mlle Fournet. From this time onward a close friendship sprang up between Mme Martin and the newly-married couple. At their house in Lisieux she spent in company with her children the few holidays which she allowed herself. To her sister-in-law were addressed for the most part those simple yet typical letters wherein she traces such charming pictures of the home-life, or gives expression to supernatural hope in the midst of tears and trials; letters which her family has faithfully preserved, and which are to us so invaluable a treasure in compiling the biography of "little Thérèse."

Neither did Mme Martin forget that, as elder sister, she had certain moral duties to her brother. Here is a novel example of her manner of persuasion.

An old pair, of the rich and egoistic type, had just built a costly house at Alençon. At the prospect of soon enjoying this grand dwelling, the wife exclaimed: "Oh, how happy I am! Nothing is wanting to me; I have health and fortune, can procure everything I wish; I have no children to disturb my peace; indeed, I know of no one so well off as I am."

Mme Martin made the following comment to her brother on hearing the remarks of this lady:

> I have always heard, "Unfortunate, thrice unfortunate, is the person who can speak thus." And, my dear friend,

> I am so convinced of this truth that, at certain periods of my life, when I had that feeling of happiness, I could only dwell on it with fear and trembling, for experience has shown beyond doubt that true happiness does not exist here below; its semblance may perchance appear on earth, but it is the herald of misfortune. I have noticed it myself. No, happiness cannot be found here; good fortune carries with it a dangersignal. God, in His wisdom, has so ordained our life that we may never forget that this earth is not our true home.[17]

In confirmation of this seemingly rigid teaching, she gives a striking example. She tells of this old couple walking one evening through their new garden, at the end of which a deep trench had just been dug, and was left unprotected save for a few planks. In the growing darkness the husband and wife stepped on one of these slender planks, and both were dashed into the pit beneath, crushed and injured.

Oftentimes, however, these more serious lessons give place to an account of some little incident in lighter vein. Now it is a story of the children's pranks as they romp around the table where the lace is being prepared, now the repetition of some ingenuous question or remark which shows already the bent of their character; often, too, comes the expression of deep intense gratitude for these treasures that Heaven has entrusted to her.

She had just put her baby, Hélène, under the care of a nurse, and in a letter to her brother she gives naïve expression to her feelings. "I went to see her a fortnight ago. I think I never experienced a greater joy than when I took her in my arms; she smiled at me so sweetly that I thought I was looking at an angel. I cannot express what I felt. Never, I think, was seen, never will be seen a child so charming. My little Hélène, when shall I have the happiness of possessing her fully? I cannot realize that I have the honour of being the mother of so beautiful a little creature."[18]

Alas! this cherished child was destined to leave, five years later, her mother's arms for ever. How deeply this would wound that loving heart the foregoing lines reveal.[19]

In the meantime a poignant sorrow, the prelude of many another, now came to Mme Martin. Captain Martin, her husband's father, who was in his eighty-ninth year, was lingering between death and life. On June 27, 1865, she wrote to her brother: "My father-in-law died yesterday at one in the afternoon, He received the last Sacraments on Thursday. He died like a saint; as was his life, so, also, his death. I would never have believed that it could have such an effect on me; I feel it most deeply."[20]

She was destined to become familiar with the sight of death. In the course of the next few years two sons were born, and were quickly taken to heaven; then she had the sorrow of losing her own father, from whom she had never been parted.

On September 3, 1868, she wrote to her sister-in-law: "If you had but witnessed his holy death! I cherish the hope, I have even the certitude, that my dear father has been favourably received by God. May my death be like to his! We have already had three Masses said for him, and intend to have many more, so that he may be speedily delivered from purgatory if anything yet remains to be atoned for. His tomb will be quite close to that of my two little Josephs."[21] And on November 1 of the same year, writing to her brother: "If the good God hears my prayer, He will admit him this very day to paradise. Poor father! He was not accustomed to suffer. For myself I do not fear purgatory; to suffer seems quite natural to me. If God so willed, I would at once agree to expiate his purgatory and my own, so desirous am I that he should be happy."[22]

Added to this sorrow was disquietude caused by the frail constitution of her daughter Léonie, and the consequent difficulties regarding her education.

This valiant woman, who in spite of her delicate sensitiveness had gone through such trials with fortitude, whom sorrow had strengthened rather than vanquished, could endure without flinching the thousand little annoyances which add weight to the burden of daily life.

But to her cares as mother, wife, and mistress of a household, were added fears regarding the health of her sister, the Visitation nun, now threatened with phthisis. She dreaded the loss of this sister all the more because her two daughters Marie and Pauline were making wonderful progress under her charge, and their growing virtue was her greatest consolation amid crosses and vexations.

The gentle and reserved nature of Marie concealed, as is usual in timid people, a depth of tenderness which only required expansion to bring out its true worth.

The gracious and prepossessing disposition of Pauline, and her natural bent for learning, made her, notwithstanding her exuberant disposition, the joy of her teachers.

More especially after her father's death did Mme Martin appreciate these happy traits of character in her children; their lovable qualities proved a wonderful solace to her in her sorrows.

Marie was asked to offer the pain of a dental operation for the soul of her grandfather: "This morning at eight o'clock," writes Mme Martin, "I took her to the dentist. She asked me if her suffering would really help 'the poor papa.' On my answering in the affirmative, she never uttered a word; in fact, the dentist told me he had never seen a child so brave." After a fresh examination, when the operation was declared unnecessary, she said to her mother: "What a pity! the poor papa would no longer have been in purgatory."[23]

Thus, in return for the pious education given to her children, this Christian mother tasted, even in the midst of hard trials, the consolations of faith. God willed to brighten with a few flowers the rough path which she trod, for, ere the end of the way be reached, more thorns still would there be to harass and afflict her.

On February 23 came the death of her fourth child, little Marie-Hélène. From the monastery of Le Mans her sister wrote: "I cannot help considering you fortunate in giving to heaven these innocent souls who, later, will be your joy and your crown. Your faith and never-failing confidence will then receive a magnificent recompense. . . . Rest assured that the Saviour will bless you; your joy hereafter will be according to the measure of the consolations refused you now; for if God, accepting your sacrifice, wills to give you *this great saint whom you have so much desired for His glory,*[24] will you not then be well repaid?"[25]

These last lines would seem to contain a presentiment of the future. The admonition of the good religious was hardly necessary in the case of Mme Martin, for we find her, shortly afterwards, writing to her sister-in-law at Lisieux, who had received a similar cross: "When I closed the eyes of my dear little children, when I laid them in the grave, my grief, though great, was always resigned. I never regretted the pain and anxiety I had endured for their sake. Everyone said: 'Better they had never been born.' I could not agree to this view. I realize that my pain and anxiety cannot be compared to the eternal happiness of my dear children. They are not lost to me for ever. Life is short and full of sorrow; we shall meet again in heaven."[26]

These and similar reflections were communicated to Sister Marie Dosithée, the fervent Visitandine, who, at the thought of such great spiritual strength in a life so sorely crossed, thus pays homage to the virtue of Mme Martin: "I have fears," she wrote to her brother, "lest her health suffer from the effect of so many shocks. Her spirit of faith, however, and her wonderful courage reassures me. What a valiant woman she is! Adversity has no power to overcome her, prosperity cannot deceive her; she is admirable."[27]

At the beginning of 1870 M. Martin handed over his watch-making establishment to one of his nephews.[28] He thought it well to give henceforward more active and practical help to his wife, whose lace industry continued to extend considerably.

A period of remarkable and unprecedented success opened for the family, until Alençon had to bow before the invasion of the victorious Prussian army. After having witnessed the sad spectacle of our soldiers suffering in the hospitals of the town from the wounds of battle or the contagion of disease, Mme Martin had to open her house in the rue du Pont-Neuf to nine German infantry soldiers, who, while refraining from insulting violence, destroyed from the commencement the beautiful order established therein by its mistress.

"They have," she wrote, "reduced the house to a deplorable condition. . . . The town is in desolation; everyone is in tears except myself."

In spite of his consternation, M. Martin showed, like his valiant wife, the greatest courage. She herself is happy in testifying to the fact: "It is quite possible that the men between forty and fifty years will be called out; I am in hourly expectation of the order. My husband is not in the least alarmed. He often says that if he were free he would soon be enlisted amongst the *franc-tireurs*."

Of a lady who had succeeded in concealing her husband and saving him from the mobilization, the heroic Frenchwoman exclaimed: "Is it possible that anyone would so act!"

The war was concluded before M. Martin was called to the colours. The evils of invasion were confined in their case to material losses; their habitual order and economy in home life brought them through this tragic period without too much privation.

With the return of peace, M. and Mme Martin decided to retire to the residence in the rue Saint Blaise, which had become theirs by the death of the grandfather, M. Guérin.

The house was situated near the church of Notre-Dame. A simpler and more retired residence would be hard to find; adjoining on one side a quiet dwelling, it was separated on the other from the neighbouring house by a garden trellis. With its ground floor pierced by only two windows, with three arched windows to light its second floor, it appeared somewhat small for a large family; but the two elder girls, who were then boarders at Le Mans, spent only vacation-time at Alençon, and the parents, always adverse to ostentation, aspired to nothing beyond simplicity and good taste in their home. With a rather larger garden for her children's play, Mme Martin would have been perfectly content.

Before the retirement of M. Martin they had been blessed with two more children. Marie-Céline, born in 1869, was to brighten the household with her laughter; but

Marie-Mélanie-Thérèse, born in 1870, had gone to join her little brothers in paradise.

Of these the courageous mother wrote: "Four of my children are already in their eternal home, and the others—yes, the others—will also go to that heavenly kingdom, laden with more merits, for they will have been longer in the fight."[29]

Christian hope healed every painful wound, and gave her that resigned attitude of mind which was visible even to strangers, and which those little versed in the wonders of God's love took for indifference or coldness.

In spite of fresh trials, destined to fortify their virtue, Louis and Zélie spent in this house six years of the purest joy and happiness.

Into this atmosphere of tender piety, of domestic peace and mutual forbearance, came on January 2, 1873, another child, hailed, like the rest, with transports of joy. It was the "little missionary," the object of such ardent longings and fervent prayers. Contrary to the expectation of her parents, or to what anyone could foresee, this frail little daughter was destined to win to God, by the power of her intercession and of her miracles, more souls than the greatest apostle of foreign lands.[30]

The two elder girls, who were home for the holidays, were sleeping in their little room on the second floor when, towards midnight, M. Martin received this new gift from heaven. He mounted the stairs with light step, and arousing them, announced in joyous tones, "My children, you have a little sister." Marie and Pauline joined him in fervent thanks to God.

To follow the life of the newly-born little one will be henceforward the unique object of our work. Before speaking of the wonders of this life, it was fitting that we should present to the reader those chosen souls whose wise guardianship partly explains its secret.[31]

2

Early Infancy of "Little Thérèse"

Marie, the eldest sister, was chosen as godmother to the child. Her future godfather, Paul Albert Boul, son of one of M. Martin's friends, although he lived in Alençon, caused some delay. Anxious on account of this delay, Mme Martin besought God that he would not allow her child to die without baptism.

At last, on the afternoon of January 4, everything was in readiness for the great ceremony, and the whole family set out for the church of Notre-Dame. This church, with its three-sided porch surmounted by gracefully pointed arches, and lighted by small apertures of highly elaborate style, with its triforium of rare elegance and its glistening stained glass windows of fifteenth- and sixteenth-century design, was a joy to artists, as well as to the faithful who came to pray and meditate within its walls smoothed by the long caress of the years. But it is not in the boldly curved arches, nor yet in the beautiful stained glass windows, each depicting an incident in the life of the Blessed Virgin,[1] that the most lively interest of the present-day pilgrim is centered.

In the first chapel to the left, near a baptismal font of rather original design, and, until quite recently, before a group representing the baptism of Christ, the flames of innumerable candles bend to the north wind which blows through the crevices made in the window by the ravages of winter.[2]

Here persons of rank and wealth come side by side with the poor, to kneel in silent prayer and to offer their *ex votos* to the blessed soul regenerated long ago in this corner of the old church.

The Sacrament of Baptism was conferred by Abbé Lucien-Victor Dumaine, a priest of the parish and personal friend of the Martin family. This priest, who became later Vicar-General of Séez, was to be a witness in the process of beatification of the child, whom he regenerated that day to the divine life. But who, on that cold January afternoon, could have predicted for her so glorious a future?[3]

In accordance with her parents' vow, this child received, like her sisters, the name of Marie, Françoise-Thérèse being added, of which the last became her usual name in the family.

Pure as the dome of heaven studded with stars, white as a snow-clad countryside, Thérèse was carried home in the arms of the faithful servant Louise, while the bells of Notre-Dame rang out in gladness. Mme Martin was now satisfied; her mind was at rest.

Weeks passed by, weeks full of radiant hope. The mother took to herself the charge of nursing her dear little one, on whose brow she seemed already to discern the divine light. But very soon her strength failed, and the child, too, began to decline. Thérèse was following in the way of the little angels who were gone. They were calling her, perhaps; another sacrifice seemed to be demanded of the poor parents. Every means was employed to avert the threatened calamity. The family doctor declared that one chance of life alone remained, to confide Thérèse to the care of a healthy nurse.

Mme Martin had already had one of her children nursed by the wife of a farmer and mother of a large family living at some distance from Alençon. Her full name was Rose Taillé, but on account of her small stature, and, perhaps too, because of her prepossessing and pleasing manner, she was called by those who knew her "little Rose." The poor mother grasped eagerly at this one chance of saving the life of her child. "If it had not been so late," she writes,

> I would have gone instantly to get the nurse. How long the night seemed! Thérèse would scarce swallow a few drops of milk; the gravest symptoms that had preceded the death of the other little ones began to

> appear. I was sorely grieved that my poor babe could get no help from me in her feeble state. At daybreak I set out to find the nurse who lived at Semallé, almost two leagues from Alençon. My husband was away, and I did not wish to entrust to anyone else the success of my errand. In a lonely part of the road I met two men, and for a moment felt frightened; but I said to myself: "Even though they should kill me, I do not care." I was sick at heart. At last I arrived at the nurse's house, and asked her if she would come with me and remain with us, but she said that she could not leave her home and children; she would stay with me eight days and then take Thérèse back with her. I consented, knowing that my child would be very safe in her care.[4]

The two women reached Alençon in the forenoon. At sight of the dying child the nurse shook her head discouragingly, evidently thinking that it was too late. Mme Martin, grieved beyond measure at the pitiful aspect of the babe, hastened to her room, and throwing herself on her knees before a statue of St. Joseph, invoked, with tears but with hope that never faltered, that patron of every hope-bereft cause.

She then returned to the room below. Unexpected joy! The child, in the nurse's arms, seemed to have come back to life. But the joy was fleeting, for, as though finally vanquished by the malady, little Thérèse fell back again on the peasant's lap; not a sign of life remained, not a breath, nothing! . . .

Amid her tears, the heroic mother's piety gave her sufficient courage to offer a prayer of thanks to God that death had come so gently to her little one.

Then, suddenly, Thérèse opened her eyes once more, her features were reanimated, and she smiled as she gazed up at her mother. St Joseph had hearkened to that mother's prayer; the child but a moment before at the point of death appeared now quite revived.

The nurse was obliged to return to her home, but carried away in her arms the little Thérèse.

As may be easily imagined, a farmhouse in *Basse-Normandie* holds few attractions for a town-dweller. One or two apartments of stone or mud, with a roof of thatch, form the dwelling. To this retreat, surrounded as it is by evil-smelling stables, situated beside a cattle-pen which is a water-logged swamp during the winter months, and in summer little more than a manure-heap with pools of stagnant water, the Bocage peasant retires after his daily labour in the fields.

To one of these humble dwellings was the little invalid brought. This simple home, a one-storied building with three openings, had still its cradle, for a child had been born to the farmer but a year before. Three other playful and happy mites gathered round to gaze on the new-comer in smiling wonder. As to the rest, the cottage was comparatively neat and clean, and Mme Martin knew from the good woman's former services that "little Rose" could be relied upon to give conscientious care to her charge. But internal troubles, so common amongst young children, are usually tenacious. Little Thérèse had been in Semallé not quite three weeks when she got a fresh attack, which awakened anew her mother's gravest fears.

We find this letter from Mme Martin to her relations at Lisieux, dated March 30, 1873:

> Since Thérèse had been taken over by the nurse she had been very well, and had even grown a good deal. But the internal irritation was only allayed for a time and has, since Friday last, attacked her throat and chest. When the doctor visited her she was in high fever. . . . He told me, however, that he did not think her in danger. To-day she is better, but I am in great fear; I doubt whether we shall be able to bring her up. . . . I have done everything I can to save her life. If now the good God wills to dispose otherwise, I will strive to bear the trial with all possible patience. There is indeed need to reanimate my courage. I have already suffered much during my life. I should wish, my dear friends, that you were more fortunate than I: it grieves me to see that trials also come your way.[5]

The concluding words of the letter refer to a recent fire which had caused great damage to a portion of the pharmacy belonging to M. Guérin. For the rest, the Martin family had not seen the last of their sorrows.

Before Thérèse had gained health, Marie, her eldest sister and godmother, was attacked at Le Mans by typhoid fever and obliged to leave school.

For weeks she lay ill at Alençon, anxiously watched over by her mother. Every day, and oftentimes the greater part of the night, were spent by Mme Martin at the bedside of her daughter. Meanwhile orders were pouring in, the workers had to be directed, and the lace delivered at the promised time. The poor mother was weighed down with the heavy burthen, but her faith did not for a moment fail. Even in her own sorrow she had a thought for the trials of others. She wrote, at this time, to Mme Guérin: "Each has his own cross to bear; some receive a heavier load than others. You have already begun to learn, dear sister, that life is not all strewn with roses. God, in His goodness, has decreed this in order to detach us from the earth, and to turn our thoughts towards heaven."[6]

She admits, nevertheless, that she herself had need of supernatural help in her great distress of soul. "I never leave the sick-room, and sometimes remain on my feet the whole night. The grace of God is surely necessary at such a time as this to keep one from breaking down."[7]

Her husband realized the necessity of obtaining that grace, or at least of prolonging its effects. We find him imposing on himself, for his daughter's cure, those primitive penances which, fifty years ago, were common in the cantons of Normandy, to obtain the intercession of some local patron saint.

On May 5 Mme Martin wrote to her daughter Pauline: "Your father sets out this morning for the ridge of Chaumont to make a pilgrimage on behalf of Marie. He goes fasting and will return fasting. He wants to do penance in order that God may hear his prayers; he has to travel six leagues on foot."[8]

God had already, at this time, answered in part the prayers of the poor parents for their two sick children. On April 20 the mother had been able to write these reassuring words: "The nurse brought our little Thérèse here today; she is quite well and strong."

Slowly, after frequent relapses, Marie too became convalescent, and once more gladness reappeared in the family circle. Sometimes little Thérèse was the innocent messenger of joy, although her visits had on a few occasions other unforeseen effects.

Thus one Sunday "little Rose" brought her, all unexpectedly, to Alençon, and without any previous announcement took her to the rue Saint Blaise. "We did not expect Thérèse," writes Mme Martin;

> the nurse arrived with her four children at half-past eleven, just as we were sitting down to table. She put the baby in my arms and went off immediately to Mass.
>
> Yes, but the little one would not have this; she cried until we thought she would swoon away. Everyone in the house was upset. I had to send Louise[9] to ask the nurse to come back immediately after Mass, as she had intended to make some delay in purchasing shoes for her children. She left before Mass was half finished and came running up to the house. I was vexed at that; the babe would not have died from crying.
>
> She became happy immediately. She is quite strong; everybody is surprised. I rocked her in my arms and walked about so much, trying to quiet her, that I had a pain in my back for the remainder of the day![10]

What a consolation for Mme Martin, after months of anxiety, to feel at last reassured about the life which had seemed so near its end.

The child's recovery could not indeed be attributed to delicate care. When the farmer's wife was going out to the fields she placed Thérèse on some straw in the bottom of her barrow, and thus wheeled her along the grassy paths through the clover and flowers to the spot where her husband was working. When milking-time came she carried the little one with her in her apron, so that Thérèse lived constantly in the open air amidst the fragrance of the fresh hay and the scent of the ripe corn. In this way she became "browned by the sun," and grew daily more robust from inhaling the chemicals given out by the harvest-bearing fields.

From constant intercourse with this peasant family Thérèse developed rustic instincts. Mme Martin had occasion to notice this almost every month when little scenes took place of which she chose to see only the pleasant side. She wrote on May 22 to her daughter Pauline:

> I saw little Thérèse on Tuesday last. The nurse brought her here but she would not stay, and cried loudly when she found herself left with us. Louise had to take her to the market where "little Rose" had gone to sell her butter; there was no other way out of the difficulty. The moment she caught sight of her nurse she began to smile, and cried no more. She remained there selling butter with all the women until midday. I know I could not hold her long in my arms without being really tired. She weighs fourteen pounds. She will be very winning and graceful later on.[11]

The trifling incidents that went to make up the early days of Thérèse differ very slightly from those which every mother may observe. Now comes what would seem to be the first manifestation of the presence of the Holy Spirit in the soul of the little child.

It was November 30, 1873; Thérèse was eleven months old. Her mother, writing to Pauline, tells of her physical development, and notices the dawning reflection on her countenance of the inward beauty of a child of God: "I expect that she will be able to walk unaided in five or six weeks more. You have only to put her standing beside a chair, and she remains quite steady—never falls. She takes her own little precautions to accomplish this and appears very intelligent. She is continually smiling; she has *the expression of one who is predestined.*"[12]

On January 11 following we find this letter: "My little Thérèse has since Thursday been able to walk alone. She is sweet and lovely as a little angel. She has a charming disposition, that is apparent already; and she has such a winning smile. I long to have her with us again."[13]

Was it not remarkable to see this frail infant, only a year old, already revealing by her sweet disposition and the unmistakable light of her countenance, the abiding presence of God in her soul, finding His delight in its innocent depths?

Thérèse had been taken back to Alençon on April 2, 1874. The danger so feared by the family seemed to have passed. Marie, too, was growing strong again; Pauline, at the Visitation Convent, proved the constant joy of her teachers and the consolation of her mother; little Céline, of a lively and amiable disposition, and very quick intelligence, triumphed over certain symptoms which had given cause for disquietude. As for Léonie, everything gave promise for the near future of the expansion and activity, hitherto indeterminate, of her good qualities.

Gladdened by the constant caresses of their children, the parents soon forgot their distress of mind. The sight alone of her who was to be the "little Queen" was sufficient to fill their hearts with joy. "Of all, except my first child, she is the most robust," declared Mme Martin. "She will be pretty; even now she has a pleasing grace; she has a tiny mouth, which I particularly admire."[14]

In the midst of his happiness, M. Martin never forgot his debt of thanks to God. In May, 1873, after the cure of his daughter Marie, he went to Notre-Dame de Chartres to offer a prayer of gratitude. In October of the same year he went on the diocesan pilgrimage to Lourdes, and brought back with him two large pieces of stone which he had detached from the rock of Massabielle, two yards distant from the spot of the Apparition.

To these pilgrimages of penance and thanks this fervent soul joined more assiduously than ever the practice of nocturnal Adoration.

Mme Martin, on her part, surrounded as she was by her devout children who seemed already to give signs of the call to religious life, encouraged in the way of self-abnegation and piety by her saintly Visitandine sister, made daily effort to progress towards union with God, after the example of her husband. She wrote freely to her two eldest daughters, who were again together at the convent, of her intention to undertake a vigilant fight against nature. We give the letter in the familiar style of her native Normandy. "I must go to Vespers to pray for the souls of our dead," she writes on the evening of All Saints Day. "A day will come when you will go also to pray for me; but I must so act now as not to have too much need of your prayers. I earnestly wish to become a saint. It will not be easy; a great deal yet remains to be 'hewn' off, and the wood is hard as stone. It would have been better to have commenced earlier in life, the task would have been less difficult, but 'better late than never.'"[15] Needless to say that we have here the language of humility, and that the struggle towards perfection had been undertaken long before.

M. Martin was a loving father, especially towards his younger children. So captivated was he by the charms of Thérèse that he called her even then his "Queen," and sought to provide many little pleasures for her.

The child must have been precocious beyond her age, for when only eighteen months old she was offered amusements which ordinarily belong to children more advanced. In June, 1874, M. Martin erected in their little garden a swing for the amusement of Céline and Thérèse. It was wonderful to see how Thérèse enjoyed the motion of the swing, imagining, no doubt, that she was floating on wings. "She acts just like an older child," writes her mother. "There is no danger that she will let go the rope; when the swing is not going high enough she calls out to us; we tie a cord in front to keep her from falling off, but notwithstanding that, I cannot feel at rest when I see her perched aloft."[16]

This exercise did, no doubt, appear somewhat violent for a child of her age; but God, who had such glorious designs for her, preserved her by means which sometimes seemed to defy the laws of nature. The following incident, related by Mme Martin, gives a striking example of this:

> Quite lately I had a singular experience with the little one. It was my custom to go to Mass every morning at half-past five. At first I did not dare to leave her alone, but, seeing that she never awakened, I decided at last

> to leave her. I put her therefore to sleep in my bed, and placed the cradle so close beside it that it was impossible for her to fall out.
>
> One day I forgot to place the cradle thus as a protection. On my return I saw no Thérèse. At that very moment I heard a cry, and looking, found her sitting on a chair close to the bed. Her head rested on the bolster, and there she was sleeping, uneasily, for she was in an uncomfortable position.
>
> I cannot understand how she fell in such a way as to get seated on that chair. I thanked God when I found that she had come to no harm. It was certainly providential; she would, in ordinary circumstances, have fallen to the ground. Her guardian angel was there keeping watch over her, and the souls in purgatory, whose intercession I ask for her every day, saved her.[17]

Up to this time, Thérèse's faculties had lain dormant in the silent torpor of early infancy. At most, the light of heaven which seems to caress the brow of every little child, as it smiles perhaps an answering smile to the angels, appeared more distinctly reflected in her innocent countenance than in that of other babies. Now her soul began gradually to awaken.

From the age of eighteen months Thérèse manifested, in her own charming and naïve way, a tender love for her mother. This was not always, be it admitted, "the perfect love" without hope of recompense; nevertheless, Mme Martin smiled with delight at these first lispings of her little daughter.

"Picture to yourselves," she wrote to Marie and Pauline, "the baby coming to embrace me and stroke my face with her little hand. I can see that she has some idea behind it all. She wants a scarf pin. . . . The poor baba, she cannot bear to leave me, and is continually at my side; she loves going into the garden, but if I am not there, does not want to stay, and cries until she is brought back to me."[18]

This good mother was soon to taste purer and deeper joy. She wished that the first words spoken by her child should be words of prayer, and on November 8, 1874, this baby, aged only twenty-two months, offered to the "good

Jesus" the love of her innocent soul with words and with a sincerity that delighted the heart of her mother.

"My little Thérèse," she said, "grows every day more charming; she prattles from morning till night. She sings little songs for us; but you must become accustomed to her in order to understand. She says her prayers like a little angel; it is ideal."[19]

Soon she was brought to church, and it was wonderful to see the interest which this child of two years took in the sacred functions; she seemed already to understand their meaning and import. Let her mother again describe her childlike actions, and her innocent remarks; we have nothing of greater worth than these accounts from so authoritative a witness to enable us to catch a glimpse of the first workings in this little soul.

> Thérèse continues always in good health: she has an air of well-being. She says very amusing things. She already knows how to pray to the good God, and goes every Sunday to a part of Vespers; if, unfortunately, she is left at home, she cries and will not be comforted.
>
> Some weeks ago she was taken for a walk on Sunday. She had not been "at Mass" as she said herself. On returning from the walk she began to cry vigorously, saying that she wanted to go to Mass. She opened the hall door and ran away, in torrents of rain, towards the church. When we had run after her and brought her back, her tears and lanentation lasted a good hour.
>
> Once she said out aloud to me in church: "I have been at Mass here, and I have prayed well to the good God too." When, on her father's return home this evening, she did not see him say his prayers, she said: "Why do you not say your prayers, papa? Have you already been to church?"
>
> Since the beginning of Lent, I go to six o'clock Mass, and often she is awake when I leave the house. Before I go, she says to me, "Mama, I am going to be very good." In fact, she never stirs, but goes off to sleep again.[20]

Allowing for the influence of example in religious exercises which affects the children of Christian families, the fact remains that a child of two years, whose attraction for the things of God was so great as to draw her towards the church in torrents of rain, manifested by her unusual courage the interior influence of the Holy Spirit urging her, even then, "to refuse nothing to Jesus."

Mme Martin's heart rejoiced at these first gleams of supernatural light; but to those joys were often added the sudden and passing anxieties of a mother; such as when Thérèse fell one day against the leg of a table and cut her forehead so badly that it was feared she would bear the mark all her life; or when, scarcely cured of one cold, she would contract another. But children, as we know, although liable to be affected seriously by the least accident, recover just as quickly. The clouds soon disappeared after each little storm, and the first smile of Thérèse, on recovering from these not very serious attacks, brought back the light anew to her mother's face.

From this time onward the family enjoyed frequent periods of tranquil happiness.

There is a painting which represents the complete group of children gathered around M. and Mme Martin in their sitting-room, in the rue Saint Blaise, during the quiet evening hours, probably towards the end of September when Marie and Pauline were on vacation at Alençon. In the subdued lamplight each one is occupied or at rest according to inclination. The father, his grave countenance rendered more venerable by his already white hair, has opened a newspaper, but he is more concerned with his children than with the news of the day, and he is speaking to Léonie, who is finishing some school task. Marie is leaning on the back of her mother's chair. Her attention is centered on little Thérèse, who, kneeling on her mother's lap with joined hands and eyes raised heavenwards, addresses herself to the little Jesus, whom she seems almost to see, as through a transparent veil. Kneeling at her mother's feet, Céline joins her prayer to that of her little sister whose dearest companion she was henceforth to be, while Pauline has interrupted her reading and sits smiling at the angelic child in converse with God. A beautiful and homely picture they make, a picture which gives an idea of the tastes and family life of the Martin household. Its members did not, it is true, form a rigorously closed circle, but their habitual intercourse scarcely extended beyond their nearest relations.

The deep affection of Mme Martin for her brother is already known to the reader. The more she knew of her sister-in-law, a woman of tender devotedness and solid piety, the more did she appreciate her friendship, and Mme Guérin became the confidante of all her joys and sorrows.

Mme Martin always made of her visit to Lisieux a special holiday; not indeed that she sought relaxation for herself, but she knew what pleasure it gave the children to have a few hours' play with little Jeanne Guérin and her sister Marie.

In the same way, the greatest pleasure of New Year's Day for the two families was the interchange of many and various presents, which on the one side and on the other aunts and uncles sent as New Year gifts to their little nieces.

One outing, however, had for Mme Martin a deeper, if not a sweeter, charm than the visit to Lisieux. She prized her day in the Visitation Convent of Le Mans above all others. This holy soul, who had at one time serious thoughts of the religious life, felt a profound attraction for the recollection and the self-abnegation of the cloister. When she found that her dearly loved sister had been attacked by phthisis, and that her days were numbered, her devotion redoubled towards the fervent religious who had, in great measure, been a mother to her two eldest children.

Mme Martin was anxious also that this dear sister should see her little Thérèse, who gave, even as a child, so great promise of virtue. Who knows? Perhaps this little daughter would one day occupy in a convent choir the place that she had thought destined for herself. So, one morning in April, 1875, they set out by train for Le Mans. "I took with me," writes Mme Martin,

> little Thérèse, who was delighted to travel by train. . . . When we had arrived at Le Mans she was tired and began to cry, but became quite bright afterwards, and behaved like a grown girl all the time we remained in

> the parlour. Why she cried when we went in I do not know; her heart was full; the tears fell freely. She was convulsed with silent weeping. Perhaps the grille frightened her. Afterwards all went well. She answered every question addressed to her, as if she were undergoing an examination.
>
> The Superioress came to see her, and gave her some little presents. When I said to her "Ask the good Mother for her blessing," she caused a general laugh by replying: '"Mother, will you come home with us?"[21]

We may smile at this little incident, but can we not see, even in this childish request, the inclination of the little soul towards everything which spoke of God, were it even the austere vesture of a religious?

But are we to suppose that Thérèse was altogether free from childish caprice, from those quick flashes of child-nature, where a word or a cry reveals the naturally self-willed temperament of all very young children? This would be the more astonishing, since, according to the testimony of Mme Martin, her husband had been inclined at first rather to spoil the little one. But even amidst childishly persistent and unreasonable demands, an ingenuous remark, an unexpected request, proved that Thérèse was losing nothing of her growing piety.

One day, when she offered some resistance, Mme Martin insisted on obedience from her little daughter. She wrote afterwards to Pauline that "little Thérèse is very lovable." Then she adds: "On Sunday, after I had gone to bed, she told me that she had not said her prayers. I replied: 'Go to sleep; you shall say them tomorrow.' But that did not satisfy her. To end the matter, her father helped her to say them. But he was not the teacher all the time. They had to say 'Grace.' He was not sure what this was for. In the end he had said everything nearly according to her ideas, and we had peace until the following morning."

Negligible details, the reader may be inclined to say at first. Perhaps so, if it were question of an ordinary child; but what seriously-minded Catholic will not be interested in searching for the first traces of divine influence in a soul which was to become afterwards so fruitful a source of supernatural charity?

The love of this innocent soul for God, and her attraction towards heaven where His presence could be eternally enjoyed, led Thérèse at times to give utterance to unexpected wishes. One day she surprised her mother by throwing her arms around her and telling her that she wished her to die. "Oh, how I wish *you would die,* my poor little mother." On her mother protesting, Thérèse explained: "But it is that you may go to heaven, since you say we must die to go there." And Mme Martin adds: "She expresses the same wish to her father in the fervour of her love for him."[22]

The desire of pleasing our Lord, or at least unwillingness to cause him pain, prompted her even at so early an age to overcome certain imperious tendencies which arose instinctively in her nature.

After leaving school Marie began to give lessons to Céline, who was three years and eight months older than Thérèse. Thérèse eagerly insisted on being allowed to stay in the room during lesson-time; nor was this without profit, for Mme Martin records that, at the end of December, 1875, before her third year was completed, Thérèse knew almost all her letters and was even beginning to read.[23]

Some months later in a letter to Pauline the mother wrote with ever growing delight: "She is endowed with more intelligence than I noticed in any of you."[24]

But the child's anxiety to learn was sometimes embarrassing. Marie, fearing that her work as teacher would be impeded by Thérèse, did not always invite her to come. But the little one was not to be denied; she came of her own accord.

"One day," Marie tells us,

> I saw her at the door of my room. She was trying to open it, but was too small to reach the handle. I waited to see what she would do; would she begin to cry, or would she call some one to open it for her? But no; she did not say a word, simply lay down outside the door in disappointment at her failure.

> I told my mother of the incident. She said to me: "She must not be allowed to do that."
>
> On the following day the same thing happened. Then I said: "Thérèse, you are grieving the Little Jesus." She looked at me earnestly. So well did she understand that never since has she repeated that action.[25]

Wonderful instance of divine solicitude; under the guiding influence of the virtues infused at baptism, virtues guarded and fostered by a mother's loving care, the fear and love of God had already sown in the soul of this child of two years seeds which were daily springing forth into meritorious acts.

Mme Martin was mindful of the ambition of her early motherhood: "That all her children might be consecrated to God." What a joy! For a long time she feared that this dream would never be realized; but her hopes began now to revive. The deep and earnest piety of Marie, supported by a ready and acute intelligence, her constant application, her simple and modest tastes, pointed undoubtedly to a religious vocation. The brilliant qualities of Pauline might have given grounds to fear vanity, but that she was as obedient as industrious and her earnest preparation of class-work was exceeded by her fidelity to religious exercises. The account of her progress at the Visitation Convent was her mother's great joy and consolation. "You are my true friend," she wrote to Pauline; "you give me courage to bear trial with patience. . . . I feel grateful to you for the joy that you are to us all. God will be your recompense in this world as well as in the next, for duty faithfully done brings its reward of happiness even here below."[26]

Despite the inequalities of an uneven temperament, Léonie showed so real an attachment to her aunt in the convent as to give rise to the thought that she might one day join her there. In 1875 Sr. Marie-Dosithée wrote to her brother, M. Guérin: "Léonie inspires me with great hopes for the future. True she is somewhat difficult to manage, but she has a heart of gold. I find in her a fund of good sense and great force of character. When this child sees her duty nothing will hold her back from carrying it out."[27]

In 1875 Céline was six years of age. "She is," says Mme Martin, "very gentle, she learns easily, and will be a charming child, if God leaves her with us."[28]

As to the little Benjamin of the family, who manifested so clearly by her unexpected remarks and precocious reflections the impress of the Holy Spirit, there was good reason to hope that she would one day be united to Him for ever.

In order to keep alive these high aspirations, Mme Martin gave her moments of leisure to the reading of some book which portrayed the joys of the religious life, joys which had at one time won her own heart, and which she desired now more than ever for her children.

"I am reading at present," she wrote, "the life of St. Chantal. I am rapt in admiration. It is all the more interesting for me, because I have a great love for the Order of the Visitation; I love it now more than ever. How fortunate are they who are called to that sacred retreat."[29]

And some weeks later we find the following: "I do nothing but dream of the cloister and solitude. Indeed, with the ideas that I have, I do not know how it was not my vocation either to remain unmarried or to enter a convent. I would now wish to live to a great age, so that I might retire into solitude when all my children have been brought up."[30]

But these hopes of long life and of peaceful old age in the retirement of the cloister were not to be satisfied.

God had other designs for that chosen one who was preparing souls to be consecrated to Him in the religious life. By the merit of suffering heroically endured she will complete the spiritual formation of her elder children, and will obtain for little Thérèse—that child already predestined—grace to become, one day, the purest victim of God's merciful love.

3

Growing Virtue of Thérèse— Her First Great Trial

"During my whole life God has been pleased to surround me with love: my earliest memories are of smiles and tender caresses."[1] Thérèse attributes her early attraction towards good, which we have already noticed in its commencement, to the influence of this holy affection and the example of every family virtue. We must add to these the austere action of trial which raised her young soul, deprived from the first of the unstable happiness of earth, towards the joys of heaven.

Before setting out to follow her progress in the path of virtue, we must first complete the picture of this family life where self-denial was the sustaining force of charity, and where the devotedness of each called forth from the others the most meritorious effort by the influence of example. Notice first these actions which, in their daily exercise by the parents before the eyes of Thérèse, must have given her little by little a high sense of duty. The traits thus described will serve to bring into clearer outline the picture of this Christian home.

We have already given the reader an idea of Mme Martin's zeal for work; but her husband, although retired from his former business, did not leave his wife unaided in her lace industry.

On the front of the house occupied by the family was a marble slab bearing this inscription: "Louis Martin, Manufacturer of Point d'Alençon," and this notice gives an indication of the very real part which the master of the house took in the work. It was M. Martin who transacted all the business outside the house and took charge of the delivery to distant places. He also often kept the accounts. These occupations gave him opportunity to practise virtues of which little Thérèse, an astute observer from her infancy, took note, and marked the progress.

Thus he would on no account take goods on credit; everything must be paid for on the spot. The workers too must be paid regularly "in order that," as he said himself, "a justly earned wage or a sum of money due for goods received may not be retained unjustly, and furthermore, to safeguard oneself from running into debt by inadvertence." Neither would he increase his income by frequent speculation, even if justifiable. He would say: "I know I could easily take large profits by the skillful manipulation of my capital, but speculation is a slippery incline, and I have no desire whatever to follow too closely the fluctuating values of those perishable securities."

His strictness in observing the rest from servile work prescribed for the Lord's Day, his scrupulous care in carrying out the Church's exercises of penance, are already known to the reader. In this respect also his wife surpassed the ordinary practice of the faithful. What an example of self-denial and sacrifice we find in this noble woman who, having come to Lisieux eight months before her death to undergo an operation for an incurable disease of long standing, refused to partake of the evening meal prepared for her "because it was an Ember Day, and she intended to keep the fast."

To such heroic souls as hers are the supernatural manifestations of heaven vouchsafed. We have seen with what tenderness Mme Martin watched over little Hélène until her death at the early age of five and a half years. Recalling afterwards a slight untruth that had escaped the child in its innocent prattling, the mother was reflecting sorrowfully one day before a statue of the Blessed Virgin that her Hélène might be in purgatory, when from this statue, which was later to play a part in the life of Thérèse, came the reassuring words: "She is here at my side."[2]

With Heaven-sent communications this devout Catholic was also to experience, after the manner of certain saints who were physically tormented by the demon, the brutality of the powers of hell raised in jealous strife against her virtues. One evening,[3] as Mme Martin was sitting alone in the lower room, a passage of an edifying work which she had just laid down led her to meditate on the trials inflicted on the servants of God by the spirit of darkness. She said to herself: "Such attacks of the evil one will never be directed against me; only the saints are destined for trials of this nature." At that moment an enormous weight, as of the claw of some wild beast, bore down upon her shoulder. After the first sensation of terror caused by this ferocious attack followed the calm of a soul which feels above all that it is in the hands of God.

Such were the lives that came daily under the notice of little Thérèse. With "her quick intelligence, her open and impressionable mind,"[4] she observed these examples attentively, admired them, and under the influence of the Holy Spirit grew to love more and more these devoted parents whom she felt to be the harbingers of the divine goodness to her in her weakness. "No one can imagine," she wrote, "how I loved papa and mama. I showed my affection for them in numberless ways, for I was very demonstrative; the ways I employed make me laugh now when I think of them."[5]

With this tender affection as its inspiration and guiding force, the piety of her young soul developed. She wished to be a joy to her parents; she knew that they owed their perfection in every good to the great love they had for God; she understood, besides, that the beneficent Being must be loved above all, his commands obeyed, everything that would displease him avoided, and she set herself with all the ardour of her nature to follow these dictates of conscience. Nor was hers the unquestioning piety of a child satisfying itself in the incoherent recital of a few prayers; the first dawnings of reason in Thérèse were applied to discerning the relation between the obligations imposed by God and the eternal recompense of heaven. Eternity of happiness is a reward—a reward which must be won by merit; this truth grasped already by the childish intelligence formed the keynote of her life. "Thérèse told me this morning," writes Mme Martin, "that she wished to go to heaven, and, to obtain this, she would always act like a little angel."[6]

Her lofty idea of the goodness of God led her to believe, in her innocence, that the Almighty would never separate a child from its mother, even should that child offend him ever so much. Hear her in this little dialogue:

"Shall I go to heaven, mama?"

"Yes, if you are very good."

"Ah, mama, if I was not good I should then go to hell. But I know what I would do, I would fly up to you in heaven, and you would hold me close in your arms. How then would God be able to take me away?"[7] And her look confirmed her conviction that God would be powerless to touch her if she were once in the arms of her mother.

Some months later she gave an example of more orthodox theology. On her sister Céline asking "How can God be in a little host?" Thérèse replied: "That is not so wonderful, since God is all-powerful." "And what does all-powerful mean?" "It means that he can do everything he wills."[8]

We have been left the following charming picture sketched by Mme Martin in one of her letters to Pauline, still at the Visitation Convent.

> Céline and Thérèse are inseparable. Two more loving companions could not be found. When Céline is taken away for lessons Thérèse is immediately in tears. Alas! what is she to do? Her little friend is going from her. . . . Marie takes pity on her and brings her also, and the poor baby sits at the table with them for two, or maybe three, hours. She is given pearls to string or a piece of cloth to sew. She does not dare to stir, and from time to time gives vent to a deep sigh, especially when her needle comes unthreaded, for she is not able to thread it and she dare not disturb Marie. Then the big tears roll down her cheeks. Quickly Marie turns to console her, threads her needle again, and the poor little angel smiles through her tears.[9]

But while her little fingers were busy her ears were open to all that was being said, and Thérèse carried away in her naturally retentive memory many precious ideas, especially regarding the things of God.

Thus she learned by listening much more quickly than by reading.

While ever showing a predilection for holy things, Thérèse set herself, at the age of four, to learn by heart little pieces of poetry which she recited in the family circle, to the great delight of everybody. As can be well imagined, Mme Martin found in these little family gatherings around Thérèse a solace in her heavy toil. Let us again hear her tell the glad thoughts that filled her heart.

"This dear little one," she wrote to Pauline,

> is the joy of us all. She will be good; the seeds of goodness are plainly there already. She speaks only of God; she would not omit her prayers for all the world. I wish you could hear her recite little verses that she has learned by heart. Never have I seen anything so pleasing. Without any help she gets the exact expression and tone of voice. This is particularly true when she recites:
>
> "Sweet little child with locks of gold,
> Where, think you, hath the Lord his Home?
> —Wide earth doth the Almighty hold;
> He ruleth, too, the great blue dome."
>
> When she comes to the last line she raises her eyes to heaven with an expression truly angelic. We never tire of hearing her repeat it, so beautiful is her rendering; there is something so heavenly in her expression that we are enraptured.[10]

The influence of this family life where all were so united in the bonds of affection and holy joy, the atmosphere of tender love and piety ruling and penetrating every word and action, had a profound effect in the formation of Thérèse's character.

To the undaunted faith and devotion of her mother, to the unfailing goodness—unmingled with weakness—of her saintly father, to the charming tenderness of sisterly affection, did this child owe, after God, her sweet graciousness as well as her desire to diffuse peace and joy around her, and her imperative wish to please, at any cost, the good Jesus whom she saw so ardently loved in her home. Before noting the final indications of the educative action of her parents, let us try to understand the part which the influence of her sisters had in the formation of her character.

We have on this subject the invaluable testimony of the saint's own words: "I remember," she writes,

> the great love which I had at this time for my dear godmother [her sister Marie], who had just finished her studies at the Visitation Convent. Without seeming to do so, I took note of all that was done and said before me; I think I judged of everything then as now, I listened attentively to whatever she taught Céline. To obtain the favour of admission into the room during lessons I was very well-behaved and obeyed her in everything. She also gave me numerous little presents, which, although of small worth, pleased me immensely.[11]

Mme Martin shows by the following incident Marie's authority over her godchild.

> Marie loves her little sister very much and finds her charming. Indeed, if she did not she would be hard to please, for the little one dreads lest she should go against Marie's wishes in anything. Yesterday I wanted to give her a rose, knowing the delight she took in flowers, but she begged me not to cut it; Marie had forbidden that. She flushed crimson with emotion. In spite of all I cut two roses for her, but she would not dare to appear with them in the house. It was useless to reassure her that the roses belonged to me. "No," she said; "they are Marie's." A very small thing disturbs the child.[12]

Notwithstanding her continual contact with the little one in her almost maternal capacity of first instructor, it was not this eldest sister who had the most marked influence on the formation and future of Thérèse. Strange to relate, it was the example of a sister who lived as yet far away from her; stranger still, it was a little word concerning the vocation of Pauline which decided the destiny of Thérèse.

She tells us this expressly herself: "From the time I commenced to speak, whenever mama asked me 'Of what are you thinking?' my invariable answer was 'Of Pauline.' Sometimes I heard others say that Pauline would be a religious; then, without knowing too well what it meant, I thought to myself 'I also will be a religious.' That is one of my first memories, and since then I never once changed my resolution. Her example it was that, from the age of two years, drew me towards the Divine Spouse of virgins."[13]

Wonderful message from the God of Love to this faithful soul through that sister who, after having unconsciously drawn her towards the cloister from her earliest years, was afterwards to be her official guide in the way of perfection. This declaration of Thérèse regarding the unusual manifestation of God's Providence towards her should be carefully borne in mind. It was this consciousness of vocation to a life of perfection, a consciousness prudently but constantly entertained, which explains the heroic resolution of Thérèse, at the age of three, never to refuse anything to Jesus.

The influence of Léonie on the education of Thérèse seems to have been less marked. Naturally a very delicate child, she had to content herself with courses of studies in the town of Alençon, so that she was little at the house. There were times, however, when her affectionate nature expanded, and she lavished her tenderness on Thérèse, whose generous heart responded with gladness. "Dear little Léonie," she writes,

> held also a large place in my heart; she loved me very much. In the evening, when she came home from lessons, she took care of me while the rest of the family went for a walk. I seem to hear even now her gentle voice in the sweet refrains with which she sang me to sleep. I can recall her first Communion perfectly. I remember also her companion, the poor child whom mother had dressed, according to a time-honoured custom among families in easy circumstances, at Alençon.

> This little girl never left Léonie's side for an instant during the whole of that happy day, and in the evening at dinner she was given the place of honour.[14]

This incident throws one more light on the picture of that charitable mother, who sought above all else to teach her children by good example.

Céline, on account of her tender years, could not have the same influence as the other sisters on the life and habits of Thérèse. Nevertheless her precocious qualities formed a real attraction for her little companion, for she also was a charming child. "I believe," her mother wrote, "that Céline will be a great consolation to me. She has an exceptionally good disposition, quite above the ordinary. She is already most anxious to find out how she should prepare for her first Holy Communion."[15]

But she was above all the confidante of her little sister, her constant companion in every childish game and recreation. It was Céline, more than any other, who was to create around Thérèse that atmosphere of radiant joy, whose memory made her ever afterwards bless "these sunny years of childhood." It was also from her childhood companionship with Céline that Thérèse learned the sweetness of a pure and tender attachment which was to prepare her to receive later into her virginal heart, already trained to the immolation of self, the outpourings of divine love.

What more pleasing than this scene from the life of the two sisters, traced by Mme Martin?

> Céline and Thérèse love one another dearly: they never require other company than themselves alone. The nurse gave Thérèse a cock and hen of the smaller variety of fowls; at once the child gave the cock to Céline. Every day, after dinner, Céline goes to catch the little cock. She catches it immediately, as well as the hen which, nevertheless, is not so easy to seize hold of; but Céline is so agile that with one bound she has it in her hands. Then they bring them in beside the fire and there amuse themselves for quite a long time.
>
> On Sunday Thérèse took it into her head to leave her own cot and go to sleep with Céline. The maid, on

> coming to dress her, found no Thérèse. She saw her at last, but the little one clung to Céline, saying: "Do leave me here, Louise; you see that we two are like two little white chicks that cannot be separated."[16]

Should Céline leave the table before Thérèse, the latter would immediately leave her dessert unfinished and go join her sister. Oftentimes thoughts of higher things, or some pious word or remark, were intermingled with their innocent amusements. "On Sundays," Thérèse relates,

> as I was too small to go to Church, mama remained at home to take care of me. Understanding the circumstances, I tried to behave very properly, and walked about only on tiptoe in order not to make any noise; but when I heard the door being opened it was the signal for an outburst of joy. I would rush to my dear little sister, saying: "O Céline, give me quickly some of the blessed bread!" One day she had none. . . . What was I to do? I could not remain deprived of it, for I called this *feast my Mass*. All at once I conceived a brilliant idea. "You have no blessed bread. Well then, make some!" Céline opened the cupboard, took out the bread, cut off a morsel, and reciting over it the *Ave Maria* in a solemn tone, triumphantly presented it to me. And I, having first made the sign of the Cross, ate it with great devotion, finding that it tasted exactly like blessed bread.[17]

Thus, in every circumstance, in the simplest actions as well as in religious rites, we find the soul of this child penetrated with sentiments of piety which fostered in her respect for the things of God.

We have passed in review some outstanding examples of religious courage and devotion, given by the parents to their children from their very infancy. The force of good example would not, it is true, have influenced Thérèse so powerfully had not these loved ones who watched over her with such solicitude surrounded her at the same time with love. It was by love that they developed divine charity within her to so high a degree—charity urging her to sacrifice and even to death.

In all Mme Martin's dealings with her daughters, tenderness was governed by virility of character. Hers was that strength of will which would never, for any consideration, foster a dangerous disposition in her children. On the other hand she was ready, when occasion offered, to shower upon them the sweetest and most touching marks of attachment.

She has alluded, herself, to the loving condescension which she showed to the childish desires of Thérèse.

"She will not go up the stairs alone," she writes, "without calling out at each step 'Mama! Mama!' Another step, another cry of 'Mama!' And if, by chance, I forget to reply at each call 'Yes, my little child!' she remains there without moving a single step."[18]

On the part of her father, we see examples of even more demonstrative affection. The moment he returns from business, Thérèse runs to him, throws her arms around him, and unceremoniously seats herself on his foot. Her delight is then to have herself carried along, mounted in this way. Mme Martin smilingly reproaches her husband for complying with every wish of Thérèse. "Well, after all," he says, "is she not the Queen?" And he forthwith takes her in his arms, seats her on his shoulder, embraces her, and showers upon her every mark of tenderness.

This upbringing by love, where the thought of God and the desire to please Him above all held so large a place, had no hurtful influence on the development of the normal qualities of Thérèse. Grace perfected nature, without destroying it. Like all children of her years, she loved play; not the more violent open-air pastimes,[19] but indoor amusements, for which she was well provided with a varied collection of playthings, toy-carriages, dolls of different models, and ribbons to adorn them.

She was delighted with a box of delicious bonbons which her uncle and aunt in Lisieux sent her on the occasion of a baptism. When afterwards someone spoke in her presence about the wealth of a rich proprietor, she clapped her hands and exclaimed that she preferred her aunt's present to all the lands of this potentate.

But beyond everything else, before her toys and even cakes, she preferred flowers: garden flowers whose rich colours filled her eyes with delight, flowers of the field above all, for her inborn love of subdued elegance and delicate beauty found its counterpart in the simple and too often unappreciated charms, the unobtrusive radiance and graceful formation of wild blossoms.

In her innocent soul were springing up and blossoming forth, promiscuously perhaps, these thoughts so beautifully expressed by a recent poet in the lines which we give here in paraphrase:

> Flowers of the meadows and woods, mountain blossoms and sweet water-flowers that are rocked to sleep by the song of the reeds. And you fair buds that bloom within orchard walls vieing with the butterflies in your tints of white and red. Flowers clothed in the purple of evening; golden and azure blossoms forming mystic censers, as you spread perfume from your white corollas. Gentle-faced flowers, and flowers with eyes of blue, heather blossoms which seem a bright reflection of the sunset on the steep hillside slopes. Primrose and lily, first-fruits of the spring, silver daisies that deck the fields with stars. Flower of the Gauls, vervain that gave to our ancestors the mystic portents of the future. The limpid stream waters you with its rippling wavelets—the virgin soil both nourish your deep-set roots. For good and for bad, for all, you exhale your perfume, sweet sisters, God's own flowers of the fields![20]

Thus it was a red-letter day for Céline and Thérèse when M. Martin brought them to the "Pavillion." It stood on the outskirts of the town, a small house, quaint with its rustic furniture, surrounded by a large garden where, during the summer months, strawberries, currants, geraniums, and beautiful deep-coloured roses abounded. Thérèse returned home laden with enormous bouquets, formed not so much of the roses from the "Pavillon" as of daisies, buttercups, and wild poppies, gathered here and there along the paths. She seems to have understood, even at this early age, the symbolism of flowers offered in token of love. And so, in surrounding with wild flowers the statue of the Blessed Virgin, held in such honour in the home, or St. Joseph's image before which her mother was wont to kneel, she intends to signify the oblation of her soul and her life. At all events, she never prayed more fervently than in the oratory prepared for the "month of Mary." Her eldest sister assures us of this in convincing language. "It is quite a ceremony," she writes to Pauline,

> this preparation for the "month of Mary."[21] Mama is so very particular about it, more particular than the Blessed Virgin herself. She wants hawthorn branches reaching to the ceiling, the walls decorated with evergreens, etc. . . . Thérèse is in wonderment at it all. Every morning she goes bounding with gladness there to say her prayers. If you knew how frolicsome and ingenious she is. I have a wonderful admiration for this little "bouquet." Everyone in the house showers affection on her.[22]

Not alone had Thérèse retained, under the action of divine grace, her childlike candour and grace of manner, but she was remarkable for the charming spontaneity of her language and the originality of her lively repartee, which showed itself from time to time in racy and piquant phrases. One morning Céline was tormenting her father to bring her and Thérèse to the "Pavillon," as he had done the evening before. In a half-jesting, half-serious tone, M. Martin said: "Are you joking? Do you imagine that I can bring you there every day?" Thérèse was over in a corner amusing herself with a little wand and seemingly quite occupied with her toy. Suddenly she turned with a nonchalant air: "Oh, we need not flatter ourselves with the notion that papa will bring us there every day!"[23] Céline hung down her head, and "papa" laughed heartily.

This atmosphere of tender affection, where the childhood of Thérèse passed quietly amidst prayer, innocent amusement, and family love, contributed, as we know, to develop her spirituality; but although we have on her own testimony that she was not really spoiled by her parents, still self-love, which, as a consequence of original sin, has root in the souls of all, even the predestined, was sometimes to make itself felt in her virginal nature.

Thérèse recognized these attempts, weak and fleeting attempts, yet sufficiently distinct to leave an imprint on her memory, which, in her humility, she has noted in the *Histoire d'une Ame.*

About the age of three she had some fits of the wayward stubbornness so usual at that age. Her mother mentions this without extenuation, but without disquietude, recognizing in Thérèse the good qualities which are its corrective. "My little Céline," she writes,

> is altogether inclined to virtue; it is in every fibre of her being. She is the soul of candour and has an instinctive horror of evil.
>
> As to the "little ferret," not much can yet be predicted about her; she is still so young, so heedless. She has a remarkable intellect and a heart of gold; she is very affectionate too, and absolutely frank. It is quaint to see her running after me to make her confession: "Mama, I have pushed Céline once and I hit her once, but I will not do it again." And so for everything she does.[24]

In spite of the precaution of the parents, who, while tenderly loving this child, never overlooked her slightest unruly caprice, Thérèse appears in a few rare instances as a spoiled child. But what touching regrets make amends for this momentary forgetfulness; with what promptitude the fault is atoned for! Let us hear her own words:

> I recall perfectly one day, when I was amusing myself on the swing, my father who was just passing by said to me: "Come and kiss me, little queen." Contrary to my usual custom, I would not stir, but replied in a defiant tone: "Come yourself, papa!" He very rightly did not listen to me. Marie was present at the time. "Bold little one!" she said to me, "how naughty to answer papa in that manner." Immediately I got down from that ill-fated swing; the lesson had gone home. The whole house resounded with my cries of contrition; I climbed the stairs in all haste, not calling "Mama" now at each

> step; I thought only of finding papa and of being reconciled to him, which was speedily accomplished.[25]

The same, or an almost similar, scene was repeated between Thérèse and her mother. Mme Martin herself recounts it.

> The other day I wished to embrace Thérèse before going downstairs, but she appeared to be sound asleep. I would not risk awakening her, and was turning away when Marie said "Mama, I am sure she is only pretending to be asleep." Hearing this, I bent down to kiss her; but she immediately hid herself under the coverlet, saying, with the air of a spoiled child, "I don't want anyone to look at me." I was not in the least pleased, and took care to make her realize it.
>
> Two minutes afterwards I heard her crying, and soon, to my great surprise, found her at my side. She had got out unaided from the cot, had come down the stairs with bare feet, tripping over her nightdress, which was too long for her; her little face was wet with tears. "Mama," she said, throwing herself down at my knees, "I have been naughty; forgive me." Pardon was quickly granted. I took the little cherub in my arms, pressed her to my heart, and covered her with kisses.[26]

Would we not be tempted to say "Happy fault which is atoned for by so touching a reparation"?

The child adopted the practice, from her earliest years, of making known even involuntary little accidents of which she might have been the cause. Let us hear her mother speak on this subject:

> As soon as she has done the slightest thing out of the way everybody must know about it. Yesterday, having quite accidentally torn a little corner of the wallpaper, she got into a pitiable state. Then papa must be told as soon as possible. When he came back, four hours afterwards, everyone had forgotten about it; but she ran to Marie and said, "Tell papa quickly that I have torn the paper." She stood there like a criminal awaiting sentence, but she has the idea in her little head that pardon will come more easily if she accuses herself.[27]

Not content with accusing herself, she makes an effort to repair the harm done, and this by means so quaint and simple as to draw an indulgent smile from her parents and redoubled tenderness from all.

One day she broke a little vase which her mother had given her. Immediately, as was her custom, she came to show what she had done, and, seeing the look of displeasure on her mother's face, she commenced to cry. A moment afterwards she came to her and said: "Do not be vexed, little mother; when I earn money of my own, I promise I will buy you another." And Mme Martin adds in her letter to Pauline: "As you can see, I shall have to wait some time for it!"[28]

Notwithstanding these little clouds, everything contributed to the joy of Thérèse. Her intelligence, her animation and charming grace of manner became every day more attractive. Her highly developed piety was, all unknown to herself, drawing wonder from those around her. But what solidity could be guaranteed to virtue, developing as hers now was, amid the smiles of her parents and sisters, scarcely interrupted by occasional gentle reprimands? Might not all her acts of devotion, now sustained by a mother's watchful love, be checked by any discouragement? Divine Providence must guide the future.

In order to increase and grow strong, Thérèse's infant piety required, like every other, the fortifying influence of trial. God, in His immutable design, early bestowed on her this chastening influence to such an extent that she could write later, she who, as a child, had been so fondled and caressed: "The Cross has never, from my cradle, ceased to accompany me."

To the little attacks of illness and physical suffering, borne smilingly without a word of complaint, Thérèse felt already the need of adding voluntary privations. Marie had brought from the Visitation Convent a special chaplet, used amongst the boarders to count their acts of virtue. Each bead was movable, and could be separated a space from the rest; every act of self-sacrifice was marked by moving on a bead. She gave Céline and Thérèse each a chaplet. From this time onward Thérèse was to be seen, almost all day, with the chaplet in her hand, moving forward a bead for every tiny sacrifice that she succeeded in accomplishing.

The two little sisters encouraged each other unceasingly to renew these sacrifices. They called their acts of virtue "practices," so that in their conversation, and even at their games, there was continual question of "practices."

One day, as they were having a very earnest discussion on this point in their garden of rue Saint Blaise, their mysterious conversation aroused the curiosity of a neighbor who leaned out of the window in a vain attempt to understand their meaning. Finally she stole down quietly to the maid to ask her what were these "practices" which seemed so deeply to interest the children.[29]

This indiscreet step did not prevent either Céline or Thérèse from reverting on every occasion to their favorite discussion. Of small importance, however, is more talk about these little privations, or even noting their number. The acquisition of solid durable virtue was the real end directing all.

Soon it became evident that Thérèse was not counting her chaplet in vain. "How happy I was at this time!" she declared afterwards. "Not only did I begin to enjoy life, but virtue had for me a real charm. I had then, I think, the same dispositions as now; I exercised already great control over all my actions. Thus I had acquired the habit of refraining from complaint when anything belonging to me was taken away; also when accused unjustly I preferred rather to remain silent than to offer excuse. In this there was no merit on my part; I simply acted naturally."[30]

These "natural" actions were none the less consciously done for God, since, according to her mother, the child "put her hand in her pocket a hundred times a day to move forward a bead on her chaplet every time she had practiced a mortification." But they were accomplished so easily and sweetly as to leave no doubt that the "little sprite" lived under the continual guidance of the Holy Spirit.

Her love of wild flowers is already known. One Sunday, when she had spent the afternoon in the country gathering cornflowers, daisies, and buttercups in abundance, she returned home, glowing with delight, and set herself to arrange in clusters her wealth of blossoms. Her grandmother, Mme Martin, too old to realize certain delicate attractions of child-nature, claimed the flowers to decorate a little altar erected in the house. Poor Thérèse felt the tears welling to her eyes, but controlled herself so well that only Céline, who knew her intimately, perceived her emotion; she gave away her dear flowers one by one to the very last.[31]

In further ways, too, Thérèse was to find that, in order to please fully her divine Lord, the mere adoption of a certain round of practices did not suffice; she must show herself ready to accept gladly His good pleasure in all things.

A little incident which took place at this time is referred to later, as symbolizing the spontaneous and whole-hearted acceptation of God's will in all things. This early recognition of the importance of generosity with our Divine Lord grew afterwards to be the keynote of all her virtue.

"One day," she writes,

> Léonie, realizing, I suppose, that she was now too old to play with dolls, came to us (Céline and myself) with a basket full of dolls' dresses, pretty bits of cloth, trimmings, etc. Placing her doll on the top of these, she said to us: "Here, little sisters, choose for yourselves." Céline looked, and chose a ball of silk braid. After a moment's consideration, I put forward my hand and said "I choose everything." And I carried off basket and doll without further ceremony.
>
> My whole life could be summed up in this little incident of my childhood. Later, when I realized what was meant by perfection, I understood that in order to become a saint, great sufferings must be endured, all thought of self must be put aside—in a word, the most perfect must be sought in all. I realized that there are in holiness many degrees, that each soul is free to correspond with the advances of Our Lord, to do little or great things for His love, to *choose* between the sacrifices that he asks. Then, as in my childhood days, I cried out: "My God, I choose all! I do not wish to be a saint by halves. I am not afraid to suffer for Your sake; only

> one thing do I fear—my own will. Take it from me, for I *choose everything* You will."[32]

These generous tendencies could only be in their commencement in the child of four years. But, to the grace of Christian education, and the influence of edifying example which had so largely developed Thérèse's piety, was now to be added the heavenly protection of her saintly aunt, recently taken from this world, and a share in the merit of severe physical suffering which for long months her mother was to endure.

On February 24, 1877, Mme Martin received from one of the Visitation nuns at Le Mans the following lines:

> The life of our dear Sr. Marie-Dosithée, that was so edifying, closed this morning by a death one might envy. She was quite conscious and preserved an admirable calmness to the end. One evening, almost the last before her death, she said to our mother: "O Mother, I have no other thoughts but of love, trust, and abandonment. Help me to thank God for it all."
>
> We can say that we have now another protectress in heaven, for it would be difficult to find a more saintly ending to a holier life.[33]

Sustained in her great sorrow by this hope, Mme Martin induced her children, and more especially Thérèse, to implore the protection of their aunt, now, she believed, among the blessed in heaven. Through the intercession of her dear sister, joined to that of the Holy Virgin Mary, she hoped for a miracle of which she personally stood in need.

In her early years she had hurt herself so severely against the corner of a table as to cause a permanent swelling in her breast. This had not been very painful in the beginning, but developed in time into a fibrous tumour. Without a word of complaint, never interrupting her fatiguing work, or failing in a single duty to her family or her religion, Mme Martin had for sixteen years felt this malady doing its fatal work. The time came when intense pain made it no longer possible to hide her condition from her family. They immediately took her to a doctor in Alençon,

M. Prévost. For the sake of form he began to write a prescription. "Of what use will it be?" asked Mme Martin. The doctor, looking at her, said in a low voice, "It is useless; I give it to please patients."

In spite of this, M. Isidore Guérin recommended an operation. For this end he took his sister to an experienced medical man in Lisieux, who declared that it was now too late.

Given up by the doctors, having no other prospect than death in the midst of terrible suffering, this courageous Christian returned to Alençon, took up again her ordinary round of life, having no other thought but to persevere unfailingly and unostentatiously in duty, to the end.

On her return home she wrote to her sister-in-law: "You are really causing yourself too much anxiety on my account; you put me to shame by it. I do not deserve that people should be so concerned about me; my life is not so precious."[34]

She gave up, however, her lace industry, well knowing that she would never enjoy the leisure thus acquired. She resigned herself to the inevitable with barely expressed regret. "I have given up in good earnest my point d'Alençon and now begin to live on my income. All things considered, I believe it is time. My greatest fear is that I shall not enjoy my retreat for long, although I can say that it has cost me dear."[35]

The image of death had become familiar to her. She looked it unflinchingly in the face, although it seemed to her that she would still be of use in this world in order to finish the education of her children now that her sister was gone. Once more she began to cherish the hope that, by the all-powerful help of the Queen of heaven, and the intercession of her dear Visitandine, a pilgrimage to Lourdes would restore her to health. She wrote to her daughter Pauline: "It was about ten or fifteen days after your aunt's death that, rightly or wrongly, this confidence which I cannot explain entered my mind, and with it a great desire to live for another few years in order to bring up my children."[36]

A pilgrimage to Lourdes from the diocese of Angers was organized for June 18, 1877. Mme Martin, with her three daughters, Marie, Pauline, and Lèonie, succeeded in being enrolled amongst the pilgrims. "The trouble and expense are considerable," she wrote; "but if I obtain the favour so greatly desired, I shall not be paying too dear for it. Moreover, it seems to me that the greater the sacrifices I shall make, the more disposed will the Blessed Virgin be to hear our prayer."[37]

Her chief reason for taking the children was the hope which she placed in their fervent prayers, for with unparalleled faith they prepared to besiege the Immaculate Mother by their supplications.

The journey was more fatiguing than had been anticipated. Overwhelming heat, unsuitable food, and the difficulty of finding proper sleeping accommodation in Lourdes all contributed to weaken the invalid.

The visits to the piscina were without success. On her return home she wrote to her relatives in Lisieux:

> I was immersed four times in the piscina, the last time two hours before we set out for home. I was in the icy water above my shoulders, but did not find it so cold as in the morning. I remained there over a quarter of an hour, hoping all the time that the Blessed Virgin would cure me. While actually in the water I felt no pain, but once out, the stinging recommenced as usual.
>
> For your sake I would have been doubly happy to be cured. Alas! the Holy Virgin has said to us as to Bernadette: "I will make you happy, not in this world but in the next."[38]

Strong in this hope, the courageous pilgrim set out on her homeward way, joining heartily in the hymns of the pilgrimage, while her daughters remained silent with grief and distress. But, on reaching Normandy, she broke down, and was forced to admit that the journey had increased her malady. Her husband, with Céline and Thérèse, was awaiting her at the station. He had passed an anxious week, hoping every day for the good news that never came. He was grief-stricken, and the little ones were astonished to find that the Blessed Virgin had not hearkened to their innocent prayers. M. Martin was, as his wife tells us, surprised to see her come back as happy as if she had obtained her desired favour. "That," she added, "reanimated his courage and restored the good spirits of all."[39]

This attitude of the sufferer was adopted out of pure charity towards her family. To her daughter Pauline, whose solid foundation in virtue was well known to her, and whom, on that account, she wished to train in unwavering acceptance of trial, she confided her real thoughts. "I wish to know," she writes to her, "what your present frame of mind is, whether you are still wroth with the Blessed Virgin because she has not made you 'leap for joy.' Do not hope for much happiness on this earth; you would meet with too many disappointments. For my part, I know by experience the fickleness of earthly joy; if my hopes were not centred on heaven I should indeed be unhappy."[40]

Nevertheless, in order to bring consolation to her loved ones and to sustain her own courage, the poor mother still continued to pray for a miracle. She greatly desired to see once more the dear family in Lisieux, always so affectionately helpful to her. She even planned to bring some of her daughters with her. Telling her sister-in-law of the children's longing to accompany her, she added: "The smallest is the most eager of them all. She will remember all her life that she was left behind at Alençon two years ago; when she refers to it, the tears come to her eyes immediately. She is a charming little creature, my Thérèse; I assure you that she will succeed."[41]

The poor child who feared that she would not be taken to Lisieux did not foresee the cruel necessity which would soon constrain her to this journey.

Mercilessly the dread malady progressed. June and July were months of intolerable suffering. No sleep or calm, not a moment's respite for the poor invalid on her bed of pain, where she passed part of her days. She realized fully the gravity of her condition, and with that faith which had been the guiding light and the mainstay of her life, she prepared for the inevitable. "I have made up my mind to it," she writes, "and am trying to prepare for death. I must not lose a moment of the short space which I have yet to live. These are days of salvation which will never return; I must, then, profit by them."[42]

In order to secure in an especial manner the grace of final perseverance, and to give even to the end a living example of devotion to religious duty, she made a final painful effort to be present at Mass in the parish church on the first Friday of August. At each step she felt as if her neck were being pierced by a stiletto. Agonizing pains all down her right side obliged her several times to stand still. She persevered in spite of all. In this condition of suffering she assisted at her last Mass, and from the Sacrifice of Calvary renewed on the altar drew courage to face the final combat.

The following weeks saw the gradual decline of the poor body sinking beneath the ravages of an implacable malady.

It was not thought well that the two youngest children, Céline and Thérèse, should witness these scenes of suffering; those two whom the devoted mother had, up to the last, tended with loving care. It was decided that they be taken to a friend's house each day. On this subject we will consult Thérèse's memoirs.

> Céline and I were like two poor little exiles. Every morning Mme X. came for us, and we spent the day at her house. Once, when we had not time to say our prayers before starting, Céline whispered to me on the way, "Shall we tell that we have not said our prayers?" "Oh, yes," I replied. Timidly she confided her trouble to this lady, who immediately replied: "Well, my little ones, you shall say them." Then, leaving us in a large room, she went away. Céline looked at me stupefied; I was no less amazed, and exclaimed: "Ah, that is not what mama would have done; she always helped us to say our prayers."
>
> In spite of the distractions which they endeavored to provide for us during the day, our thoughts were ever returning to our dear mother. I remember once when Céline was given a delicious apricot, her leaning towards me and saying, "We will not eat it, we will

> give it to mama." Alas! our poor mama was now too ill to eat the fruits of this earth. She was never more to be satiated except by the glory of God in heaven, when she would drink with Jesus the mystic wine of which He spoke at His last supper, promising to share it with us in the kingdom of His Father.[43]

One last earthly joy was yet in store for this mother who was so anxious about the proper education of her children. Marie had continued to act as instructress to Céline and Thérèse; and at the commencement of vacation, knowing the encouragement that would result for her little pupils, and also in order to bring some consolation to her parents, she conceived the idea of imitating at home a school distribution of prizes. We have a description of the little scene in a letter to her aunt at Lisieux.

> I assure you it was quite a pretty sight. I had decorated my room with garlands of vinca, intermingled with bouquets of roses. Wreaths of flowers hung from the ceiling. The rostrum was covered with cloth, and two armchairs were in readiness for the presidents of "the august ceremony," Monsieur and Madame Martin.
>
> Yes, mama also took part in our distribution of prizes. Our two little girls were in white, and you should see with what a triumphant air they came up to receive their books and wreaths. Papa and mama gave out the prizes, and I, of course, called forward my pupils.[44]

This was the last gleam of happiness before Death made a break in the family circle. Mme Martin went from the president's chair to her bed of suffering. Eight days later she writes: "My strength is at an end. . . . If the Holy Virgin does not cure me, then my term of life is over; God wills that I find my resting-place elsewhere than on this earth."[45]

This last message to her brother at Lisieux was dated August 16. On the 26th, Holy Viaticum was judged necessary. M. Martin had the courage to go himself to the church, and to accompany to and from the house the Divine Saviour, who came to fortify the dying mother in her last journey.

The holy Unction, with its saving effects of purification and renewal of grace, was administered to the departing soul. Thérèse was present; she knew that a solemn separation was soon to take place, but she realized that by the mercy of the Almighty her heroic mother would not leave her for ever by returning to God.

"The touching ceremony of Extreme Unction," she writes, "has left a lasting impression on my mind. I see again the spot where they placed me on my knees, I hear once more the sobs of our poor father."[46]

The soul thus prepared broke its bonds August 28, 1877, half an hour after midnight. She had passed here below forty-six years of toil and trial, which give every ground for hope that she enjoyed the eternal peace of heaven after her death.[47]

Before her mortal remains disappeared for ever from the eyes of Thérèse, M. Martin took the little one in his arms. "Come," he said, "and kiss your dear mother for the last time." And without uttering a word, the orphan touched with her lips the icy-cold forehead of the dead.

This little child, hitherto so lively and laughter-loving, so full of the joy of living, seemed transformed and suddenly matured by the terrible vision of death. She shed no tear; she looked on and listened in silence, but understood everything. She had been left by herself for a moment, and, while alone, was confronted with the sight of the coffin lying in the corridor. She had never seen one before. Instead of fleeing at the sight, she contemplated the dismal object sadly for several moments, raising her head to examine its form more closely, and to familiarize herself with this narrow bed, the last resting-place of poor crumbling humanity.

After the religious ceremonies in the Church of Notre-Dame the family returned home plunged in sorrow. "The whole five of us," says Thérèse,

> stood together in a group mutely gazing at one another in our grief. The maid seeing us thus was moved to compassion, and, turning to Céline and myself, she exclaimed: "Poor little children, you have no longer a mother." Then Céline, throwing herself into Marie's

> arms, cried: "It is you who will be mama for us now." And I, accustomed as I was to follow Céline in everything, would also have imitated this action, so beautifully appropriate, but I thought that Pauline would perhaps feel sorrowful and forsaken, having no little daughter. I looked up at her tenderly, and leaning my little head on her heart, I said: "As for me, Pauline will be my mama."[48]

The child of four and a half years was far from realizing to what an extent this chosen sister was to prove a mother to her, what a spiritual guide God was preparing for her in the person of Pauline.

The two elder sisters made every effort to show their earnest acceptation of the delicate duty entrusted to them in order to lighten for the two little ones the cloud of sorrow that had come upon their home.

The days following the burial were full of desolation and sadness. The grief-stricken family went out only to visit the cemetery. M. Martin was winding up his commercial affairs; his time was occupied by these and other cares of the same kind. What was to become of his orphan children, more especially the two youngest, now deprived of a mother's guiding hand?

Friends at Alençon and elsewhere proffered advice, and offered their help regarding the education of the children. M. Martin thanked them, but could not reconcile his rigid principles with their suggestions.

He remembered then that during her last agony, being no longer able to utter a word, his wife had turned to her sister-in-law with a long look of mute appeal, as though to confide to her the care of her children, and that Mme Guérin had promised to be a mother to them. He resolved to accept the kindly offer of his friends in Lisieux.

The sacrifice was bitter; he had to bid adieu to all the old associations, to friends of his childhood, to his "Pavillon," to every cherished custom and time-honoured habit. Above all, he had to leave his beloved graves.[49] He did not hesitate, however, but asked his brother-in-law, M. Guérin, to look out for a house at Lisieux which would be large enough for him and his family.

On September 10, following, a suitable residence was found. The necessary preparations were quickly accomplished. M. Martin remained behind at Alençon for a time, to settle some matters of business, but during the first fortnight of November he took his daughters to their new home selected by M. Guérin, which bore the pleasing name of "Les Buissonnets."[50]

4

Lisieux—Les Buissonnets

Lisieux, a group of picturesque steep-roofed houses, dominated by the bold spire and severe façade of a towering Gothic cathedral; a quiet retreat for the wood-carvers of Normandy, whose fine arabesques and fantastic monsters are displayed on the worm-eaten doors and window frames along the sides of the narrow streets; a melancholy little town in spite of its verdant surroundings and gaily-coloured flower gardens—such was to be henceforward the retreat of the Martin family after their great bereavement at Alençon.

The children's first impression on their arrival was one of sadness. Besides the fact that they carried everywhere with them the thought of their dear one departed, the smoke-blackened porches of Lisieux with their grimacing figures, the high factory chimneys covered with a pall of thick smoke, contrasted unfavourably to them with the pretty, attractive homes of Alençon.

Little Thérèse alone left the house in the rue Saint Blaise without regret, and she accuses herself of this later where she naively says "Children love change." Moreover, the welcoming smiles that awaited her at her uncle's house kept her from remarking the rather depressing appearance of the old city.

M. Guérin's house, a high, solidly constructed building of the old type, stood at the corner of the Grande-Rue and what is now called "Place Thiers."

With the master of the house we are already acquainted; some further traits will help to complete the sketch previously outlined.

M. Guérin, who at this time still conducted a flourishing pharmacy, was a man of medium height and distinguished demeanour, a man whose keen look, decisive manner, and equally decisive speech, betokened unfailing honesty and uprightness. Imbued with the best traditions of Christianity, endowed with an open and vigorous mind, he had early extended his studies beyond the circle of technical knowledge required for his profession, and had become so well versed in religious matters as to prove on occasion a formidable polemical opponent of the Church's enemies. He had, moreover, a heart of unchangeable devotedness, as easily touched as it was constant in its friendship.

With her tender, affectionate nature, her readiness to lend an ever helping hand, Mme Guérin was the unobtrusive but warming ray of sunshine in this grave and somewhat austere household. A descendant of one of those thoroughly religious families, which had given priests and even martyrs[1] to the Church, Céline Fournet became, as we know, the intimate friend of her sister-in-law, and her promise to prove a mother to Mme Martin's children had cheered the last moments of the dying woman. But she counted especially on the loving-kindness of her daughters Marie and Jeanne to bring a ray of joy to the hearts of her youngest nieces now so pitifully left orphans.

The welcome given to the children was tender in its sincerity. Mme Guérin with her daughters stood at the door to receive the five exiles as they came accompanied by their uncle to the house. Thérèse must naturally have felt the least at home since it was her first time in Lisieux, but her aunt's caresses soon brought a smile to the timid little face.

After a quiet night's rest the orphan children were taken to their new home.

From the Pont L'Evêque road, on the east of Lisieux, we ascend by a rugged, winding path to a dwelling situated midway on the slopes of a hill. The town with its tiers of steep-roofed houses and its grey steeples spreads below. This is the house called Les Buissonnets. A pleasant home, nestling amidst a wealth of foliage and commanding an extensive view of the varied landscape, it joined the advantages of comfort to its rural situation. In front spread a smiling little lawn studded with trees; at the back was a sufficiently large garden surrounded by an ivy-grown wall. No other sound broke the stillness save the clear notes of the nightingale from the lilac hedges or the shrill symphony of the crickets in the newly mown hay.

The sight of this dwelling surrounded by the fresh foliage of fir and ash trees in sombre bloom was for Thérèse a real joy. But even this could only lighten in small measure the abiding impressions of sorrow left by her great loss. "Immediately after my mother's death," she writes, "my happy disposition changed completely. I, who had been so lively, so expansive, became timid and shy and sensitive to excess; a look sufficed to make the tears flow; I dreaded notice; I could not bear the company of strangers, and only recovered my former cheerfulness in the bosom of my own family."[2]

This trial continued for several years, becoming even more pronounced. It was alleviated for the moment by the tenderness of the Guérin family and the charm of that verdant home which was to be from henceforth the scene of the "little Queen's" development.

Meanwhile the house is yet without its master. But M. Martin was already acquainted with this little nest, where he sought to shelter all that remained to him of his happiness; he had paid a visit there in September before completing arrangements with the owner. In a letter of November 16, his daughter Marie gives her first impressions: "We are installed in Les Buissonnets. It is a delightful home with a smiling and cheerful aspect and its large garden where Thérèse and Céline can enjoy their play. Only the staircase, and also the approach to the house, leave something to be desired."

His daughter omitted to mention that although pleasing in appearance it was nevertheless a very old building, badly proportioned in construction, with very low ceilings. She refrained above all from calling the attention of this fervent Catholic to the long distance which separated it from the church; but she noticed the narrow pathway leading to

Les Buissonnets; this path which M. Martin called later "the way to Paradise."

As to the rest, she promised him peace and happiness in this quiet home. "I feel assured, dear father," she says, "that you will be contented here. Yes, we will endeavour to be so good, and to make your life so pleasant, that you will be compensated for the great sacrifice you have made for our welfare."[3]

On November 30, M. Martin arrived at Les Buissonnets. Without further delay they organized their new home-life.

A room on the ground floor opening on the garden at the rear of the house was given to Céline and Thérèse. It was there that the "little Queen" was to offer so many innocent prayers to Jesus and his Blessed Mother.[4] But later on, when she was attacked by the severe illness of which we are soon to speak, her sister Marie brought her to her own room situated on the left front of the house and bathed in the light that streamed in through two large windows. It was in this room, now transformed into an oratory, that Thérèse was to contemplate the heavenly smile of the Virgin Mother of consolation. She was to share it with Céline after the departure of her two elder sisters for the Carmel.

Céline, who now seemed possessed of her little sister's lost vivacity, was sent with Léonie as day-boarder to the Benedictine Convent. Marie and Pauline, who remained at Les Buissonnets, looked after the home and took charge of Thérèse's education. The latter required to be urged forward with spirit, for although she had in earlier days learned her letters quickly, yet when the time came to form these into words, at about the age of three and a half years, she had returned to her games as if decided to end her learning at this point. From that time onward, it is true, she became more favourably disposed towards her books, but this entailed constant effort.

On Pauline, for the most part, devolved the charge of the child's formation, a duty which she performed with tact and devotedness.

Having kissed the little innocent face upturned to her on awakening, she would make Thérèse kneel by her side to say her prayers. The morning was then begun with a reading lesson. The word "*cieux*" was the first that Thérèse could read unaided, and she ran joyously to announce this grand achievement to her father, who was in the room at the top of the house called the "Belvedere," which he had chosen for himself. To this room she came, in fact, every day after lessons to show him the marks obtained, and to enjoy his affectionate recognition when it was a question of success.

M. Martin, whom sorrow had rendered prematurely grey, had no longer any other thought but to sanctify his remaining years by prayer, by works of charity, and by the education of his children. Little Thérèse was the special object of his care. After daily Mass at the Cathedral, some time was given to working in the garden. Long hours were devoted to meditation and reading in the "Belvedere," where he felt so close to heaven. Then each day he paid a second fervent visit to our Lord in the Tabernacle. Accompanied by Thérèse, he would go to one or other of the churches where the Blessed Sacrament was reserved. It was thus the little one entered for the first time, while as yet her sisters did not even know of the existence of a Carmel at Lisieux, the chapel of that monastery where nine years later she was to take the veil.

These afternoon outings were given to Thérèse by way of reward. Her teacher was as firm as she was devoted. She required a definite amount of study done. If application to work was remiss, the evening walk was irrevocably cancelled. Pauline never went back on a decision once given, and M. Martin, at whatever cost, always ratified her verdict.[5]

These prohibitions made Thérèse appreciate all the more the long walks which were allowed her during the fine season.

The child's early preference for the simple flowers of the hedgerows still continued. What joy it was to her to gambol through the thick copse amidst the woodland flowers and wild orchids. How triumphantly she returned in the evening, laden with bright-coloured bouquets and sweet-smelling garlands to decorate her little altar in the corner of the garden in honour of the God of Love.

Sometimes Thérèse went out with her father along the banks of the Touques, and, with her little line, made cunning attempts to imitate him in throwing the hook. It was easy to see, however, that her mind was otherwise occupied, and soon, leaving her line and hook, she would sit down amid the flower-strewn grass. "There," she writes, "I became immersed in deep thought, and without even knowing what meditation meant, my soul plunged into mental prayer. I listened to the distant sounds and the murmur of the wind. At times the music of a military band in the town reached me in faint and undecided notes, filling my heart with a sweet melancholy. Earth seemed to me a place of exile, and I dreamed of heaven."[6]

We find expression of the same or even deeper impressions when, on one occasion, a sudden storm filled the skies with lightning flashes. "I turned now to the left, now to the right," declared the little one, "in order to lose nothing of that brilliant spectacle. I saw a thunderbolt fall into a neighbouring meadow, and far from being terrified, I was enchanted at the sight; it seemed to me that the good God was quite near."[7]

Sometimes along the rugged paths leading to Les Buissonnets, as well as in the streets of the town, were to be met old men looking for alms. Thérèse always went up to them smilingly and offered the money that her father had entrusted to her. One evening, meeting a man who was in a particularly miserable condition, she resolved to pray for him on the day of her first Holy Communion, for she had heard that God grants every favour demanded of Him on that day.

But it was especially at her own home that the gentle child lavished her tokens of compassion on the poor who came every Monday to Les Buissonnets. At each sound of the bell Thérèse went to open the garden gate. Then, quickly returning to her sister, she would say: "Pauline, it is a poor old crippled man. It is a poor woman with a family of little children; one of them is an infant in arms, and the mother looks pitifully pale. What shall we give them?" And deep was the pity visible in her eyes. She ran immediately to the mendicants with the bread or money that had been given her. At times she came back radiant with joy. "Pauline, that poor person said to me, 'God will bless you, my little one.'"

The graces consequent on union with God were visibly increasing in this ingenuous child who sought our Divine Saviour with her whole soul. "As I grew up," she declares, "I loved the good God more and more, and I frequently made Him the offering of my heart, using the words mama had taught me.[8] I strove to please Jesus in all my actions, and I guarded with great care against ever offending Him."[9]

She strove no less to make those around her avoid the smallest faults. The servant, by way of fun, one day let slip in her presence some little untruths. "You know well, Victoire," she said, "that this offends the good God."

In this child of five years certain remarkable traits were already present, which some theologians have attributed to mystic intuition.

All have especially remarked the impression which she received when returning in the evening with her father from M. Guérin's house. "I well recall," she says, "that I watched the stars with inexpressible rapture. . . . I noticed with especial delight one group of golden pearls (the belt of Orion) in the vast firmament, finding that they formed a T, and I would say to my dear father as we walked along: 'See, papa, my name is written in heaven!' Then, unwilling to look any longer on this miserable earth, I would ask him to lead me, and, heedless where I trod, would turn my little face upwards, never tired of contemplating the starry skies."[10]

Childish perhaps this trait may be called, but place it side by side with the statement which Thérèse was later to make: "The certitude of one day leaving this land of darkness far behind had been given me *from my infancy*. I did not merely believe this because of what I had heard from others, but I felt even then in my heart by intimate and certain inspiration, that another land, a more beautiful country, would one day be my lasting dwelling-place, just as the genius of Christopher Columbus inspired him with a presentiment of the New World."[11]

While waiting to call her into solitude to speak more intimately to her heart, God revealed himself to her in the mirror of sensible objects. In this way her walks through the sunlit countryside, which seemed to have no other purpose than to serve as a distraction for Thérèse and to fill her soul with joy, had their invisible and sublime profit.

On her return from her walk, the little one set herself to write out the exercises set by Pauline in the morning. She then passed the remainder of the day in frolicking around her father when she did not go with him to the "Belvedere," to contemplate once more the tranquil expanse of the blue firmament, where she could already read secrets so sublime.

The Christian formation of the child was continued in the evening when the family were gathered around a sparkling fire in the dining-room, where even today are the massive round table and austere-looking oak chairs which were silent witnesses of Thérèse's early years.

After an animated game of draughts, Marie or Pauline would take the *Liturgical Year* of Dom Guéranger and read some pages relative to the ecclesiastical season or an approaching feast. They then passed on to some other attractive and instructive reading, so that both soul and mind had each their special nourishment.

Seated on her father's knees, "little Thérèse" listened attentively but quietly to everything, and when the reading was finished, M. Martin, with his fine voice, would sing some melodious refrain as though to lull her to sleep.

Then all went upstairs for night prayers, and Thérèse, on her knees beside her father, "had but to look at him to realize how the saints pray."

Once in bed, the little one invariably asked Pauline, as formerly she had asked her mother: "Have I been good today? Is the good God pleased with me? Will the little angels come to hover round me?" The reply was always "Yes"; otherwise Thérèse would have passed the night in tears.

Evenings such as these presented scenes more angelic than earthly; but sweeter still was the supernatural charm of Sundays and feast-days.

Sunday, what a day of gladness for Thérèse! It was not merely the day of rest, the weekly holiday. Rather was it the splendour of the ceremonies under the solemn arches of the cathedral whose clear-cut lines and sober decoration presented a *chef d'œuvre* of harmonious simplicity. Above all, it was the vision of Jesus in the Sacred Host.

At the appointed hour, the whole family went to the High Mass and took their places in one of the chapels at the Epistle side. This chapel being far from the pulpit, it was necessary to change their place during the sermon so as not to be deprived of the word of God. Each Sunday, then, might be seen a white-haired man holding by the hand a child of wondrously sweet countenance coming down the nave in search of a favourable position, while her uncle, M. Guérin, seated in his church-warden's pew, looked on, happy, as he said himself, to see his "little ray of sunshine" appear.

Thérèse listened attentively to the sermon, endeavouring to follow the preacher. A sermon on the Passion of our Lord was the first she understood, and she was vividly impressed. Her age was then five and a half years. From that time onward she was able to grasp and appreciate the meaning of all the instructions.

The enchantment of sacred music and divine ceremony extended ordinarily to Compline. As the evening shadows spread through the old church, Thérèse reflected sadly that this celestial day was soon to end, and the morrow would bring its monotonous train of work once more. Then she dreamed of a never-ending Sunday, when the music of heaven's choirs would continue without interruption. Everything seemed to raise her thoughts more and more above the things of earth, and by reason of a special grace, bring her into contact with supernatural reality.

Sometimes, Sunday evening was spent with the Guérin family, where each of the five sisters was received in turn. When Thérèse came Mme Guérin and the two cousins redoubled their attentions, making special efforts to give her pleasure, the more so because they feared that the little one would be made to feel ill at ease by her uncle's serious conversation.

But the precocious development of Thérèse had not been taken into account. Not only was she not wearied, but she listened with unsuspected eagerness to the grave and instructive remarks of M. Guérin. Her joy was mingled with a slight feeling of fear, when, to amuse her, M. Guérin seated her on his knee and sang "Barbe-Bleue" for her in a stentorian voice.

Above even the happiness of Sunday the "little Queen" loved the gladness of the principal feasts. She welcomed every succeeding holyday with redoubled fervour, for Pauline had taken care to explain to her the mystery commemorated on each festival. Especially when the time for Blessed Sacrament processions drew near did the soul of Thérèse thrill with exultation. Other children, it is true, are delighted with the sight of splendid banners which reflect the azure sky, of white veils, of beautiful lace and golden copes, all ranged in splendour around the wayside altars on the Feast of Corpus Christi. But none of these imposing or beautiful objects could fully charm Thérèse. Far higher went her admiration, her homage, and more especially her loving prayers. If she was happy in taking her place in the procession, among the little flower-girls carrying baskets laden with bright-tinted petals, her graceful costume or the kindness of her amiable companions counted for nothing in her joy. "What happiness," she writes, "to strew flowers in the path of the good God! But before letting them fall I threw them high in the air, and was never so happy as when I saw my rose petals touch the sacred Monstrance."[12]

In her devotion to the Blessed Virgin she gives evidence of the same tender love. The little child of five was thought too young to assist every evening at the May devotions. But that makes no difference. She will have a chest of drawers in her elder sisters' room converted into a madonna altar, with its tiny flower vases and its illumination consisting of wax vestas to serve as candles. Victoire, the devoted servant, will alone form the congregation at these ceremonies, of which the principal exercise will be the recitation in common of the *Memorare.*

Although the family scarcely held communication with anyone beyond its own circle, yet the virtues of little Thérèse Martin began to attract attention.

An old lady who had often met her at the church, and who had remarked the ecstatic expression of her countenance in presence of the Blessed Sacrament during the processions, said to one of her neighbours: "That little one is an angel. I shall be greatly surprised if she lives long; but if she lives, you will find that she will be spoken of later on as a saint."

A woman who came to work at Les Buissonnets one day insistently pleaded to be allowed to cut off a lock of the child's hair, and carried it away as a treasure.

Whenever she accompanied her sisters in their walks through the town the passers-by turned and gazed as if fascinated, not by her physical grace, though this too was striking, but by a supernatural charm which seemed to radiate from her.

Withal, Thérèse, who, more evidently from this time onward, lived in the continual presence of God, had nothing in common with those timorous devotees who, according to St. Teresa of Avila, "do not dare to stir for fear their devotion should fly away."

She remained full of eagerness for games suited to her age, and the weekly holiday on Thursday was always heartily welcomed as permitting her to resume her old sports with Céline. They gambolled around the flower-beds in the garden, they entered into competitions of skill in arranging bouquets, then Céline would start class with her dolls.

Having but small attraction for dressing dolls, Thérèse willingly entrusted hers to Céline, who, having ranged them in good order beside her own collection, gave her little regiment course of morals or orthography. Thérèse greeted these tirades with peals of laughter; but she applauded still more when Céline, wishing to reward one of her speechless pupils, brought her to her sister, saying to the privileged one: "My dear child, go and kiss your aunt."

It was but proper that in this predestined life the simple and artless amusements of infancy should play their part. While giving herself daily more and more to Jesus, this little saint of five years had her hours of exuberance, with all the freshness and charm of early childhood.

Little Thérèse had learned from Pauline that the sacraments are the principal channels whereby Jesus gives Himself to souls. She longed ardently to receive nourishment from the Divine Host which she had seen shining in the golden Monstrance. The practice then in vogue prevented her from approaching the Sacred Table for yet a long time; but knowing that the sacrament of Penance must be received in preparation for Holy Communion, she asked to be allowed at least to go to Confession as soon as possible. She was granted this privilege at the age of six. What was this child to tell the priest, this candid soul which had never from the age of three refused anything to Jesus? In her examination of conscience she had recourse to Pauline, who told her that she was about to speak to our Divine Saviour Himself in the person of the priest. So convinced was Thérèse of this truth, that she asked whether she should not in consequence say to her confessor that "she loved him with all her heart."

The confessor before whom she presented herself was the Abbé Ducellier, then parish priest of Saint Pierre, who, at the time of his death in 1917, was arch-priest of the same parish. He was an ecclesiastic of grave demeanour, little inclined to confidences. With all this he could not but be moved by the exceptional candour of this angelic soul. After having heard her confession, wherein he found great difficulty in discerning real faults, he exhorted her with fervent words to imitate the Queen of Virgins. Then, in conformity with the practice of the time, he gave her simply a blessing.

Thérèse was so small that she had to stand in the confessional. She succeeded, however, in passing her rosary through the grating to have it blessed, and came out radiant with happiness. It was dark outside, and Thérèse stopped beneath a street lamp and examined curiously the rosary that had just been given back to her.

"What are you looking at, Thérèse?" asked Pauline.

"I want to see what a blessed rosary is like," she said.

From that time onward she sought more than ever to please Jesus, in order to prepare for him in her soul a choice dwelling for the day when it would please him to come there in his corporeal presence.

She was seven years of age when the time came for Céline, then a day-boarder at the Benedictine Abbey, to prepare for her first Holy Communion. During the intervals of school hours, Pauline undertook her remote preparation. Thérèse was admitted to the first instructions, and she listened, eager to prepare her soul already for the great day which she had wished to bring nearer. She was told later that, on account of being too young, she must cease attending, and she remained away with a heavy heart, for it seemed to her that four years would not be too much to spend in preparation to receive her God.

Obliged thus to fall back sometimes on her own thoughts, she restrained with difficulty her longing to receive the Holy of Holies. She conceived the idea of asking her sisters whether she could not join them secretly when they were to have the happiness of receiving Holy Communion. One Christmas Eve, before midnight Mass, she said to Marie: "Oh, if you would only bring me with you tonight! . . . This is what I would do, so that I, too, might receive the good Jesus. I would slip in amongst the others, quite near to you; I am so small that no one would notice me." Her eyes shone with her desire, and she went away sadly when told that such a thing could not be thought of.

The Guérin family liked spending a holiday at Trouville during the fine season. Thérèse was nearly six when in August, 1878, she went to join them there, accompanied by her father and sisters.

It was her first sight of the sea, and, susceptible as always to things sublime in which she discerned the image of God, she gazed enraptured, her eyes full of fervent and ingenuous admiration.

Passers-by were not slow to notice this tall man with snow-white hair framing a face still young, holding by the hand a child whose sweet and clear countenance, long golden tresses and angelic smile, made one think of a seraphic vision. One day a lady accompanied by her husband could not refrain from saying in a low tone as they passed: "What a pretty little girl!" And she asked M. Martin if the child belonged to him.[13] The father, though pleased, signed to these passers-by not to address compliments to his little daughter. But she had so well profited by Pauline's teaching, which had long aimed at fortifying her against all vanity, that she paid no attention to the flattering remark.

Having gone on the promenade *des Planches* one evening, accompanied by the other members of their party, this resort was abandoned, and she ventured to the isolated point of the *Roches Noires* which overhang the *Jetée des Anglais*. There again she enjoyed moments of contemplation which made her realize still more the divine presence. The following gives her own account of the impression received at that time: "Just when the sun seemed to bathe itself in the vast expanse of waters, marking out before it a sparkling pathway, I sat beside Pauline on a lonely rock. I contemplated for a long time this golden pathway, which she had told me was an image of grace lighting the way for faithful souls here below. Then I pictured to myself my own heart as a frail little barque with snowy white sail in the middle of this way, and I resolved never to wander away from Jesus' sight."[14]

Thus, then, at an age when ordinarily the first rays of reason struggle through the clouds of infancy, God was gradually taking possession of this little soul already inundated at times with supernatural light. Assuredly it was the work of Divine Providence, who in His wisdom gives His gifts to whom He will; but much was also due to the Christian family who collaborated so actively in the divine work.

We have dwelt on the part played by her mother in the formation of Thérèse. Pauline, whom the little one had chosen as her "new mother," set herself especially to continue this labour of love.

She took care, as we know, that this love should be without weakness. While refraining always from unmerited reproach, she never went back on a decision once given, and never passed over in silence the slightest imperfection in her little sister. She carried this firmness to the extent of making Thérèse impervious to fear by sending her in the dusk to look for a forgotten object in some dark corner.

But with these apparent severities, what devotion, what affection and common-sense she displayed, more especially when there was question of instilling into the young mind some abstract truth.

One day Thérèse asked her why it was that God did not give equal glory in heaven to all His elect; she feared that the less favoured would not be truly happy. Pauline sent her for her father's tumbler, and placing it beside Thérèse's tiny thimble, she filled both with water to the brim. She then asked the child which of the two appeared the fuller. Thérèse replied that they were both equally full, since neither could contain any more. "Thus," said the 'little mother,' "will it be with the elect. Each will receive in accordance with his capacity, and having therefore no cause to envy the others will be in his own sphere perfectly happy." Thérèse grasped this truth immediately; the apt illustration had carried the lesson home.

Though less manifest perhaps and less clear in detail, the father's influence was, however, far reaching. This influence was primarily exercised by example. This fervent Christian had carried with him to Lisieux his cherished practices of Alençon, and Thérèse, as she grew up, became each day more capable of appreciating their meaning and merit.

During the first years M. Martin, rising early, went every morning in all weathers to six o'clock Mass, to which his daughters Marie and Pauline accompanied him. They afterwards induced him to change the hour to seven o'clock. He did so with regret, for he loved to be there in company with the poor, who went to the earlier Mass, and whom he looked upon as God's favourite children.

Mass and thanksgiving ended, they returned to their rather distant home. The father walked in silence and recollection. Marie asked him one day what occupied his thoughts so completely. "I continue," he said, "to commune with our Lord."

It was natural that the charity of such a soul should extend, as formerly, beyond the family circle. Scarcely had he settled in Lisieux, when he persuaded M. Guérin to establish, in cooperation with the clergy of St. Pierre, a society for Nocturnal Adoration, and he became, as at Alençon, one of its most devoted members.

Little Thérèse saw and understood everything. She kept these precious lessons in her heart, in order to make them her rule of life. Her father had, however, other and more personal influence on his daughter.

Besides the country walks which provided numberless occasions for counsel and instruction, there were the little meetings in the "Belvedere." Thérèse often joined him there, and would it be rash to think that she owed, in part, to these intimate conversations her unflinching faith, and her maturely developed disregard for earthly things? We can form our opinion from the following lines, the only fragment left to us of the reflections with which M. Martin loved to animate his fervour:

"Men," he writes,

> torment themselves with anxiety, and make as much effort to preserve their life on the eve of death as if they had yet many hundred years to live. They act similarly in regard to everything else in the world; there is nothing that they will not do in their endeavour to immortalize themselves.
>
> God, however, disregards their diligence. He knows the moment, decided by him from all eternity, when these things shall be no more.
>
> This divine decree does not exclude all solicitude, but only undue anxiety, and extraordinary and exaggerated precaution. Let us do what we are able and leave the rest to Providence. The Abbé de Rancé was right. "In vain does the sea rage and foam in its wrath, in vain do the waves hurl themselves aloft and roar, in vain is the vessel tossed to and fro. If the breath of Divine Providence fills its sails it cannot be wrecked; nothing will prevent it from coming to port."[15]

Written perhaps near the large windows of his "Belvedere," from whence could be seen every day the darkness strive for mastery against the dying light of evening, spreading out before the eye illuminated by faith a type of universal decay, these lines express the serene faith and tranquil hope which were ever the foundations of Thérèse's piety. She learned, too, in these intimate conversations with her father, the lesson of tender love which was to be the guiding light in her relations with her divine Master. The following is an example of the outpourings of love which M. Martin borrowed from the saintly Mère Barat, and which expressed his own feelings at the foot of his crucifix. "My well-beloved Saviour, when I first bound myself to Thy service, I did not know the happiness that comes from belonging wholly to Thee; but today I know all that Thou art to me; and, with this experience, I wish to declare that before all earthly joys I prefer the honour and happiness of serving Thee."[16]

We see they were kindred souls, this fervent Christian and his little daughter who was already so decidedly drawn into the way of divine union.

It happens occasionally, by the secret ordination of Providence, that new relations are established in mysterious ways between two souls, sometimes by presentiments or visions of the future, which enlighten them in their mutual way of sanctity, but which often remain unexplained for long years.

Little Thérèse, at the age of six, was the recipient of a communication of this kind.

Her father sometimes went on business to Alençon. One day when he had gone there, the child had a prophetic vision, which she relates as follows:

> My father was away on a journey, and was not due to return for some time. It was about two or three in the afternoon; the sun was shining brilliantly, and all nature was in festal array. I was standing alone at a window which over-looked the garden, my mind occupied with joyous reflections, when I saw in front of the laundry opposite to me a man dressed exactly like papa, equally tall, and with the same bearing, but very bent

and aged. I use the word *aged* to describe his general appearance, for I did not see his features, as his head was covered with a thick veil. He walked slowly with regular step past my little garden. Immediately a feeling of unearthly fear took possession of me, and I called out loudly with trembling voice: "Papa! Papa!" But the mysterious personage did not seem to hear me; he continued his walk without even turning round, and went towards a clump of fir trees which divided the principal path in the garden. I expected to see him reappear on the other side of the trees, but the prophetic vision had vanished.

The whole thing had taken place in a moment, a moment so deeply graven in my memory that the impression is as vivid today after many years as was the vision itself.

My sisters were together in a room adjoining. Hearing me call papa, both experienced a feeling of fear. Hiding her emotion, Marie ran to me. "Why do you call papa thus, my little one, when he is at Alençon?" I related what I had just seen, and, to set my mind at rest, they said that very likely the maid wanted to startle me and had covered her head with her apron.

But Victoire, on being questioned, assured us that she had not left the kitchen. Besides, I could not banish the truth from my mind: *I had seen a man, and that man resembled my father absolutely*. Then we all went to look behind the clump of trees, and, finding nothing, they told me to think no more about it.

Think no more about it! Ah, that was beyond my power. Often and often did my imagination bring up before me the mysterious vision. Often I endeavoured to lift the veil which hid from me its meaning, and deep down in my heart I held the conviction that it would one day be fully revealed to me.[17]

It was, in fact, destined to be revealed, and Thérèse had little notion of the martyrdom she was then to endure. But the prophetic vision of her father "bent and aged" was from that time onward all the more painful to her, since, on her own avowal, she had not then the courage to dwell without terror on the thought that her "dear king" could die.

To draw her more closely to Himself, the Well-Beloved continued to detach her by means of trials from the fascination of earthly joy, and even directed her on the way of severest sacrifice.

5

The Benedictine Convent—Strange Malady—First Communion—Sudden Spiritual Transformation

The years between 1877, the date of Mme Martin's death, and Christmas, 1886, which marked a profound transformation in Thérèse's character, marked, too, an epoch of trial scarcely interrupted by the joy of her first Communion and the tender affection of her family.

These trials, as we have already mentioned in passing, form the strife through which God leads the souls of His predestined first away from sensible things, later from every other earthly attachment, on to intimate union with Himself.

Céline has delineated in remarkably precise terms the condition of her little companion at that time, a state into which, by divine permission, she fell back even after the marked development which we have described.

"Thérèse," she declares,

> underwent (between these two dates) a period of darkness. There seemed to be a veil thrown over those qualities that the Saviour had bestowed on her. . . . In the world she passed unnoticed. This impression of effacement was caused chiefly by her excessive timidity which made her hesitating in manner and paralysed every activity. She sometimes left herself open, it is true, to unfavourable interpretation by the fact that she hardly ever said anything in her own defence, always letting others speak. She suffered at this period from continual headaches, but her extreme sensibility and the delicacy of her feelings were to her the most

> fruitful source of pain—pain, however, which she bore uncomplainingly.
>
> It is important to note that, even during these years, she was, in spite of her apparent weakness, truly strong. This remarkable strength was shown to me by the fact that her troubles never in the least degree turned her from the path of duty. For my part, I have never discovered in her during this period instability of character, never heard a sharp word, nor noticed a falling away from virtue. She practiced mortification at every moment and in the smallest things. She seemed to me to lose no opportunity of offering sacrifices to God. . . .
>
> She regarded the trials of her youth as the special providence of God, who wished to form her in humility. "I had all the more need of this austere formation," she writes, "as I was not insensible to praise."
>
> By reason of her extreme sensitiveness mentioned above, Thérèse cried at the least thing that pained or distressed her, and when she had been consoled, she cried for having cried. She herself realized that this was great weakness, and she calls the sudden change which took place in her on Christmas night, 1886, "her conversion."[1]

This acute sensitiveness existed in the child, as we know, from the death of her mother. Her passing sorrows were, it is true, partly assuaged by the loving atmosphere of Les Buissonnets, where every little family feast-day gave Thérèse occasion for joyous expansion. But she had reached an age when the formation received at home ought to be completed by a more systematic education, and, moreover, covering a wider field. Léonie was just about to leave the Benedictine Abbey where Céline had been admitted with her, and M. Martin being satisfied with the intellectual and moral training given at this convent, decided that Thérèse should replace Léonie there, and the two youngest sisters found themselves together as day-boarders. It was to be, then, for the family only an apparent separation. Nevertheless, the entrance of Thérèse into this convent school, worthy of all esteem, marks a new phase of the long trial she had suffered since 1877.

The Benedictine Abbey of Notre-Dame-du-Pré, of Saint Désir, is situated in a suburb of Lisieux at a considerable distance from Les Buissonnets. Founded in 1011, it was for a long time devoted exclusively, as were the other convents of the same name, to the contemplative life; but in the seventeenth century its community began to give instruction to the young girls of the neighbourhood, and set up a boarding-school at the convent. Resuming its work after the interruption caused by the Revolution, the convent experienced during the nineteenth century periods of great prosperity. Its importance was, however, diminished later on by the competition of new educational establishments.

In October, 1881, when Thérèse first went there, it counted about sixty pupils from the town of Lisieux and the best families of the neighbourhood. The instruction given there was solid and rather above the ordinary. Its system of education was simple and thoroughly religious, displaying even maternal kindness. For the rest, the nuns could not avoid bringing together the daughters of the farmer class and the children whom city life had rendered more refined, whence arose a certain amount of friction to the annoyance of the latter. On the whole, a good spirit prevailed, piety was in honour, peace and joy were the general rule.[2]

We already know the delight that Thérèse took in the beauties of nature, and what a radiant picture Les Buissonnets presented to her when she came to Lisieux. Great was the change on her entrance to the boarding-school. High grey walls ranged around in geometrical precision, faultlessly neat but somewhat austere-looking classrooms, a chapel built in Louis-Philippe's time, inadequately compensating for plainness by its commodious arrangements, a spacious garden, but hemmed in from any outlook—such was the retreat offered to the child of eight and a half years, this child who so loved the sun and the flowers, who had revelled and grown strong in the open air of the country, who had been unceasingly surrounded with family affection. Happily, the welcoming smile of her teachers brightened from the first the severe appearance of the school; more fortunately still, Thérèse was to return every evening to Les Buissonnets.

Her two cousins, Marie and Jeanne Guérin, also attended the convent school. It was arranged that Céline and Thérèse should join them each morning at the pharmacy, and all four go together to the Abbey accompanied by a servant of M. Guérin's.

This servant, who later became a Benedictine,[3] loved to recall after thirty years her relations with Thérèse at this time.

> When the little one found herself alone with me on the way to the convent or in the house, she became affectionate and confiding, and freely told me her little secrets. These intimate conversations centred, quite naturally, on spiritual things. For her age she was exceptionally intelligent and reflective. I remember in particular how, even before her first Holy Communion, she explained to me as an excuse for some workmen whom she heard blaspheming, that we must not judge of the hidden things of souls, that these people had received much less grace than we, and that they were more unfortunate than blameworthy.[4]

On account of her remarkable precociousness, the nuns had no hesitation in putting their new pupil immediately in a class composed of girls much older than herself, some of them even fourteen years of age. Thérèse's success soon justified this measure.

If certain classmates equalled or even surpassed her in arithmetic or orthography, she quickly succeeded, despite the difference of age, in placing herself amongst the first.

She had a special attraction for Sacred and Church History. As for catechism, she grasped the doctrine with wonderful facility, but the literal recital of the text was at first a difficult effort.

At the class for religious instruction she never failed to reply with perfect exactitude and precision to the questions of M. l'Abbé Domin, the chaplain of the convent. Her knowledge was so precise in the case of difficult questions that the good priest had named her "his little Doctor." She seemed endowed with marvelous intuition, especially as regards heaven and everything that pertained to the life beyond. Nevertheless, it happened at rare intervals that she obtained even in religious doctrine something less than her usual success. The poor child was then inconsolable, for she could not bear to think that her father would have less cause for joy that evening when he examined her notes.

Other incidents caused her painful surprise. There were in the Abbey, as in every other educational establishment, children of a naturally turbulent disposition, who profited by a momentary absence of supervision, especially in the corridors or on the staircases, to abandon themselves to relaxation which was quickly repressed. Thérèse, invariably adverse to anything which could displease God, could not understand this and would look on dumbfounded. Her silent disapproval, which was almost always taken note of, was the first penalty for these small acts of insubordination.

But at that age censure, even if silent, is not willingly tolerated from a companion. Still less would they admit the intellectual superiority of a child several years their junior, and care was taken that the new-comer should be made aware of the fact. "There was one pupil in particular, aged fourteen," relates Thérèse, "possessed of little intelligence, able, nevertheless, to pose before the others as better than she really was. Seeing me, so young, almost always first at composition and beloved by all the nuns, she became jealous and made me pay in many ways for my little successes. With my timid and delicate nature I knew not how to defend myself, and simply wept in silence."[5]

A poor means of defence, truly, especially against the temptation so common to a number of children grouped together, to torment collectively the rival by whose superiority they are eclipsed.

Thérèse offered other vulnerable points to the taunts of certain companions. She seemed to have little relish for exuberant demonstrations and noisy recreation, and the others felt this keenly. Finding her joy in unpetalling roses and strewing the petals in front of the Blessed Virgin's statue, or decorating with flowers the little altar before which she prayed, she was unskillful in handling a racquet or a croquet mallet, and more than one stupid or idle pupil took revenge for Thérèse's success in the classroom by triumphing over her awkwardness at the physical exercises in which they indulged.

Another observed fact created unjust prejudice against her. Subject to frequent illness, she was obliged to remain at home on certain class-days, but even on these days she made every effort to complete the composition exercises that had been set. This led some of her companions to suspect that she remained at home purposely in order to have more leisure to study the matter set for competition.[6]

From this state of affairs arose a mutual constraint, often obliging Thérèse to spend her recreations apart from the animated and joyous groups around her, either alone with her catechism in an endeavour to memorize the literal words or in the company of some model children who understood her better than the others and felt drawn by her simple virtue.

One of the older pupils, afterwards a Benedictine nun, has made known the object of this silent child's constant preoccupation, even while only two paces away from a noisy and turbulent group of companions. "As I was president of a pious association," says Sœur Marie du Saint Rosaire,

> Thérèse came during recreation, according to the custom of the school, to ask advice. She was then about ten, and I was greatly surprised at her question. She asked me to explain to her the method of meditation. She also described to me then, as far as I can remember, how she herself made mental prayer on holidays. She hid behind her bed-curtain the better to recollect herself, *"and there,"* she said, *"I think."* This word expresses clearly enough the state to which Thérèse had arrived in her soul's intercourse with God, and how little need she had therefore of the methods offered to beginners in the spiritual life.

She felt little need of a missal or other manual containing set prayers for the faithful. Her teachers remarked that she hardly ever followed the method given in the prayer-book for assistance at the Holy Sacrifice. Sometimes they drew her attention to this fact by a word or look. She thanked them with a smile, but the next instant it could plainly be seen that her gaze, far from giving any indication of vague abstraction, fixed itself on heavenly reality. She prayed "without noise of words."

The nuns realized in part the value of the treasure confided to their care, without however esteeming it at its true worth. Dispositions of soul which in the estimation of those around her were faults, and which constituted in reality a trial from Providence, prevented them from discerning the degree of union with God to which this timid and reserved child whom they saw every day in their classrooms had attained. One of them has given the following picture of Thérèse Martin.

"A winning and delicate smile was her habitual expression of countenance, as soon as her tears, too ready and too frequent it must indeed be said, were dried. Sweet and gracious manners, tender piety, obedience in even the smallest things, a shrinking from turbulent and noisy associates or games, such were the characteristics of her school life. All this was, however, veiled by the excessive timidity and sensitiveness already noted."[7]

As in the past, God vouchsafed to His well-beloved child some rays of joy in her night of trial. The daily return to her father's home, the re-union each evening of the "little Queen" and her "dear King," as she called M. Martin, were to her a sweet alleviation of her daily troubles. There were also the holidays, and never did Thérèse find them so joyful as when they were spent at Les Buissonnets with Céline. Sometimes, too, she passed a few hours with the Guérin family, enjoying very much the company of her little cousin Marie.

They played at "solitaries," and became for the moment penitent anchorites dividing their time between contemplation and exercises of the active life. Sometimes, unfortunately, the hard facts of modern life intervened to remind the two hermits that they did not live in the desert.

One evening as they were returning from the Abbey they wished to imitate the modesty of hermits. Thérèse said to Marie, "Lead me; I am going to close my eyes." "I want to close mine too," said her cousin, and thus blindly they walked along on the footpath which was crowded with wares. Soon there was an unexpected collision as the two hermits tumbled over cases containing the early vegetables exposed for sale by some honest grocer. He was furious, and fumed and threatened as he gathered up his scattered products. The two blind solitaries promptly recovered their sight, in order to run away with all possible speed.

Our little predestined soul could not but inspire the enemy of man with ferocious jealousy. God permitted that he should endeavour to cut off this life which was so pleasing in the sight of the Eternal Father.

We know the place that Pauline held in the heart of Thérèse, Pauline whom she called, and who with so much affection proved truly "her little mother." Since she became exposed to the numberless small vexations of school-life, she appreciated more than ever the tenderness of this elder sister who had brought her up, instructed her, and unceasingly watched over her with loving care.

One day, as Pauline and Marie were talking together, she heard them speak of Pauline's intention of very soon entering Carmel.

What picture could Carmel present to the eyes of Thérèse?

Pauline described to her the life in the cloister, its austerity and renunciation, but also the infinite sweetness and intimacy established between the divine Master and chosen souls who have left all to follow Him.

Thérèse kept these thoughts in her heart, seeking from them a light for her future. Then, one evening, she discerned clearly, by sudden illumination, that Carmel was really the "distant desert" of which she had so often dreamed, and in which the ineffable peace of companionship with God is to be found. She realized that *there* would be her refuge for ever, realized it with such force "that from that day onward there was never the least doubt in her mind."[8]

Pauline, far from discouraging this hope, induced Thérèse to present her request to the Mother Prioress of the Convent of Lisieux. This good Mother listened to the "great confidences" of the child, and while not denying the existence of her vocation, told her that she did not receive postulants of nine years, and that she would have to wait until her sixteenth year before dreaming of admittance.

Pauline, then, was going away, and forever. The family re-union, grouping, each evening, the five daughters around their father, was to be dismembered.

The separation was intensely painful, and harder still were the first visits, at the end of which Pauline, now become Sœur Agnès de Jésus, could give scarcely more than two or three minutes to her poor little sister.

The child's health, which had long been precarious, was not proof against this trial. The demon was going to profit by her weak condition to obtain from God a certain short-lived mastery over her body, to treat it with such cruelty as would even have shattered the delicate organs had God so permitted.

Pauline entered Carmel in October, 1882. The months following were for Thérèse a period of bitter sadness and physical suffering which tended to increase day by day.

In March, 1883, M. Martin was in Paris, and, accompanied by Marie and Léonie, he was introducing them to the wonderful ceremonies of Holy Week in the great churches of the capital, when he was suddenly called back to Lisieux.

Thérèse, who, with Céline, had been left in Mme Guérin's charge, was suffering from a sharp and disquieting attack. After a conversation with her uncle, who was speaking about her departed mother, she had wept silently. Later in the evening she was seized, without any apparent cause, by fits of violent trembling.

She was taken back to Les Buissonnets, and here her condition became decidedly critical. Terrifying visions drew from her cries of distress which struck fear and compassion into those who stood around. Strange words which she seemed to articulate in spite of herself, then long hours of prostrate suffering, all seemed to denote the action of an evil spirit who had received external power over the little sick child.

This impression was increased when, one day, she tried to climb over the bed-rail to throw herself to the ground. Her sisters had to prevent her by force. "One Sunday," relates Léonie, "I had remained alone to take care of her during High Mass. Seeing her very calm, I ventured to leave her for a few moments. On returning I found her stretched on the floor between the bed and the wall. She might have been killed or badly hurt, but, thanks to God, she had not even received a scratch."[9]

Sometimes the most familiar objects assumed terrifying forms. Nails driven in the walls of her room suddenly appeared to her as huge fingers burnt black, and she cried out, "I am frightened! I am frightened!" Her face, usually so calm and sweet, wore then an indescribable expression of terror.

One evening her father came and sat close to her bed holding his hat in his hand. She looked at him at first without uttering a word, then suddenly her expression changed, and fixing her eyes on the hat with a look of horror, she cried out in a choking voice: "Oh, the big black beast!" The poor father went away in tears.

It happened sometimes that she did not even recognize her own relatives; sometimes, too, she would hit her head violently against the sides of the bed. Dr. Notta, a conscientious practitioner, declared unhesitatingly on witnessing these strange happenings: "Science is powerless in face of these phenomena; nothing can be done."[10]

Thérèse has written later that even during the most severe crisis she never lost the use of her reason, that she heard and understood perfectly everything that took place around her; a further proof that while retaining the full use of her faculties she was under the action of a hidden power, whose author, realizing the obstacles that she would put to his influence in the future, made attempts on her life.

The date fixed for Pauline's reception of the habit was drawing near. It was not spoken of in Thérèse's presence, lest regret at not being able to assist at this touching ceremony should aggravate her illness. But the little one declared that she would be able to accompany her sisters.

She was in fact able, when the day came, to embrace her "little mother," sit on her lap, hide under her veil, and receive her caresses. Perhaps, too, she contemplated with feelings of envy the joy of this fiancée of Jesus. But her hours of rapture passed quickly away. Soon they had to get into the carriage and return to Les Buissonnets, and the following morning saw the poor child struck down by a fresh attack of even greater violence.

Once more, they had to keep continual watch beside her. Marie, in particular, tended her with unwearied kindness, and the little invalid would hardly let her leave the room, except to go to Church or to the Carmel.

M. Martin, grieved at the failure of every remedy, but ever confiding in the power of the Queen of Heaven, requested a novena of Masses for the cure of his little daughter at the Church of Notre-Dame-des-Victoires, Paris.

Such supplication could not but touch the heart of the Immaculate Virgin. The scene which followed must be related by the inspired pen of her who contemplated "the holy Virgin's smile." Thérèse writes:

> On Sunday, during the novena, Marie went out into the garden, leaving me with Léonie who was reading near the window. After a few minutes I began to call in almost a whisper "Marie, Marie." Léonie, accustomed to hear me continually calling in that way, paid no attention. I then cried out loudly, and Marie came back to me. I saw her perfectly as she came in, but for the first time failed to recognize her. I looked searchingly all around, gazed anxiously into the garden, and began again to call "Marie, Marie." It was unutterable suffering, this inexplicable and constrained strife, and Marie suffered even more perhaps than her poor Thérèse. At last, after vain efforts to make herself known to me, she turned to Léonie, whispered a word to her, and went out pale and trembling.
>
> Dear Léonie quickly carried me near to the window; then I saw Marie in the garden again without recognizing her. She walked slowly, holding out her arms

> to me, smiling and calling me in her tenderest tone: "Thérèse, my little Thérèse." This last attempt having also failed, my beloved sister, weeping, threw herself on her knees at the foot of my bed, and turning towards the Blessed Virgin she implored her with the fervour of a mother who begs with *insistence* for the life of her child. Léonie and Céline followed her example, and this was a cry of faith which forced the gates of heaven.
>
> Finding no help on earth and almost dead from grief, I also turned towards my heavenly Mother beseeching her with all my heart to have pity on me.
>
> All at once the statue became animated. The Virgin Mary became so beautiful that I shall never find words to express that heavenly loveliness. Her countenance breathed sweetness, goodness, and ineffable tenderness; but what penetrated to the depths of my soul was her *ravishing smile*. Then all my pain vanished; two big tears gushed from my eyes and fell silently.
>
> Ah, those were tears of unalloyed celestial joy. *The holy Virgin advanced towards me. She smiled on me . . . how happy I am*, thought I. *But I will tell no one, for then my happiness would vanish*. Then I lowered my eyes and without effort recognized my dear Marie. She was looking at me lovingly, and appeared deeply moved; she seemed to have guessed the great favour I had just received.[11]

Seeing the child's countenance transfigured before the statue, Marie had in truth conjectured that a miracle was taking place. She questioned Thérèse, who confirmed the reality of the glorious apparition, and then both realized that all trace of illness had disappeared.

The joyous news must be made known at the Carmel. Marie told it immediately though discreetly, and Thérèse herself some time afterwards. The latter had intended to confide the secret only to her "dear little mother," but the nuns having heard rumours of a miracle, questioned her in the parlour, and the little one's very reserved account soon became a subject of conversation amongst the nuns at the risk of being modified or amplified. Thérèse began to fear that she had given rise to these little inaccuracies by a clumsy account of the miracle, and her mind became tortured with anxieties, which were quieted only years afterwards before another statue of the Mother of mercy.[12]

Be it as it may concerning this passing cloud, the demon was conquered. Once more the Immaculate had crushed him with her heel. By this terrible trial, borne with so much Christian fortitude, the child had progressed in union with God. Her first Communion was to strengthen still more her bond of union with the Well-Beloved.

Before the great day, and, doubtless, to completely restore her health, M. Martin believed that he should accede to the wishes of some old acquaintances who offered Thérèse a holiday in the country. He took her to Alençon to these friends who received them in their respective chateaux of Saint-Denis, Grogny, and very probably Lanchal.

The season was most favourable and the scenery enchanting. Everywhere the welcome was delightfully cordial. Fêted continually, and petted even to emulation by all in these beautiful places, Thérèse admits that she allowed herself to yield for the moment to the charm of attentions lavished on her with so much affection. But the temptation touched merely the surface of her soul already completely surrendered to the guidance of the Holy Spirit. Serious thoughts counteracted "the bewitchment of trifles" so completely that the memory of this delightful holiday will inspire her later with no other reflections than these: "Alas! how well the world plans to combine the joys of earth with the service of God. How seldom it thinks of death."

The vanity of those things which had for the moment charmed her, inclined her more than ever, on her return to Lisieux, towards closer union with the Friend who remains when all the rest are gone.

We know how she had for years longed to partake of the celestial banquet. When told that in the early Church fragments of the consecrated Host were given to quite little children, she exclaimed with astonishment: "Why is it not so now?"

But the Diocesan laws had to be obeyed. By these regulations a child, in order to be admitted to her first

Communion, must complete her eleventh year within the year of admission. Thérèse was born on January 2, 1873; she was, therefore, two days short of the required age when, in the Spring of 1883, came the usual time for first Communion. Seeing her companions preparing for the great event, the dear little one deplored these two unlucky days which kept her away from the holy table.

Meanwhile, being one day in Lisieux with her sister Marie, she saw the Bishop of Bayeux, Mgr Hugonin, who was going towards the station accompanied by one of his Vicars-General. "Oh, Marie," she said eagerly, "shall I run and ask his permission to make my first Communion this year?" Her elder sister had considerable difficulty in preventing her from carrying out her purpose.

Thérèse, now definitely restored to health, had returned to the Benedictine Abbey. Preparation had to be made for her first Communion, at all events for the following year, and therefore only a few months distant. Marie, who since Pauline's departure supplemented the work of the nuns with Thérèse, early undertook her remote preparation. This was all the more easy as the little one, possessed of an ever increasing desire for the sacred nourishment, had moreover a marked taste for instruction in religious doctrine.

Each evening, then, Thérèse's room, or the garden of Les Buissonnets, was the scene of a long and intimate colloquy where the elder sister instilled into her mind the inestimable value of the "gift of God."

Behind the grilles of Carmel Pauline followed the supernatural work and took part in it by prayer. She did more. Recalling the chaplet of "practices," which had so happily contributed in former years to the sanctification of Céline and Thérèse, she prepared a beautiful little notebook for the latter, advising her to write down day by day the number of her sacrifices and aspirations of love, which she exhorted her to multiply in order that she might belong entirely to the Well-Beloved whose advent was so near. At the end of three months the booklet noted 818 sacrifices and 2,774 acts of love.

The angelic child wished to go further in her endeavours to draw nearer to her Divine Master. Led by the Holy Spirit at an early age into intimate, easy, and almost spontaneous communication with God, she desired, during these last weeks of preparation, to consecrate regularly a half-hour each day to this familiar communion with Jesus.

She expressed the wish to her elder sister, who did not consider it prudent to agree. "Then," relates Marie,

> she asked my permission for at least a quarter of an hour's mental prayer every day. I did not grant this either. Seeing her so fervent, and that she comprehended in so exalted a manner the things of heaven, I thought it better to act with very great reserve on this point.
>
> The dear little one submitted with her usual docility; but innocently, and without suspecting that she was thus giving herself up to real contemplation, she used to hide herself in a corner of her room which could be easily closed in by the bed-curtains, and there she would spend a long time on the half-holidays "thinking about the good God, about the shortness of this life, and about eternity."

The week for the final retreat came at last, and Thérèse was invited to stay day and night at the Convent. She long retained happy memories of the supernatural tenderness showered on her by the nuns during that period. Each evening the first mistress, filled with holy admiration for the openhearted child, came with her little lantern, gently drew back the bed-curtains, and respectfully kissed her forehead. Seeing herself the object of so much care, the little one ventured one day to remark to her: "O Madame, I love you so well that I am going to confide to you a great secret." And she showed her the precious booklet, Pauline's gift, where she noted down her offerings to the divine Master, and which she kept hidden under her pillow.

The week was passed in religious exercises, in fervent and tender prayer, also classes in the study hall, where the solid instruction of Abbé Domin was recapitulated.

"At last," writes Thérèse,

the happy day of all days dawned for me. What ineffable memories the least details of those celestial hours left in my soul. The joyous awakening at break of day, the tender and respectful kisses of my mistresses and bigger companions, the dressing-room filled with snowy vesture in which each child clothed in turn; above all, our entrance to the chapel to the strains of the matin-hymn: "O sacred altar girt with angel-guard!"

But I do not wish to, nor could I describe all. . . . There are things which lose their perfume when exposed to the air; thoughts that cannot be translated into earthly language without losing their profound and heavenly meaning.

Ah, how sweet it was, this first kiss of Jesus to my soul! Yes, it was a kiss of love. I felt that I was loved, and I said in return: "I love Thee; I give myself to Thee for ever." Jesus did not ask for anything; He claimed no sacrifice. For a long time already had He and little Thérèse regarded and understood one another. . . . On this day, our meeting could not be called by the simple name of regard but of *Fusion*. We were no longer two; Thérèse had disappeared like the drop of water which is lost in the ocean's depths; Jesus alone remained: He was Master and King. Had not Thérèse asked Him to take away her liberty? Her liberty had caused her to fear; so weak and frail did she feel herself, that she longed to be eternally united to the Divine strength. . . .[13]

So great was her joy and so profound that she could not restrain it. Tears of happiness fell from her eyes, to the great astonishment of her companions, who said to one another afterwards: "Why did she cry? Had she some scruple of conscience? No, it was because she had not her mother near her, or her Carmelite sister whom she loves so much." But no one understood that this exiled heart, weak and mortal as it was, could not, without tears, contain all the joy that came to it from heaven.[14]

This great love was to express itself in act. Thérèse knew, that after the joys of Thabor, the Master would recall her to her daily task, and she determined to make manifest by her actions that she had drawn strength from the Source of life.

On the evening of the great day, she wrote in her little notebook the three following resolutions: (1) "I will never give way to discouragement." (2) "I will say the *Memorare* every day." (3) "I will endeavour to humble my pride."[15]

The second of these resolutions was connected with the Act of Consecration to the Blessed Virgin, which Thérèse had recited that afternoon in the name of all. The little one remembered the smiling vision of Mary, when so recently she had cured and delivered her, and so her whole soul entered into this offering of herself, which was at the same time a filial appeal for the constant protection of the Queen of Heaven.

This day, opening with the Saviour's kiss, was to be completed for Thérèse by the sweet contemplation of the spiritual union which Jesus had deigned to establish, almost at the same hour, with her "little mother," a union she continually dreamed of for herself. After the ceremony at the abbey, M. Martin took his little daughter to the Carmel to see her dear Pauline, that morning professed, "wearing a white veil like her own, and crowned with roses." No longer did the pangs of separation tear the heart of Thérèse. Rather was it envy of Pauline's lot and the cherished hope of soon sharing the same joy that made her heart expand.

They returned finally to Les Buissonnets, where all were united in common gladness at the family repast. Afterwards M. Martin, in accordance with custom, made his "little Queen" a present of a pretty watch.

The day had been so full of happiness, her intercourse with her Divine Lord so sweet, that gladly would Thérèse have approached the Holy Table again on the following morning. She had, however, to wait eight days. On May 15, the feast of the Ascension, she was able to participate in the sacred banquet for the second time, accompanied by her father and her eldest sister. But, alas! the greater feast days, when alone it was possible at that time for her to communicate, were but few. She experienced then the hunger for this celestial food which was the lot of many pure souls before the happy intervention of Pius X. But she compensated for the relatively small number of communions by the fervour of her preparation.

Marie always helped her to prepare a worthy dwelling for the Holy of Holies. In one of these little talks before Communion, Marie spoke to her of the rôle of suffering, adding that perhaps God would not lead her by that way. After Holy Communion the little one felt her heart inflamed with desire for the cross, with an inward conviction that her desire would be granted. "Then," she declares, "my soul was flooded with consolation such as I have never again known in my whole life."[16] The Most High had commenced to prepare his little victim.

But Thérèse felt at the same time that she would inevitably fail under trial without the help of her divine Master. Thus she disposed herself with unusual care and earnestness to receive the sacrament of Confirmation, whose dignity and fruit were apparent to her with a vividness unknown to most children. Hear Céline's words on the subject:

> She received the sacrament of Confirmation on June 14, 1884. The days immediately preceding are in particular deeply graven in my memory. Thérèse, usually so calm, was no longer the same; a sort of enthusiasm and holy rapture were perceptible in her exterior. One day, during her preparatory retreat, I expressed my astonishment at seeing her thus. She explained to me what she understood regarding the power of this sacrament, of the Holy Spirit taking possession of her whole being. There was in her words such conviction, in her countenance such ardour, that, penetrated by a sense of the supernatural, I came away profoundly moved. This incident so struck me that I can see even now her actions, her attitude, the place where she stood, and the memory will never be effaced from my mind.[17]

After vacation, she resumed with more success than ever her religious and literary studies. A mere child in age, and also perhaps in sensitiveness, she was no longer such to anyone who observed the wonderfully developed maturity of her judgement. From henceforth, nothing childish entered into her intellectual development or the formation of her will.

Her very recreations had the stamp of gravity. For instance, she loved to give "honourable burial," as she said, under the large chestnut-trees of the Abbey to the little birds that had fallen accidentally from the nest. She took a delight, too, in telling stories, and told them so well that the older pupils readily formed a circle around her until the Sister in charge, who wished to see play rather than discussion, broke up the momentary group.

With her affectionate and refined tenderness, Thérèse naturally had friends. There were two whom she regarded with special predilection among the souls that she loved for God. Of those two attachments one was no doubt so fleeting as to have left no definite trace in her life. She has confided to us the course of the other. After an absence of some months, imposed by various circumstances on her little friend, Thérèse received from her on her return merely a look of indifference, which revealed to her for the rest of her life the inconstancy of human friendship. "But," she says, "the good God has given me so faithful a heart, that when it has once loved it loves always; so I continue to pray for that companion, and I love her still."[18]

Rendered wise by this experience, she was on her guard against those attachments conceived by some of the pupils for one or other of the mistresses, attachments too often also passing and vain when founded on merely natural attraction.

In recalling these memories later she wrote: "How I thank God for having allowed me to find nothing but bitterness in earthly friendship. With a heart like mine I should have let myself be captured and my wings cut. How then could I fly away and be at rest!"[19]

Having kept her treasure of tenderness inviolate for Jesus, she renewed, in May, 1885, with her young companions, that solemn Communion which in the preceding year had brought her the most fervent emotion of her life. Alas! the Master refused her, this time, the joyous consciousness of this Presence. She had been tormented with scruples for several days, and this heavy trial was to last for many months.

To afford her some necessary relaxation, her aunt, Mme Guérin, took her to Deauville with her own children on the day following the ceremony.

The kindness of this second mother, the charming vivacity of her two daughters Marie and Jeanne, the sight of the great sea, calm as a beautiful lake or terrible in its sudden fury, helped the child to raise her soul to the Almighty whose majesty extends over the abysses.

The family took a villa situated on the quay *de la Touques*, called then "Châlet Colombe." The church of Notre-Dame-des-Victoires was a long distance away. They went, nevertheless, every evening to the devotions for the month of May. If the distance or some other motive sometimes caused hesitation, Thérèse insisted in favour of the daily homage to the Mother of God, and never did the fatigue, however great, prevent her undertaking this long walk. It was also her happiness to assist, in spite of storm and rain, at early Mass in the church consecrated to the holy Virgin.[20]

In September, Mme Guérin made a second visit to Trouville-Deauville, staying this time in a house in the rue Charlemagne. M. Martin having set out some weeks before on a long journey of which we shall speak later, she invited her nieces to join her. This second visit to the Normandy coast was marked by two little incidents, which Thérèse has noted in her autobiography.

While providing abundant distractions for her little niece in order to make her holiday beneficial, Mme Guérin took care to preserve her from all that could weaken her moral strength.

One evening when the family were together in the little sitting-room, Marie Guérin, who was then about fourteen years of age, complained of a headache. Her mother, yielding to tenderness that made her over-anxious, began "to fondle her, addressing her in the most affectionate terms without obtaining anything but tears."

For the moment, Thérèse allowed herself to yield to the attraction of these tender words. She, too, has frequent headaches. She has never complained of them; but is not the experiment worth trying? A few days afterwards, she retires into a corner of the sitting-room, sinks down on a chair and commences in her turn to cry. On being questioned she answered like Marie, "I have a headache."

What! No one bestirs herself to sympathize with her. Her aunt gravely reproves her as one grown up who wished to play the spoiled child. Even Jeanne, her cousin, corrects her in a slightly sarcastic tone, insinuating that Thérèse does not wish to tell her aunt the true cause of her tears. "Thérèse," she says, "is wanting in confidence and simplicity. She is, in all probability, tormented by some big scruple and does not dare admit it."[21] The lesson had gone home. "In fine," declares the little one, "I was paid back in my own coin, and I firmly resolved never again to imitate others, for I understood now the fable of 'The Ass and the Dog.' I was the ass who, on seeing the lap-dog petted, placed his unwieldy hoof on the table to be kissed in turn. If I was not driven away with blows like the poor animal, I received, nevertheless, the price of my folly, and this price cured me for ever of the desire to attract attention."[22]

Another day Mme Guérin, with her usual kindness, had given the little one some "sky-blue" ribbons to tie her beautiful golden hair. Thérèse, for the moment, was highly pleased. But had she the right to pander to self-love by this vain finery? This problem placed her in a difficulty, and her extreme delicacy of conscience forced her to confess, even at Trouville, "this childish pleasure which, to her, seemed a sin."[23]

Thérèse passed the remainder of the vacation at Les Buissonnets, where she had to suffer a privation which she had never known before and which she certainly must have felt very keenly: the prolonged absence of her father. At the earnest desire of a priest of Lisieux, the Abbé Marie, parish priest of Saint-Jacques, M. Martin was persuaded to go on a tour through Germany, Austria, Constantinople, and Italy. This event, which was of some note in his peaceful life and indirectly in that of his family, calls for a few details.

We possess a series of letters written by M. Martin to his daughters at different stages of the journey, which lasted six weeks. Munich with its museums, Vienna with its marvellous bridges "unequalled in the traveller's experience even in Paris," Constantinople with the splendours of Santa Sophia and the dazzling panorama from the tower of Galata presented to his eyes unsuspected wonders whose charm he describes to Marie, "his Diamond," to the "good Léonie," to "the Intrepid" Céline, to Thérèse, the "Queen of his heart," not forgetting Pauline, "the delicate Pearl" of Carmel.[24]

These beautiful sights did not, however, make him forget Les Buissonnets, and in reply to feast-day wishes which his daughters had sent for August 25, 1885, he wrote from Vienna: "I seemed to see you all around me in the Belvedere, and to hear Thérèse's sweet and sympathetic voice murmur a little compliment to me. It so moved me that I wished to be back at Lisieux, to be there in good earnest to embrace you all."[25]

The tour was completed in Italy. Naples, "that enchanting city"; Pompeii, with the poetry of its ruins; Rome, with the wonders of St. Peter's, which are in truth "the most magnificent in the world," were successively the objects of M. Martin's enthusiastic descriptions.

Rome, above every other place, had for him the most compelling attraction. Near to the tomb of the Apostles, within a few paces of the Pontiff prisoner whose word and influence cease not to rule the world, he could scarcely contain his gladness. He wrote to Marie: "It is certainly here that I experience the greatest joy. Tell 'my Pearl' (Pauline) that my happiness is too great to last."[26]

Is there a presentment in these words? At all events, when in Milan on the eve of re-entering France, M. Martin experienced still more vividly the impression of the instability of human joy, and his tour ended with an aspiration towards the beauty of the eternal Fatherland, which cannot be dimmed by sad foreboding. "Everything I see is splendid," he writes, "but with earthly beauty; our heart is never satisfied as long as it sees not the Infinite Beauty.

. . . Welcome the intimate joy of family life! It is this which brings us nearest to the beauty above."[27]

When M. Martin returned to Lisieux, Thérèse had already for some days attended the classes at the Abbey, which had re-opened in October. She returned alone this time, as Céline had finished her studies at the end of the preceding school-year.

Her scruples, far from being calmed, had, alas, redoubled. Moreover, the little one who worked with great diligence suffered so much from headaches, that her father felt obliged, after a few months, to interrupt her studies and withdraw her from the too sedentary life of the boarding-school.

This was at the beginning of the year 1886. It was then decided that Thérèse should be brought several times a week to a lady of good position, from whom she would receive excellent lessons, and combine the double advantage of instruction on the one hand, and on the other, of bringing her into contact with the world for the first time.

There, then, we find the little one seated before a desk "in an antiquely furnished room, surrounded by lesson- and copy-books where numbers of well-meaning ladies came daily in search of distraction." One would go into ecstasy about the new pupil's beautiful hair; another would ask in a whisper who was this pretty little girl. Thérèse was, to all outward appearance, studying, but she heard and understood all, and she was not slow to conclude that, in order not to make shipwreck of her humility, she had need of special assistance from the Queen of heaven.

There was an Association of the Children of Mary at the Abbey of Notre-Dame-du-Pré. She will ask to be affiliated to this band of young girls specially devoted to the imitation of the divine Mother, and in order to be admitted she will accept a new term of probation among the older pupils of the convent.

As one of the conditions, she had to assist, two or three times a week, at a lesson in manual work given at the Abbey. For the rest, Mother Saint-Placide, directress of the boarding-school, had said to the members of the Sodality on receiving her request for admission: "We shall never have to regret her name on our list."

Thérèse came, then, without enthusiasm it is true, and even with a certain amount of weariness, "for she had not, like the others, a favourite amongst the mistresses." She worked in silence until the end of the work lesson, "and then, no one noticing me," she writes, "I went up to the tribune of the chapel until my father came for me."[28]

Thérèse deceived herself in imagining that no one thought about her. Among her companions, one of the senior girls who was afterwards to become a Benedictine under the name of Sœur Jean l'Evangéliste, observed her during her silent work, and such was her admiration for the gentleness and continual recollection of the aspirant, that she watched, on coming out of the room, for an occasion of talking with her. But Thérèse would disappear too quickly; she was before the Tabernacle in converse with Jesus, and usually remained there for more than an hour.[29]

She became a Child of Mary officially on May 31, 1887. This was the last notable favour that she owed to the solicitude of the Benedictine nuns. She retained all her life a feeling of deep gratitude for the solid Christian education received at their convent and signified this to them at every opportunity.[30]

Thérèse had nearly attained her fourteenth year, when in October, 1886, her sister Marie, who had become her principal confidante, believed her now sufficiently courageous to bear a new separation. She did not fear, then, to carry out a project formed some months previously of joining Pauline at the Carmel.

Thérèse who herself aspired to the same destiny certainly could not blame her.

But while awaiting the time to imitate her sisters in their supreme sacrifice, what was to become of her? Who would now guide her in her troubles of conscience? She commenced by shedding tears. Then, seeing herself deprived of all human support, she thought of appealing for help to the four little angels who, born before her, had passed so soon from her mother's arms and gone before her into the arms of God. In the name of the affection that they would have shown her here below had they lived, and which their entrance to heaven could not have extinguished, she conjured them to obtain peace of mind for her, thus proving that "up there they still know how to love."

The answer of these little brothers and sisters to the prayer of Thérèse was not slow in coming. A delicious peace filled her soul hitherto so tormented. She was loved in heaven; her scruples had ceased.

It now remained to conquer that excessive sensitiveness which, even yet, often betrayed itself by floods of tears. This little miracle—for it needed a miracle—was worked by the Babe of Bethlehem on Christmas night, 1886. "On that holy night," Thérèse declares, "Jesus, the sweet Infant of an hour, changed the night of my soul into floods of light. In making Himself weak and little for my sake, He made me strong and courageous. He clothed me with His armour, and since then I go from victory to victory, advancing, as it were, *with giant strides*. The fountain of my tears was dried up, not to be reopened save rarely and with difficulty."

She afterwards describes the occasion and the precise moment when this precious and unexpected grace was accorded to her.

> On arriving at Les Buissonnets after midnight Mass, I knew I should find my shoes on the hearthstone filled with gifts, as in my infant days—which proves that I had been, till now, treated like a little baby. Papa himself loved to see my happiness, to hear my cries of delight as I drew out each new surprise from the enchanted shoes, and his gaiety further increased my pleasure. But the hour was come when Jesus willed to free me from the failings of childhood and also to withdraw from me its harmless joys. He permitted that my dear father, contrary to his usual habit of indulging me in everything, should this time feel annoyed. Going up the stairs to my room I heard him say these words, which pierced me to the heart: "For a big girl like Thérèse, this is too childish; I hope this will be the last time."
>
> Céline, knowing my extreme sensitiveness, said to me in a low tone: "Do not go down immediately; wait a

little while; you would surely cry when looking at the presents before papa." But Thérèse was no longer the same; Jesus had changed her heart.

Driving back my tears, I went down quickly to the dining-room, then, endeavouring to quell my beating heart, I took the shoes and drew out *joyously* all the gifts, looking as happy as a queen. Papa laughed; no trace of displeasure appeared on his countenance; Céline thought she was in a dream. Happily it was a sweet reality; little Thérèse had regained for ever her strength of soul lost at the age of four and a half years.

In that luminous night began the third period of my life, the most beautiful of all and the most full of graces from heaven. In an instant Jesus, pleased with my good will, accomplished the work that I had failed to do in many years.[31]

The trial ordained by Providence was at an end. The child who had borne it with undiminished virtue was to become one of the most valiant souls to be found in the "Lives of the Saints." Henceforth she could aspire to giving herself wholly to God in the religious life.

Her childhood, too, was ended. In spite of the clouds of sadness which from time to time had bedimmed her skies, she never disclaimed, even when wearing the Carmelite veil, those youthful years when her soul opened in joyous candour to earthly beauty, the figure and symbol of Heavenly splendour. She never in her after life wrote anything more charming than the following lines in imitation of a well-known poem of Chateaubriand:

Oh, well-beloved memory,
The joyous days of infancy!
To guard my innocence inviolably,
Our Lord enclosed me from above
With love.

I loved the plain, the hillside green,
The waving wheatfield's golden sheen;
Breathless my joy with sisters mine to glean

Through the long summer hours
Sweet flowers.

I loved the little daisy white,
The Sunday walk of pure delight;
Birds warbling 'mid the boughs in sight,
The radiant azure as it dyes
The skies.

Oh, memories, ye breathe repose,
Full many a picture ye disclose,
The evening meal, the perfume of the rose,
The summer-day at Buissonnets
So gay.[32]

When Thérèse bade this sweet and melancholy adieu to the ever dear past, she had had, for many years before, no other horizon except the grey walls of the cloister; but then had commenced that period rich in grace which she proclaims, in spite of all, the most beautiful of her life. It is now time to show how she endeavoured with a maturity beyond her years to leave behind the charm of earthly beauty, and to follow in the odour of His perfumes the Well-Beloved who was calling her to the desert.

6

Vocation to Carmel—Struggle against Exterior Obstacles which Restrained Her—Journey to Italy

Thérèse herself unfolds with heartfelt gratitude the effects of that singular grace, which, according to her own admission, had transformed her on Christmas night, 1886. She summed them up in these words: "Charity entered my heart with the need of entire forgetfulness of self; from that time forth I was happy."[1]

Charity certainly dwelt in this virginal soul from the moment of baptism. But the gift of self to the Saviour even to the desire "of entire self-forgetfulness" is an act so perfect and rare that the child could not but have noted the precise moment when this grace, one of the greatest gifts of the Divine Master, was given to her. She was to appreciate all the more dearly this sacred hour because it brought her the "perfect joy" extolled by the seraphic beggar of Assisi as the reward of supreme self-abnegation.

Here, then, is this child of fourteen years determined to serve her Creator even to the extent of forgetting self always, to become a choice stone in the mystic city built, according to St. Augustine, by those who know how to love God even to the extent of utter contempt for self.

Moreover, Thérèse felt, ever more insistently, that the Crucified demanded this total surrender of herself without reserve, the only return which corresponds to the bloody sacrifice of Calvary.

"One Sunday," she relates,

> in closing my book at the end of Mass, a picture representing Our Saviour on the cross slipped out a little from the pages, showing me one of the Divine Hands pierced and bleeding. I experienced then a new and inexpressible feeling. My heart was rent with grief at the sight of this precious Blood falling to the earth with no one eager to gather it as it fell, and I resolved that in spirit I would stand continually at the foot of the cross to receive the Divine dew of salvation and to pour it out on souls.
>
> From that day the cry of the dying Jesus, "I thirst," resounded in my soul at every instant, inflaming it with an unknown and intense ardour. I longed to give my Saviour to drink; I felt myself devoured with the thirst for souls, and I desired at all costs to snatch sinners from eternal flames.[2]

Without doubt, she foresaw as one of the surest means of rescue for these unhappy ones the immolation of self, which her sisters were already practising behind the grilles of Carmel, and of which her dear Pauline had made known to her the powerful influence. But had not the Prioress declared that at her age it was not yet time to think of entering a convent?

While waiting in order to answer the pressing appeal of the Master, she must in every way and by every means devote herself to her neighbour, thereby gaining him to God.

This neighbour was to be found in the first instance in the family circle. Having left school, and secretly aspiring to the life of Carmel, Thérèse had at present the duty of sacrificing herself joyously in the interests of those around her.

"At this period," her sister Léonie declares, "Thérèse, being constantly at home, was in truth the joy of the family. The very servants had a great love for her; everything about her breathed of peace, goodness, and consideration for all. She always forgot self in order to bring pleasure to others. Her evenness of temper was so simple and seemed so natural that no one would believe her perpetual renunciation cost her anything."[3]

In speaking of this period of her life, she was to write later to one of her sisters: "I had great compassion for those in service. In noticing the difference between masters and servants, I said to myself: 'How well this proves that there must be a heaven where each will be placed according to his interior merit. How well then will the poor and lowly be recompensed for the humiliations which they have endured in this life.'"

After her own family came the poor. When each Monday they rang at the garden gate, they assuredly appreciated the piece of white bread which Thérèse handed to them; but how much more did they love the smile of the little one and the care she took to protect them from barking Tom, the faithful watch-dog who made himself an object of terror to beggars. In the town, where she now accompanied her father more frequently than before, an appeal was made almost at every street-corner to M. Martin's purse to help some poor wretched person crouching under the shelter of a sculptured gable.

To relief of the body she joined charity for souls. Mme Guérin's maid, who later became a Benedictine, has noted some manifestations of this distinctive love of her neighbour which gave evidence, even then, of Thérèse's vocation to the life of Carmel. "When she was scarcely fourteen years of age she visited poor little girls and taught them their catechism. I went with her several times to these families. I was then witness of her joy and of the gratitude shown her by the children."[4]

Thérèse herself has spoken in charming words of her friendly relations with two of these children: "During the illness of the mother of a family," she writes,

> I looked after her two children, the elder of whom was only six years old. It was a real pleasure to see with what simplicity they believed all I said to them. Holy Baptism must, indeed, plant the theological virtues deep in souls, since from very infancy the hope of future good suffices to make sacrifice acceptable. When I wished to see my two little ones very amiable to one another, instead of promising them toys or sweets, I

> would speak to them of the eternal recompense which the Little Jesus would give to good children. The elder child, whose reason had commenced to develop, would turn to me with an expression of animated joy, asking me many charming questions about Jesus and His beautiful heaven. She afterwards promised me with fervour that she would always give way to her sister, adding that she would never forget the lessons of the "grand lady," as she called me.[5]

Mme Guérin's servant received from her in turn delicate and affectionate spiritual help of a different nature. The little one repeatedly spoke to her of the goodness of God to those who love Him, and of the consequent love that we should have for Him. The poor girl was then drawn to reveal an interior trouble of soul to Thérèse. "As I did not at all feel this love," she writes, "I mentioned the fact to her, saying that I had not this love for God by any means. She explained to me that love does not consist in sentiment, but in the practice of virtue."

Thérèse could not speak thus openly to everyone whom she wished to instruct and sanctify. There were the obstinately impenitent, the hardened sinners who held aloof from her sweet voice as well as from every Christian influence. For these she had but one resource, unceasing prayer, and, if need be, unwavering suffering. She preluded then her heroic act of charity, which, on her deathbed would be the résumé, as it were, of her life's aspirations. "I beseech the good God that all the prayers which are offered for me serve not to allay my sufferings, but may be entirely for sinners."[6]

No degree of perversity or obduracy could restrain the ardour of her charity. This was made evident when, in 1887, the newspapers recorded the fate of a great criminal who, after having astonished his judges by his cynical attitude, grieved by his impiety the chaplain who was charged with preparing him for execution.

M. Martin did not allow his daughters to read the newspapers, not even *La Croix*, to which he was a subscriber, but the topics of the day were discussed in the family circle.

In the latter part of June, 1887, everybody was speaking about the hateful circumstances accompanying the murder of two women and a girl in the rue Montaigu, Paris, by a man named Pranzini. Since then, the assassin had given no sign of repentance, and it was soon known that, even on the near approach of the supreme punishment, he refused all help from religion.

The thought of eternal punishment in store for the miserable man after the shame of the scaffold, moved Thérèse to unbounded compassion, and she resolved, she a weak child living at fifty leagues distance from the guilty man who was entirely unknown to her, to attempt the impossible in order to rescue his soul from damnation. But we must hear her give in her own words the prelude of the attempt.

"In order," she says,

> to succeed in preventing the irremediable misfortune, I employed every spiritual means imaginable, and, knowing that of myself I could do nothing, I offered for the ransom of this unfortunate man the Infinite merits of Our Saviour and the fruits of the Church's treasury.
>
> Need I say that I felt in my heart the certitude of being heard? But in order to give myself courage to continue to strive for the conquest of souls, I offered up this naïve prayer: "My God, I feel assured that You will pardon the unfortunate Pranzini; I would believe this even if he did not go to confession or give any mark of contrition, so great confidence have I in Your mercy. But this is my first sinner; for that reason I ask but *a sign* of repentance for my own consolation."[7]

From that time, Thérèse thought it allowable to glance at the newspaper each day in order to find out as far as possible the fate of her protégé.

On September 1, she read the following lines in the *La Croix*:

> (Upon awaking) the condemned man was taken to the Office of Registration and handed over to Deibler and his assistants who were waiting for him.
>
> There his hair was cut off, his neck bared, his hands bound, and at two minutes to five, while the

> birds sang in the trees around and a confused murmur rose from the crowd, the order "Sabre au clair" rang out; the click of irons was heard, sword-blades gleamed, and at the opened door of the prison the assassin appeared with livid face.
>
> The chaplain places himself in front to hide from him the fatal machine; the assistants help him along; he repels both priests and executioners. He now stands before the guillotine. Deibler pushes and throws him forward on to it. An assistant on the other side seizes hold of his head and draws it under the knife, holding it there by the hair.
>
> But before the final stroke—it may be that a lightning flash of repentance penetrated his conscience—he asked for the chaplain's crucifix, and three times he kissed it. And when the knife fell, when one of the assistants lifted up by one ear the separated head, we said to ourselves that if human justice is satisfied, perhaps too this last kiss will have satisfied Divine Justice which demands, above all, repentance.[8]

On reading this Thérèse's tears betrayed her emotion, and she was obliged to run away.

"I had then," she continues,

> obtained the desired sign, and this sign was very consoling to me. Was it not in presence of the wounds of Jesus, watching His Divine Blood flow, that the thirst for souls had penetrated my heart? I wished to give them this Immaculate Blood to drink in order to purify them from their stains, and the lips of "*mon premier enfant*" were pressed to the Divine Wounds. Ah, what an ineffable response! My desire to save souls increased each day since this wonderful grace. I seemed to hear Jesus whisper to me as He did to the Samaritan woman: "Give Me to drink." It was a veritable exchange of love; for souls I offered the Blood of Jesus, to Jesus I offered those same souls refreshed by the Dew of Calvary; thus I thought to quench His thirst; but the more I gave to Him drink, the more did the thirst of my poor soul increase, and I received this burning thirst as the most delicious recompense.[9]

With such dispositions one question absorbed Thérèse: In what way could she best find an outlet for her all-consuming zeal? Was it her vocation to be a foreign missionary nun, or a Sister devoted to the care of the sick, or yet a priests' helper in parish works? Did she not sometimes smile at herself, so a thirst for sacrifices which would save sinners? There can be no doubt, and she herself will declare afterwards, that she felt in her heart the flame which nourishes apostolic labourers; but an interior voice kept ever repeating to her that the life where unceasing prayer united to mortification perfected the entire immolation of the creature, would give more complete satisfaction to the *Sitio* of the Divine Saviour, and the attraction which from early childhood had inclined her towards Carmel became more pronounced than ever.

"The Servant of God," declares Sœur Geneviève de la Sainte-Face (Céline),

> has herself confided to me the reason of this preference. It was in order to suffer more, and by this means to gain more souls to Jesus. She reasoned that it is more difficult to nature to work without seeing the fruit of its labour, without encouragement, without distraction of any kind; that the most painful of all tasks is that of conquering self.
>
> Thus it was this living death, most fruitful of all for the salvation of souls, that she chose to embrace, "longing," as she said herself, "to become a prisoner as soon as possible, in order to give the beauty and freedom of heaven to souls." Finally, in entering Carmel, her special object was to pray for priests and to immolate herself in the interests of holy Church.[10]

"The smallest movement of pure love is more useful to the Church than all works combined." Without the help of any human stimulus, without even the aid of a director, this maxim of St. John of the Cross was adopted by Thérèse as the directing principle of her future, and she decided to go where she would be able to give most to God, in the first place, and then, indirectly but really, to her neighbour.

Besides, nothing could be more natural than that she should feel drawn towards the cloister where her two elder sisters were already living in penitence and peace. But if Pauline, who still remained her dear confidante, did not hesitate to encourage her, in spite of her tender years, to follow her austere vocation, it must be remembered that Marie, with her authority as eldest sister, considering her too young, opposed the idea of her immediate entrance.

The little one could speak but rarely and with difficulty about her future to her two elder sisters, separated as they were from her by the convent grille. She was more at ease with Céline, the "dear companion of her infancy," in whom she had for some time noticed those aspirations towards the perfect life which she herself experienced so forcibly and so clearly. This dear sister, suppressing her own desire for the sake of Thérèse's happiness, willingly consented to let her go first.

Every evening, when the day's round of study and domestic duty was over, the two young girls conversed freely of the austere joy of the cross enjoyed at Carmel, which gives here below a foretaste of heavenly peace.

Seated in the "Belvedere" with hands linked together, watching the towering trees bathed in the silver light of summer twilight, together they turned their gaze towards the azure firmament studded with stars, and there behind the light and transparent veil of creation they discerned the presence of the Well-Beloved, and repeated in the words of the Divine Canticle: "Having found Him without, He has given us His kiss so that no one can despise us."[11]

They had to descend from these heights, for M. Martin considered that, notwithstanding their tender years, the two children could with profit devote themselves to the different duties that fall within a woman's sphere, and acquire the knowledge necessary for good housekeeping.

As before, Céline and Thérèse always began their day by assisting at Mass. Thérèse communicated usually in that beautiful chapel of the fifteenth century which formed the apse of the cathedral, and which, according to a tradition, sometimes denied, had been built by Bishop Cauchon in expiation of his blameworthy part in the trial of Joan of Arc.

Did Thérèse find a special charm in receiving her God in this framework of beauty? Very probably yes, for earthly splendour which she instinctively appreciated had never hindered her soul from soaring towards the magnificence of the invisible world. But what interested her most in this church, where she had watched the Holy Table with so much envy, was the possibility of often participating here in the sacred Banquet. Struck by the purity of this soul, her confessor, contrary to the custom of that time, allowed her Holy Communion several times in the week. Not content with giving her Well-Beloved her time, her work, and her sacrifices, she gave him in an embrace of ever increasing sweetness her being, person, and entire life.

Long since delivered from scruples, and cured of her excessive sensitiveness by the grace of Christmas night, Thérèse was now a young girl of an exceptionally keen and reflective mind, inclined towards deep study by her desire for knowledge.

She continued to attend the classes of the teacher whom her father had chosen for her on leaving the boarding school. That lady was very proud of so promising a pupil; but Thérèse's eager desire for knowledge continually carried her beyond the limits of her teacher's programme. Such a disposition would have been perilous had not God taken care to guide his soul who saw in Him the climax of all human knowledge.

By a preference worthy of attention, this young girl, eager to make special progress in the science of the saints, chose for her manual of spirituality the book which, after the Gospels themselves, is commended above all others to the meditation of the simplest Christians—namely, the *Imitation of Christ*. In these pages, humble in composition but rich in doctrine and deep observation, impregnated above all with an unction which seems borrowed from the sacred writings themselves, Thérèse found a language adapted to the aspirations of her upright soul, filled as it was with love and gifted with perfect understanding. She made it her constant companion, even to the extent of learning it by heart in a few months, and being able to repeat entire chapters from memory.

Amongst the books which nurtured and strengthened her fervour at this time she mentions with special praise a volume which does not seem to have received from the Catholic public the same appreciation: *Conferences on the End of the World and the Mysteries of the Future Life*, by the Abbé Arminjon. "The reading of that book," she declares, "brought to my soul a happiness not of earth. I foresaw already what God has in store for those who love Him, and seeing how great is the eternal recompense compared with the trifling sacrifices of this life, I longed to love Jesus, to love Him ardently, and give Him a thousand marks of tenderness while it was yet in my power."[12]

In other words, this child of fourteen, who shrinks from receiving, unmerited, the recompenses of another life of which she had already caught a glimpse, must hasten to Carmel, there to immolate herself.

But how was she to force the convent gates, since neither the Mother Prioress nor even her eldest sister judged that the time had yet come to open these gates to her?

"I found but one soul," she declares, "to encourage me in my vocation: that of my dear Pauline. My heart found in hers a faithful echo, and without her, I would certainly never have arrived at the sacred shore which she had reached five years before."[13]

A difficulty more poignant if not more unsurmountable than the opposition from the Carmel itself, was the prospect of leaving M. Martin in loneliness, which could not but sadden his heart. He was then sixty-four years of age. Outwardly he retained all appearance of health and vigour, although in reality he was weakened by an attack of paralysis, from which he had quickly recovered, it is true, but which left his friends apprehensive of a possible recurrence. Besides this, he had once been stung while fishing by a poisonous fly, and had never been cured of a small excrescence left on his neck which resisted all remedies and sometimes caused him great pain. His life, then, was threatened with a twofold danger, and it was in these circumstances that he must be asked to part with his "little Queen."

Thérèse trembled at the very thought of broaching the subject to him. The months, meanwhile, were slipping by. She was now fourteen and a half, and had decided that if she overcame the obstacles raised against her project, she would enter Carmel at the coming feast of Christmas, the day on which a year previously she had received the "grace of conversion."

Having chosen the Day of Pentecost on which to make her "great disclosure," she resolved to speak after having invoked the holy Apostles, renewed and fortified by the infusion of the Holy Spirit.

The family had assisted as usual at the long ceremonies at the cathedral. After Vespers M. Martin, a little fatigued, was seated at the entrance to the garden at the back of the house, and there, with his hands joined he was contemplating the wonders of nature glowing in the May sunshine.

The evening was glorious; the last rays of the setting sun shone golden on the leaves of the tall trees, and the birds filled the clear air with their adieu to the declining day as with an evening prayer. M. Martin's noble countenance reflected the serenity of holy thoughts.

Softly, with her eyes full of tears, Thérèse came, and without a word, sat down beside him. He looked at her with touching tenderness; then, drawing her to his heart, he said: "What is it, my little Queen? Tell me . . ."[14] And rising to hide his emotion, he commenced to walk slowly, keeping his arm still around her.

Amid tears Thérèse revealed her secret. . . . She felt called to Carmel, and she desired to enter soon within its walls.

The first shock was severe for the poor father. Did he in looking towards the future see his fireside deserted, his house empty, his old age abandoned to the care of hired servants? At all events, like the Saviour on the eve of His bloody sacrifice, he felt his soul torn with grief—and he wept.

Nature had claimed her tribute of tears, but in an instant the great Christian soul recovered possession of itself. He first of all pointed out to Thérèse that she was still very young to make so grave a decision; then he listened to her reasons, which she, having become more sure of herself, laid before him with calmness. Then approaching a wall where grew some tiny white flowers, which in form and colour resembled the lily, he plucked one and offered it to his daughter as a symbol of the virginal purity that she wished to consecrate to God. These two hearts were henceforth united in their aspirations towards the same ideal; the step which cost Thérèse the most had been successfully taken.

But from the time of her mother's death, she had had a guardian, and it would not be right to leave her home without having first obtained his consent.

M. Guérin, in his affection for his niece, was surprised and greatly troubled, and showed himself at first adverse. "This would be," he declared, "a unique case in the whole of France. It would, in fact, be almost a scandal for a child of fifteen years to enter Carmel." As for him, he would oppose it with all his power, and to alter his opinion a miracle would be necessary.

Such a reply filled Thérèse with consternation. She besought her heavenly patrons to change her uncle's resolve; but Heaven remained deaf to her pleading, and for three days she felt abandoned by God and man. Nature was in unison with her soul; dense inky clouds covered the sky, betokening sadness and fear. Despite all, she prayed in her distress of soul.

On the fourth day she returned to her uncle, and great was her surprise to find him completely changed. "A miracle is no longer necessary," he said; "I have prayed to God to give me an unbiassed inclination of heart, and my prayer has been granted. Go in peace, my dear child. You are a little privileged flower that the Saviour wills to cull for Himself; I will not stand in opposition." And he embraced his niece with the tenderness of a father.

The horizon was cleared; Thérèse could from henceforth make direct appeal to the Carmel.

Although formerly she had discountenanced the ingenuous request of the postulant of nine years, the Mother Prioress, who had since seen Thérèse many times in the parlour and had learned about her from her sisters, was now quite disposed to welcome her. But before deciding finally to admit her, she had to consult the ecclesiastical superior of the community, who represented the Bishop in her regard.

This superior, M. le Chanoine Delatröette, was then curé in the parish of Saint-Jacques, in which the convent is established. A man of lively faith, of a disposition in the main benevolent, but with rigid, definitely moulded convictions, this priest, ignoring the just observations of the Prioress, constituted himself, in an exaggerated way, the inflexible guardian of the Rule which he believed it his duty to maintain without modification or exception.

He held that no one should be allowed to enter the Carmel before the completion of their twenty-first year.[15]

Mother Marie de Gonzague had tried without success to induce him to change his decision. She made another attempt in an indirect way. One day, when this formidable Superior had come to the infirmary to visit the venerable Mother Geneviève de Sainte-Thérèse, foundress of the Carmel of Lisieux, she, on the suggestion of the Prioress, renewed the petition that Thérèse Martin be admitted as a member of the community. A veritable outburst followed. "Again this young girl," exclaimed M. Delatröette. "To hear you talk, one would think that the salvation of the community depended on the entrance of this child. There is no danger in delay. Let her remain with her father until she has reached her majority. Besides, do you believe that I would persist in refusing without having consulted God? Let no one speak further to me on this affair."[16]

The above scene gave an idea of the reception that awaited the one chiefly interested when she should present herself to plead her cause. Therefore M. Martin, who now not only accepted as a fact but intended to foster his daughter's vocation, decided to accompany her to the house of the redoubtable Canon.

A sharp and decisive "No" to the opening words of Thérèse cut short the little speech she had prepared. But the conscientious priest said to them in parting: "However, I am only the delegate of Monseigneur. If he allows you to enter, I shall have no more to say."

They came away from the presbytery in torrents of rain. Like the heavens, Thérèse's soul, too, was sad. Yet the Superior's last words gave her a ray of hope. Recourse to the Bishop of the diocese was possible. Without hesitation, M. Martin offered to take her to Bayeux, and Thérèse found solace in the thought of this further attempt, from which, nevertheless her habitual timidity made her shrink.

Mgr. Hugonin, the prelate in question, was a man of gentle and benevolent disposition. Of studious habits and already advanced in years, he left part of the administration of his diocese in the hands of his Vicars-General.

Associated with him in this quality was a priest of sterling piety and devotedness whose action was to have a momentary influence on Thérèse's destiny.

Successively parish priest of Vaucelles de Caen, military chaplain, curé of Saint-Pierre, Caen, and Vicar-General of Bayeux, the Abbé Reverony had gained everywhere the reputation of an earnest apostle and an enlightened director in matters of conscience. As humble and disinterested as he was charitable, he had refused the Episcopate, his only ambition being to minister to souls to the end, in the diocese where he had received the priesthood. He was in the confidence, too, of Mgr. Hugonin, who hardly ever took an important step without consulting him.[17]

It was this confidential counseller of the prelate who assigned October 31, 1887, to M. Martin as the date of his interview with the Bishop.

Thérèse set out accompanied by her father. It was the first time that the young girl had gone to visit anyone without her sisters, and now she was to begin by visiting a Bishop. Added to this, she who never spoke except to reply to the questions of others, found herself obliged to explain before a prelate her reasons for seeking a strange and almost unheard-of favour. What a trial for her excessive reserve!

Meanwhile she endeavoured to put the best face on matters. In order not to appear as a child in the eyes of Mgr. Hugonin, she had put up her hair which, till then, fell on her shoulders in natural curls. In spite of all, when she had entered through the majestic gates and saw herself within two paces of those solemn walls behind which her fate was to be decided, she felt her emotion rising. But let her relate herself the interview on which her heart had founded so many hopes.

> The Abbé Reverony was very friendly, although he looked slightly surprised. Noticing the tears in my eyes, he said to me: "Ah, I see diamonds. You must not show these to Monseigneur."
>
> We then passed through large state-rooms, which made me feel as insignificant as a tiny ant, and I asked myself what I should dare to say. Monseigneur was at the moment walking in a corridor with two priests. I saw the Vicar-General exchange some words with him and come back in his company to the room where we were waiting. There three enormous armchairs were ranged in front of a brightly burning fire.
>
> On seeing Monseigneur enter, papa knelt with me to receive his blessing; then his lordship motioned us to be seated. M. Reverony offered me the central armchair. I excused myself politely. He insisted, telling me to show that I was capable of obedience. I immediately submitted without further hesitation, and had the mortification of seeing him take an ordinary chair while I found myself buried in a monumental seat where four girls like me might sit at ease—certainly more at ease than I was, for I was far from feeling at home.
>
> I hoped that papa would open the conversation, but he told me to explain the object of our visit. This I did as eloquently as I could, though fully realizing that a simple word from the Superior would have done me more service than anything I could say, and that his opposition must certainly tell against me. Monseigneur asked me if I had long had the desire to enter Carmel. "Oh yes, Monseigneur," I replied, "a very long time."

"Let us see," said M. Reverony smiling, "certainly not as long as fifteen years."

"That is true," I answered; "but it is not much less, for from the age of three I have desired to give myself to the good God."

Monseigneur, believing that he would be expressing my father's wishes, tried to explain that I ought to remain at home with him for some time longer. What was his lordship's surprise and edification to see him immediately take my part, adding with respect and gentleness that we were going to Rome on the diocesan pilgrimage, and that I would not hesitate to speak to the Holy Father if I had not obtained before then the permission I sought.

Meanwhile a discussion on the matter with the Superior was considered indispensable before giving us a final decision. I could have heard nothing more disquieting, for I was well aware of his declared and decided opposition. So, disregarding M. Reverony's warning, I did more than *show my diamonds* to Monseigneur, *I gave them—shedding tears*. I saw clearly that he was moved. He came and caressed me—a favour that no other child had ever, it appears, received from him. "All is not lost, little one," he said to me, "but I am pleased that you are going to Rome with your father; you will thus confirm your vocation. Instead of weeping you should rejoice. Besides, I am going to Lisieux next week; I shall speak to the Superior about you. You shall certainly receive my reply in Italy." His lordship then took us into the garden.[18]

The audience was finished, and Thérèse had, alas, accomplished nothing.

Moved by the child's candour and generosity, the venerable Bishop did not wish to discourage her openly; but the step appeared to him as well as to his Vicar-General both inopportune and unusual, and apparently they decided on withholding their approval, at least until the case had been more thoroughly examined.

One last resource remained, a petition made in person to the Sovereign Pontiff, if that were possible.

But what was this pilgrimage to which M. Martin had alluded and on which he counted to facilitate his "little Queen's" entrance to religion?

We are writing of that epoch when the recent spoliation of Italian convents, added to the position of the Sovereign Pontiff, who found himself virtually a prisoner, made the faithful of the whole world shudder, and more especially the Catholics of France. The Bishops of the most loyal dioceses wished to protest against these sacrileges, and to console the Holy Father by leading to his palace legions of pilgrims eager to make known their respectful attachment to him.

Amongst the most ardent protestations against the usurpations of the Italian Government was that of the Bishop of Coutances, Mgr. Germain.

It was he, apparently, who had initiated the pilgrimage in which the Martin family were to join, and which had the avowed object of honouring the sacerdotal jubilee of Leo XIII.

Mgr. Germain had a Vicar-General well adapted to second him in his undertaking. A successful organizer of religious pilgrimages, of active disposition and ultra-montane tendencies, the Abbé Legoux, who bore the title of Pope's chamberlain as reward of his many acts of devotion to the Holy See, set about finding among the clergy and the wealthy families of that part of the country a sufficient number of pilgrims to form an imposing body in the halls of the Vatican.

In order to increase their numbers, it was decided to make the projected journey both an act of filial loyalty to the Holy Father and at the same time a magnificent pleasure trip. The programme published in the Diocese of Bayeux appeared so attractive that there also numerous families enrolled themselves as pilgrims, so many that Mgr. Hugonin, wishing to have his flock officially represented at the Vatican, sent at their head his Vicar-General, M. Reverony.

Everything was in readiness for the approaching departure. The preliminaries of this long excursion had been exceptionally well thought out. Cares for the material side of the journey were reduced to the minimum, permitting each pilgrim to give himself without anxiety to the enjoyment of the wonderful sights. The economic organization of the pilgrimage had been given to the "Agence Lubin" who, for an agreed sum payable in advance, guaranteed to provide the railway journey, hotel accommodation and meals, and sight-seeing tours by vehicle in the principal towns. M. Martin had always a great love for travel. From the first he had been tempted by the charm of this pilgrimage which would enable him to see a second time the most beautiful sights in Europe, to view the most splendid monuments of Christian art, while at the same time bringing to the Pontiff prisoner the homage of unwavering fidelity. After his interview with Mgr Hugonin his resolution was strengthened by a new motive.

He left Lisieux accompanied by his two daughters on November 4, for Paris, where all the pilgrims were to meet.

Thérèse soon remarked that certain pilgrims were obsessed with other preoccupations than those of piety. In these carriages decorated with religious emblems were assembled the flower of the Normandy nobility. In this brilliant reunion, at the commencement of a tour which promised as much enjoyment as edification, each one made willing display of his titles and family prerogatives.

The little one was shocked by this worldly ostentation at the very beginning of the pilgrimage. "Far from dazzling us," she says, "all these titles of nobility appeared to our eyes as smoke and vanity. I recalled these words of the *Imitation: 'Pursue not the shadow of a great name.'*[19] I understood that true greatness is not to be found in a name but in the soul."

Nothing reveals the little failings or whims of good people more than the continuous close intimacy of life on a pilgrimage. Thérèse esteemed the many edifying Normandy priests with whom she travelled; edifying they were, in truth, though not wholly freed, as she saw, from every weakness of human nature.

This continual association inspired Thérèse, after a few weeks, with the following reflections: "For the past month I have met many holy priests, and I have seen that if their sublime dignity has raised them above the angels, they are, as men, still subject to human weakness and frailty. If, then, holy priests whom Jesus in the Gospel calls the *salt of the earth,* show that they have need of prayer, what of those who are tepid?"[20]

She now understood what had hitherto escaped her—namely, that prayer for priests was one of the highest and most salutary services rendered by Carmel, and she resolved to place this, later, in the first rank of the duties involved by her state of life.

November 7 was fixed for the gathering together of the pilgrims in the Basilica of the Sacred Heart, Montmartre.

While awaiting the departure for Italy, M. Martin thought it well to take his daughter to see the principal monuments of Paris.

In Thérèse's opinion, nothing equalled the little church of Our Lady of Victories. She felt that in this sanctuary which had witnessed so many spiritual favours, Mary had something to reveal to her, and she held herself in confident and peaceful expectation at the foot of the white statue which represented so well the maternal countenance of the Blessed Virgin.

Our Lady of Victories made her understand clearly, first of all, that it was in very truth she who had smiled on her and cured her. This assurance was of inestimable worth for Thérèse. It will be remembered that the searching questions of some of the Carmelites had troubled the "little one" to the extent of making her lose in part the joy of her supernatural cure. The Queen of Heaven set her mind at rest on this subject so completely that she could open her soul in gratitude and consolation unalloyed.

Such condescension on the part of the Blessed Virgin induced Thérèse to ask for new favours. She feared that the tour through Italy, with its spectacle of purely pagan art or of art too directly inspired by paganism, would not be without danger to her modesty. Having no knowledge of evil, she dreaded to discover it. Thus she besought the Immaculate Virgin to guard her unceasingly. After she had addressed the same prayer to St. Joseph, "the father and protector of virgins," she felt that her prayers were heard.

The time had come to rejoin the pilgrimage. After the consecration of the members to the Sacred Heart in the Basilica of Montmartre, they set out for Switzerland, through which they had to pass before entering Italy.

Each compartment of the train was, at the outset, placed under the patronage of a saint, the idea being to choose the patron of the presiding priest of each compartment or that of his parish.

Mgr. Legoux had already remarked the fervour of the three pilgrims from Lisieux. Approaching their group with animation, he announced in a loud tone the name of their patron as *St. Martin.* Thérèse's father smiled and thanked him. He was to experience, during the journey, less agreeable incidents.

He was accustomed to hear hymns sung on former pilgrimages. He thought that when travelling through the level plains of Champagne, where nothing worth notice was to be seen, some moments at least could well be devoted to united praise of God; but card-playing often occupied a greater number of hours than prayer, even in M. Martin's compartment. When he was asked to join in this pastime he excused himself, saying that in his opinion it would be better to devote more time to devotional exercises. Vexed at this remark, although it was made in the most courteous manner, one of the persons concerned cried out: "Fortunately, Pharisees are rare." The humble M. Martin did not utter a word; he pretended not to have heard the remark, and, soon afterwards, found an occasion of shaking hands with the man who was so utterly wanting in respect for his grey hairs.

This was one of the numberless incidents which served for the sanctification of each according to his measure, and made of the beautiful tour, in spite of everything, a pilgrimage of penance.

The first halting-place was Bâle. As the pilgrims arrived at nightfall they were unable to visit the town, and after a few hours' delay at the station set out again in the middle of the night for Lucerne.

Switzerland had till then veiled its splendour; but when suddenly the lake of the Four Cantons came in view, the travellers perceived, beneath the clear rays of the sun, the deeply indented shores bathing their rugged or smiling promontories in the crystal waters; when they beheld the imposing heights of the Pilatus and the Righi with snow-capped summits veiled in cloud, there was a universal cry of admiration.

Thérèse Martin rivalled in enthusiasm her most animated companions. These splendid sights had lasting powers of enchantment since, she could write after the lapse of many years: "What good it did my soul to see those beauties of nature spread out thus in profusion! How they raised it to Him who is pleased to scatter His wondrous works over this land of exile which lasts but for a day."[21]

On leaving Lucerne, the town of historic bridges, of which the majestic setting made one rather forget their archaeological value, the railway followed the course of the Reuss. This is the most picturesque portion of Switzerland, so rich in magnificent scenery. Thus Thérèse found at every turn occasion for a new hymn of praise to the Creator. "At times we were carried up nearly to the summit of a mountain. Below the awful precipices seemed ready to engulf us in their unfathomable depths. Or again, we would pass through a charming hamlet with its châlets and its graceful belfry, above which the fleecy clouds hung softly. Then, an immense lake with calm and crystal waters mingling their azure tint with the gold of the setting sun. How express in words my impressions of so poetic, so imposing a spectacle? I had there a foretaste of the wonders of heaven. . . ."[22]

And again: "I said to myself, 'Later on, in the hour of trial when, a prisoner in the Carmel, I shall be able to see only a little corner of the heavens, I will recall this scene, and the remembrance will give me courage. I shall no longer be preoccupied about my own petty interests when thinking on the grandeur and power of God. I will love Him alone, and shall not be so unfortunate as to become attached to trifles, now that my heart foresees something of what He has in store for those who love Him.'"[23]

Such was the spiritual profit of this rapid excursion through Switzerland and its renowned scenery.

Beyond the Saint-Gothard tunnel new scenes of enchantment awaited them. They were now in the plains of Lombardy, resplendent in the sun, offering to the astonished eyes of the Normandy visitors, who had just left behind them leafless trees and leaf-strewn roads, the glory of summer growth and verdant fields as yet hardly touched by the autumn blast.

Here, on the edge of transparent waters which throw back the reflection of its white houses, Lugano raises its cupolas in the centre of an elysian countryside. Here is Como with its lake sleeping peacefully in the moonlight, and its blue crown of hills wreathed in mist. Here, also, is Milan, the proud capital, which was reached at nightfall, and of which nothing but the broad boulevards with their sparkling lights could be seen.

The pilgrims had to await the morrow for their visit to the "Duomo," that incomparable cathedral with its lace-like white marble and its innumerable statues.

This church holds the body of St. Charles. M. Martin and his daughters did not fail to assist at the early Mass celebrated by Mgr. Germain before the precious shrine. As pilgrims were allowed to ascend to the top of the edifice, Thérèse, whose admiration was not exhausted by the Swiss landscapes, undertook, with her sister, the ascent of dome and turret in order to see from this vantage-point the wide panorama of the city and the Lombard countryside. They continued to mount upward until the people in the streets below appeared "as small as ants."

The programme of excursions included a visit to the Campo-Santo of Milan. In the north of Italy, every large town has its monumental cemetery, where the tombs of the wealthy are usually of marble adorned with finely executed sculpture. Appreciating works of art, as well as Nature's grandeur, Thérèse was struck with admiration for the perfection and finish of these statues which almost seemed to palpitate with life. "What masterpieces!" she exclaimed. "Here is a little child strewing flowers on its father's tomb; the lifeless marble is forgotten; the delicate petals seem to slip from the fingers. Here the light veil of the widow, and ribbons woven through young maidens' hair, seem to float and shimmer in the breeze."[24]

One pilgrim, however, tried to suppress this joy. He was an old gentleman who grumbled and found fault with everything, and who could in no way endure enthusiasm of any description in his fellow-travellers. It would have been better for him to remain at home, as Thérèse frankly declared. But she refrained from complaining. She rather made this a subject of observation from which she purposed to draw profit. "What an interesting study," she writes, "is the world to one who is on the eve of leaving it."

On the following day the pilgrims took train for Venice, and arrived there at nightfall, about ten o'clock. Their entry into this singular town was lugubrious. On leaving terra firma, the solid ground of the station, they were handed over to the gondolier who had been engaged to bring them to the hotel selected beforehand; all this in the darkness. The gondolier, with whose language you are generally unacquainted, rows you along in silence over the marshy waters of the canals. Your route lies at times between high walls, dark and sinister-looking, intensifying by their shade the inky blackness of night which hangs over the stagnant waters. Through numberless unknown windings you are finally taken to the hotel, where you regain with some difficulty your sense of security.

Such was the first impression received by the Normandy pilgrims on entering the city of the Doges. Was it the memory of this cheerless arrival which drew from Thérèse the following unenthusiastic appreciation? "This city," she says, "has many charms, but it is melancholy."

Perhaps it did not sufficiently present the attraction which, in her eyes, surpassed all others, that of sanctuaries specially venerated for their precious relics or the miracles wrought within their walls. Assuredly, incomparable marvels of art were in evidence at the palace of the Doges, at St.

Mark's, in the museums, on the façade of the palace near the Grand Canal; but all was solemn with the silent solemnity of a necropolis. And then there were the underground prisons, dungeons where so many victims pined away their lives in former days, the sight of which inspired Thérèse with horror and pity.[25]

The cathedral of Padua was a compensation to her fervour. Only after venerating the precious relic of St. Anthony, did she turn to admire the splendid sculptures of Donatello lavished on the tomb of the humble Franciscan.

The next break in their journey was at Bologna. Without delaying over the details of San Petronio Cathedral, or the masterpieces of Francia within its walls, Thérèse hastened to the church of St. Catherine. The future Thérèse de l'Enfant Jésus could not fail to contemplate with devotion the mortal remains of this little Collettine of the fifteenth century, whom the Divine Infant had loved with predilection, and on whose dead face still remained the imprint of His kiss. She venerated those limbs, pliant still in spite of death and the blood liquid after 400 years. The pilgrims saw in this preservation the glorification of the saint's purity and humility, this saint who, before entering the cloister, had shone as a lady of honour at the Ferrara court. Once more Thérèse raised her heart in gratitude to the Almighty who seemed thus to recompense the virtues He loves best.[26]

But Loreto was a real joy to her. There one can venerate the humble dwelling where the Word was made flesh, those walls which were silent witnesses of the play as well as the rude toil of the Child Jesus.

After a delightful journey along by the Adriatic studded with little triangular-sailed fishing barques, then through plains where, as in Virgil's time, the vine is mated with the elm and the cherry-tree, the pilgrims could at last climb the slopes of the holy hill.

As if the corner of the earth where the Santa-Casa lies should participate in the humility of this artisan's dwelling, Loreto is a simple village where a house of some appearance or a comfortable hotel would be sought for in vain. The home of the King is surrounded, as of old, by lowly dwellings. This very fact formed an additional attraction for Thérèse. In this, she declares, lay the charm of Loreto.

The Holy House, enclosed now in a gorgeous basilica, contains, as we know, certain objects well calculated to excite devotion in the pilgrim; for example, a little wooden vessel called "the bowl of the Infant Jesus." Thérèse did not fail to touch with her rosary beads this relic held sacred by a graceful tradition; but the Santa-Casa had a yet more precious possession, an altar; and at this altar, so near to the place where Our Saviour lived, the two sisters, Thérèse and Céline, by a holy daring, succeeded in receiving Holy Communion.

Some hours later the train departed for Rome. The weather was exceptionally favourable; the Umbrian countryside, bathed in the transparent autumn light, produced in the souls of the pilgrims a feeling of deep peace. Each beautiful little village seemed to them a terrestrial paradise, as it emerged from the clusters of evergreen pines or yew-trees, crowning hills, the rounded summits of which seemed to succeed one another in infinite line.

As for Thérèse, she delighted more than any other in the charms of this enchanting country. Were not these the farewell smiles of well-beloved nature to which she was about to bid adieu?

It was night-time, and she was asleep in a corner of the carriage, when the porters ran along the train crying out, "Roma, Roma!" She had reached the end of the journey; the home of the Sovereign Pontiff, whose authority she was about to invoke, was not far away.

Through the noisy modern streets which enclose ancient Rome within a circle of ugly commonplace houses, Thérèse and her two companions were driven to one of the vast hotels which the agency had procured for the pilgrims. This was the Hotel du Sud, where she stayed during her brief sojourn in Rome,[27] while Mgr. Germain, Mgr. Legoux, and the majority of the pilgrims from Coutances went to the Hotel Minerva.

An inquisitorial eye had noted the actions and demeanour of Thérèse since they left Normandy, and did not cease to observe her during each halt in the journey. It was that of the Abbé Reverony. Though a little embarrassed at finding herself the object of this prolonged solicitude, which she foresaw would grow more vigilant when they visited the Vatican, yet Thérèse went on her way without constraint, and joined in the excursion arranged for the pilgrims before the day fixed for the Papal audience, with perfect freedom of spirit and childlike wholeheartedness.

To visit the places of interest, the pilgrims had been divided into five groups. That to which the Martin family belonged began by visiting those the most celebrated of the Campagna.

More than mere curiosity inspired Thérèse and Céline to examine the gigantic circus which, under the name of the Coliseum, had been the theatre of the cruel Roman games; they had a genuine veneration for its arena, red with the blood of martyrs. With real joy, then, they set out for the amphitheatre, that imposing ruin which forms one of the wonders of the papal city.

Their ambition was to kiss the ground where the Christians had fallen torn by the teeth of wild beasts, and, if possible, to gather some grains of this sacred dust. But they had not taken into account the ravages of time, through which, in the course of centuries, the original soil had been covered up at a depth of at least 25 feet.

Excavations had, however, been carried out in one part of the arena, and a gaping hole protected by a strong barrier gave access to depths where, perhaps, the soil sanctified by martyr-blood could still be found.

Notwithstanding the barricade, the two sisters approached this opening and Thérèse, leaning over the edge, believed she saw a way of getting down: "Come, follow me," she said to Céline; "we shall be able to get down." But we must hear her own account of this exploit:

> We set ourselves immediately to the attempt, climbing over ruins which crumbled beneath our feet, while papa, astonished at our daring, called out to us from the distance. But we no longer heard anything.

> As warriors feel their courage rise according as the peril increases, so did our joy grow greater in proportion to our fatigue and the danger we had to face in order to attain the end in view.
>
> Céline, more far-seeing than I, had listened to the guide. Remembering that he had described a certain stone marked with a cross, as indicating the place where the martyrs fought, she set herself to find it. She soon succeeded, and we knelt down on this sacred ground, our souls united in the selfsame prayer. . . . My heart throbbed with emotion as I touched with my lips the dust empurpled with the blood of the early Christians. I asked the grace that I, too, might be a martyr for Jesus, and I felt deep down in my heart that my prayer was heard.
>
> All this occupied but a few moments. Having collected some small stones, we returned towards the walls to resume the perilous part of our enterprise. Papa, seeing us so delighted, could not chide us; I even saw that he was proud of our courage.[28]

It was during this expedition through the Campagna that the two sisters visited the catacombs of St. Calixtus. They had as guide a Trappist of Norman origin, Père Marie-Bernard. His kindness proved a considerable help in reaching this labyrinth of underground galleries, lighted only by the flickering flame of a torch.

This catacomb contains, as we know, the sarcophagus where the body of St. Cecilia was discovered. In order to show their veneration for the martyr's last resting-place, Thérèse and Céline lay in turn in this loculus of stone which had guarded through so many centuries the body of the gentle saint, "the Queen of Harmony."[29]

This moment marked for Thérèse the beginning of a new devotion. She felt for St. Cecilia not only veneration, but the real love of a friend. "She became," says Thérèse, "my saint of predilection, my intimate confidante. What above all gained my love was her perfect abandonment to God, her unlimited confidence, which enabled her to convert to virginity souls who had never a thought before but to seek their joys in the things of earth."[30]

At the tomb of St. Agnes she experienced the same emotion. She picked up and carried away with her a small fragment of the ancient mosaic as a souvenir for her dear Pauline (Sœur Agnès de Jésus).

The days following the expeditions to these celebrated places where Thérèse sought only food for her fervour, were devoted to visiting the principal churches and other monuments that history or art has immortalized.

It was proposed, and had even been made the subject of a wager, that they should see in six days the most famous wonders at least of the Eternal City. Thus, to fulfil their programme, they had usually to hasten along after a guide who too often allowed but little time for prayer even in the most venerated places.

To make matters worse, the rain never ceased to harass the pilgrims; every cupola and obelisk had for background a leaden sky.

Visited under these conditions, the greater basilicas, including St. Peter's, then the Scala-Santa and the Mamertine prison, without counting the museums and private galleries, do not seem to have left any vivid impression on Thérèse, since she does not mention them in her autobiography.[31]

"At Rome," she writes,

> in the church of the Holy Cross of Jerusalem, we venerated several fragments of the true Cross, two of the thorns, and one of the sacred nails. In order to examine them more at leisure, I managed to remain last, and as the religious who had charge of the precious treasures was preparing to replace them on the altar, I asked him if I might touch them. He replied in the affirmative, though appearing doubtful that I should succeed. I then put my little finger through an opening in the reliquary, and was thus able to touch one of the precious nails once bathed in Our Saviour's Blood. I acted towards Him, as can be seen, like a child who believes that everything is allowed her, and who regards as her own the treasures of her Father.[32]

Besides, she became more and more preoccupied by the thought of the Pontifical audience fixed for November 20, and of the petition which she was to address to the Holy Father.

Early on the morning of the appointed day, the carriages arranged for by the Agency came to the hotels beneath a continuous downpour of rain and took the different groups of pilgrims to the Vatican. At half-past seven, all had assembled under the leadership of Mgr. Germain and the Abbé Reverony, with the Bishops of Nantes, Séez, and Vanne in a vast hall hung with red damask, and occupied at one end by an altar of surprising simplicity. Here the Sovereign Pontiff was to celebrate the Holy Sacrifice, after which he had promised to receive the members of the pilgrimage.

Exactly at eight, Leo XIII appeared, wearing a flowing red mantle over his white woollen cassock. Having given a silent blessing to the assembly, he knelt to prepare for the Holy Sacrifice, and the pilgrims realized how this great Pope, so renowned for powerful doctrine and great governing ability, was, at the same time, a man of prayer and recollection in presence of the Saint of Saints.

With deathly pale countenance, ascetic in its worn appearance, and eyelids lowered over the dark eyes, ordinarily so sparkling with light, he communed with his God. His lips moved slowly as in that prayer where a few words sustain the intensity of inward feeling. He rose from prayer, and one noticed that, although his frail frame was scarce bent by age, he had to lean his already trembling hands on the arms of his chaplains to ascend the altar.

The Papal Mass was to console Thérèse for all the prayers said perforce so hurriedly during the preceding days. To see Leo XIII at the altar was better than any sermon. He pronounced the Latin in a slow and measured voice. His Italian accent sometimes prevented the French congregation from catching the words perfectly. But what faith, what tender piety was in his tone, in his attitude, even in his least action. What unction, above all, in the prayers after Mass, which he had himself composed and prescribed for the universal Church.

Leo XIII impressed Thérèse as a truly saintly Pontiff, and when after the Mass of thanksgiving celebrated by one of the chaplains, he went into the Audience Chamber to receive the pilgrims, the young girl felt strongly drawn to speak to him as to a father.

The audience commenced without great formality, almost with the intimacy of a family reunion. Mgr. Germain presented in turn every member of his flock, giving name and rank, and, in certain cases, their title to a special blessing from the Holy Father, who, himself seated on an ordinary armchair raised on one or two steps, and wearing his soutane and camail, took the hand of each one, spoke a few fatherly words, gave fervently his blessing, and presented a commemoration medal.[33]

Next in turn came the Bayeux pilgrims; but Mgr. Germain did not present these. M. Reverony, with a little less good grace perhaps, watched to see that the formalities of the audience be, above all, scrupulously observed. Had he a suspicion that Thérèse Martin, in a full public audience of the Sovereign Pontiff, in presence of the high dignitaries who surrounded him, and in sight and hearing of over a hundred people, would dare to address to Leo XIII the petition deferred by the Bishop of Bayeux?

Be that as it may, when he saw the two sisters, with calm and resolute faces beneath their black mantillas, approach the Pontifical throne, he announced in a loud voice that he absolutely forbade anyone to speak to the Holy Father. What was to be done? Thérèse looked imploringly for a sign from Céline. To obey the injunction would mean seeing destroyed in one instant the hope that had sustained the two during a journey of 500 leagues. "Speak!" said her elder sister.

A moment afterwards Thérèse is at the feet of Leo XIII. She quickly kisses the Pontiff's foot, grasps his extended hand, then, with eyes bathed in tears, exclaims: "Most Holy Father, I have a great favour to ask."

The Pope bent down his head until it touched Thérèse's mantilla. His dark piercing eyes sought to read those of the child.

She continued: "Most Holy Father, in honour of your Jubilee, permit me to enter Carmel at fifteen."

Here was the famous petition feared by M. Reverony. No doubt he did not wish it said that what had been refused at Bayeux had been obtained in Rome. Standing, as he was, beside the Sovereign Pontiff, he believed that he should interfere. "Most Holy Father," he said, "this is a child who desires the life of Carmel, but the superiors are, at the moment, considering the question."

This was almost a dictation of the Pope's answer.

"Well, my child," said His Holiness, "do whatever the superiors shall decide."

Thérèse joined her hands and resting them on the Pontiff's knees said in a suppliant voice: "O Holy Father, if you only said yes everyone else would agree."

Leo XIII looking at her fixedly and with kindness, said in an earnest voice: "Well, my child, you shall enter if it be God's will."

This reply, though evasive, was not a refusal, and left room for the Bishop's authorization.

The other pilgrims were waiting their turn. Thérèse was preparing to renew her petition when two of the noble guard told her to rise. As she still remained kneeling, hoping for a favourable answer, they took her by the arms, and M. Reverony had to come to their aid before she would relinquish her post at the knees of the Sovereign Pontiff.

It was over; the journey had failed in its object, at least until Mgr. Hugonin should again intervene. The poor child retired in desolation. When her father, who had received the Pope's blessing before her, met her coming out from the audience, she was bathed in tears, which she made no effort to dry. . . . The dark mass of cloud over the city continued to pour down torrents of rain, and Thérèse remarked once more the harmony between her soul and the heavens which seemed as though wishing to share in her griefs as well as in her joys.

This time her disappointment was profound; but despite her bitter sadness, Thérèse remained mistress over that pure region where her will, dominating the lower faculties, insured that serene happiness which results from union with God's holy will.

The young girl had done all in her power to answer Heaven's call. The Almighty had judged fit to overthrow her calculations and hopes; the trial was hard, but, interiorly, she experienced great peace. A simple reflection made her, moreover, accept lovingly this Divine providence in her regard. She had offered herself some time before to the Infant Jesus as His plaything—"His little ball," as she expressed it. It was, then, only natural to see herself tossed to right or left, driven here and there or even pierced, according to His good pleasure. The treatment, apparently so rigorous, which had been meted out to her was the consequence of her offering. Jesus had accepted that offering. Will not his acceptance be the source, was it not already the presage of that "perfect joy" promised, in spite of dire tribulation, to those who give themselves to God without reserve?

Thérèse returned with her father to the hotel. Some days later M. Martin went to visit a venerable religious, Brother Simeon, founder, and, at that time, Superior of St. Joseph's college.

He met there the Abbé Reverony whom he gently reproached for not having aided Thérèse in her difficult enterprise, and he made known in a few words to Brother Simeon his daughter's heroic attempt. "That never happens in Italy," said the old man. These words were meant, perhaps, as an indirect lesson for the Vicar-General, so little inclined to favour this noble and generous design. M. Reverony did not defend himself. He believed he had interpreted his Bishop's wishes; that, to his conscience, was sufficient. It is probable, too, that his long-standing habits of administrative prudence suppressed the enthusiasm which was, no doubt, required before taking part in this apparently rash project.

The day following the Papal audience had been chosen for a visit to Naples and Pompeii. They set out at early morning. In a few hours, after a passing sight of Aquino, the native place of St. Thomas, and the celebrated monastery of Monte Cassino, the travelers reached Pompeii.

The sadness of this ruined city corresponded to the state of Thérèse's soul. She would have liked to wander alone through the abandoned streets and ruined palaces, to meditate at leisure on the decay of earthly splendour, but she had to follow the merciless guide, surrounded by the pilgrims who had been caught in a shower of rain, and were little disposed to stand still admiring roofless houses.

The departure for Naples was a happy diversion. Thérèse, who so lately was deeply impressed by the sight of the sea during her holiday at Trouville, would naturally be enraptured on beholding the Bay of Naples, dominated as it is by the great Vesuvius and its threatening crater.

The town shelters beneath a hill on which stands a noble convent, now, alas, bereft of its monks. Its halls, adorned with fine frescoes, sculpture, and mosaic work, have been converted into a museum, so that, at the San Martino monastery, the traveller can enjoy priceless treasures of art and the still more astonishing marvels of nature.

The view from this beautiful spot would assuredly, at another time, have greatly delighted Thérèse, but, on the morrow of her disappointment at the Vatican, she felt keenly the powerlessness of earthly things to bring joy to her soul. Nor did the wondrous Bay of Naples any more than its rich hotels awaken feelings of gladness within her, for she writes later, recalling this excursion: "I felt truly that joy is not to be found in the things that surround us; it resides in our inmost soul. We can possess joy in the depths of an obscure prison as well as in a royal palace."[34]

A threatened accident had, it is true, helped to cloud her visit to Naples. Coming down the hill from San Martino the horses took the bit between their teeth and ran away; she owed it to the protection of her angel guardian that she arrived safe and sound at the hotel where they were all to pass the night.

The desire to return to France took possession of the Martin family, and it was with pleasure that Thérèse saw, on the following day at Rome, preparations for the homeward journey.

Their departure was fixed for November 24. The train left at six o'clock in the morning for the north of Italy. At one of the first stops Mgr. Legoux came to the door of the carriage where Céline and her sister alone remained. He looked attentively at Thérèse, then smiling, said to her: "Well, how is our little Carmelite?" The poor child, who had thought that her petition to the Holy Father was known only to those who were quite near at the time, now understood that all the pilgrims knew her secret. This made her suffer all the more, but only, in truth, because of her scrupulous reserve and modesty, for, on her own avowal, the revelation won for her some "sympathetic" glances, which never went beyond the bounds of discretion, as her perfect reserve during the journey had gained the respect of all.

The writer of these lines had heard since the departure from Rome the touching history of this young girl of Lisieux, who had dared to ask Leo XIII for permission to bury herself at fifteen in an austere convent. The incident was spoken of in his compartment with curiosity, but also with unfeigned admiration, so much so, that he became greatly desirous of seeing this child, so impatient to leave all for God. But the train continued on its way without a stop; interesting sights succeeded one another; soon the charms of the beautiful pilgrimage gave place to the ordinary cares of everyday life, so that after long years it required the fame of St. Thérèse's miracles to recall to her present humble biographer that he had lived for a whole month in her immediate vicinity.

After skirting the beautiful lake of Pérouse, the pilgrims alighted on a clear sunlit evening at the foot of the hill at Assisi.

The traces of the "poor one" who had found "perfect joy" in complete renunciation had naturally an attraction for a young girl drawn to the lowly poverty of Carmel. So great was her ardour in seeking these out at the convent of Assisi, that she mislaid, in her distraction, some small articles of dress, and when the time came for departure, she was so preoccupied in looking for them that she let the carriage which was to take her to the station go off without her.

There remained but one more conveyance, that of M. Reverony, and this was already full. On pain of missing the train, Thérèse had to reveal her critical position to the priest whom she instinctively dreaded more than ever.

The Abbé Reverony was a man capable of generosity, and, at times, of a certain delicate kindness. Conscious of the pain that he had caused Thérèse, he asked one of his companions to sit with the driver, and placed the child opposite to himself in the best seat.

She felt "like a squirrel caught in a trap." He, determined to make her feel at ease, spoke to her continually about Carmel, promising to do all in his power to realize her desire of entering at fifteen.

These words cheered her for the rest of the journey. She avows, however, that after so many disillusions "she had lost confidence in creatures, and could no longer rely on anyone but God alone."

Be that as it may, her soul had regained its calm when she reached Florence on her homeward way. Here again nature displays splendours which would have delighted the pilgrims; but, once more, dark rain-clouds hid the horizon. They had to content themselves with a visit to the principal buildings. While her fellow-travellers wandered through the galleries of the Uffizi or the Pitti Palace, which contain the richest collections of art in the world, Thérèse, feeling, even amidst these marvels, the attraction of Carmel, hastened to the convent where St. Magdalen of Pazzi had lived, and kneeling before her tomb, she begged the saint to obtain entrance for her into that house of her Order, where she unceasingly asked to be admitted.

Numerous pilgrims wished to touch with their rosary beads the relics of the saint. Thérèse's hand alone was found small enough to pass through the grating which protected the venerated body. She rendered service thus to each one who passed their rosary beads to her, and this "noble office," as she tells us, made her feel very proud.

A short delay only was made at Pisa and Genoa. They were anxious to return to France, and Thérèse, in her autobiography, makes merely a passing reference to these towns. But her poetic soul could not refrain from paying a final tribute to the Italian coast, along which lay their way to the French frontier: "We returned to France," she says, "by a splendid route. We now skirted along by the sea, and one day during a storm the railway ran so close to the water's edge that the waves seemed almost to reach us. Further on, we travelled through plains covered with orange-trees, olives and graceful palms. At evening-time the numerous seaports gleamed with brilliant lights while, in the firmament above, the first stars faintly sparkled. Yet, without regret, I watched this fairy-like tableau vanish away; my heart aspired to greater things."[35]

Having venerated Notre-Dame de la Garde at Marseilles, and Notre-Dame de Fourvière at Lyons, the pilgrims hastened towards Paris, where they arrived on December 2. The dispersion of the various groups commenced immediately; the pilgrimage was ended.

M. Martin was, as we know, a born traveler. Whether to console Thérèse after her recent disappointments, or to shorten the period of waiting which, seemingly, was to be imposed on her before entering Carmel, he offered, probably during the journey from Paris to Lisieux, to take her on a pilgrimage to Jerusalem; but this proposal held no attraction for the young girl. Instead of contemplating new horizons, she wished to be shut in between the four walls of a cell. Moreover, in spite of every bitter failure, she had not yet given up her old and cherished idea of entering Carmel on December 25.

No sooner had she reached Lisieux than she hastened to the convent to tell her sisters the result of the journey. Having exhausted in vain all her resources, she asked for advice and support, especially from Sœur Agnès de Jésus, who had always encouraged her desire to consecrate herself to God without delay. This sister reminded her that the Bishop of Bayeux had promised her a written reply, a reply that one might hope would be favourable, and which had not yet been received. She consequently advised her to write to the Bishop asking to be allowed to enter the cloister at the coming feast of Christmas. She did so, but Mgr. Hugonin remained silent.

However, on January 1, 1888, Thérèse received from the Prioress, Mère Marie de Gonzague, a letter informing her that the Bishop had addressed his reply to the monastery on December 28, that he sanctioned her immediate entrance, but that she herself thought it better to defer her entrance until after Lent. Thérèse learnt later that the Mother Prioress had imposed this slight delay in order to soothe the susceptibilities of M. Delatroëtte, who still maintained his opposition, and also to spare the postulant from undergoing, at the very beginning, the rigour of a Carmelite Lent.

At first this decision was extremely painful to Thérèse. But she found means of sanctifying those months of waiting by endeavouring more than ever to forget self for others.

She thus prepared herself beforehand for the life of renunciation which was soon to be imposed on her by the rule, and tied herself down in advance to the austere practices of the novitiate, which had such an attraction for her generous spirit.

7

The Carmel of Lisieux— Thérèse As Postulant, and Her Reception— Terrible Trial—Progress in Detachment

Towards the centre of old Lisieux, not far from the church of St. Jacques, in a narrow street bordered in part by antique wood-stayed houses, stands the convent which Thérèse Martin was to render famous all the world over.

The beautiful chapel, embellished and enlarged in honour of her who has become its glory, though unchanged in its essential parts, did not present, at Thérèse's entrance, the same aspect as today. As to the rest, the cloister has not changed, and the saint who lived there would, if it were given her to return, recognize its every detail.

Nothing could be more simple than the austere and geometrical architecture of this convent, built of red brick and surmounted by a little slate-roofed dome. Its garden, closed in between the muddy waters of the Orbiquet river and the adjoining properties, occupies but a narrow space, and the perfect arrangement of its walks does not take away the impression of smallness.

This monastery had heroic beginnings, almost equal to the first Spanish Foundations of St. Teresa of Avila.

Established in 1838 in a small thatched house lent them in the Chaussée de Beuvillers, the first four Lisieux Carmelites, trained and governed by two nuns from Poitiers, experienced the rigours of extreme poverty.

With their accommodation consisting of little more than two miserable garrets, a poor oratory and a room eighteen feet square divided into three compartments, they lacked even the most necessary furniture.

A box in the kitchen served as a cupboard; a chimney-board, placed in a corner, did duty for a larder, while the stone floor had to be used as a serving-table. The plates and other utensils were so scarce that it was necessary to wash the dishes during dinner for use again at the same meal.

It was from this stable of Bethlehem that Mère Elizabeth de Saint-Louis, the Prioress, and Mère Geneviève de Sainte-Thérèse, whom we shall meet later on, took their little band to an old house in the rue de Liverot, which was to be replaced by the present convent.

Here also long years of great hardship were endured, so much so that more than once the sisters had to dine on fried leeks. But the fervour of the community grew in proportion to its privations. It was blessed, moreover, by the prolonged government of one of those first nuns from Poitiers, Mère Geneviève de Sainte-Thérèse, chosen as Prioress after Mère Elizabeth's death. She was a religious of consummate humility, who, by dint of application, had accustomed herself to carry out the ordinary duties of daily life with rare and supernatural perfection.

Her eminent virtue drew down blessings on the convent, and with the arrival of new postulants came a much needed increase in material prosperity. Mère Aimée de Jésus, future Prioress of the Carmel of Coutances, who for three years governed the house of Lisieux after the temporary deposition (enjoined by the rule) of Mère Geneviève, was able, in 1858, to have the first large wing of the present convent built, and Mère Marie de Gonzague, who later succeeded Mère Geneviève, undertook in 1876 the building which was to give the convent its definite form.

The Carmel of Lisieux was therefore, when Thérèse Martin entered, a house already sanctified by heroic sacrifice, where the most humble practices of the Carmelite rule were ennobled and hallowed by the memories that clustered around them.[1]

April 9, 1888, had been chosen for Thérèse's entrance. Her last days of freedom were passed at Les Buissonnets, hallowed by the tender love of her father and her two sisters, Léonie[2] and Céline. Before parting with his "little Queen," M. Martin sought every occasion of giving her pleasure. Returning from one of his country walks, he brought her a little lamb only one day old, all white and frizzly. Céline and Thérèse were delighted; they instinctively loved these frail little creatures, seeing in their delicate grace the smile of God; but, alas, their poor lambkin died that same day. Meditating on this disappointment, Thérèse wrote to her sister Marie: "We should not become attached to anything on this earth, not even to things most innocent, for they fail us at the moment we least think. Only the eternal can fully content us."

On the evening of April 8, the family, consisting of the father and the three sisters, to whom were added M. and Mme Guérin with Jeanne and Marie, had taken their places around the old oak table at which Thérèse was to sit for the last time. Everything in this room spoke to the young girl of the happy past; a veritable sanctuary it was, where so many affectionate words had been interchanged, so many conversations inspired and blessed by God. There were the two armchairs which had generally been used by her parents during the intimate and restful gatherings on winter evenings. There was the hearth, the centre of attraction for all, from whose sparkling flames radiated heat and joy. Even the walls themselves, silent witnesses of so much quiet happiness, of so many loving confidences. To all these mute objects, which yet seemed this evening to give expression to their grief, she had to bid farewell.

But what was this separation from inanimate things in comparison to the parting that awaited Thérèse on the following morning? "Then, just when one would wish to be forgotten," she wrote later, "words of the deepest tenderness are on all lips, as though to make the sacrifice of separation more keenly felt."[3]

The hour had come to leave all for God.[4] "That morning," continues Thérèse,

> after a last glance at Les Buissonnets, the charming nest of my childhood, I departed for the Carmel. I assisted at holy Mass, surrounded, as on the eve, by my dear ones. At the moment of Communion, when Jesus descended into their hearts, I heard nothing but the sound of weeping. As for me, I did not shed tears; but as I walked on before the others to the door of the cloister, my heart beat so violently that I asked myself whether I was not about to die. Ah, what a moment! What agony! One must have experienced it in order to understand.
>
> I embraced all, and knelt before my father to receive his blessing. He too knelt and, weeping, he blessed me. It was a sight to make the angels smile for joy—the old man presenting his child to the Saviour while yet in the springtime of her life. At last the doors of Carmel closed behind me, and there I received the embrace of the two beloved sisters who had each been a mother to me, and of a new family whose loving devotedness is unknown to the world.[5]

The thought of living henceforth under the same roof with Marie, her ever devoted elder sister, and Pauline, her "dear little mother," the hope of being formed in part by their example in the life of immolation, had no share in the joy that inundated the soul of the postulant from the moment of her entrance. Solely with the enthusiasm inspired by sacrifice willingly undertaken, did she look forward to the rude austerities of the religious life. Everything in the monastery charmed her; she believed herself transported into the desert which had been the dream of her childhood; her cell above all, with its cold bare walls, had an attraction for her which made her say from the very first hour with a sigh of contentment: "Now I am here for ever."

That she retained this happy impression speaks all the more highly for her when we consider the words of salutation with which M. Delatröette thought fit to greet her entrance into the convent. In presence of M. Martin, the enclosure door being wide open, this unyielding Superior had said dryly: "Well, my Reverend Mothers, you can now chant a *Te Deum*. As the Bishop's delegate, I present to you this child of fifteen whose entrance you have desired. I trust she may not disappoint your hopes, but I remind you that if it should turn out otherwise, the responsibility will be yours alone."[6] All the Sisters were chilled by the attitude of this venerable priest who seemed to set himself up as a prophet of evil.

This was the first mortification of Thérèse in the cloister to which she came to pray, suffer, and make reparation.

Happily, the sad forebodings of M. Delatroëtte did not influence the judgement of her companions. On the contrary, they felt from the outset the power of that virtue which, all unconscious of itself, shone forth even in the physical aspect of the postulant. "From her entrance," her Novice mistress has declared, "the Servant of God surprised the community by her bearing which was marked by a certain majesty that one would not expect in a child of fifteen."[7]

What has been referred to as *majesty* "did not exclude either simplicity or a charming readiness to render service," since, on the testimony of the same religious, "she set herself to every duty with an admirable grace."

Before following the details of her daily life, let us give a rapid glance at the life she had chosen.

To commence here below, as perfectly as may be possible, the life of contemplation led by the blessed above, such is the aim of the Carmelite. And as the life of heaven can be summed up in three actions which are the eternal occupation of the saints—namely, to see, love, and praise God—the Carmelite applies herself here on earth to acquire a knowledge and love of the Divine Majesty, as well as to praise Him, borrowing for hymn and psalmody words dictated by the Holy Spirit Himself. By the recitation of the Roman Breviary, to which the rule obliges her, by her reading and meditation, she has on her lips, during six and often seven hours a day, the word of God, and these inspired words must create in her heart divine affections. Zeal for the glory of God and the salvation of souls, the end and object proposed by St. Teresa of Avila to her daughters, must ever urge them on.[8]

On the other hand, religious perfection is not obtained without an entire detachment from creatures and a deeply rooted distrust of self; and so the Carmelite practices, during her whole life, many exercises of mortification, of penance, obedience, and humility. Her rule enjoins a continual fast from September 14 until Easter, in addition to the prescribed fasts of the Church; every Friday of the year and numerous vigils are added to this, with perpetual abstinence except in cases of sickness. Obliged also to profound silence save during the two hours of daily recreation, spending a considerable portion of the day in her cell or in the office assigned to her, where in solitude and recollection she does her appointed work, clothed in coarse serge, she has but a hard palliasse supported on three planks on which to repose after her prolonged vigils. And to these austerities of the rule it is occasionally allowable to add those voluntary penances which have been at all times familiar to the saints.

These austere mortifications are ordinarily insignificant in comparison to the assaults directed against self-love and the caprices of the imagination. Acts of humility publicly performed, the obligation of never excusing herself though perhaps unjustly accused, or reproached without cause, prompt, absolute, and unquestioning obedience, even in the minutest details, to every superior commanding in the name of God—such are the arms unceasingly employed to bring her nature under subjection and lead her to the happy state of a spouse who loves God even to the extent of wholly immolating herself for His glory.

Not in vain is this struggle against the old enemy carried on in these shrines of joyous suffering. Little by little, souls become detached and purified and more Christ-like. There is, perhaps, no place in the world where peace so abounds, where happiness so reigns, as in the enclosures bounded by the sombre walls of Carmel.

Such was the life that Thérèse Martin had just embraced in the hope of thus compensating for the insults launched by the world against her well-beloved Saviour.

Mortifications were not slow in coming to this child, who had made the offering of herself with disinterested love. Providence permitted that she should find in the character of certain superiors and companions a source of suffering in addition to the rigours of the rule.

The monastery had now, for two years, been governed by Mère Marie de Gonzague, who succeeded, in a fourth term of three years, the venerable Mère Geneviève de Sainte-Thérèse, still living but weighed down with infirmities.

Daughter of a noble Calvados family,[9] the prioress in office had, in the past, given proof of initiative and administrative ability. These qualities, joined to a great heart and a charming personality, due in part to careful education in early years, had no doubt determined the choice of the community.

But this active and richly endowed nature was not without some defects. Very impressionable, and of somewhat distrustful character, predisposed to melancholy, she did not always possess that even-balanced judgement which makes rule beneficial and inspires subordinates with confidence.

Besides, although she had greatly desired the entrance of Thérèse Martin to the Carmel, she judged, as it would seem, that a vocation so premature required to be specially tested. As a result of this theory, and in consequence of a certain natural impulsiveness not always held in check, she made the child's early religious life painful.

Note the frank admission of the postulant: "From the first," she says,

> my way was strewn with more thorns than roses. Bitter dryness was the daily food of my soul. Then the Saviour permitted that I should be very severely treated by our Mother, even unconsciously; I could never meet her without receiving some reproof. Once, when I had left a cobweb in the cloister, I remember her saying to me in presence of the whole community: "It can be easily seen that our cloisters have been swept by a child of fifteen. Too bad! Go, sweep away that cobweb, and learn to be more careful in future."
>
> On the rare occasions when, for spiritual direction, I spent an hour with her, I was reprimanded nearly all the time, and what distressed me most was that I did not understand how to correct my faults, for example,

> my slowness and insufficient assiduity in the various duties.
>
> One day, I said to myself that our Mother would, no doubt, like me to be employed at work during the free time usually devoted to prayer, and I plied my little needle without raising my eyes; but no one ever knew of it, as I wanted to be faithful and to act always for Jesus alone.
>
> When I was a postulant, our Mistress would send me at half-past four in the afternoon to weed in the garden. This cost me a great deal, especially as I was almost sure to meet Mère Marie de Gonzague on the way. She said on one of these occasions: "After all, this child does absolutely nothing. What sort of novice would she be who must be sent out every day for a walk?" And it was thus that she acted towards me in all things.[10]

Such was the treatment which Thérèse was to receive for long years, the rigour of which, allowing for some intervals of calm, was scarcely relaxed, even during her last illness.

How she acted under this undoubtedly heavy hand which was for her, nevertheless, always the hand of God, we learn from the testimony of the Prioress herself. "Mère Marie de Gonzague," declares R. P. Godefroy Madelaine,[11] "confided to me that, in order to exercise Sœur Thérèse's virtue, she had studiously sought to try her by affecting towards her a certain indifference and severity. She has, moreover, testified to me that this apparently harsh treatment had certainly been very painful to the Servant of God, but that no pain had ever caused her to deviate in the least from perfect obedience."[12]

We shall revert to this obedience, which attained an heroic degree in later years, and will ever be numbered amongst the most meritorious virtues of the young nun.

After the Mother Prioress, to whom she felt at first drawn by a sympathy so soon checked, the mistress of novices, Mère Marie des Anges, contributed to the formation of Thérèse.

She was a good and pious religious of superior education who had known Thérèse as a little child, having seen her from the age of nine come to the parlour to visit her sister Pauline.[13] She had conceived for her a real affection, which was increased by admiration for her virtues. "From her entrance," she declared, "Thérèse grew in grace and wisdom before God and before the community by a very constant correspondence with Divine grace. This it is which explains to me the rapid ascent of so young a child to the highest sanctity. Even quite lately a venerable and holy nun said to me in referring to Thérèse's novitiate: 'In truth, we had never seen anything like it.'"[14]

From the outset, she too had procured for her novice an increase of merit by unintentionally exercising her patience. Not understanding, just at first, the special grace of the little saint, which was that of interior silence, she gave her during the early months long exhortations, of which the fervour did not lessen the monotony, and which rather impeded Thérèse's intimate communing with Jesus and hindered her soul from "expanding."

But the esteem with which the virtues of this good mistress inspired all the sisters soon triumphed over this embarrassment.

It was to her, notwithstanding the difficulty at first of expressing her feelings, that Thérèse made known the pain caused her by the Mother Prioress's severity—not that she dreamed of criticising or complaining—but through a need of her affectionate and loyal nature. "I see her still," said Mère Marie des Anges, "as she came one day to confide to me the grief of her heart, without, however, letting the least murmur of complaint escape her. She discerned the providence of God regarding her soul, and smiled in spite of everything."[15]

Seeing her pained, and sometimes physically weakened by the austerities of the rule, the mistress of novices tried to procure her some relaxation, in allowing her, for instance, to prolong her sleep. Unfortunately, the poor Mother was often absent-minded. Having forgotten to give her this alleviation for whole weeks together, she would then oblige her, without sufficient reason, to rest for fifteen consecutive days, and the Mother Prioress, not seeing the novice at morning meditation, blamed Thérèse, who did not then know whom to obey.

The child hoped for a time to find support and light in the counsel of the former Prioress, the venerable Mère Geneviève de Sainte-Thérèse, now definitely confined to bed, a prey to cruel suffering. But it was decreed that no human consolation should ever enter to lessen the merit of her generosity. Mère Geneviève was a saint favoured with supernatural lights. Nevertheless, Thérèse did not receive from her the help that she desired for her spiritual advancement. This good Mother had, in more than one instance, prophetic visions of the future; she did not, however, divine the sublime destiny which awaited the humble postulant. She was even frightened by the hardihood of her ideas, and disconcerted her by certain remarks; this, however, did not prevent her from consoling Thérèse in the exterior trials with which she saw her afflicted.[16] Thérèse profited by the inspiring example given her by the piety of the Foundress; but, excepting one instance which we shall mention, she received from her few words of encouragement in her ascent to the heights of perfection.

There remains to note the influence of the confessor, on whose help Thérèse had the right to count on entering the cloister. Abbé Youf, chaplain to the Carmel of Lisieux, was a priest of true piety and austere virtue, but whose spiritual activity was restricted by ill-health. It was impossible to obtain from him direction properly so called. He was not long, however, in noticing the rare qualities of the new-comer; he did not hesitate to speak most highly of her, and favoured, as far as discretion permitted, her desire for daily Communion.

Up to this time Thérèse does not seem to have felt real need of a spiritual director. During the two years preceding her entrance to Carmel, God did not make use of an intermediary to instruct her regarding her vocation; at most He had given her a certain insight into convent life and the spirit of the Order by means of her sister Pauline, who was already a religious. But once across the threshold of the cloister, this light became dim; trials of darkness and aridity were added to the other sufferings sent her by the Divine Master for the purification of her soul. Henceforth, she sought counsel from the priests who came to the monastery.

Excepting the chaplain, who was but feeble support to her, she saw only, and that at rare intervals, the preacher of the retreat.

All did not understand her. Père Blino, of the Society of Jesus, a holy man undoubtedly, and well versed in the ways of spirituality, considered rash her ardour for self-immolation, and in his opinion, these outbursts of love were scarcely compatible with a religious formation which was yet only in its commencement.[17]

Another Jesuit saw further and more clearly. Born in the vicinity of Alençon, at Carrouges, Père Almire Pichon was an eminent religious who excelled in his particular work as preacher of Retreats.[18]

Sent by his superiors to Canada in 1886, he returned to France in 1887 for some months. Thérèse was then fourteen. On the advice of her sisters, whose director he was, she told him of her desire for the religious life, and he was probably the only ecclesiastic to encourage her project of entering the Carmel without delay, even if, to obtain permission, she must have recourse to the Sovereign Pontiff.

During the year 1888, Père Pichon came to give the Exercises at the Carmel of Lisieux, where he again met Thérèse, and he thought that he had only to encourage her in the way of trustful love, the safety and efficacy of which he everywhere dwelt upon in his preaching. This was, alas, the time when the poor child, plunged as she was in aridity, asked herself with bitter disquietude if she were worthy of love or hatred.

The Father commenced by restoring peace to her soul. But let us hear her tell of the benefits of his direction, though given but in passing.

> R. P. Pichon was himself surprised, two months after my entrance, at the work of God in my soul; he thought my fervour quite childlike and my way very sweet. This little conference with the good Father might have brought me great consolation but for the extreme

> difficulty which I felt in laying open my heart. I, nevertheless, made a general confession to him, after which he spoke these words: "In the presence of God, of the Blessed Virgin, of all the Angels and Saints, I declare that you have never committed a single mortal sin. Render thanks to the Saviour who has given you this grace gratuitously without any merit on your part."
>
> Without any merit on my part! Ah, I had no difficulty in believing this. I felt how feeble and imperfect I was; gratitude alone filled my soul. The fear of having stained the white robe of my baptism had caused me much suffering, and this assurance, coming from the lips of a director who, according to the desire expressed by our Mother St. Teresa, "joined knowledge to virtue," seemed to come from God Himself. The good Father also said to me: "My child, may Our Saviour be always your Superior, and your Novice Master." He was so, in truth, and my Director too. . . . Hardly had Père Pichon taken charge of my soul than his superiors sent him to Canada. Reduced, henceforth, to receive from him but one letter a year, the "little Flower" turned towards the Director of directors.[19]

Some time afterwards, Thérèse met another priest who came to give a Retreat, and who perfectly understood the state of her soul; but his help was also to be but passing, so that she had again to implore the aid of her heavenly Director.

She then accustomed herself to seek guidance and consolation either in the Holy Scripture or in writings where the doctrine and general tone more vividly recalled the word of God.

On the testimony of her sister Céline, who was later to have her as novice mistress, "she studied the Sacred Scriptures in order to know the *character* of the good God. The different senses of Scripture distressed her. 'If I had been a priest,' she said, 'I would have diligently studied Greek and Hebrew, in order to know the Divine thought as God deigned to express it in our human language.'"[20]

It would appear, too, that the light of the Holy Spirit supplied for her want of knowledge of Eastern languages, for, if we rely on the testimony of Sœur Marie de la Trinité, who made her novitiate under Sœur Thérèse's direction, "she interpreted the books of Holy Scripture with unheard-of facility. One would have said that these Divine books had no meaning hidden from her, so well was she able to discover all their beauty."[21]

Thus is her love for liturgical prayer explained, a love that began on her entrance to the convent, and which was to go on increasing until her death. She affirms this herself in enthusiastic words which show the clearness with which she perceived, through these sacred writings, the radiance of the Spirit of God. "How happy I was," she says, "when, officiating at the Divine Office, I said the prayers out loud in the centre of the choir. I reflected then that the priest recited the same prayers at Mass, and that, like him, I had the right to pray aloud before the Blessed Sacrament, and to read the Gospel when I was First Chantress. I can say truly that the Divine Office has been, at the same time, my joy and my martyrdom, for I had a great desire to recite it without fault, and yet, in spite of all my application, I made mistakes."[22]

Together with the Sacred Scriptures, Thérèse had to make a deep study, at the commencement of her life in the convent, of the writings of St. Teresa and St. John of the Cross,[23] which are considered as classics in the Carmelite Order. She loved the beautiful and mystical lyrics of this latter, and became very deeply imbued with his doctrine.

The novice's predilection for the *Imitation* is already known; she had no need to re-read it, as she knew the whole book by heart. But the fruit that she had drawn from it inspired her with the thought of studying another book, which is nothing else but its commentary.

The work formerly published by Père Surin under the title *The Foundations of the Spiritual Life, drawn from the Imitation of Christ*, presents, among other merits, that of participating in the admirable simplicity and penetrating unction of the text that it expounds. It constitutes, moreover, a perfect manual of detachment, since it inculcates above all, contempt of the world, detachment from all earthly riches, mortification of the senses, and self-abnegation. This was sufficient recommendation for Thérèse, already practised by the Divine Master in every degree of patience, to make of this book her constant companion.

Another work, simple in style but remarkably lucid, which had for her an equal charm, was the treatise of Mgr. de Ségur, entitled *Piety and the Interior Life*. The saintly prelate therein insists on the idea that the chief means of living the life of Jesus is diligent meditation on His Gospel. No doctrine could be more adapted to the long-standing and ever increasing attraction of Thérèse for this Divine book, which, in the end, absorbed all her attention, to the exclusion of every human book. A word on the place which it held in her interior life.

After her entrance to the convent, the fervent Carmelite succeeded in finding the four Gospels in one volume small enough to allow of its being carried constantly near her heart, and she was faithful to this practice until her death. Furthermore, at a time when she was undergoing grievous temptations against faith, she wrote the entire *Credo* with her blood in this book, as counselled by one of her confessors.

To her most intimate confidantes she explained this devotion. She wrote, for example, to the Mother Prioress: "It is the Gospels, which, above all, occupy my mind during mental prayer. From them I draw everything necessary for my poor little soul. I ever discover there new lights, hidden and mysterious meanings."[24]

And again: "When I read certain treatises where many obstacles to perfection are shown, my poor mind grows tired very quickly; I close the learned book which wearies my head and dries up my heart, and I take instead the Holy Scripture. Then, everything appears to me in clear light; a single word opens out infinite horizons to my soul; perfection seems easy to me; I realize that it is sufficient to recognize one's nothingness, and to abandon oneself as a child in the arms of God."[25]

These last words show clearly where Thérèse found the idea of the "little way" of perfection, which she was afterwards to recommend to every soul. It was in the Gospel itself, in the Gospel clearly understood, which preaches unceasingly the way of abandonment and filial love towards our Heavenly Father. Could we find, in truth, a doctrine more frequently inculcated in the sacred text than that of our Divine sonship? And if we are really and literally the sons of God, is it not our first duty to become as little children towards Him? And consequently, shall we not be pleasing to Him in such measure as we show ourselves little and humble and trustful? It is important to note in passing the purely evangelical origin of this way of perfection which, in a few years, led the young religious to the highest degrees of Divine union.

Exercised in detachment by the Mother Prioress, formed by the mistress of novices in the practices of cloister-life, instructed by the occasional counsel of an experienced director, and by the study of a few ascetical books, Thérèse de l'Enfant Jésus had, above and beyond all these, as principal and soon as sole teacher, the Divine Saviour Himself, making known in His Gospel the secret of sanctity.

She could have equally relied on the help of her own two sisters in religion to initiate her into the spirit of Carmel. But the postulant's relations with her elder sisters were altogether different from what friends outside expected. On seeing this charming, intelligent, and gentle-mannered child of fifteen enter the Carmel, the natural conclusion, judging from a worldly point of view, was that she would be the "pet" of the community, and that her two elder sisters could never show her enough affectionate attention. Her real position in regard to them would have caused astonishment had it been known outside the Carmel. Persuaded that in the religious life more than anywhere else, perfect charity requires the sacrifice of natural affection, at least as regards its external manifestation, Thérèse, loving, sensitive, and tender as she was, mortified herself to the extent of never seeking the company of Sœur Agnès de Jésus or Sœur Marie du Sacré-Cœur. At recreation, she took her place indifferently beside whoever came first, or rather, made sure of being near to one who seemed to her forlorn.

If one of her own sisters were sick, she did not feel that she had any right to go to see her until other nuns had been before her in this little act of kindness.

Certain admissions reveal, it is true, the cruel constraint she put on herself in such cases. During her last illness she was asked what she would have done if one of her sisters had been ill instead of herself.

> "Would you have gone to the infirmary during recreation?"
>
> "No, I would have gone straight to recreation without making any inquiry; but I would have done it quite simply, so that no one would notice the sacrifice I was making."[26]

As regards visits to the parlour, she practised the same self-effacement, the same voluntary privation of family affection. With the exception of her beloved Léonie and Céline, whom she knew she ought to console in their loneliness by showing her tenderness for them, Thérèse allowed her visitors to talk on while she listened, saying scarcely a word, and was the first to leave when the appointed time came.

But in this school of renunciation, she learned that love renders every suffering sweet; she enjoyed profound peace, even in the apparent abandonment of creatures, even under heavy trials which, humanly speaking, should have dismayed her. The following lines, bearing the date of this period, are addressed to Céline at Les Buissonnets:

> You are right, life is often oppressive and sad; it is hard to begin the day's work, especially when Jesus hides Himself from our love. What is He doing, this sweet Friend? Does He not see our distress, the heavy weight that presses upon us? Where is He? Why does He not come to console us? Céline, have no fear; He is there, quite near. He is looking at us. It is He who asks of us this suffering, these tears. . . . He has need of them for the sake of souls, for our soul, as He wants to give us so glorious a reward. Oh, I assure you that it costs Him a great deal to plunge us thus in bitterness; but He knows

> that it is the only way of preparing us to *know Him as He knows Himself, to become as gods ourselves*! What a destiny, how great is our soul! Let us rise above passing things, let us hold ourselves aloof from earth; high up the air is so pure! Jesus may hide Himself, but one divines His presence. . . .[27]

A child who, at fifteen, soared to these heights, could still be wounded by the thorns on the way in her intermittent contact with earth, but she could neither be brought down nor slackened in her flight.

This rare virtue, moreover, quickly gained the secret admiration of the superiors who had believed it their duty to try her. Mère Marie de Gonzague, always so strict in regard to her, declared freely that she was a treasure for the Carmel, "the best of the best; an angel." What was of greater value, she permitted her to take the holy Habit—not, it is true, at the normal time, that is, after six months as postulant—but on January 10, 1889.[28]

The preparatory retreat for her clothing was passed by Thérèse in that aridity of soul by which Jesus was pleased to purify her. But the following lines, addressed at the time to Sœur Agnès de Jésus, reveal to us her perfect comprehension of this Heaven-sent trial.

> . . . In my soul's intercourse with Jesus there is nothing, nothing but dryness and sleep! Since my Well-beloved wills to remain asleep, I will not prevent Him; I am too happy in seeing that He does not treat me as a stranger, that He is not constrained with me. . . .
>
> I am happy, yes, truly happy to suffer . . . O mother, if you knew how ardently I wish to become indifferent to the things of earth. What is created beauty to me? I should be exceedingly unhappy in its possession. Oh, how great my heart appears when I compare it to the goods of this world, since all these united could not satisfy it. But when I consider it in relation to Jesus, how small it then seems.
>
> How good He is to me, He who will soon be my Fiancé. How divinely lovable He is in not allowing me to become captive to anything here below. He well

> knows that if He sent me even one ray of earthly happiness, I would become attached to it with all the energy, all the power of my heart's affection, and He refuses me this ray. . . . He prefers to leave me in darkness rather than give me a false light which would not be His.
>
> I do not wish creatures to possess a single atom of my love; I want to give all to Jesus, since He has made me understand that He alone is true happiness. Everything shall be for Him, everything. And even when I shall have nothing to give Him, as this evening, I will offer Him that nothing. . . .[29]

"Even one ray of happiness Jesus refuses me." What, then, was the great distress of soul which could draw this cry of grief-stricken resignation from the postulant? We know her secret privations. We realize the truth of her words when she affirms her growing indifference for the beauty of created things. But stronger and sweeter ties still bound her to her loved ones. Jesus was now preparing to cut to the quick, so that the betrothal of Thérèse, sealed in the blood of her sacrifice, would be for ever indissoluble.

It will be remembered that, shortly before the departure of his youngest daughter for the Carmel, M. Martin had suffered his first attack of paralysis. He recovered almost completely, and it was in the spirit of joyous thankfulness that he had offered his child to God. He wrote at that time to one of his friends: "Thérèse, my little Queen, entered Carmel yesterday. God alone can claim such a sacrifice, but He helps me so powerfully that, in the midst of my tears, my heart abounds with joy."

How admirable were these dispositions, dispositions which were to carry him to the heights of heroism. One day he came to the Carmel and said to his three daughters: "My children, I have just returned from Alençon, where I received, in the church of Notre-Dame, such wonderful graces and consolation that I made this prayer: 'My God, it is too much; yes, I am too happy. It is not possible to get to heaven in this manner; I want to suffer something for Thee . . .' And I offered myself . . ." The tender father did not dare to finish the sentence, but they understood. He had offered himself as a victim.

Shortly afterwards, a second attack of paralysis seemed to indicate that the holocaust had been accepted.

In spite of all, the feast of Thérèse's reception was an occasion of joy and happiness for the whole family, more especially for M. Martin.

Thérèse for the last time crossed the threshold of the cloister, arrayed in her bridal robes. To honour the King of Heaven to whom his "little Queen" was about to be publicly betrothed, M. Martin wished that she should wear a dress of white velvet, bordered with swansdown and enriched with point d'Alençon. Her long fair hair fell over her shoulders in natural curls, and pure white lilies were her only ornament.

"Papa was waiting for me," she writes,

> at the enclosure door. Advancing towards me, while his eyes filled with tears, he pressed me to his heart, saying: "Ah, here is my little Queen." Then he gave me his arm, and we made our solemn entrance into the chapel. This day was his triumph, his last feast on earth. All his offerings were made; his children belonged to God. Céline having confided in him that, later on, she too would abandon the world for Carmel, this exemplary father had replied in a transport of joy: "Let us go together before the Blessed Sacrament to thank the Saviour for the graces that He showers on our family, and the honour He has done me in choosing spouses from my house. Yes, the good God greatly honours me in claiming my children. If I possessed anything better, I would hasten to offer it to Him." This better thing was himself. . . .[30]

We shall see under what form God desired the holocaust. Meanwhile, the heavenly Spouse was pleased, on the morning of the nuptial feast, to respond with Divine solicitude to a desire of His new fiancée. Snow had a particular attraction for Thérèse. "The first time her infant eyes beheld the earth, snow was its raiment," and she wanted to see it on the day of her reception clothed, like herself, in white. But the extreme mildness of the temperature seemed to show clearly that her hope was not to be realized.

However, the ceremony in the church being concluded, the nuns welcomed the newly received novice at the enclosure door, and led her in procession to the choir.

"The moment I entered the cloister," says Thérèse, "my eyes instinctively turned to my dear little Jesus,[31] who was smiling on me amidst flowers and lights. Then turning towards the quadrangle, *I saw it all covered with snow.* What tenderness on the part of Jesus! Fulfilling the desires of His little fiancée, He gave her the snow. What human being, however powerful, could make a single snowflake fall from heaven to charm his beloved?"[32]

This desire of Thérèse was known in the community and elsewhere. The unexpected appearance of the snow was hailed as a symbol of the virginal soul who was giving herself to God, and everyone who knew about it spoke of the "little miracle" which had signalized Sœur Thérèse's reception.

The hour had come, however, for the great trial which was to plunge Thérèse and her family in long and bitter sorrow.

M. Martin's second attack of paralysis had given cause to fear some brain trouble. The third, which came a month after her reception, realized their gravest fears. The young novice who, at the time of the previous threatenings of trouble, had said to Mère Marie des Anges, "I suffer much, but I can still suffer more," wrote after this terrible attack, "Ah, I did not say then that I could suffer more. Words could not express our agony; I shall not try to describe it. . . ."

That keen intellect darkened, that tender affection wrecked, perhaps irremediably—was not this the end of all human happiness for M. Martin's daughters?

The hand of God was visible here. He demanded from this family heartrending sacrifices in order that, every earthly tie being broken, nothing might stay these souls in their flight towards the heights of perfection.

On February 12, 1889, M. Martin left Lisieux to receive special treatment in a Home chosen by his family. He remained there three years.

The daughters of this great Christian, this voluntary victim, were to climb with him his steep and rugged path of suffering. Undoubtedly, for the three Carmelites as well as for the two young girls now alone in the world, the blow had penetrated to the very heart's core. But Thérèse and her sisters repeated, in heroic submission, these words of the poet, worshipping, even in their bitter moment of grief, the Divine good pleasure.

> I come to Thee, my Saviour, by faith in Thee inspired;
> I bring Thee pacified
> The fragments of this heart by Thine own might all fired
> Which Thou hast severed wide.[33]

The thought of giving pleasure to Jesus by suffering for love of Him, the ever-growing sense of detachment which became more and more easy according as the Divine Hand severed the final bonds, the remembrance of a victim's sacrifice so visibly accepted, the almost sensible vision of God who came to purify, to strengthen, to inflame—all this brought to the five sisters, weighed down as they were by severest tribulation, a wealth of supernatural joy, so much so, that Thérèse did not hesitate to write: "The three years of my father's martyrdom seem to me the dearest and most fruitful of our life; I would not exchange them for the most sublime ecstasies."

Recalling later the thoughts which at this time she had exchanged with Céline, the "little sister of her soul," Thérèse added: "As formerly at Les Buissonnets, we lifted not alone our eyes but also our hearts beyond space and time, and, in order quickly to enjoy eternal happiness, we chose suffering and contempt here below."[34] We have here the echo of her conversations in the parlour. The letters of the novice to her dear Céline reveal the same sublime choice.

"We have now nothing further to hope for on this earth; the *fresh mornings are gone*,[35] naught is left to us but suffering. Oh, what an enviable lot! The Seraphim in Heaven are jealous of our happiness."[36]

And again: "Céline, far from making any complaint to Our Saviour of the cross He has sent us, I cannot comprehend the infinite love that has urged Him to deal thus with us. Our father must be greatly loved by God, since he has so much to suffer. What a delight to share in his humiliation!"[37]

To be deprived of those dearest to us, how hard so ever it may be, is less painful for a fervent soul than apparent abandonment by her heavenly Spouse. In order to complete the work of detachment, Jesus veiled Himself more and more from the eyes of the novice, and by this abandonment her suffering was greatly increased. But, at the same time, she experienced the sweetest spiritual joy in showing her Divine Master that she loved Him for His own sake, not for any sensible favours that He grants or withholds at will.

"I found no consolation," she avows, "either from heaven or from earth; and, nevertheless, amidst these waters of tribulation, for which I had so longed and prayed, I was the happiest of creatures."[38]

In this state of mingled grief and consolation was passed the first part of the novitiate before her vows.

Her recent trials had made her more than ever capable of healing the wounds of others. If a postulant was suffering under some heavy trial, she was sent to Sœur Thérèse to receive words of consolation. Moreover, even before her profession she was given the charge of encouraging and stimulating the efforts of one of her companions, a further proof of the secret esteem which Mère Marie de Gonzague, in spite of her severity, had for Thérèse's discernment and piety.

Once more, however, Thérèse was to experience contradiction in regard to her most cherished desires. At the end of her year's novitiate, she was not called to make her vows; the still inflexible ecclesiastical superior opposed it. Far from murmuring, the saintly child attributed the imposed delay to her insufficient merit, and addressed to her heavenly Fiancé this touching prayer: "I no longer ask Thee to let me make my profession; I shall wait as long as may please Thee; but I must not allow my union with Thee to be delayed by any fault of mine, so will devote all my care to preparing for myself a robe enriched with diamonds and every precious stone. When Thou dost find it rich enough, I am sure that nothing will prevent Thee from taking me as Thy spouse."[39]

And she redoubled her ardour in the practice of religious perfection. She had as companion in the novitiate a young lay-sister of rather difficult character. Instead of avoiding this sister, Thérèse chose her company by preference, and, by dint of kindness, obtained over her a considerable influence for good.

But nothing could equal her tender charity towards another lay-sister, old Sœur Saint-Pierre, of a disposition which infirmity had rendered very exacting, and whom it was necessary to lead each evening to the refectory, with numberless precautions in order not to irritate her. Sœur Thérèse had hesitated about volunteering for this office on account of the difficulty of pleasing the poor invalid. Her generous heart carried the day, and she succeeded, though not easily, in getting her services accepted. Each evening, towards the end of prayer, when the aged Sister shook her hour-glass, Thérèse knew that this meant, "Let us go now."

"Summoning all my courage," she says,

> I rose, and quite a ceremony commenced. Her seat had to be removed and carried *in a certain way*, and above all there was to be no hurry. Then we set out. One had to follow the good sister, supporting her by her girdle. I tried to do this as gently as I could, but if unfortunately she chanced to stumble, it seemed to her that I was holding her badly and that she was going to fall. "You go too fast, I shall break my bones," she would say; and if I then tried to lead her more slowly, "Now you are not following me; I do not feel your hand; you are loosening your hold; I shall fall. . . . Ah, I was right in saying that you were too young to take care of me."
>
> At last, without further mishap, we arrived at the refectory. There other troubles arose. My poor invalid had to be very skilfully helped into her place, in order not to hurt her; after that her sleeves had to be turned up, always *in a certain way*. I was then free to go. But I soon noticed that she had much difficulty in cutting her bread, so I never left her without rendering that final service. As she had not asked me to do it, this attention

> greatly touched her. It was by this means, unsought, that I quite won her confidence, and especially—as I learned later—that after all my little services I gave her *my sweetest smile.*[40]

From that time onward, the invalid never ceased to extol Thérèse's charity. Thus it was that the young Sister, even before her profession, endeavoured to be an angel of peace and good-will in the convent that had opened its gates to her.

The "bejewelled robe" was gradually enriched. It shone with the rarest gems of charity and patience. It now remained to add those of religious poverty and humility. Before giving in detail the outstanding actions which mark the rapid progress of Thérèse in these two virtues, let us here dwell for a moment on the first victories gained in Carmel over her natural tendencies.[41]

Thérèse Martin had brought to the convent, together with her delicately refined nature, an inborn love for the beautiful and a strong predilection for order. As a postulant it gave her pleasure to have for her use things that were nice, and to find at her hand whatever was required for her work. "Jesus," she says, "suffered this patiently, for He does not wish to disclose all to the soul at once; He ordinarily gives His light little by little." This light became more and more vivid during the course of the novitiate. Her Divine Master also provided her with numerous occasions of practicing the virtues He demanded.

One evening, Thérèse searched in vain for her little lamp on the shelf where it was usually kept. Evidently, some Sister had taken it in mistake for her own. But it was after Compline; the *Great Silence* had commenced: how was the mistake to be righted? On the other hand, must she pass a whole hour in darkness, when she had counted on doing much work that very evening? The Holy Spirit reminded her that true poverty consists in the voluntary privation, not only of things that are pleasing, but also of things necessary. "And," she concludes, "amid the exterior darkness, my soul was filled with Divine light." She was still more imbued with this doctrine when, by order no doubt of the Mother

Prioress, a large jug, much damaged, was substituted for the one she had till then been using. Far from any thought of complaint, she joyously accepted this new and unsightly object. Aided from above, she had arrived at the state of preferring the ugliest and least serviceable utensils.

The observance of another point of the Carmelite rule already mentioned was more difficult. "Amongst all the virtuous practices enjoined by our holy Constitution," we read in a collection of the Statutes of the Order, "that of never excusing oneself is one of the most important in order to advance in the practice of humility."[42]

We shall see with what admirable generosity she overcame her repugnance and seized the first opportunity for self-renunciation on this point. A little vase left behind a window had been broken. The novice-mistress, believing Thérèse accountable for not having put it in its proper place, spoke severely to her, and reproached her with failing altogether on the point of order. The novice was in no way responsible for the accident; with one word she could have cleared herself, but without saying anything she kissed the ground, and promised to be more careful in future.

Acts of humility like this were to go on increasing in number during the whole course of her religious life. The nuptial garment had now acquired enough brilliancy to charm the Divine Spouse. After eight long months added to the usual term of the novitiate, Thérèse de l'Enfant Jésus was admitted to profession.

8

Profession—Apparent Severity of God, and the Disinterested Love of His Servant—Gracious Gift of Jesus to Thérèse—Poetry of the Young Carmelite—Correspondence on Spiritual Matters—Céline's Entrance

On September 8, 1890, Thérèse was to bind herself for ever by the vows of religion. The Almighty still kept her in that darkness, as of night, well known to those whom He invites to climb the heights of the mountain of love, and she herself affirms that her retreat for profession was, like its successors, "a retreat of great aridity." But this absence of consolation was to make still more perfect the gift of self, and never perhaps did she love her Divine Master more whole-heartedly than in this path of darkness that He had chosen for her. She has described by means of striking imagery the cold and cloudy atmosphere in which she was condemned to live, an atmosphere which, far from extinguishing, seemed to foster and strengthen the fire of love in her heart.

We refer to the letter addressed to Mère Agnes de Jésus a few days before her profession. In no other place is portrayed more clearly the delicate purity of the dispositions which she brought to her Well-Beloved. "Before setting out," she says,

> my Betrothed asked me through what country I wished to journey, what route I desired to follow. I replied that I

had but one desire—to reach the *summit of the mountain of Love*. . . .

Then Our Saviour took me by the hand, and led me into a subterranean way, where it is neither hot nor cold, where the sun never shines, into which neither rain nor wind find entrance, a tunnel, where I see nothing but a half-veiled light, the brightness radiating from the down-cast eyes of the Face of Jesus.

My Betrothed utters no word, nor do I, save only to assure Him that I love Him more than myself, and I feel in my heart that this is true, for I am more His than my own.

I could not see that we were advancing, since our way lies underground; and yet it seems to me, without knowing how, that we are approaching the mountain-top.

I am grateful to Jesus for making me walk in darkness; I am in profound peace; willingly I consent to remain during the whole of my religious life in this sombre tunnel which He has made me enter; I desire only that my darkness may obtain light for sinners.

I am happy, yes, truly happy in having no consolation; I should feel ashamed if my love resembled that of earthly fiancées who look for presents from the hands of their betrothed, or eagerly watch his face for the loving smile that delights them.

Thérèse, the little fiancée of Jesus, loves Jesus for His own sake; she wishes to look upon the face of her Well-Beloved only that she may catch sight of the tears that delight her with their hidden charm. She wants to dry those tears; she would fain gather them as priceless diamonds to enrich her nuptial robe.

Jesus! How I wish to love Him, to love Him more than He has ever yet been loved. . . .

I wish, at all costs, to win the palm of St. Agnes. If this cannot be by blood, it must be gained by love. . . .[1]

Thérèse had, as we know, charge of decorating the statue of the Child Jesus which stands in the cloister near one of the entrances. On the evening before her profession, she placed around the Divine Infant the same waxen tapers as on the day of her reception. And when Sœur Marie du

Sacré-Cœur expressed astonishment that she should reject the beautiful rose-tinted candles prepared for the great day, she received from Thérèse this note which gives touching expression to her faithful remembrance of family joys and to her lively faith: "The others (candles) speak to me of the past. They commenced to burn on the day of my reception; they were fresh and rosy then; papa who had given them to me was there, and all was joyous. But now their rosy hue is gone. . . . Are there still any rose-coloured joys here below for your little Thérèse? Oh no, there remain for her now but the joys of Heaven; joys where the created, which is nothingness, gives place to the uncreated, which is reality."[2]

With soul unburdened by this magnificent detachment, Thérèse de l'Enfant Jésus saw the morning of the great day dawn. Nature was in festal array to celebrate the mystic nuptials. A radiant sun shone from a cloudless sky on the procession which accompanied her to the marriage-feast of the Lamb. As the community went in procession to the chapter-room where the novice was to make her vows, a veritable *cloud* of swallows passed rapidly over the monastery, almost touching the walls in their flight, seeming to portray by their swift and unhindered soaring the eager flight of the bride to her Spouse.

During the ceremony an opportunity presented itself for a particularly meritorious act of abandonment. The Prioress, Mère Marie de Gonzague, had counselled Thérèse to ask God, when prostrate during her act of self-immolation, to grant her father's cure. She contented herself with saying, "My God, grant that papa may recover if it be truly Thy Holy Will, since our Mother has told me to ask this." Thus did she unite submission to the Divine Will, filial love and holy obedience.

Another interest which she deemed of higher importance than even her father's health because it was of the spiritual order, was, during these precious moments, the object of a less conditional petition to Jesus in return for her holocaust. She was anxious about the future of her sister Léonie, whose poor health had, so far, defeated her hopes of the religious life. Thérèse had the courage to address this prayer to her Divine Master: "As regards Léonie, grant that by Thy will she may become a Visitation nun, and, if she has not the vocation, I pray Thee to bestow it on her; Thou canst not refuse me this."

Many others too were included in her supplications on the day of her profession. Her heart expanded so as to include the whole world. "I did not forget anyone," she says; "I desired that every sinner on earth might that day be converted, that purgatory might no longer hold a single captive."

For herself she made the following petitions:

> O Jesus, my Divine Spouse, grant that my Baptismal robe may never be stained. Take me to Thyself rather than allow me to sully my soul here below by the smallest voluntary fault. May I never seek or find but Thee alone. May creatures be ever as nothing to me and I as nothing to them. May my peace never be disturbed by earthly things. O Jesus, I ask only peace. . . . Peace and above all Love, unbounded, illimitable Love. Jesus, may I die a martyr's death for Thee. Grant me martyrdom of heart or of body. . . . Ah, rather, give me both. Grant that I may fulfil my promises perfectly, that I may count for nothing here below; may I be unnoticed and trampled under foot like a little grain of sand. I offer myself to Thee, my Well-Beloved, in order that Thou mayest accomplish perfectly Thy holy Will in me unhindered by any created obstacle.[3]

An interior trial, on the eve, had shown that the Master accepted her offering. After Matins, during the hour of prayer which preceded the dawn of the great day,[4] her vocation to Carmel appeared suddenly to Thérèse as a dream, an illusion which it was time to renounce. By a final artifice, the father of lies endeavoured to persuade her that she was not called to the religious life and should return to the world. Terrified, and enveloped as she was in dense darkness, the poor child conceived the happy idea of confiding this temptation without delay to her novice-mistress, whom she therefore asked to come with her out of the choir. Hearing the account of her illusion, Mère Marie des Anges laughed heartily and completely reassured Thérèse. The demon was conquered. Thérèse felt this immediately by the light which entered her soul.

Nor did the Divine Master refuse his faithful spouse the peace given to those who serve God even without sensible joy and consolation. "On the morning of September 8," she says, "a river of peace inundated my soul,[5] and in that peace, 'which surpasseth all understanding,'[6] I made my holy vows." And she adds: "At the end of that happy day, it was without sadness that I laid my crown of roses, according to custom, at the feet of the Blessed Virgin; I felt that time would never take from me my joy. . . ."[7]

But her crucified Spouse was to hearken fully to the remaining petitions of her heroic prayer. Martyrdom of heart, so ardently desired, was granted to her while awaiting the other.

The great act of profession is completed at Carmel by the symbolical ceremony of taking the veil. The date fixed for Thérèse was September 24. A slight improvement had given reason to hope that her beloved father would assist at the coming feast, and the thought of his dear presence brought her great joy. But, at the last moment, those in charge feared that the aged man's malady would be increased by strong emotion, and M. Martin did not come.

The generous-hearted child, so brave ever in adversity, could not now restrain her grief; she shed torrents of tears. To add to her disappointment, those around her expressed astonishment at her apparent weakness, and she was forced to make this painful admission: "My tears were not understood." But her valiant soul soon mastered its emotion, and she wrote to Céline:

> Everything was ready for the nuptial feast. Yet do you not think that something was lacking? Jesus had, it is true, already put many jewels in my casket, but one of incomparable beauty was undoubtedly wanting. This precious diamond Jesus has given me today; papa will not be here tomorrow. Céline, I own that my tears flowed fast; they are falling now while I write; I can hardly hold my pen. You know how ardently I longed

> to see our beloved father again. Now I realize that it is God's will he should not be present at my feast. He has permitted this solely to test our love. Jesus wants me to be an orphan; He wills that I be alone with Him alone, in order that He may unite Himself more closely to me. He will also repay me in Heaven the innocent joys He has denied me in exile.
>
> Today's trial is a sorrow difficult to understand. A joy had been offered to us which was quite possible and natural. We stretched out our hands . . . and could not grasp the longed-for consolation. But this is the work of no human hand, it is Jesus. Céline, understand your Thérèse. Let us both accept willingly this thorn presented to us. Tomorrow's feast will be for us a feast of tears, but I feel that Jesus will be so consoled. . . .[8]

Everything, in fact, combined to make Thérèse's veiling a feast of tears. Mgr. Hugonin, who had been counted upon to preside, did not come; several other incidents filled the day with bitterness and grief. The peace of God was ever, it is true, at the bottom of her chalice, and this thrice happy peace enabled the young religious to console Céline, grief-stricken too by their father's continued illness. Nothing could be more impressive than her words of comfort: "I understand all that you suffer; I understand your anguish for I share your grief. Ah, if I could but impart to you the peace that Jesus has infused into my soul even amidst bitter tears. Be consoled! All things pass away, our former life is gone; death too will pass, and then we shall enjoy life, true life for endless ages, for ever and ever."[9]

This appeal to the eternal recompense did not always assuage her sister's sorrow. When by her tender words of comfort in the parlour, Thérèse found herself unable to bring calm to the grief-rent heart, the fervent Carmelite would beseech the Divine Master Himself to console her sister, to shed light on the truths necessary for her soul's peace. She then remained calm and confident, persuaded that God had heard her prayer. It was even so, for at the next meeting she always found Céline serenely peaceful, with soul enlightened, inundated with joy which even she herself could not account for.

Thus began that religious apostolate which, after a few years' exercise on earth, was to perpetuate in heaven the good begun here below. Its influence was to extend far beyond the family circle.

During the canonical examination which preceded her profession, Thérèse Martin was asked to state the motives that had drawn her to the cloister. "I have come to Carmel," she said, "to save souls, and more especially to pray for priests."

This spiritual charity towards priests dated chiefly, as we know, from her pilgrimage to Italy; its activity increased according as the young nun realized more and more fully the greatness of the priesthood. She desired, as she said, to help in preserving the salt of the earth, by becoming in all humility an apostle of apostles, and in securing for them the grace of fruitful ministry in word and example. At times, carried away by her dream of love, she would fain be herself a priest in order to preach the Gospel to the most abandoned nations, and, as she has said, to die a martyr for Jesus Christ.[10]

This all-conquering ardour was soon to associate her, by means of prayer and sacrifice, in the work of two young missionaries who shall appear later in these pages.

At the moment, the unhappy state of one particular priest claimed all her compassion and assistance. She had heard of the celebrated Père Hyacinthe of the Carmelite Order, of his widely known defection from the Church, and of the errors to which he persistently adhered. She resolved to bring back this erring soul to God by prayer and sacrifice. She was destined to labour for his conversion till the very end of her life, offering even her last Communion for the unfortunate apostate. Events did not appear to justify her hope, for Hyacinthe Loyson died without at least public reconciliation with the Church. But the immediate witnesses of the end, which was terrifying to behold, said that at the last moment the dying man touched with his lips a cross which he continually carried, and expired with the words "O my sweet Jesus!" on his lips. Was not this a sign of long-delayed return to that God whom he had denied? Did not this last invocation express an act of repentance obtained by the unknown religious who had sacrificed herself for him?

The vocation to sacrifice which Thérèse had always distinctly felt since she had abandoned herself to Divine love, became more definite from the time she entered Carmel. Without doubt, the name Thérèse de l'Enfant Jésus which had been given her from the age of nine when she manifested her desire of becoming a Carmelite, corresponded now more than ever to a reality,[11] for her devotion to the Divine Child ever increased.[12] But, as she loved to contemplate in its entirety the Sacred Humanity, she could not separate the mysteries of the Crib from the Cross of Calvary. This it was which made her receive with joyous eagerness the favour of adding to her name in religion the title "of the Holy Face."

If her love for the Child Jesus led her to surrender herself into His hands as a plaything in the hands of an infant, she saw in the Holy Face the symbol of every humiliation endured by the Saviour, and she drew from such contemplation the ever-constant wish to suffer and to be humiliated for His sake. The sight alone of that Divine Face bruised and bleeding moved her to inexpressible tenderness. Her sister, Mère Agnès de Jésus, one day said to her as they stood before the traditional image which is venerated at Tours: "What a pity that the eyes are lowered, that we cannot see His gaze." "Oh no," Thérèse replied, "it is better so, for otherwise we could not look on His Face without dying of love."[13] She always kept a picture of the Holy Face in her Breviary, and she placed it near her in her stall during prayer; she was to have it hung later on her bed-curtain during her prolonged agony.[14]

Habitual contemplation of the Saviour's tortured features, and the very name she had adopted, were continual sources of encouragement to Thérèse in her way of redemption by suffering. The rôle of victim, so joyously undertaken in her very childhood, so courageously fulfilled in the novitiate, was to grow more defined, to take a fuller signification, until, by an authentic act, she consecrated herself for ever in this quality to God's merciful Love.

The ardour of the young nun in the Master's service was stimulated at this time by a conversation, in itself apparently indifferent, with one of her cousins in the parlour. Jeanne Guérin had married an excellent Catholic, Dr. La Néele, eight days after Thérèse received the veil, and during her next visit at the Carmel she spoke of the attentions that she lavished on her husband. The newly-made spouse of the King of kings was stirred to emulation by what she heard. "It shall not be said," she told herself, "that a woman in the world will do more for her husband, an ordinary mortal, than I for my well-beloved Jesus." Then she resolved more firmly than ever that she would offer her flowers of abnegation to the heavenly Bridegroom to rejoice and console Him, while she alone should feel their thorns.[15]

The first mortification which she was destined to undergo at this time was a renewal of the troubles of mind endured in the course of her novitiate. Père Pichon was no longer there to encourage her secret aspirations towards absolute confidence in God. She was suffering from interior difficulties which she made the matter of continual sacrifice, when a Recollet from the monastery of Caen, Père Alexis, came to preach the Retreat of 1891. This religious was widely known and appreciated throughout the country for his apostolic work, but up to that time his name had been more associated with the conversion of working-men and servants than with spiritual success in giving retreats to nuns. Thérèse, who knew him by reputation, feared that she would not be able to lay before him her numerous difficulties which he, no doubt, would consider scrupulous in the extreme. But, through the hidden workings of the Holy Spirit, she was soon undeceived and reassured. From the very first interview she felt that she was understood, and confided unhesitatingly in the worthy religious. The result was as remarkable as it was immediate. "The Father," she says, "launched me under full sail on the waters of confidence and love which attracted me so powerfully, but on which I had not had the courage to go forward. He told me that my failings did not displease the good God. 'I hold His place at this moment,' he added, 'in your regard. Well then, I assure you that He is well satisfied with your soul.'"

To say that the faults of even a Carmelite "would not displease God" leaves room for misinterpretation. But Thérèse did not deceive herself. She recalled to mind that a mother is ever ready to pardon the little failings of her child, that she is not grieved by these slight faults for she knows they are involuntary, and remembering that Jesus is infinitely more tender than the best of mothers, she was fully reassured on the state of her soul. The heavenly Spouse found therein, it is true, nothing but failings and frailties which are inseparable from human nature. These would never separate Him from her. What relief and joy in that thought. . . . Such pacifying assurance enabled her to face unwaveringly and even with joy another series of trials.

The short sketch which we have given of the life at Carmel shows that the mortifications and penances enjoined by rule are severe; but even in the most fervent communities, it is not these austerities which cause the greatest suffering to human nature.

"My greatest penance," St. Bernard has said, "is community life." Who is there, in fact, who does not know that diversity of character, difference in education, the play of natural sympathies and natural antipathies which we can counteract but which we are unable wholly to suppress, form, for the most fervent religious, innumerable and continuous occasions of suffering? And if this source of trial is to be found amongst religious who have access to the world outside their community, what of those who are cloistered, where a small number of persons, always the same, live together and constantly meet one another? Not only was Thérèse de l'Enfant Jésus not spared this mortification, but it was increased by two choir sisters whose difficult characters made her early days in the religious life harder still.

The Mother Prioress was not entirely unaware of the sufferings which the young nun might experience from this source, but, foreseeing, no doubt, the eminent virtue to which Sœur Thérèse would attain, she appeared desirous of affording her occasions for merit. In this she judged correctly of her daughter, for the generous Carmelite always surpassed the expectations of those who seized occasion to humiliate her. Not with the lips alone but from her heart had she said to Jesus, "May no one ever give me a thought, may I be trodden under foot like a little grain of sand."[16]

Now, more than ever, was this heroic desire to be fulfilled to the letter. Not that ordinarily her Sisters had the intention of making her suffer; rather was it by reason of that instinctive tendency to accept the services and overlook the privations of those who never complain.

Thus we find Thérèse, ever ingenious regarding means of self-sacrifice, offering her services in winter for such portion of the washing as was to be done in the open air with cold water, a task which cost her a great deal, and, in summer, remaining by preference in the steaming hot laundry, where she willingly received full in the face the soapy water with which the Sister opposite frequently, though inadvertently, splashed her. Thus it was also that she expressed the desire to help in her duties one of the two Sisters mentioned above whose gloomy disposition made her a burden to the whole community.

These things mortified above all self-love and the tendency of nature to seek bodily ease; others of a different kind affected more directly her health. The Carmelite fare, one may suppose, was frugal enough, but the young nun found means of adding to the ordinary privations. As she never complained, and left uncontradicted the impression that she was of robust constitution, she was treated without any special regard to her health by the Sisters in the kitchen who, for example, simply passed on to her the indigestible foods which others were unable to take.

As regards clothing, the same spirit of mortification was apparent. Not alone did Thérèse seek to obtain the poorest material, but her "alpargates" were nearly always in a quite worn-out condition. These "alpargates" are a kind of sandal, the soles are made of plaited hemp sewn together, and they are in themselves fairly well calculated to exercise the virtue of patience. What must they have been when much worn and all out of shape?

Treated with severity by the Mother Prioress, her self-love humiliated, deprived of her sisters' companionship, except during the occasional visits in the parlour, submitted to continual bodily mortification, and above all a stranger now to spiritual consolation, was Thérèse then without comfort, was she without joy in the monastery where she had hoped to find the place of her rest? Far from it, for the greater part of her suffering was welcomed as the fulfilment of her own desires and wishes, and was accepted with eagerness for love of the Spouse whose divine liberality thus satisfying her thirst for immolation, she recognized in every trial. She walked henceforth joyously in the "little way of spiritual childhood" which we shall describe later on, and which she knew how to "strew with flowers of little sacrifices" even to the end. Besides the fact that she never, even in moments of deepest tribulation, lost that peace which, on her own admission, "surpasseth all understanding," she lived in the society of souls for the greater part most fervent whose example and counsel were to her a perpetual *Sursum corda.*

She was later to form a truly spiritual friendship with certain of these, and she loved to record the last counsels of such as, after a life of austerity, seemed on the eve of receiving their crown. Thus it was that through charity, as well as for her own edification at the sight of a holy life now drawing to its close, she visited in the infirmary the venerable Foundress, Mère Geneviève de Sainte-Thérèse. One Sunday, the invalid noticing that Thérèse was discreetly retiring in favour of some older visitors, said to her, "Wait, my little one, I have just a word to say to you. You are continually asking me for a spiritual bouquet. To-day, then, I give you this: *'Serve God in peace and joy; remember, my child, that our God is the God of Peace.'"*

It so happened that, on that very day, Thérèse was suffering keenly under the weight of an interior desolation. The words of the venerated Mother appeared as a response from heaven to her anxious soul, and joy exceeding great filled her heart as she came away. It was one of those smiles given by the Well-Beloved in return for her sacrifices. He continued to multiply His marks of encouragement, without, however, suppressing the trials.

When, some time later, Mère Geneviève was in her last agony, Sœur Thérèse for two hours watched with the Community beside the death-bed. By a design of Providence, she felt overpowered by a sort of insensibility which distressed and saddened her. "But," she says, "at the moment of her birth in heaven, my interior disposition changed completely. In an instant, I was filled with joy and indescribable fervour as if the sanctified soul of our holy Mother had at that moment given me a share of the happiness she enjoyed, for I am convinced that she went straight to heaven."[17]

Out of tender respect, Thérèse conceived the idea of obtaining an almost imperceptible relic of the saintly Carmelite. During her last agony a tear had glistened in her eyelash and remained there even when she had been laid in the Choir as is customary after death. Sœur Thérèse took a little piece of fine linen, and approaching stealthily in the evening, she carried away from the death-cold face this impalpable relic of the deeply-regretted Mother who had done her so much good. She desired to surround the dear remains with every attention even to the end, and being Sacristan at the time, she had the privilege of arranging round the coffin the flowers sent as tokens of veneration by the inhabitants of Lisieux. This she was doing with filial care, when a lay-sister, yielding for the moment to ill-humour, so far forgot herself as to say, "Ah, you know well how to put in the foremost place the wreath sent by your own family, while you leave in the background the bouquets of the poor." Nothing could be less justified than this reproach. Thérèse, nevertheless, replied with infinite sweetness, "I am thankful to you, Sister. You are right. Give me the moss-covered cross sent by the workmen; I am going to place it in front."[18]

Thus did Jesus mingle wormwood in every cup for the young religious, even in those that had held the promise of a fleeting joy.

This admirable fortitude in the face of disappointments was equalled by courage in act. Employed, since her entrance, in the humblest, and at times the most fatiguing tasks, such as sweeping the stairs, refectory and other community rooms, she never shirked the burden of labour.[19]

In the beginning of 1891 she was assigned as assistant to the Sister sacristan, having care of the vestments, and preparing the sacred vessels for the Holy Sacrifice. No duty could be more in harmony with her devotion to the Eucharist. Before placing the particles destined to become the Body of Christ in the Ciborium, she loved to see her own reflection at the bottom of the golden vessel where the Holy of Holies was soon, to repose. When, one morning, after Mass, she discovered a tiny particle of the Sacred Host on the paten, she called a few of her companions, who she knew would be pleased, and adored with them the Sacred Species with the deepest reverence, carefully leaving the Particle on the paten for the priest himself to remove.

But she was destined to be taken from her daily duties by a terrible calamity. The infectious and serious illness known as "*la grippe*," or influenza, which, during the last thirty years, has so many times decimated the world, made its first appearance, as we know, in France about the year 1890. This visitation of the dread malady was particularly virulent and proved fatal in numerous cases.

In the last days of 1891, the epidemic broke out in the Carmel of Lisieux. All the Sisters were attacked except two who entirely escaped contagion, and Sœur Thérèse de l'Enfant Jésus who was only slightly affected. Nothing could be more pitiful than the condition of the community during this awful visitation. The more seriously stricken were nursed by others who were scarcely able to drag themselves along. Death hovered over the monastery, and when a sister had succumbed, she had to be abandoned immediately in order to attend to those most in danger. In this house of sickness Thérèse, who was then scarcely nineteen and herself attacked by the malady, gave proof of remarkable resource and unbounded devotedness. Though unaided in the Sacristy to prepare for the funeral ceremonies which took place three times within a few days, yet she so managed as to give also the help needed by the sick.

One morning she had a presentiment that one of the Sisters was dead. She hastened to the cell through the darkness, and found her already clothed and extended on the bed, motionless in death.[20] "I was not in the least afraid," she declares, "and running to the Sacristy, I quickly brought a blessed candle, and placed on her head a crown of roses. Amidst all these trials, I felt the Hand of the good God; and that His Heart was keeping watch over us. Without effort our dear Sisters passed to a better life; on their faces there was an expression of celestial joy; they seemed to rest in a sweet sleep."[21]

Meanwhile, the inexorable Superior of the community, M. Delatröette, came to visit his daughters in their trial. He saw the lately professed nun at her work, she whose entrance he had signalized with such disquieting prophecy. Obliged to recognize her mature formation and rare virtue, he rid himself of all prejudice, and afterwards, with tears in his eyes, spoke in terms of admiration of her whom he had at first so little understood.

About this time, the saint's self-denial was to be rewarded by a sweet and intense happiness. The Abbé Youf, who was well aware of her great longing to communicate frequently, felt grieved at not being able to allow her to approach the Holy Table daily. But, on this point, Mère Marie de Gonzague, insisting on the rights which tradition in French convents gave to superiors, proved inflexible. Nevertheless, on the occasion of the unavoidable disorder caused by the epidemic, the confessor took it upon himself to allow the fervent child the spiritual support of daily communion. The privilege lasted for some months after the influenza had disappeared. "Ah, how sweet it was," writes Thérèse, ". . . I had not sought this exception, but I was happy indeed to be united each day to my Well-Beloved."

This was in truth the most Divine of those joys which uplifted the heart of the young nun, making her forget many sorrows. But it must also be remembered that Thérèse was never egoistic in seeking heavenly consolation. On her own testimony, she desired her Saviour's visits not for her personal satisfaction, but solely "for the pleasure given to

Him." Hence her communions were most fervent, but usually brought her very little sensible consolation.

Immediately on receiving the Sacred Host, she invited, as she so simply tells us, all the angels and saints to come and chant in her heart, and with her, canticles of love. It seemed to her that Jesus would then be pleased at seeing Himself so magnificently received, and she shared in the joy of the Divine Guest, no matter how great might be her own aridity and spiritual darkness.

For Sœur Thérèse, the first stages of the religious life had been strewn with more thorns than roses. But later, with purpose, no doubt, of encouraging her on the steep path of sacrifice, the heavenly Spouse was pleased to grant a number of her desires, and even childish longings of which, with her happy familiarity, she had told Him. The essentially artistic soul of the young nun had always felt the attraction of beauty in its various forms, and, even before making the trial, she felt convinced that the æsthetic realization of these beloved visions would not be impossible to her. In truth, "all the Muses dwelt within her," silent as yet, but ready to burst forth in song. She was ten years of age, when her father one day told Céline that he was arranging about drawing-lessons for her, and asked Thérèse would she too like to learn. She was just going to answer joyfully in the affirmative when her sister, Marie, remarked that she had not the same aptitude as Céline. M. Martin yielded to her opinion, and the little one, realizing that this was a good opportunity of offering a great sacrifice to Jesus, remained silent. But, even after her entrance into Carmel, she still wondered how she had the strength to refrain from speaking on that occasion.

Seeing her sister Pauline, her "little mother," paint charming miniatures and compose sweet verses, she greatly desired to imitate her, even though she had no previous training. The Divine Master, while recalling to her mind the vanity of these human accomplishments, and how powerless they were to bring her perfect joy or even to express her boundless aspirations, deigned to give her that creative gift which constitutes the power and charm of the artist.

Thus we find the young Carmelite executing at the first attempt and almost without lessons, minute paintings on church ornaments, or on little vellum leaflets for circulation. Moreover, she undertook out of pure obedience the decoration of an interior oratory where the fresco from her brush still excites admiration by its grace and delicacy of execution, and at the same time, encourages devotion by the angelic expression of the cherubim there represented.

But the nuns were still more surprised on reading the first verses composed by Sœur Thérèse de l'Enfant Jésus at the demand of her superiors, poems inspired by piety, deeply penetrated with thoughts from nature or the poetry of the past. Often she composed hymns of lofty poetic thought and expression destined to commemorate a profession, a clothing, or some other Carmelite solemnity. The words were usually adapted to an air already known, which was decided on beforehand.

How did Thérèse find time to compose these hymns which from the first had power to charm the community? Who had taught her the science of prosody so as to handle with perfect ease the most varied metres? No leisure was ever specially given her for literary composition. At the request of a superior or a companion, she mentally grouped her thoughts together in sweet and flowing verse while polishing a floor or arranging the chasubles in a press,[22] and as she did not wish to take from the time allotted to ordinary work, she had to wait until evening to pen, in the silence of her cell, on some loose slip of paper, the couplets which she had retained in her memory.[23] On Sundays alone did she find a little more opportunity to compose her verses, during the few hours left at a Carmelite's own disposal. As to rules of versification, she must undoubtedly have been instructed by the Divine Artist Himself, for her sister, Pauline, only found it necessary to correct in her first poems a few mistakes in prosody.

What, then, is the true value of these compositions which profane writers, incapable of real appreciation, have thought might be classed with the little pious objects usually made by nuns, works of ingeniousness or patience wherein art, in its true sense, is lacking? We notice first of all that the hymns, intended by Thérèse as an incentive to greater fervour in her companions, have considerable doctrinal value. In them we can see the influence of Sacred Scripture, and at times of St. John of the Cross, whose lyric fervour visibly inspires certain pages. The poem *"Jésus, rappelle-toi"* is simply a résumé in poetical language of the principal mysteries of our Saviour's life. Like the hymns of Blessed Grignion de Montfort, the young Carmelite's poetry almost always drives home some dogmatic truth. This fact alone should be sufficient recommendation to pastors who want really instructive hymns for the use of their flocks. But Thérèse's compositions possess also a literary value far superior to the majority of hymns now used in our churches.

Elaborate finish or research will be sought for in vain in her poems. Intended as they were to be sung, they claim on that account considerable liberty of composition. She must be forgiven the multitudinous comparisons taken from flowers because of her predilection for those symbols of joy and innocence so graciously fashioned by the Hand of God. Notwithstanding all this, what a singular charm there is—a charm which Racine would have appreciated—in the purity and freshness of these soulful or nature-inspired poems.

Neither is there anything artificial in Thérèse's compositions. Her whole soul springs forth in streams of sweet and touching melody. We find in them the expression of her own childlike candour together with her refined and profound realization of spiritual things. Her songs tell of her entire abandonment to her Well-Beloved, and her numberless devices to obtain from Him blessings or marks of tenderness; her happy contemplation too of Divine mysteries, and her unbounded desire for the conversion of the infidel and the sinner. We see in them her perfect detachment from self, and above all her love for her heavenly Spouse, that love which was "an abyss of which she could never sound the depths."

Flowers, as we have remarked, hold a large place in her poetry, and in fact, as Père Jubaru says, "her verses fall like a shower of petals, fresh and lightly floating, delicately coloured and sweet with an exquisite perfume. They are not of marble or onyx, creations like impersonal Parnassian sonnets; they are living productions."

And he writes again: "Thérèse's heart sang in the out-pouring of her spiritual joy as sings a nightingale in the midst of the flower-strewn fields of May. Her heart sang in the severe constraint of trial as sings the crystal stream amid the rocks of a rude ravine."[24]

We shall give some of these verses when relating the circumstances in which they were composed. Let us note just now another of those gracious surprises which seemed to the loving saint as marks of tender affection from her loving Saviour. We know how wild flowers delighted her. There is no doubt that, in making herself a prisoner at fifteen, she had counted as one of her greatest sacrifices that of giving up her rambles in springtime through the hawthorn thickets and the green fields studded with innumerable flowers. She expected in the convent nothing more to feast her eyes on than the red-bricked cloister walls or the bare and un-adorned whiteness of her cell. But scarcely had she entered Carmel, when from friends, known and unknown, came a profusion of sweet-scented flowers destined to honour the Child Jesus, whose statue she had the charge of decorating, and also that she herself might enjoy the sight of familiar flowers again. Never before had she handled so many corn-flowers, poppies, and daisies. One flower, however, was wanting, the humblest among the humble, but one which, for that very reason, she had gathered with predilection. This was the corn-cockle, hated by the farmer as it damages his crops, but charming to the artist-eye which discerns its graceful beauty.[25] Thérèse was just regretting that she might never again see this little flower, when she caught sight of its mauve corolla peeping from a bouquet left for her in the parlour—a new instance of the solicitude of her Divine Spouse, He who had sent her the snow for her reception-day. Her joy was childlike, tempered, however, by a vivid realization of the nothingness of these passing satisfactions, even of these gifts which have no value except as a means of giving praise to eternal Love.

With her characteristic confidence, Thérèse had expressed to her Well-Beloved another desire, higher and of deeper import, since she thought it concerned in some degree the glory of the Almighty. She wished to see Céline join her very soon in her holy retreat, so that she might initiate her into the joys of perfect immolation.

But how could such a hope be entertained, since Céline was so necessary in the world as the devoted nurse and angel-guardian of her father who was still plunged in the dark night of suffering? When the paralysis had become general, M. Martin was taken back to Lisieux, where he lived with his daughters Léonie and Céline in a house near the Guérin family. There the ever deepening lethargy gradually gained dominion over all his faculties. It was possible, however, to take him once to the Carmel for a last farewell to his daughters. At the moment of parting, he raised his eyes, and pointing towards the eternal meeting-place, he said simply in a voice choked with emotion, "In Heaven."

Far from fainting under the long-continued weight of this cross, Thérèse set herself to sustain her sisters' fortitude. She encouraged Céline especially in her filial devotedness, fostered her hopes regarding the religious life, and did everything possible to preserve her against the attacks of the spirit of the world. With this end in view, she wrote to her sister as often as the rule permitted. Hence that correspondence so full of poetic thought, so penetrated with the sacred unction of Scripture, that it enabled Céline, while yet outside the convent walls, to share beforehand in the happiness of the cloister.

Thérèse unhesitatingly proposed to her sister the highest doctrines of perfection, and preached to her the virtues of whose efficacy she herself had become convinced in following her "little way of childhood." First of all her own favourite virtue, love of lowliness and oblivion. Céline must be "the dew-drop which refreshes for one night the 'Lily of the valley,'" a figure of the hidden God.

"Happy little dew-drop, known to God alone, do not stay to contemplate the rivers of the world in their noisy course; envy not even the clear rivulet winding through the meadow. Undoubtedly its low, sweet song has charms, but it can be heard by creatures, and the calyx of the Flower of the fields could not contain it. How little we must be in order to approach Jesus. Oh, how few souls there are who desire to be little and unknown."[26]

Notwithstanding how feeble the means at her disposal, the young girl did not hesitate in face of the great apostolic mission so little understood by ordinary Christians. "What a mystery!" exclaims Thérèse.

> Is not Jesus all-powerful? Do not all creatures belong to Him who has created them? Why has He humbled Himself to say: "*Pray ye the Lord of the harvest that He send labourers. . .*"? Ah, His love for us is so incomprehensible, so tender, that it is His will to do nothing without associating us in the work. The Creator of the universe awaits the prayer of a poor little soul to save a multitude of others redeemed like herself at the price of His blood. Our vocation in Carmel is not to go as reapers into our Father's harvest. Jesus has not said to us: "Cast down your eyes, reap the fields"; our mission is still more sublime. "Lift up your eyes and see . . ." See that in heaven there are empty places; it is for you to fill them. . . . You are as Moses praying on the mountain; ask from Me labourers, and I will send them; I wait only for a prayer, a sigh from your heart.[27]

Though transported to these heights and associated in these sublime purposes, Céline experienced, nevertheless, the bitterness of aridity. Her loving Carmelite sister then unfolded to her the secret of turning to profit these hours of anguish:

> Dear little sister, sweet echo of my soul, your Thérèse does not dwell on the mountain heights at this moment. But see, when I am plunged in aridity, unable to pray or practise virtue, I look for little occasions, insignificant opportunities, to give pleasure to Jesus. A smile, for instance, or a kind word when I want to remain silent and to show weariness. If I can find no such occasions, I at least tell Him many times that I love Him. This is not difficult, and it helps to keep the fire burning in my

> heart. Even should the fire of love seem extinct, I would still throw little straws on the ashes, and I am quite sure that it would revive.[28]

Each summer from this time onward, M. Martin with his two daughters spent some months with his brother-in-law at the château de la Musse, which belonged to the Guérin family, and was situated near Évreux. If the vast solitudes and enchanting landscapes which Céline could there enjoy were, in Thérèse's opinion, well calculated to elevate her mind, it was, on the other hand, difficult to exclude completely every worldly influence from the hospitable and beautiful château.

At Lisieux, also, there were chance occurrences more or less dissipating for souls desirous of living continually in the presence of God. Once, on the occasion of a marriage, Céline thought that she could not well refuse an invitation to be present at a dance. Thérèse, having heard of this, became anxious immediately, and summoned her sister to the parlour to give her advice. Céline, thinking her precautions a little exaggerated, remarked that it was not necessary to "make herself ridiculous." Then Thérèse, usually so affectionate towards her sister, did not hesitate to speak in words of indignant sorrow. "O Céline," she entreated, "think of the three young Hebrews who preferred to be thrown into the fiery furnace rather than bend the knee before a golden statue. And you, the spouse of Jesus by your vow of chastity,[29] would you imitate the folly of the age and adore the world's golden statue by giving yourself to dangerous pleasures? Take heed of this warning given on behalf of God."

Insistence was unnecessary, for Céline was not in the least attracted by the dance. Obliged, nevertheless, to be present at the *soirée,* to which her uncle brought her, she refused for a long time, even at the risk of offending several, to join in the amusement. In the end, she was, to use her own expression, "literally forced" by a young cavalier. But, astonishing to relate, both one and the other found themselves immediately as though paralyzed, so that they were not able to go through a single movement of the dance. In vain did Céline endeavour to follow the music in order to save her partner from confusion; she could not succeed. The two dancers, held by an invisible force, could do nothing but walk "with solemn steps," until the young cavalier, having conducted Céline back to her seat, quietly slipped away much abashed, and did not dare to appear again. Céline ever afterwards believed that she owed this intervention to the prayers of her dear Thérèse.[30]

This incident was the only diversion of any importance in her life while she was nursing her father. Her sorrowful duties as nurse were soon to end. On July 29, 1894, her father died at M. Guérin's house, the château de la Musse, after repaying her devotion and tender care with a last look of loving gratitude. Her filial task had been long, and generously accomplished. She was now free to enter the haven for which she had longed through so many years.

But the question arose: was the Carmel of Lisieux to receive four sisters of the Martin family? Would not this be against the traditions, or even the spirit of the Order? Mère Marie de Gonzague, then Mistress of novices and Council Sister, strongly encouraged the Prioress, Mère Agnès de Jésus, to make this exception. She adduced the exceptional dispositions of the four sisters in support of her recommendation. However, the fear of creating a precedent which might later open the door to abuses, seemed to haunt the mind of the one nun who made no secret of her opposition to Céline being admitted.

Faced with this obstacle, Thérèse set herself with fervent hope to invoke her father, now with God in His Kingdom, he who had been so anxious while living to consecrate all his daughters to Him. The dear saint begged Jesus to remove the obstacle quickly. She even dared, one day, to ask after Holy Communion, that this might be granted as a sign that her father had entered at once into the joys of heaven. Scarcely had she finished her thanksgiving, when she met the nun who had held out in opposition to Céline's entrance. This Sister called her and as though almost ashamed of her former attitude, told her earnestly how happy she would be to see Céline in the Carmel.

Nothing now prevented the young girl from rejoining the dear companion of her childhood in her holy retreat. Did Thérèse fear that with Céline's desire for immolation in an austere Order was mingled some small share of human joy at the prospect of being once more with her sisters? In any case, she wished to communicate to the future postulant a presentiment she had of the days to come, which was well calculated to overthrow any dreams of a long and happy reunion of the four sisters beneath the convent roof.

When everything had been arranged, she wrote to Céline:

> This is perhaps the last time, my dear little sister, that my pen must serve me for a talk with you; the good God has granted my dearest wish.
>
> Come, we will suffer together, and then *the good God will take one of us*, and the others will remain a little while longer in exile. Now *hearken to what I am going to say to you. Never, never will God separate us. If I die before you, do not think that I shall ever be separated from your soul; never shall we have been more united*. Do not, above all, be troubled by my prophecy, it is but childishness. I am not ill; I am strong as iron; *but God can break iron as easily as potter's clay....*
>
> Our dear father is making us feel his presence in a way that is profoundly touching. After five long years of deathlike separation, what joy to find him as of old, and even more fatherly. Oh, how well will he repay you for all your care of him. You have been his angel; he will now be yours. See, he has not yet been a month in heaven, and already by his powerful intercession all your projects succeed. It is now easy for him to arrange what concerns us, therefore has he had less trouble for Céline than he had for his poor little queen.[31]

Not quite a month later, on September 14, 1894, Céline was received into the Carmel, where she was to become Sœur Geneviève de la Sainte-Face et de Sainte-Thérèse.

Jesus had royally fulfilled the desires of His mystic spouse. Her supernatural love of suffering had been, and was to be to the very end, superabundantly satisfied; that interior voice which, from her earliest years, made the "little flower" believe that she would be plucked in the springtime of her life seemed an answer to the secret aspiration which made her hail death as a messenger of joy. She had now nothing further to wish for except that she might love Jesus even to folly. This love without reserve, without limit or condition, will be henceforth the sole guiding force of her actions and her life, as her only attitude towards the merciful and all-powerful Saviour will be that of abandonment, of supreme and perfect self-surrender.

9

Interior Life at the Carmel—Divine Love the Source of All Thérèse's Perfection—Qualities of This Love and Its Principal Manifestations—Thérèse's Devotion to the Blessed Virgin and the Saints

With Céline's entrance into the convent closes, so to speak, the external biography of Thérèse de l'Enfant Jésus. What remains to be noted before her happy birth into life eternal cannot be classified as events, a name not to be given to the minute details which made up her life as refectorian, portress, linen-keeper, or even sacristan. Only her office as assistant-mistress of novices gives matter for varied and striking narratives. Thus we shall henceforth be solely occupied with the consideration of the Saint's life of love within these walls which cut off earthly horizons and oblige her to keep ever fixed on Heaven her eyes, withdrawn from the vanities of earth.

We have described the awakening and early growth of this life, in delineating her ingenuous childhood and youth, filled with eagerness for her spiritual espousals with Jesus. It remains for us to give the characteristics of this union, the principal actions which rooted it firmly in the "garden enclosed" of the Spouse, and its consequent fruits whether for the glory of the Well-Beloved, or for Thérèse's own happiness, or for the good of the souls around her.

To this enumeration will naturally be joined a rapid glance at the principal traits which characterized her love for her neighbour, the second object of the Master's great commandment.

Her other supernatural qualities being in the Saint's own estimation only the expansion of love, we shall have to describe later her growth in monastic virtues, properly so called, under the influence of Divine charity. Then we shall make known the "little way of spiritual childhood" that she believed it her duty to reveal at the end of her life, with the different means of sanctification therein inculcated which she herself had continually practised.

Certain spiritual writers give love as the culminating point of all the other virtues. Such is not Thérèse's theory; on the contrary, she makes all advancement in the ways of God proceed from love. "You ask of me," she wrote to her cousin, "a way to arrive at perfection. I know of only one—Love."[1]

Concerning her methods of progress she was one day questioned: "You must have had to strive hard in order to conquer self so completely?" "Oh, it is not that," she said. And we find elsewhere the explanation of her answer. "Certain directors advise us, I know, to count our acts of virtue in order to advance in the way of perfection. But my Director, who is Jesus, does not teach me to count my acts, He directs me *to do all through love.*"[2] On the eve of her death she was able to say: *"I have never given the good God anything but love."*

Her confidence in this method was inspired by its perfect conformity with St. Paul's teaching according to which the most perfect of gifts is nothing without love,[3] and also by its intimate connection with this maxim of St. John of the Cross: "The smallest movement of pure love is of more benefit to the Church than all other works put together." She could have found the same teaching, had she read the writings of St. Francis de Sales, in a characteristic reply given by the eminent doctor to a nun of his time: "I wish," she said, "to acquire love by humility." "I," he replied, "wish to acquire humility by love."

Besides, the wish to make love the basis of every action had come to Thérèse as the effect of grace. She had so perfectly corresponded, even from earliest childhood, to the appeals of the God of love that Divine charity, infused into her soul at baptism, had power ever since the dawn of reason to control all her actions.

Moreover, this constant love which was to be the law of her life must not be taken for simply a series of affective emotions. We have seen with what generosity she conquered herself while yet in the world, in order to please Jesus. As a Carmelite, self-effacement, self-conquest, and self-sacrifice will be now, more than ever, the continual exercise of her love.

Let us consider some of those actions which reveal the energy, generosity, disinterestedness, and delicacy of her charity, particularly in the years that followed her profession. We have seen Thérèse Martin as a young girl, and even as a child, combat with indefatigable courage the little faults and imperfections over which grace had not yet obtained the mastery. Even in Carmel she had to strive, at least in the beginning, against her natural tendencies, not yet completely subdued.

We know how much it cost her to observe the rule of never excusing oneself. She tells of another point which caused her many a struggle, in which she gained victories from the first. "During my novitiate," she says, "I found it very difficult, on account of my great timidity, to ask permission for certain mortifications customary in our convents. But I was always most faithful in doing this."[4]

She was asked to undertake almost without any preparation little works of painting. She consented heartily, but it happened sometimes that, in her absence, an absent-minded companion threw her brushes and other instruments into disorder, mislaying perhaps a ruler or penknife. On perceiving this, Thérèse, so methodical by nature, very nearly saw "her patience abandon her." But she hastened to "take hold of it with both hands" and gently reclaimed the missing articles.

The religious life also held for Thérèse combats of a different order, wherein she won, for love of Jesus, more difficult victories. In the cloistered and silent life of a Carmelite nun, nature finds some relief in speaking to the only person with whom the rule allows conversation outside recreation hours, the Prioress of the convent. With her extremely sensitive soul, Sœur Thérèse de l'Enfant Jésus would have become attached to Mère Marie de Gonzague, if the good mother had not thought it necessary, for motives no doubt praiseworthy, to discourage her. In spite of all, the young religious loved these little conferences with her Prioress, and if she had listened to her natural inclinations, she would, in order to approach her, have resorted to the "pretext of having numberless permissions to ask." Her heart urged her on, but scrupulous fidelity to duty forbade her to yield to its promptings. At times, the temptation was so strong that Thérèse had, as she tells us, to pass rapidly by the Mother Prioress's cell. She would even "cling to the banister of the stairs so that she might not return."

This natural attraction was conquered. Another victory undoubtedly more meritorious was gained over a strong and persistent antipathy. A certain nun was a continual source of trial to Thérèse, and we know what a burden, and how depressing constantly recurring little contrarieties can become when there is not much to divert the mind. But the dear saint did not neglect such an opportunity of offering a fine sheaf of sacrifices to her heavenly Spouse. "I set myself," she says "to do for this Sister what I would have done for the person I loved best. Every time I met her, I prayed to the good God for her; but I did not content myself with that, I tried to render every possible service, and when tempted to answer her in a disagreeable manner, I hastened to give her instead an amiable smile. When the demon tempted me too violently, and if I could do so without her perceiving my inward struggle, I fled from the fight like a deserting soldier."[5]

It was not alone the natural tendencies of character that had to be combated, but also a violent and distressing temptation with which the demon by Divine permission afflicted Thérèse. She had experienced in the world, as we know, periods of spiritual darkness; but one would naturally expect that in the convent, wholly devoted to her life of love, she would no longer find veiled from the eyes of faith the Divine realities which she adored and praised. Yet such was not the case, and the following acknowledgment made only a year before her death reveals interior anguish infinitely more distressing than all the mortifications of community life. "When I sing of the happiness of heaven, of the eternal possession of God, I feel no joy, for I sing simply what I wish to believe."

Did the fervent nun abandon herself to this obsession which lasted long months? She tells in her Autobiography how hard was the struggle, but also of the indomitable efforts which secured her peace of soul.

> When the enemy wishes to entice me to combat, I behave on every occasion as a brave soldier should. Knowing that to fight a duel is an unworthy act, I turn my back on the adversary without even looking him in the face and run to my Jesus. I tell Him that I am willing to shed my blood to testify to my belief that there is a heaven. He knows well that, although I have not the consolations of faith, I strive to work by faith. I have uttered more acts of faith during this one year than in all the rest of my life.[6]

After a period of combat wherein all the graces of the religious life strengthened her resistence, nature was at last conquered. Thérèse's soul was ready for the highest ascents; she set forth on her career of love with a generosity which from that time onward was to be one of the characteristics of her life of immolation in Carmel.

This prodigality in giving herself was not of recent date, for at the age of three she formed the habit of never refusing anything to Jesus, and shortly before her first Communion she wrote: "I try every day to make a great many little sacrifices. I do my best to let no opportunity escape me."[7]

But when once impregnated with the maxims of St. Teresa, and entirely surrendered to the spirit of Carmel, she did not fear to say: "Complete immolation of self is the only thing worthy to be called love," and she acted accordingly.

There is no true love here below without suffering. Whoever really loves Jesus must, in the words of St. Paul, consummate in his own flesh the work of Calvary.[8] He must also associate himself in the Divine work of expiation for abandoned souls, remembering that the salvation of souls is won by the shedding of blood.[9]

Now Thérèse, as we know, longed to offer Jesus an efficacious love, she wanted to love Him "as never before had He been loved." Thus it was that she embraced with ever growing ardour the most rigorous mortifications, to advance His kingdom and to give Him pleasure. First of all by physical suffering. We are already aware of the privations imposed by the Carmelite rule itself, all of which Thérèse embraced without the least relaxation. She also found means of supplementing in her own case the rigours of the ordinary observance in order to unite herself more closely by love to her Saviour, humiliated, torn by stripes, and expiring on a gibbet.

The privations in question appear slight if taken separately; the real mortification consists in continual practice, therefore she faithfully observed the minutest recommendations and customs of religious life, as, for instance, never to lean for support against anything without permission, to hold oneself erect, to avoid raising the hands to the face in choir, never to seek a too easy position, not even for the sake of rest.

Except in case of absolute necessity, she never wiped away the perspiration which, during certain heavy manual labour, rolled down her face. This would have been, in her opinion, a means of showing that she felt oppressively hot, and so of calling attention to her sufferings. Then, in winter, she exposed to the cold without any precaution her poor hands, usually all swollen and covered with painful chilblains.

The Carmelite rule itself enjoins real penances, such as the frequent use of the discipline. One day, when Thérèse was speaking on this subject to a novice who needed to be urged forward in the spiritual life, the latter made the observation that persons who use these instruments of penance, instinctively avoid certain movements which inflict greater pain. The saint, astonished at the remark, made this confession: "As for me, I find that it is not worth doing things by halves. I take the discipline to make myself suffer, and I wish that it should inflict as much punishment as possible. . . . Nevertheless," she added with characteristic kindness, "I do not counsel you to do this. Act therein with great simplicity."

But she admitted that at times this penance caused her such suffering that tears came to her eyes. She quickly drove them back, however, and forced herself to smile, so that her countenance reflected the feelings of her heart, overjoyed as it was to suffer for the Well-Beloved in order to win souls to Him.[10]

Here is an example of heroic patience. A Sister, one day in readjusting the saint's scapular, drove into her shoulder the point of the large pin used to keep the scapular in place. Thérèse made no remark but left it so, and continued her work. This incident occurred during her novitiate. When it was made known near the close of her life she was asked how long she had endured the pain. "Several hours," she replied simply. "I went to the cellar to refill the bottles, and brought them back in their baskets. I felt very happy. But, in the end, I began to fear that I was not acting according to obedience, since our Mother knew nothing about it."[11]

Thérèse had wished, moreover, to use another instrument of penance every day on which the rule did not prescribe the discipline. She wore for a long time on her breast a cross furnished with sharp iron points, and only when ulceration set in did she part with this penitential jewel.

Her mortification in the matter of clothing is already known. To give some further examples: Thérèse was glad when the Sister in charge of the linen gave her what was oldest and much patched; and when opportunity occurred she laughingly encouraged her to do so. She was content with a habit which was most unskilfully cut, and wore it without showing the least sign of discomfort or repugnance.

Not alone in supporting passing mortifications, however trying, did the saint wish to suffer for Jesus. She longed for martyrdom, a longing which became more and more ardent the nearer she approached to the end.

The last years of the nineteenth century witnessed the growing strength of freemasonry against religious congregations, and irreligious sects of every denomination began to threaten openly. The Mother Prioress thought it right to speak to Thérèse about the coming storm. The saint radiant with delight went immediately to find one of her companions. "Our Mother," she said, "has just told me of the persecution already raging against religious communities. . . . What joy! The good God is going to realize the grandest dream of my life. . . . Ah, let us no longer trouble ourselves about the petty miseries of the present; let us endeavour to bear them generously that we may merit so great a grace."[12]

Bodily suffering is small in comparison to martyrdom of the heart which the generous child accepted or desired. We know with what constancy she endured the terrible trial of her father's illness, which she ever looked on as a blessing from the God of merciful Love.

We know too of her self-imposed reserve in regard to her own sisters from the time of her entrance. This severity towards herself was to cease only with her last hour. Shortly after her death, a nun asked Sœur Marie du Sacré-Cœur why she had not appeared to seek more the companionship of her angelic sister. "Alas," she replied, "how could I? I often longed to do so, but through fidelity to the rule, she would not have liked to speak to me."[13]

Towards her other relatives she maintained even stricter reserve, and to this mortification of the heart she remained faithful to the end, continually recommending the practice. Realizing the gravity of her illness, she said one day in private to her sisters: "When I am gone, take care that you do not 'lead a family life.' Be watchful never to refer without permission to conversations you have had in the parlour, and do not ask for permission except when there is question of something useful, not merely amusing."[14]

Thérèse de l'Enfant Jésus had sacrificed to her heavenly Spouse the joys of family life. But there remained to her this adopted family to which she was attached by bonds that became ever dearer and closer. There were in the Carmel kindred souls, the fragrance of whose virtues filled her with happiness. Then it was, that a French Carmel, just founded in the vicinity of Hanoi in the pagan territory of Tonkin, asked for subjects from the Lisieux monastery.[15] Mère Marie de Gonzague had at one moment thought of singling out Thérèse for this mission of devotedness. Carried away by the desire of going to die for Jesus alone, far from all she loved here below, but fearing that her health, even then greatly shaken, would be an obstacle, she wrote in her private notes: "I am loved here, and this affection is, to me, very sweet. For that reason I desire a monastery where I should be unknown, where I should have to suffer *exile of heart*. . . . I would go to Hanoi to suffer much for God; I would go there in order to be entirely alone, to have no consolation, no joy on this earth." Mark to what a degree of generosity this young virgin had attained in giving herself without the smallest reserve to her only Beloved. Do we read of anything more heroic in the lives of the most renowned saints?

Not alone by prodigality in sacrifice will her courage henceforth be measured, but by energy of action. Speaking to a novice in whom she confided, Thérèse said: "When in the world, my thoughts on awaking in the morning went instinctively to the probable events of the coming day, and when I foresaw annoyances, I rose with sadness. Now it is quite the contrary. I rise all the more joyfully and full of courage, the more occasions I foresee of proving my love for Jesus and saving souls. Then I kiss my crucifix and say to Him: 'My Jesus, Thou hast laboured enough during the thirty-three years of Thy life on this miserable earth. To-day, take Thy rest; it is my turn to strive and to suffer.'"

Are these traits, giving, as they do, a true picture of Thérèse, showing the strong character of her virtue, are they sufficient to destroy the legend of a little saint with pleasing airs, too often occupied in strewing flowers or bestowing smiles?

If it be necessary to accentuate still more the efficacious force of this charity which led her to dare all and to sacrifice all for Jesus, we would dwell on the absolute disinterestedness of the love lavished unceasingly on her Divine Spouse.

Certain facts in addition to the examples already cited will bring this into the full light.

From the commencement of Thérèse's religious life, her Saviour insistently deprived her of the sense of His Presence. He concealed Himself and fled from her, leaving the young saint abandoned in that dark tunnel which she has described as mournful solitude. Still withal, she declares: "I am only too happy to see that Jesus does not treat me as a stranger, that He is not constrained with me, for I assure you that He goes to no trouble to hold conversation with me."[16]

And confiding to the Blessed Virgin her patience in this latter trial, keenly felt but generously loved, she tells her in one of her hymns:

Each gift of His to me can Jesus claim again;
Tell Him to be in naught constrained with me;
He may conceal His Face, in patience I remain,
Till faith shall fade in bright Eternity.[17]

Some weeks before her death, she said in confidence to her sister, Marie du Sacré-Cœur: "Suppose God were to say to me, 'If you die immediately, you shall have very great glory in heaven. If you die at eighty, your glory will be much less, but My pleasure much greater.' Then, I would not hesitate to reply, 'My God, I wish to die at eighty, for I do not seek my own glory but Thy pleasure.'"[18]

At the very height of her prolonged trial against faith, which, as she declares, took from her every feeling of joy, she cries out again: "Lord, Thou has filled me with joy by every act of Thine . . . for can any joy be compared to suffering for Thy love?" She strives to hide her trouble from others that so her patience may be pleasing to her Divine Master, and says to Him: "The more intense the suffering, the less it appears outwardly, the better is it fitted to draw a smile from Thee, O my God. And if, by impossibility, it were hidden even from Thee, I would still be happy to suffer, in the hope that, by my tears, I could prevent or expiate a single sin against Faith."[19]

Our saint's all-absorbing desire was to console Jesus, to bring a smile to His Sacred Face, even if it might cost her the most cruel martyrdom. Moreover, she will make it her study to smile at sacrifice. Useless to speak to her of earthly exile, of the valley of tears, of the battlefield of life. "We must sing," she says; "our life should be a melody." And again:

Smiling I face war's armoury,
And in Thy arms, Saviour Friend,
Singing on battle-field I'll die
With sword in hand.[20]

The harder her sacrifices the more joyous will she be. "Yes, I will sing, I will sing always, even if I must gather my roses from the midst of thorns; and my song shall be all the sweeter the longer and sharper the thorns."[21]

This gladness in suffering she justifies by a new motive of delicate consideration for her Beloved. "The good God has already enough sorrow, He who loves us so much, in being obliged to leave us on earth to fulfil our time of trial, without our constantly reminding Him that we are suffering; we should pretend not to notice it."[22]

She desired that a novice to whom she had been assigned as "angel" to initiate her into the practices of Carmel, should also bear the Saviour's yoke with gladness. Finding her one day in tears, she gently reminded her that she must form the habit of not allowing her little troubles to appear. "That is true," replied the young Sister; "I will shed no tears in future except in the presence of God alone." "Take care not to do that," replied the saint. "This good Master has but our monasteries to rejoice His Heart. He comes to us that He may forget the constant complainings of His friends in the world, and would you act like the commonest of mortals? . . . Jesus loves the cheerful heart. When will you know how to hide from Him your sorrows or to tell Him in joyous song that you are glad to suffer for Him?"[23]

Love, when it has attained to this degree, is not divided; thus it is to Jesus alone that Thérèse has given her whole heart. This exclusive gift dates from her early girlhood. We remember her dispositions, avowed by herself, during these years of mingled sadness and joy. "Jesus was my only Friend; I could speak to none but Him alone."

She writes of these dispositions more explicitly during her retreat for reception of the holy habit. "I wish to give all my love to Jesus, since He has made me understand that He alone is perfect happiness, even when He seems to be absent."[24]

This conviction became stronger later on, and, after two years' experience of the religious life, Thérèse again wrote to her sister, Agnès de Jésus: "We must with jealous care keep all for Jesus. How good it is to work for Him alone. . . . How full of joy the heart is then and how buoyant the spirit. . . ."[25]

The affection lavished by Thérèse on Jesus was all the more meritorious as she rarely enjoyed consolation. Her love for her Saviour, exceptionally strong, generous, delicate and disinterested, was, at the same time, even in the midst of aridity, tender and burning, equal to the love which consumed the most ardent lovers of the Crucified. It could well be said of her that "she loved God as a child loves its father, with outbursts of incredible tenderness."[26]

In fact, she did not hesitate to call the Almighty, "*Papa, le bon Dieu,*" just as she instinctively referred to the Blessed Virgin as "*Maman.*" But what reveals more clearly the depths of her soul, than do these loving names, is the intensity of feeling with which she spoke to the young Sisters, when charged with their formation, of the great duty and charm of divine Love. She could never refer without emotion to the following maxims of St. John of the Cross: "At the close of life, you will be judged according to your love. Learn then to love God as He deserves, and leave yourself out of the question." And again, "It is of the highest importance that the soul should be well exercised in love, that so, being rapidly consumed, she will tarry but a short time here below and quickly attain to the vision of God face to face."[27]

So intimate had Thérèse's union with God become, that according to Mère Agnès de Jésus, one would have said that she saw the Almighty continually. At all events, she tells us herself that her thoughts never wandered far from the Object of her love. Her eldest sister had the following conversation with her one day:

> "How do you manage," said Sœur Marie du Sacré-Cœur, "to think always about God?"
>
> "It is not difficult: we think naturally on those we love."
>
> "Then, you never lose the sense of His presence?"
>
> "Oh, no! I believe I have never been three minutes without thinking of Him."[28]

Her permanent state then was that "fusion" of which little Thérèse had experienced the joy on the day of her first Communion.

Such a degree of charity brought as a necessary fruit perfection in the religious spirit. Need we recall the respect shown by Sœur Thérèse for sacred things, more especially for the sacraments?[29] Let us note simply some new characteristics of her devotion towards the Holy Eucharist which brought her not only assistance and grace, but the adored person and burning heart of her Saviour. During her last illness, she was shown for her consolation the chalice of a young priest who had just said his first Mass. She looked, as she had so often done before, into the sacred vessel and said to her companions: "My image is reflected at the bottom of this chalice where the Blood of Jesus has been, and into which this precious Blood will again so many times descend. I thank you for procuring me this joy, so much appreciated when I was sacristan."[30]

She desired ardently to receive her Saviour every day. "It is not to remain in the golden ciborium," she has written, "that Jesus descends each day from heaven, but to find another heaven, the heaven of our soul where He takes His delight."[31] We know of the obstacles opposed to her aspirations by the custom of that time. With what a sense of relief, then, did she welcome the decree of Leo XIII giving, even in communities, the right to confessors of deciding the frequency of the Communions. She was not destined, alas, to enjoy to the full the longed-for liberty. Save during the epidemic already mentioned with all its attendant sufferings, she was never in her life able to receive daily Communion. During her illness, it needed heroic courage to avail herself of the community's ordinary days for Holy Communion.

To see her then dragging herself with painful exhaustion to the chapel was a sight to draw tears.

But she counted on obtaining for her companions, when she would be with God in His kingdom, the gift that had been refused her here below. Guided by prophetic light, she even predicted the change so ardently desired.

One day, as she was speaking to Sœur Marie du Sacré-Cœur of this privation which had made her suffer so keenly she added: "It will not be always so. A time will come when we shall have perhaps as chaplain M. l'Abbé Hodierne, and he will allow us Holy Communion every day."

At this time, no human circumstance pointed to the future destination of this priest, referred to by Thérèse. "Why," asked her sister, "do you think of the Abbé Hodierne as our future chaplain?" "I hope," answered Thérèse, "that he will come, and we shall be very fortunate to have him."

A few days after Thérèse's death, Abbé Hodierne was appointed chaplain to the Carmel, and he took as text for his first instruction the words: "Come and eat my Bread." It was an invitation to daily Communion, a privilege that he counted on extending to the community, without their having as yet expressed to him the desire.

The above conversation was of a private nature. But it was in presence of several nuns that Thérèse, already stretched on her bed of suffering, promised, that once in the glory of paradise, she would cause "a shower of roses" to fall upon the earth. Can we not recognize in the abundance of Eucharistic Bread, distributed daily immediately after her death, one form of this beneficent shower in which she obtained that her dear community should participate from the first?

This passionate lover of Jesus could not fail to have a very special devotion towards the most expressive symbol of His love, the Sacred Heart. She judged, in fact, that it is impossible for anyone inflamed with this devotion to be lost and to its power she attributed the most wonderful effects. She said of a certain person whose failings disconcerted everybody: "I assure you that on account of her devotion to the Sacred Heart, God will have pity on her." And of another whose salvation was in danger: "Because of her devotion to the Sacred Heart, she will be saved, yet, so as by fire."

Besides, she could not meditate on the Sacred Heart of Jesus without thinking of His divine action on her soul. Her devotion had a particularly intimate and personal character. The Heart that she adored was to her ardent and all-embracing love the Spouse to whom she had given herself, and to whose advances she corresponded with increasing tenderness.

In 1890, Céline received from her at Paray-le-Monial the following lines: "Pray fervently in the holy sanctuary. You know that I do not look on the Sacred Heart in the same way as others do. I simply consider that the Heart of my Spouse is mine alone, just as mine is His alone, and I speak to Him heart to heart in this delicious solitude while waiting to contemplate Him one day with no veil between."

Her adoration of the divine Heart found its complete and crowning expression in her devotion to the Holy Face which was, as we know, for her the mirror reflecting the soul of her Beloved.

Thérèse's heart, so inflamed for her celestial Spouse, naturally cherished a tender affection for the Mother who had given this Saviour to the world. Besides, she did not forget that Mary had saved her from imminent death, and her devotion had that character of filial and childlike confidence which had already won for her the predilection of the Almighty. We have this exemplified in the following beautiful words: "I love to hide my pain from the good God, for with Him I wish to appear happy, pleased at everything He does. But from the Blessed Virgin I hide nothing; I tell her all."[32]

Her splendid confidence was founded partly on what, she tells us, she herself had noticed, and concerning which she counselled others thus: "When we address our petitions to the saints, they make us wait a little while; we feel that they have to go and present their request. But when we ask a favour of the Blessed Virgin, we receive immediate help. Have you not remarked this? Try it and you will see."

Relying absolutely on this help, she had recourse to the Mother of God with charming freedom and familiarity. When charged with the formation of the novices, she would bring them to the miraculous statue of our Lady, and say: "It is not to me, but to the Blessed Virgin, that you are going to avow those things which cost you most." And to encourage these young souls in the path of virtue, she sometimes wrote little letters to them in the name of the holy Virgin, their Mother and Mistress.

When already very ill, she said to her dear Céline, now Sœur Geneviève de la Sainte Face: "I have still something to do before I die. I have always longed to express in a hymn to the Blessed Virgin all I think of her." And she composed her verses "*Why I love thee, Mary.*" It is a poetic résumé of the Queen of Heaven's life, and concludes with a trustful prayer:

> Soon shall I hear it, this sweet harmony;
> Soon in bright heaven find thy vision clear.
> Thou who at morn of life didst smile on me,
> Give me thy smile again; the eve is here.

The holy angels, more especially her angel guardian, had also a high place in Sœur Thérèse's devotion. She confided to one of the novices that it was through respect for her heavenly guardian she always tried to bear herself with becoming dignity and avoided, for instance, even knitting her brows or contracting her features. "The countenance," she said, "is the reflection of the soul. Yours should be always calm and open as that of a little child, even when you are alone, for you are constantly in the sight of God and His angels."[33]

We know of Thérèse's filial affection for St. Joseph, whom she had made (before her pilgrimage to Italy) the guardian of her virtue, and to whose intervention she always attributed the salutary decree of Leo XIII regarding frequent Communion.

She honoured all the saints in general, but amongst them she had special patrons. St. Martin, St. Francis de Sales, St. Teresa and St. John of the Cross received regularly the homage which she considered was in all justice due to them. She had besides her saints of predilection.

First amongst these was St. Cecilia, whose expressive and sweet countenance, as seen in the catacomb of St. Calixtus in Rome, had strongly impressed her, and whom she named "the saint of abandonment." Then came St. Joan of Arc, whose pure, high-souled features could not fail to attract her. She had also a marked devotion towards a young missionary martyred at Tonkin, Blessed Théophane Vénard, whose Life she had read with delight. "I love him," she explained, "because he is a quite simple little saint who cherished devotion to the Blessed Virgin and had such sincere affection for his family, and who, above all, lived in loving abandonment to God."

Finally, the fervent nun, who held in so high estimation the life of spiritual childhood, invoked with faith the Holy Innocents, who in her eyes were most naturally the patrons of Christian childhood.

Thérèse multiplied her marks of devotion to the blessed in heaven, for she saw in them the most perfect image of Jesus. Always it was God whom she loved in His saints; but according to the great precept of the law of love, her charity was to extend to less privileged beings. We have seen her in the world surround with tenderness the weak and poverty-stricken. The time has come to admire the generosity with which she continued in the cloister to devote herself to others for the love of God.

10

Charity of St. Thérèse de l'Enfant Jésus towards Her Neighbour—Her Devotion to the Novices under Her Direction—Her Spiritual Help to Two Missionaries

During the summer of 1897, when already wasted by the malady which was to bring her life to a close, Sœur Thérèse de l'Enfant Jésus was often to be found in the garden of the monastery enjoying the glorious sunlight of those her last months on earth, and completing the autobiography as desired by her Mother Prioress. The novices and a lay-sister often at work in the garden came continually, under numberless pretexts, to interrupt her in her task. She welcomed each in turn with such unfailing patience that at last Mère Agnès de Jésus was amazed. Then Thérèse disclosed the secret: "I am writing," she told her, "on fraternal charity. Now is the time to practice it. Oh, fraternal charity! It is everything on this earth. We love God in the measure in which we practice it."

In order to have a correct idea of her teaching on love of the neighbour, it is necessary to read Chapters IX and X of her *Histoire d'une Ame.* Nothing could be more impressive than the saint's glowing words on the joy of self-devotion to souls wounded and suffering; nothing which better recalls the divine unction of St. John, or St. Paul's all-conquering energy. In fine, Thérèse's teaching on fraternal charity can be summed up in one sentence: "It is chief amongst virtues."

From all this we can realize what admirable examples she must have left in the monastery where her devotedness to others had full scope. Let us simply note a few incidents of these years which constituted a perpetual act of charity.

The very effectual faith of our saint inspired her with a mother's love for souls, for every soul redeemed by our Saviour's blood. She called them "her children," and laboured unceasingly "in order," as she said, "to earn for them eternal life." We shall note the chief characteristics of her charity for souls in general before speaking in detail of her mode of practising it with regard to her Sisters in the cloister and those priests whom she strove to aid in their ministry.

One day, when the community was engaged in washing, a novice was walking leisurely towards the laundry, calmly admiring the flowers in the garden. Sœur Thérèse, who followed with step more alert, soon overtook her, and said with joyous animation: "Is it thus people hasten when they have children to provide for, when they have to work for their livelihood? Let us get quickly to our task, for if we amuse ourselves, our children will die of hunger."[1] The "children" whom there was question of keeping alive by force of sacrifice were none other, as may easily be guessed, than abandoned souls.

It was natural that she who gave herself generously to those unknown souls for love of Him who had redeemed them on Calvary should especially devote herself to those who, delivered from earthly bonds and assured of possessing in glory Him whom they had served here, are nevertheless kept far from Him to satisfy divine Justice for the relics of sin.

Sœur Thérèse manifested a tender and effectual compassion for the souls in purgatory. She sought to relieve them by every means in her power, especially by gaining indulgences. With this end in view, she made the Stations of the Cross several times a week. She wished to persevere till death in reciting every day six *Paters* and *Aves*, a practice which she had been told was very efficacious in relieving the poor souls, and when during the latter part of her illness she was urged to dispense herself, she begged that she might be left free, saying: "I can do nothing but this for the souls in purgatory, and it is so little."

Very early she had made the "heroic offering" for the dead, and placed in the Blessed Virgin's hands all the merits of each day to apply to them as she considered best.

But she had nothing so much at heart as the sanctification of priests. She felt bound in duty to offer her prayers, mortifications, and penances for those souls on whose virtue depended the salvation of so many.

Even in convents, there are at times acts of charity more difficult than prayer and penance. We have already spoken of the self-renunciation imposed by community life. Sœur Thérèse experienced, as we know, these interior struggles, especially in the beginning of her religious life. Sensitive by nature, she was destined to suffer more than others in this way. An arrow that would scarce graze a thick skin buries itself deep in delicate flesh. Great indeed must have been the young saint's strength of character to enable her to triumph, as she did, over her natural tendencies. "One day," says her sister Céline, "in order to encourage me to overcome personal antipathies, she made known to me that she had long done violence to herself in this matter. The admission was a revelation to me, for she so perfectly controlled herself that no effort was apparent, and I was still more amazed when she told me the name of the Sister who was the occasion of this daily struggle. In fact I always saw the Servant of God so amiable and obliging to this particular Sister, that I would have taken her for her best friend."[2]

Thérèse knew equally well how to keep in check her natural sympathies, so that, in her relations with those who most attracted her, everything was directed by grace and subordinated to God's good pleasure. She had a tender affection for the novices so early entrusted to her direction, as we shall see. But her dealings with them were always spiritual. She took care to reprimand them for every failing. "I owe you the truth," she said to them, "and the truth I will tell you until my death."[3]

With such dispositions, seeing God in everyone around her, loving them for God alone and therefore solely with a view to their good, she naturally on all occasions gave them proof of that generous and deeply-rooted charity of which her divine Master was both the principal object and the inexhaustible source.

From the first, she loved her Mother Prioress with an affection always proved by acts. Although the changeable character of Mère Marie de Gonzague deterred her once more from leaning on creatures, Thérèse, nevertheless, ceased not to speak and act in favour of her authority, so as to maintain submission and a good spirit in the convent.

Certain admittedly brilliant qualities in this reverend Mother did not conceal the defects in her character nor the inperfections in her government. Our saint's keen intellect perceived those defects even more clearly than did others, but she understood also how much the Prioress suffered from the silent reproach manifested at times in the attitude of certain Sisters, and she strove, as did none other, to heal those wounds. She studied to show the poor Mother every tender consideration, to console and even to enlighten her, so that Mère Marie de Gonzague was able to proclaim from experience the truth of those words of Holy Scripture: "Truth comes from the mouths of children." The esteem of the Prioress for the young saint was to go on increasing until her last hour. Meditating a short time before her death on God's judgements, Mère Marie de Gonzague declared in all humility: "I am sustained by hope in spite of my faults, for I have my little Thérèse to intercede for me. I am sure that I shall owe my salvation to her."

Devoted as she was to her Mother Prioress, and pre-occupied as well with the spiritual advancement of her novices, Thérèse took care that none of those under her charge should let charity degenerate into an effeminate affection. She feared the effect of that sympathetic affection sometimes lavished blindly by an ingenuous soul on a companion who is considered more amiable or more fervent than the others. This had been her attitude from the time she entered; nothing can better exemplify it than the following episode related by Thérèse herself to Mère Marie de Gonzague in one of the memoirs of her *Histoire d'une Ame.*

"On entering Carmel," she writes,

I found in the novitiate a Sister eight years my senior. Despite the difference in years, we became intimate companions.[4] In order to favour affection which seemed to promise fruits of virtue, we were given permission to confer together on spiritual matters. I was charmed by my dear companion's innocence, her open and expansive character. But, on the other hand, I was astonished to notice how different her affection for you, Mother, was from mine. On many other points, too, her behaviour appeared to be regrettable. God, however, had already taught me that there are souls for whom His mercy wearies not of waiting, to whom He gives His light little by little, and I guarded against anticipating His own good time.

Thinking, one day, over our permission to confer together, in order, as written in our holy Constitutions, "that our hearts might be inflamed with greater love for our Divine Spouse," I realized with sadness that our converse did not tend towards the end desired, and I saw clearly that it became necessary either to speak out fearlessly or to give up altogether the conversations which had begun to resemble those of friends in the world. I besought Jesus to put gentle and convincing words on my lips, or rather to speak Himself for me. He heard my prayer, for "those who look unto Him are enlightened,"[5] and "to the upright a light is risen in the darkness."[6] I applied the first text to myself, the second to my companion who certainly had an upright heart.

When we next met to talk together, the poor little Sister saw from the first that my manner was changed. Her face flushed as she sat down beside me. Then, pressing her to my heart, I tenderly expressed my thoughts concerning her. I showed her in what true love consists, and proved to her, that in loving her Mother Prioress with mere natural affection, she was only loving herself. I told her of the sacrifices that I had been obliged to make in this matter at the commencement of my religious life, and soon her tears mingled with mine. She humbly admitted that she was wrong, recognized the truth of what I said, and promised to begin a new life, asking me, as a favour, always to warn her of her

> faults. From this moment, our affection became altogether spiritual; in us was realized that word of holy Scripture, "A brother that is helped by his brother is like a strong city."[7]

We know how faithfully Thérèse maintained the greatest reserve in her relations with the other members of her family in the convent. It was, in truth, no common thing to find four sisters in the same Carmel, to whom a first cousin was soon to be added. In a community of only twenty nuns, the above group could, humanly speaking, assert a considerable amount of influence. They could have formed a party in themselves if the "four sisters," as they were called, had not been gifted with sound judgement and a proper monastic spirit.

Thérèse made superhuman efforts to maintain fraternal union in the community, although her heart suffered cruelly in consequence of the privations she imposed on herself.

The dear saint seemed to make up for this constraint by redoubling her charity towards the other members of the community. We have already quoted more than one characteristic incident in her humble life, showing with what an excess of abnegation she gave herself to the service of all. A young Sister related certain details which she had noted.

One day in winter she asked Thérèse whether it were better to go and help to rinse out the linen in cold water (in the open air) or remain in the laundry for the washing with hot water. "Oh," she replied, "it is not difficult to judge. When it costs you something to go to the cold water washing, that is a sign that it must cost others something too; go then on that account. If, on the contrary, the day is hot, remain rather in the laundry, thus allowing some one else to enjoy the coolness of the water outside. In choosing the worst, we practise mortification for ourselves and charity towards others."

She wished to see her novices go regularly to recreation, not so much for their own enjoyment as to give pleasure to others. "There, more perhaps than anywhere else," she would say, "do we find opportunity for renunciation in order to practise charity. For instance, if some one relates a tedious story, let us listen with every sign of interest, just to please her. Let us try to make ourselves agreeable to all. Success therein, it is true, can be attained only by constant renunciation."

Cheerfulness, so important but oftentimes so difficult in community life, had become habitual with Thérèse, almost, in fact, second nature, through the fervour and force of her charity. When she was absent from recreation, the nuns expressed their disappointment: "Sœur Thérèse is not here; we shall have no laugh to-day."

The interior peace of her soul it was which thus shone in her countenance, leading others to smile with her. "I am always gladsome and content," she said, "even in my sufferings. We read in the lives of some saints that they were grave and austere, even at recreation. . . . I am more attracted by Théophane Vénard who was ever and everywhere joyous."[8]

All Thérèse's counsels to others were practised by herself with a perfection which no obstacle could impede. Should some service be asked of her which disturbed her at her work or forced her to interrupt an interesting occupation, she agreed with as gracious a smile as if she herself were the debtor. Should a Sister come to trouble her even at an inopportune moment, when she was deep in some arduous task, far from complaining, she left all there, to give the desired help which, often enough, the Sister in question, spoiled by so much charity and good will, came to regard as merely her due.

On the approach of the Prioress's feast, some of the Sisters brought divers little objects to Thérèse in order that, decorated by her brush, they might become acceptable little presents. It sometimes happened that a certain Sister, considering her gift less well finished than that of another, found fault with it instead of thanking Thérèse. But the improvised artist always consoled herself with such reflections as this: "When we work for God, we expect no thanks from creatures, and these reproaches cannot rob us of our peace." She even carried condescendence so far as to paint something that was ridiculous and not in good taste for the satisfaction of one who oftentimes mortified her. For her, too, she executed some little paintings a few months before her death, and it was in her service that she used her brush for the last time.

For two or three years, Thérèse worked with an invalided Sister whose wearisome whims and fancies exercised the patience of the whole community. A novice who one day took Thérèse's place, irritated by the Sister's remarks, retorted with some vivacity, thereby drawing from her complaint and protestation. "Never, Sister," said the astonished nun, "has Sœur Thérèse de l'Enfant Jésus spoken to me as you have done."

These words were repeated by the guilty novice to our saint. "Oh," she replied, "be very kind and gentle to this poor Sister; she is ill. And then, it is an act of charity as well as an exercise of patience to let her believe that she interests us. . . . We must guard against allowing our irritation to get the better of us; rather let us calm our souls by charitable thoughts. After that, the practice of patience comes naturally."[9]

Her example in this matter during long periods of her monotonous life as a recluse never belied her words. "For a long time," she says,

> I was near a Sister who unceasingly rattled her beads or some other thing during prayer. Perhaps I was the only one to hear it, for my sense of hearing is extremely keen; but it would be impossible to tell how much this noise disturbed me. I would have liked to turn and look at the offender in order to make her cease. In my heart, however, I felt that it was better to suffer patiently for God's sake, and also to avoid giving her pain. I therefore remained quite still, though, at times, perspiration broke out on my forehead and I was obliged to make simply a prayer of suffering. At last I strove to suffer in peace and joy at least within my soul. Then I tried to love this disagreeable little noise. Instead of endeavouring not to hear it—a thing impossible—I listened attentively to it as if it were a delightful concert. My prayer, *which was not "the prayer of quiet,"* passed in offering this concert to Jesus.[10]

The following exemplifies a far greater measure of abnegation than is ordinarily met with. We shall give it in the words of Sœur Généviève de la Sainte Face.

> Thérèse's charity extended, one might almost say, even to the extent of sacrificing her spiritual interests. Having found a book which was doing her a great deal of good, I have seen her pass it on to the other Sisters without having read it through, with the result that in spite of her desire to finish it, she was never able to do so. She sacrificed in the interests of others her personal tastes, even as regarded spiritual matters. For instance, in order to stimulate virtue in a companion of the novitiate—a lay-sister whom she was trying to help—she pretended to have need herself of a complicated system of "practices" suited to this Sister, while in reality all such methods were quite contrary to Thérèse's own tastes. She wrote to me on July 23, 1893 when I was still in the world: "I am obliged to have practice beads."[11] I have adopted this out of charity for one of the Sisters, but feel myself as though entangled in the meshes of a net.

Nevertheless, she adapted herself with such good grace to the spiritual level of her companion as to persuade the latter that she, Thérèse, was also benefited by this method.[12]

When unable to bring some comfort by words to a soul under trial, she compensated for that by other exercises of charity, which, no doubt, were not less pleasing to God, nor less efficacious. "When I see," she said, "that one of the Sisters is suffering, and I have not permission to speak, I ask Jesus to console her Himself." And she urged others to follow her example, telling them that it was a sure means of pleasing Our Lord.

When doing work in common, she placed herself by preference near those who appeared somewhat sad. As the rule forbade her to speak, she sought to give them at least an affectionate smile, and seized every opportunity of rendering them a service.

♦♦♦

We have up to the present studied Sœur Thérèse in ordinary relations with her companions. We shall now see her at work in her difficult and delicate duty as assistant mistress of novices, which was allotted to her three years after her profession. In February, 1893, Mère Marie de Gonzague had completed the term of office as Prioress allowed by the rule, and the nuns elected Thérèse's sister, Pauline (Sœur Agnès de Jésus), to succeed her. What was to become of Mère Gonzague, whose past years of Superiority and experience, and also certain material services rendered to the monastery, seemed to mark out as one destined always to rule? The new Prioress met the difficulty by appointing her mistress of novices. As that duty, however, required an evenness of disposition, sometimes lacking in the former Prioress, Mère Agnès de Jésus decided on giving her an assistant, and for this office she chose Thérèse, who was still in the novitiate.

With the consent of Mère Marie de Gonzague, our saint was charged from the very first with watching over her companions, two lay-sisters whose formation required special attention and unremitting devotedness. In reality, Thérèse was invested with the duties of novice-mistress without the corresponding title. A most difficult charge, for one could not but expect that the character of Mère Marie de Gonzague, with its tendency to doubt and to take offence, would be found more than once in conflict with the views of her assistant.

The situation became more serious still when, after three years, the former Prioress was again placed at the head of the community, and wished to retain, together with the direction of the monastery, the functions of novice-mistress, leaving still to Thérèse the care of forming, under her control, the young religious. Through love for her convent, and through obedience as well as love for souls, the young saint submitted to all.

She commenced by giving the novices an admirable example of humility. When her own term of probation was completed, she was entitled to rank among the professed nuns of the chapter, but at her own request she remained in the novitiate that she might thus be more on an equality with her companions, who soon reached the number of five. Thérèse was to retain this charge, as also this humble rank, until her death.

It will not be out of place to give a few maxims and certain acts of her spiritual direction. Therein we shall see charity shine forth side by side with watchfulness, prudence and firmness, proceeding, as did every movement of her soul, from divine love. Never did she permit herself to give advice or reprimand to her novices save with a view to their perfection or to gain more love for her Saviour.

Before entering, so young, on the difficult duty of guiding souls, Thérèse's first care was to turn for help to God, the Father of lights and dispenser of every perfect gift. She has told with her usual grace how she compelled the Holy Spirit to guide her in this work so disproportioned, humanly speaking, to her natural abilities.

"As soon," she writes,

> as I entered into the sanctuary of souls, I realized immediately that the task was beyond my strength, and, quickly throwing myself into the arms of the good God, I followed the example of a child who, terrified by some fear, hides its head on its father's shoulder. "My Saviour," I said, "Thou seest that I cannot feed Thy children. If Thou willest to give to each what she needs, then fill my little hand, and I, without leaving Thy arms, without even turning my head, shall distribute Thy treasures to each soul that comes to me for food. When she finds it according to her taste, then, not to me but to Thee will she be indebted. If, on the contrary, she complains, and finds bitter the nourishment offered, that will not disturb my peace; I shall try to persuade her that it comes from Thee, and carefully avoid seeking any other for her."
>
> Thus convinced that I could do nothing by myself, my task appeared simplified. I strove solely to unite myself interiorly more and more to God, knowing that the rest would be given me abundantly. Never has my trust been deceived. As often as nutriment has been required for the souls entrusted to me, I have found my hand full.

And in self-distrust inspired by faith, the humble nun, addressing her Prioress, adds: "I tell you, Mother, that had I acted otherwise, had I relied on my own strength, I should very soon have had to lay down my arms."[13]

If Thérèse de l'Enfant Jésus felt so imperious a need of help from above, this arose from the fact that with her innate fineness of perception and supernatural intuition she had quickly realized the formidable complexity of the task imposed upon her. "From afar," she says,

> it seems easy to do good to souls, to make them love God more, to mould them according to our own ideas and views. But coming closer, we find, on the contrary, that to do good without God's help is as impossible as to bring the sun back during the night. We feel that we must absolutely forget our own tastes, our personal ideas, and guide souls, not by our way, but by the particular path which Jesus points out. And this is not the chief difficulty. What costs me most is being obliged to observe every fault and slightest imperfection, and to wage deadly war against them.[14]

These concluding words give an indication of her energy in directing her novices, energy inspired, like everything else, by love for God and souls, that love, "prudent, strong, prompt, vigilant, and discreet," spoken of in the *Imitation,*[15] which will henceforth govern all her spiritual activity.

Firmness of direction was called for especially in the beginning, for the first novices confided to her care had need of vigilant and thorough formation if they were to become true Carmelites. In no way discouraged by their lack of spiritual culture, she bravely made war on their failings. She reprimanded them, not harshly, but with precision and, at times, with an innocent raillery which emphasized the unseemliness, futility, or absurdity of certain acts and gestures. Her severity in the matter of sensible affections we know; she combated with no less energy the tendency to pity themselves and to draw attention to their slight sufferings. She wished the young Sisters to act in all things with vigour, without self-indulgence or complaint. "In a community," she said to them, "each one should try to be self-sufficing, and not seek services that she can well do without." And again: "In order to guard against asking dispensations or permissions except as a last resource, say to yourselves: 'Suppose everyone were to do the same. . . .' The answer you must give will show you immediately what disorder would result, and will indicate the golden mean that you should follow."[16]

She volunteered, moreover, to justify according to principles of faith what might appear austere in her mode of action. "Our kindness," she confided to Mère Agnès de Jésus, "should never degenerate into weakness. When we have given a just reprimand, we ought to leave things as they are and not yield to trouble of mind for having caused pain or tears. If we run to offer consolation to her whom we have corrected, we do more harm than good. By leaving her to herself, she is led to expect nothing from creatures and to turn to God, to recognize her faults and to humble herself."[17]

To these principles which, from the beginning, she made the law of her spiritual government, she adhered faithfully to the end, and, in her last conversations with her sister who had already held the office of Prioress, she bequeathed them to her as a sort of last testament. "In the work of spiritual direction," she said, "let us never pass things over for the sake of our own ease. Let us fight unceasingly, even if we have no hope of gaining a victory. What matter about success? If we find a soul not well-disposed, let us not say: 'Nothing can be done for her. She does not understand. She will have to be abandoned; I can do no more.' Oh, it is cowardly to speak thus. Our duty must be done until the end."[18]

And, on an occasion which called for energy, she said: "I have striven hard; I am indeed fatigued, but I am not afraid of the fight; I am as much at peace there as when at prayer. It is God's will that I should fight until death. With souls under our direction we must speak truthfully what we think. I always act thus. If I am not liked, what matter! Besides, I do not seek for that. Let them not come to me if they do not wish to be told the entire truth."[19]

Such, then, were the desires and demands of the tender, humble, and affectionate Sœur Thérèse.

She well knew, besides, that recommendations and counsels have no chance of being obeyed unless she who receives the counsel can feel that it springs from a compassionate and maternal heart which suffers for the pain inflicted on a beloved soul. "In order that a reprimand bear fruit," she affirms, "it must cost in the giving; the heart must be free from the least shade of passion."[20]

In the person charged with the direction of others, there must also be clearly shown an entire detachment from self, and an all-absorbing desire to benefit, even at her own expense, the soul whose tendencies she opposes. Sœur Thérèse de l'Enfant Jésus knew this, she who revealed so candidly to her Mother Prioress her plans of government. "When I speak to a novice," she told her, "I am careful to mortify myself. I avoid asking her questions which would gratify my curiosity. If, having commenced to talk on an interesting subject, she passes on to some other, irksome to me, I guard against calling her attention to this interruption, for it seems to me that one can do no good by self-seeking."[21]

Consistently until the end, the saintly mistress asked as a grace from her Saviour that she might not be loved with mere human affection. Her prayer was heard, for spiritual affection alone entered into the novices' relations with her. But she was loved, loved even to veneration, and by those souls, too, who in the beginning had tried her patience, and of whom she succeeded in making excellent religious. She was esteemed for her uprightness, for her constant demand for truth,[22] for her entire abnegation of self, which permitted her to exercise always discerning and inexhaustible charity. Such, indeed, was the spiritual enlightenment of this nun of twenty years that others, grown old in the practices of the life in the Carmel, came to her to ask furtively the secret of a higher perfection and a more rapid advancement.

Her first novices, who found some difficulty in understanding her, were soon followed by souls more open and more generous by nature, who did not hesitate to go forward gladly on the path she pointed out to them. This marked the beginning of a period of special fervour in the Carmel of Lisieux which was never afterwards to know relaxation.

Such success, however, cannot be fully accounted for by the energy or prudence of the saintly novice-mistress. From a heart "strong as the diamond, but more tender than a mother's heart," came her exhortations to her novices. She treated them with such delicate considerateness as to draw tears of emotion and gratitude. Here is the testimony of one who profited most by Thérèse's teaching:

> Sœur Thérèse de l'Enfant Jésus, as the rule enjoins, never raised her eyes in the refectory. I had much difficulty on this very point, so she composed the following prayer, which was for me a revelation of her humility, because she asked for herself a grace that was wanting to me alone:
>
> > Jesus, Thy two little spouses resolve to keep their eyes lowered in the refectory, in order to honour and imitate the example given by Thee when standing before Herod. Though this impious prince mocked Thee, O Infinite Beauty, no complaint passed Thy lips; Thou didst not deign even to fix upon him Thy adorable eyes. O Divine Jesus, Herod did certainly not deserve to be looked on by Thee. But we who are Thy spouses, we long to make Thee turn Thy Divine eyes towards us. We ask Thee to reward us by this look of love each time we restrain our desire to raise our eyes. We even pray Thee not to deprive us of Thy tender glance when we fail, for most sincerely shall we humble ourselves before Thee.[23]

To encourage her novices to punctuality or other mortification, she sometimes did not hesitate to cite her own example, doing so, however, with a candour which excluded every suspicion of vanity. To a young Sister, whom she considered reliable and sensible, she said: "We must mortify ourselves when the bell rings, or when a knock comes to our door, and not delay even to put in another stitch[24] before answering. I have practised this, and I assure you it is a source of peace." Later on, when the same novice hastened to perform some urgent duty, she commended her heartily for this act of generosity. "At the moment of death," she said, "you will be happy to find this before you. You have just done a more glorious act than if by some skilful measures you had obtained the good will of the government for the religious communities, and all France hailed you as a second Judith."[25]

But her great lever for raising souls was the consideration of the love and mercy of Jesus. By recalling unceasingly to her novices the Saviour's adorable attributes, she almost always succeeded in renewing their courage, stimulating their good will and strengthening their love and hope of perfection.

A young nun asked her one day if our Saviour was not displeased at seeing all her failures and imperfections. "Be reassured," Thérèse said to her.

> He whom you have taken for spouse has truly every perfection that could be desired; but, if I may dare to say it, He has at the same time one great infirmity, that is, *blindness*, and there is one science He does not know, namely *arithmetic*. These two great defects, which would indeed be grave in an earthly spouse, make ours infinitely lovable. If He saw everything clearly and knew how to reckon, think you that, confronted with all our sins, He would not cast us back again into nothingness? But no; His love for us renders Him absolutely blind. For behold, if the greatest sinner on earth, repenting on his death-bed, expires with an act of love on his lips, immediately, without counting on the one hand the numberless graces abused by the unfortunate man, and on the other all his crimes, He considers and takes into account only this last prayer, and receives Him at once into the arms of His mercy. But in order to render Him thus blind, to prevent Him from making the smallest calculation, we must know how to gain His heart; this is the point where He is defenceless. . . .[26]

She profited by every incident to strengthen the novices' filial trust in God whose joy it is to pardon. One of them, having grieved her, came to ask pardon. With evident emotion Thérèse replied:

> If you but knew what I feel! I have never before understood so well the love with which Jesus receives us when we ask His pardon for a fault. If I, His poor little creature, feel so much tenderness towards you the moment you return to me, what must pass in the Heart of the good God when we return to Him! . . . Yes, He will undoubtedly forget more quickly than I have done all our falls, never more to recall them. . . . He will do more; He will love us even better than before our fault.[27]

In order to preserve souls from the attraction of created things, and to detach them from those insignificant trifles which custom could easily make dear to cloistered nuns, the wise novice-mistress related charming incidents, not hesitating to bring herself sometimes into the picture with her habitual simplicity. The following occurrence reveals the persistence of her love for silvan beauty, and at the same time the energy with which she mortified herself. . . . "One Sunday," she said,

> I set out in gladness, going towards the chestnut walk. It was springtime. I wished to enjoy the beauties of nature. Alas! what a cruel deception; my dear chestnut trees had been shorn of their branches. Those branches, already laden with verdant budding shoots, were there, lying on the ground. . . . It went to my heart to behold this disaster, and to reflect that I must wait three years to see it repaired. My grief, however, did not last long. "If I were in another monastery," thought I, "what would it matter to me if the chestnut trees of the Lisieux Carmel were entirely cut down? I will trouble myself no more about passing things, my Well-Beloved shall take the place of all else for me. I will ever walk to and fro in the groves of His love, groves which none can touch."[28]

To detach souls from exterior things was the primary and fundamental work in Carmel as in other convents. It was also necessary, and a more ungrateful task, to detach them from their own judgement. To attain this end, Thérèse knew how to use with good effect a little gentle irony. A novice boasted in her presence of having been able "to make her own opinion prevail." "Ah," replied the saint, "you wish then to push yourself forward. . . . As for me, I take good care to avoid that rôle. I prefer to repeat with our Saviour: 'I seek not my own glory; there is one that seeketh and judgeth.'"[29]

In her little group of novices, each soul had its own special trials. Some experienced habitual and sometimes exaggerated fear of God's judgements; others passed like herself through long periods of aridity. Now it was question of some inordinate attachment that had to be fought against—now a natural aversion—so hurtful in community life—that must be overcome. The humble novice-mistress had even to bear at times the mortifying and unjust expression of discontent against herself or her direction.

To all these souls desirous of progress, but at times disquieted, troubled or prejudiced, she gave herself unsparingly at all times, until her strength was finally exhausted. The bell, calling her to some community exercise, alone could interrupt her tender and consoling exhortations. True, she ever obeyed this signal instantly; but then, she prayed God Himself to help the soul that had come to her for consolation, and often her prayer was answered in a marvellous way.

"Before my profession," a religious tells us,

> I received through my saintly mistress a very special grace. We had been all day at the washing and I was extremely tired, overwhelmed too with interior trials. In the evening before mental prayer, I wished to speak to her, but she replied: "There is the bell for Prayer; I have no time now to console you. Besides, I see plainly that my efforts would be useless; God wills you to suffer alone for the moment."
>
> I followed her to prayer in a state of such discouragement that for the first time I began to doubt my

> vocation. "Never shall I have sufficient strength to be a Carmelite," I said to myself, "the life is too hard for me."
>
> I had knelt for a few moments, in strife, a prey to these sad reflections, when suddenly, without having uttered a prayer, without having even wished for peace, I experienced an instantaneous and extraordinary change in my soul. I could not recognize myself as the same person; my vocation appeared beautiful and lovable; I saw the charm and the immense worth of suffering. Every privation and fatigue in the religious life seemed to me infinitely preferable to worldly satisfactions. In a word, I came out from prayer absolutely transformed.
>
> On the following day, I told Sœur Thérèse de l'Enfant Jésus what had happened, and, as her emotion was evident, I asked her the reason. "Ah, how good God is," she replied. "Yesterday evening I had such pity for you, that for some time at the beginning of Prayer I never ceased praying for you, asking Our Saviour to console you, to change the state of your soul, and to show you the worth of suffering. He has heard me."[30]

Thus did the dear saint labour for the sanctification of her novices even at times when apparently she could not occupy herself with them.

The young novice-mistress's disinterestedness far surpassed any ordinary measure. Not content with renouncing every temporal possession or advantage, she surrendered to other souls her spiritual riches, usually so dear and precious even to those capable of sincere generosity. What more touching than the following avowal of Thérèse, possessed, like St. Paul, by the desire not only to devote herself to souls, but to be despoiled and consumed in their interest? "If I had been rich, I could not have beheld a poor man without giving him to eat. It is thus, too, in my spiritual life. According as I gain anything, I know there are souls on the point of falling into hell. Then I give them my treasures, and have never yet had a moment when I could say: 'Now I am going to work for myself.'"

Such liberality did not confine itself within the limits of Carmel. We know the tender regard which Thérèse de l'Enfant Jésus ever retained for the members of her family remaining in the world, even after Céline had entered the convent. While waiting until her cousin, Marie Guérin, should come to join her in Carmel, she saw her regularly in the parlour, also her uncle and aunt, her cousin Jeanne, now become Madame La Néele, and the latter's husband, as fervent in his religion as he was charitable in his practice as doctor. Although at these meetings, the saintly child kept herself ever in the background leaving the conversation to her sisters, her reliable judgement and spirit of justice were so appreciated, that all looked eagerly to her, to obtain wise counsel or efficacious consolation. She always endeavoured to restore peace to afflicted hearts. Should she fail in this, she turned for help to the inexhaustible Source of all joy, and thus did she arrive at restoring calm to souls, as is shown by the following avowal:—

"Formerly," she writes, "if one of my family was in some trouble, whom, during their visit, I had not succeeded in consoling, I went from the parlour with an aching heart. But Jesus soon made me understand that I was incapable of pacifying a soul. From then, onward, I never felt downhearted when they went away sad. I confided to the good God the sufferings of those dear to me, and felt convinced that I was heard. Then, at our next meeting, I would find out that so it was, in truth."[31]

Thérèse's charity extended even to those who were admitted within the cloister to carry out repairs or other work. Unable to speak to these poor workers to exhort them to piety, she contrived that they should at least carry away with them a medal of the Blessed Virgin carefully concealed in their clothing. In a word, far beyond the bounds of her convent, her family and native province, Thérèse's compassionate love went out to every soul that had need of prayer, sacrifice, or pardon.

This discreet, ingenuous, and active charity, visibly radiating from the love which ruled her whole life, the attraction of a soul at once recollected and expansive, the reflection of spotless innocence that shone from her whole being, all this joined to natural gifts gave her an exterior charm which even strangers were forced to recognize.

From temporary information, we are enabled to give the following picture of the saint: "She was tall of stature and slight, with golden hair and grey-blue eyes, eyebrows very slightly arched, a small mouth, refined and regular features. Her face, fair as a lily, was well proportioned, ever bearing the imprint of sweet serenity and celestial peace. Her every movement was full of dignity as well as simplicity and grace."[32]

♦♦♦

Her great heart was unlimited in its tenderness, but certain spiritual afflictions made special demand on her pity. They were those of the unfortunate tribes and peoples living apparently abandoned by God and man in the depths of savage solitudes, in lands as yet closed to the Gospel.

The desire to labour more generously for the salvation of infidels had strongly attracted her to the Carmel of Hanoi. The same inclination, together with her old and ardent desire to participate in the priestly apostolate, made her towards the end of her life join in a bond of spiritual fraternity with two missionaries. One of these had been assigned to a dangerous mission in pagan China, the other to the bush-district in Central Africa.

The first, Adolphe-Jean Roulland,[33] became acquainted with the young saint in 1896. He had just been ordained at the Foreign Missions' Seminary. Before leaving France, to which he had then no hope of returning, he petitioned the Carmel of Lisieux through his compatriot, Père Norbert of the Premonstratensians of Mondaye, that one of the community might be charged to pray very specially for him and his missions. Sœur Thérèse de l'Enfant Jésus was chosen for this by Mère Marie de Gonzague. The young priest came to celebrate Mass in the convent, and both before and after the holy Sacrifice, was able to speak in the parlour with the Carmelite who undertook to share his immolation.

What was the subject-matter of their conversation? The modest reserve of both, no doubt, did not permit prolonged confidences. Thérèse waited until writing later to her spiritual brother, to explain that their meeting was an answer from Heaven to a prayer addressed to God on the day of her profession. Alluding no doubt to a confidence of the priest, she wrote to him:

> On September 8, 1890, your missionary vocation was saved by Mary, Queen of apostles and martyrs. On that very day, a little Carmelite became spouse of the King of heaven. Her one aim was to save souls, above all, souls of apostles. From Jesus, her divine Spouse, she asked particularly an apostolic soul. Debarred from becoming a priest, she desired that some priest should receive in her stead the Saviour's graces and that he should have aspirations and desires like hers. You know the unworthy Carmelite who thus prayed. Do you not think, as I do, that our spiritual union, confirmed on your ordination day, began on 8th September? I believed I should never meet, except in heaven, the apostle I had asked of Jesus. This well-beloved Saviour, lifting a little the mysterious veil which hides the secrets of eternity, has deigned to give me, even in exile, the consolation of knowing the brother of my soul, and of working with him for the salvation of poor infidels.[34]

The missionary set out for his district of Su-Tchuen, and not for a single day did Thérèse forget the duty she had accepted of helping in the work of ransoming souls. But she had reached the term of her earthly career. She was only able to write six letters to the apostle whose generous and intrepid helper she had become. How intense the fervour that runs through these lines; with what ardour she must have fired the priest's brave heart. Before Père Roulland's departure, she obtained his promise to address this petition each morning to the Almighty: "My God, permit Sœur Thérèse to gain souls to Thy love."

When on the point of leaving France, he received this note from her: "I am truly happy to work with you for the salvation of souls. For this end am I a Carmelite. Unable to become actually a missionary, I have longed to be one by love and penance. . . . Ask Jesus in your next Mass to inflame me with the fire of His love, so that I may then help you to enkindle that flame in other hearts."[35]

When the young priest had set out on his journey, he appreciated more than ever the generosity of the soul which had devoted itself to his needs. "I should wish," she wrote, "that my brother might always have the consolations, and I the trials. This is perhaps egoistic; but no, for my only arms are love and suffering united." And again: "I would be most happy to work and suffer long for Jesus; but I ask Him to please Himself in all that regards me, that is to say, not to heed my desires, whether of loving Him in suffering, or of going to enjoy Him in heaven."[36]

But she had a presentiment that the time of the eternal nuptials was near. This happy expectation extinguished neither her ardour nor her hopes. On March 19, 1897, she wrote further to the missionary:

> I sincerely hope that, when I quit this exile, you will not forget your promise to pray for me. I do not desire that you should ask God to deliver me from the flames of purgatory. St. Teresa said to her daughters when asking them to pray for her: "What matters it to me to remain in purgatory till the end of the world, if, by my prayers I save a single soul. . . ." These words find echo in my heart; I long to save souls and to forget self for them. I want to save them even after my death. Therefore, I would wish you to say then a prayer which will ever be fruitful. "My God, permit my sister still to make Thee loved."[37]

Four months later, Thérèse felt that the help she could give while here below was about to end, but she assures her spiritual brother that her aid to him from above is on the eve of commencing. "I shall be of much more assistance to you in heaven than on earth. . . . You will thank the Saviour for giving me means of helping you more efficaciously in your apostolic work. I quite count on not remaining inactive up there. My desire is to labour still for the Church and souls. I ask this of the good God, and I am certain He will hear me."[38]

Then comes the last farewell and final testament of the nun to the priest who continued to labour on a far-off shore. "On the eve of appearing before God, I understand more than ever that there is but one thing necessary, to work for Him alone, not doing anything for oneself or creatures. Jesus wants to possess your heart completely; for that, you must suffer a great deal. . . . But then, what joy will inundate your soul when you reach the happy moment of your entrance into heaven. . . . I do not die, I enter into life . . . ; everything that here below I cannot tell you, I will make you fully understand from Heaven above."[39]

A few weeks later, the saint had finished her earthly task; once received into the arms of God she devoted herself to the Christians of China to whom Père Roulland had given his life.[40]

Another missionary had been given as spiritual brother to Thérèse. The two last years of her life were hallowed by an interchange of prayers and mutual encouragement with a young cleric of the Society of the White Fathers, who owed to her influence his rapid advancement in the way of perfection.

This correspondence will repay examination here. The dear saint has written nothing more impressive than these letters; their exquisite simplicity recalls the sublime conferences of St. Scholastica and St. Benedict. Abbé Belliére was still at the Seminary and had not yet received the Sub-diaconate, when Mère Agnès de Jésus, then Prioress, assigned him Thérèse as spiritual helper. He was a young man of twenty-one, full of ardour and enthusiasm for the evangelization of infidel Africa, but at times overwhelmed with grief at the thought of quitting his family for endless exile. Sœur Thérèse de l'Enfant Jésus, having long before made a like sacrifice, and having lived for several years in an austere Carmel, was able to assume in his regard, sometimes at least, the rôle of counsellor. She accepted this duty with a confidence inspired by faith. She exercised it with an impressive and affectionate simplicity which was destined to unite these two valiant souls for several months in the charity of Christ.

The correspondence commenced in October, 1896, when Abbé Belliére, tortured by the thought of his approaching departure, asked Thérèse to pray for his "mother."[41] The Carmelite's tone is dignified, compassionate and pre-eminently religious.

> Monsieur l'Abbé, your part is in truth noble, since the Saviour has chosen it for you, since He too has touched with His own lips the cup that He presents to you. A saint has said: "The greatest honour that God can confer on a soul does not consist in giving it a great deal but in asking from it a great deal." Jesus treats you as one highly privileged; He wills that you commence your mission now, and that, by suffering, you save souls. Was it not by suffering and death that He Himself redeemed the world? I know that you aspire to the happiness of sacrificing your life for Him; but martyrdom of heart is no less fruitful than the shedding of blood, and from now onward, that martyrdom is yours. So I can say in very truth that your part is noble, that it is worthy of an apostle of Christ.[42]

Encouraged by these words, the seminarist unfolded freely not only his trials and fears, but also the ardour of his zeal and hopes of perfection. Thérèse, on her side, saw in him one of those upright souls which only requires gentle urging to advance rapidly in love of God. She initiated him little by little into the way of filial abandonment which she felt it her mission to make known and followed. She claimed in return an exchange of services. Like Père Roulland, the Abbé Belliére must say for her each day a prayer of which she herself suggested the formula. "Merciful Father, in the name of Thy sweet Jesus, of the Holy Virgin and all the saints, I ask Thee to inflame my sister with Thy spirit of Love, and to give her the grace to make Thee greatly loved."[43]

This communion of spiritual goods between a seminarist full of the future and an invalid then on the eve of death has something of heaven in it, like the intercourse of two pure spirits. We must see with what supreme delight

Thérèse speaks of her approaching end to him whom she henceforth called "her brother."

> You have promised to pray for me all your life. Undoubtedly it will be longer than mine, and you cannot sing like me:
>
> My exile will be short; that hope is mine.
>
> Neither is it permitted to you to forget your promise. If the Saviour takes me soon to Himself, I ask you to continue every day the same little prayer, for I shall desire in heaven that which I have longed for on earth, to love Jesus and make Him loved.
>
> You must think me strange, Monsieur l'Abbé. Perhaps you regret having a sister who, it seems, wishes to enjoy eternal repose while leaving you to work alone. But be reassured. The only thing I desire is the will of God, and I admit, that if in heaven I could work no more for His glory, I should prefer exile rather than the Fatherland. I have no knowledge of the future. Nevertheless, if Jesus realizes my presentiments, I promise to remain your little sister in heaven. Our union, far from being broken, shall become more intimate. Then there will no longer be grille or enclosure, and my soul can fly to you in your far-off missions. Our rôles shall remain the same. For you the weapons of an apostle, for me prayer and love.[44]

While awaiting her departure for the eternal Fatherland, Thérèse applied herself to the task of leading rapidly to the summit of perfection the fervent seminarist, whom she had never seen, but who, through the medium of his "short formal" letters, had made her realize his aspirations towards perfect union with God. She both urged him on and gave him encouragement:

> I have had the same thought as your director. You cannot be a saint by halves. You must be one entirely or not at all. I felt convinced that yours was an energetic soul, and on that account I was happy to become your sister. Do not imagine that you will frighten me by speaking of your "best years wasted." No, I thank Jesus, who has

> turned on you a look of love as formerly on the young man in the Gospel. More fortunate than he, you have corresponded faithfully to the divine Master's call; you have left all to follow Him, and in the golden days of life, at eighteen years.[45]

Not content with combating his fears, she endeavoured to launch him on the way of trustful confidence. "Ah, my brother, since it has been granted me too, to understand the love of the Heart of Jesus, I avow that it has banished from my heart all fear. The remembrance of my faults humbles me, leads me to distrust my own strength which is but weakness; still more does that memory speak to me of mercy and of love. When we cast our faults with filial confidence into the devouring furnace of divine love, how should they not be consumed for ever?"[46]

Such is the apostleship exercised by a young Carmelite almost at the point of death towards a future apostle. Her exhortations were destined to bear fruit, for, shortly afterwards, the Abbé Bellière besought Sœur Thérèse to ask for him the grace of martyrdom.

This correspondence, ever growing more and more simple, candid, and free from human alloy, was to continue until the last days of our dear saint. In noting her parting thoughts and preoccupations, we shall give the ardent exhortations, the words of hope which she continued to send until the end to the future missionary.

♦♦♦

Notwithstanding the exclusively supernatural character of this correspondence between Thérèse and the two ecclesiastics whom her superiors had assigned her as brothers, she was not without discerning the untoward consequences which might result later on from such relations if the example were followed. Thus, she wished before her death humbly to counsel circumspection to Mère Agnès de Jésus. "Later on," she said,

> a great number of young priests, learning that I was given as spiritual sister to two missionaries, will ask the

> same favour at this Carmel. This may become a danger. Only by prayer and sacrifice can we be useful to the Church. Correspondence should be rare, and should not be permitted at all to those who would become preoccupied by it, believing that they would accomplish marvels, while in reality they only harm their own souls, and perhaps fall into the subtle snares of the demon. What I say to you, Mother, is very important; do not forget it when I am gone.[47]

Thus, our saint had the wisdom to realize that apostolic charity must always be regulated by prudence. The love she outpoured generously on her neighbour as the expression or consequence of her love for her crucified Saviour was indeed the "vigilant and circumspect love" which the author of the *Imitation* requires.

Her endeavour to act according to God aimed above all at that virtue which is at the summit of moral perfection, namely, divine love. By her exceeding generosity, she had given a shining example in this virtue, and it was this heroic practice of charity which recently enabled the sovereign Pontiff Pius XI to present little Thérèse as a model to the clamorous and restless world of today. "The spirit of our time," says the Holy Father,

> is, as all know and feel, that of movement, of continuous and hurried action. . . . And in this course, in this feverish occupation of every instant, people too easily overlook the real substance, the true value of all action and of all sanctity. It is Charity. The Heart of God has deigned to reveal it to us.
>
> There are, in truth, many other virtues necessary; but Charity is the greatest of all, *Major horum caritas*,[48] and this virtue makes up for deficiencies which may be found in the exercise of others. Charity is truly the love of God, and, with this motive, it is also love of the neighbour. For if we really love God, we cannot help loving those whom God Himself has loved to the extent of giving His life for them, as He has given it for us.
>
> Now, consider the Venerable Thérèse de l'Enfant Jésus, a true flower of love come from heaven to earth to astonish both earth and heaven. Hers is a heart, a

> soul, tenderly childlike, and at the same time apostolic even to heroism. She is all filled, all vibrating with love of God and of Jesus, a love tender and strong, simple yet deeply rooted, which inspires her with transports of filial abandonment and with the magnificent actions of apostle and martyr.[49]

Her apostolic actions we have already noticed in part. But as "there is no living in love without some sorrow,"[50] we must mention with new details the diverse phases of the martyrdom she endured because of her tender love for Jesus.

11

Suffering's Rôle in the Providence of God Discerned and Interpreted by Thérèse—Her Perfect Practice of Monastic Virtues Properly So Called: Poverty, Chastity, and Obedience—Her Love of the Cross the Condition and Consequence of Her Love for Jesus

God did not make pain; it is the fruit of sin. But by a merciful disposition of His infinite goodness, affliction can become the remedy of sin and a preservative from sin.

Suffering has the power of expiation. Sœur Thérèse de l'Enfant Jésus was not unaware of this power when she resolved to enter Carmel in order to atone for sinners. Suffering enlightens, undeceives, and sets free. The great, the only obstacle to the love of God is a blind and inordinate love of creatures. This inordinate love, dangerous to the soul at all times, is particularly so in periods of prosperity and success. "Our life on earth," says Mgr. Gay,

> is full of delusions. The more worldly we are in spirit, the more numerous do these delusions become and the more power have they to captivate us. We admit at times that we have been deceived and betrayed; but at heart we are pleased, and as long as suffering holds aloof from our life of delusion, we find therein charms which in our mind throw into the shade, and too often even eclipse, the joys of paradise. . . . To this mirage add

> the illusions by which we continually, but more especially in time of prosperity, deceive ourselves. How full of vain assurance and presumption is man, so long as nothing crosses or afflicts him. How many things he forgets and how many others he imagines. What self-complacency in regard to his state! Should he remain thus for but a few years without physical or moral suffering, life then seems to him a sort of heaven, and he is not far off regarding himself as a god. In a word, that man is blind. This is the worst condition that ever could befall a creature whose law is to advance, and who under pain of death should never leave the straight way. Then sorrow comes—comes through God's mercy—life takes a serious meaning and becomes austere and penitent; it assumes its true character.[1]

Sœur Thérèse had long understood this doctrine, she who at the age of fourteen wrote: "It is indeed true that the drop of gall should be mixed with every cup we drink. But I find that thorns help greatly in detaching us from earth; they make us look upwards, beyond this earth."[2]

She would never, of course, think of imputing to God the will to make His creatures suffer without the ultimate design of love. "Oh, no," she writes, "never do our sufferings make Him happy; but this suffering is necessary for us; He then sends us sorrow while, as it were, turning away His Face."[3] And again: "It costs Him much to make us drink at the source of tears, but He knows that it is the only means of preparing us to 'know Him as He knows Himself, to become as gods ourselves. . . .' We are not yet in the fatherland, and temptation must purify us as gold in the furnace."[4]

This clear perception of God's loving designs it was that made her accept with cheerfulness, even before her entrance into the convent, the little crosses of her life at school, her troubles of conscience, too, which were often severe, and later, at the Carmel, her violent temptations against faith.

To souls blinded by the "fascination of earthly trifles," as to those called to higher perfection, God usually sends some great trial, often at an unexpected moment, which reveals His divine Hand either in breaking the power of darkness or severing the last bonds which hold them back from scaling the heights.

Thérèse had gathered early the firstfruits of suffering. "Trial," she declares, "had matured and fortified my soul to such a degree that nothing here below could any longer distress it."[5]

It remained for her to cast herself wholly and entirely into the arms of God, convinced of the frailty of her most reliable human supports. Thus it was then that Providence sent her father that great trial which was to effect her so deeply. She understood its meaning and import from the first moment, as these lines addressed to her sister Céline show: "How has Jesus acted to detach our souls from everything created? Ah, He has stricken a heavy blow, but it is through love. . . . God is admirable, but He is above all lovable."[6]

Such sorrows manifest assuredly the nothingness of earthly joys and have powerful influence in drawing souls towards heaven; they cannot, however, eradicate from the soul, be it ever so sincerely given to God, the three concupiscences, always deep rooted in the sons of Adam since the Fall. These natural tendencies are for ever striving to make the poor heart return little by little to what it has renounced, so that the surest means of strengthening our union with the Sovereign Good is to engage earnestly in unrelenting conflict with these undying foes.

Hence we see the use and high import of the religious vows. Sœur Thérèse de l'Enfant Jésus, who had "never given God anything but love," and who wished to advance, to her last hour, in that sacred intimacy, naturally took the means of establishing herself irrevocably in those blessed dispositions. She had pronounced with joy the vows which bound her to the Divine Master; cost her what it might, she must now fulfil—and with heroic fidelity—the engagements which held her fast in His love. Their observance was for her a further gift of love to Jesus. Let us note some characteristic details of her religious life which, added to those already cited, will show with what vigour she strove to maintain the combat against all inclinations tending to divide her affections.

We have shown striking examples of her religious poverty. All these, however, give but an inadequate idea of the saint's detachment from earthly things.

From the first, she distinguished herself by patience in enduring privations not imposed by the rule itself, and which could have been spared her by more attentive charity on the part of others. Far from complaining, she even reassured Mère Agnès de Jésus, who was sometimes distressed at this negligence. "Do not torment yourself on my account, I beg of you; I am already too well cared for."

She was intensely sensitive to cold, and admitted, during her last illness, that she had suffered at Carmel in this respect "even to death." "When the weather was very severe," one of her sisters tells us,

> the Servant of God, having been benumbed with the cold during the whole day, would go to the community-room for a few moments after Matins to warm herself. But in order to reach her cell she had to walk about fifty yards in the cloisters, in open air; then go up the stairs and along an icy corridor, which completely robbed her of the little warmth so sparingly accorded. Thus, when she lay down on her paillasse wrapped in two poor blankets, her sleep was broken and unrestful. She often spent the entire night shivering with cold and unable to sleep. If she had told this to her novice-mistress during her first years at the Carmel, she would have obtained relief immediately; but she preferred to accept this severe mortification uncomplainingly, never mentioning it until she lay on her deathbed.[7]

By force of virtue and in spite of her natural instinct for elegance, she arrived as we know at absolute indifference in the matter of clothing. Not that she wore her habit with affected negligence, but she accepted it, such as it was, without showing the least sign of displeasure. She had been given a habit which fitted her very badly, and when asked if she did not feel some vexation, "Not the least," she said. "No more than if it were that of an inhabitant of China two thousand leagues away."

Sœur Thérèse de l'Enfant Jésus, who had a natural repugnance to unsightly objects, chose deliberately to keep them in preference to others. She also sought out for her own use the things that were least convenient. Thus during her whole religious life, she used a little lamp in which the wick could only be raised with a pin. On Céline's entrance, Thérèse passed on to her her own serviceable inkstand and holy water font, replacing them by others long disused and relegated to the garret, where she went to look for them. Her pens she continued to write with after they had become unfit for service, and for the manuscript of her autobiography she utilized two series of miserable exercise-books which the last and least in the ranks of school-children would have felt inclined to reject.

In regard to her poems, there was the same spirit of detachment. Her verses were scribbled on old envelopes or waste paper. She would have loved to keep a copy in order to sing them while at work, but she gave them away to every comer, retaining none herself, and so was unable to use her compositions for her own satisfaction or devotion.

This holy poverty was practised by her till the end with the same rigour. During her last illness, she begged that they would not give her costly remedies. She even refrained from asking for the iced water or grapes that had been offered to her, saying that she could not seek those things which were simply pleasing to the taste and not necessary.[8] As long as it was permitted, she passed her nights on the hard paillasse of her cell, far enough from the rest of the community, happy in the thought that she would not disturb other Sisters by her frequent attacks of coughing, as she would if she were in the infirmary. All the comfort afforded her in this little cell is told by her sister Céline. "After the cauterizing needle had been applied—one day I counted five hundred of these applications—she went at night to lie on her paillasse. Not having permission to give her a mattress (I was then assistant infirmarian), I had no other resource but to fold a large blanket in four and place it under her sheet."[9]

Submissive to all the constraints suggested by strict poverty such as gathering up used matches or scraps of paper, Sœur Thérèse endeavoured to leave no moments unemployed. She wished her novices also to be very strict in this matter, "because," as she said, "time does not belong to us."

But we have evidence of what is of greater merit than mortification in the material order. It happened sometimes that, at recreation or elsewhere, a Sister, more or less unconsciously, availed herself of reflections or inspired thoughts of the Saint, giving them out as though they were her own; Thérèse suffered this in silence, never asserting her rights, and acknowledging with sweetness that "the thought did not belong to herself but to the Holy Ghost."

Thus it was, that having renounced every earthly possession, she sacrificed also the fruits of her mind which formed an integral part of herself, a deprivation which is ever a real mortification.

A word now on the precautions which the extreme delicacy of her chastity always suggested to her against the seductions of the flesh.

From early childhood this most pure soul felt exiled and constrained in her prison of clay. "I have always been ill at ease in my body; even when still very young, I felt embarrassed by it." Her presence conveyed an impression of holy reserve, and she inspired all with profound respect.

She was, in truth, so pure and so simple that one could confide to her any kind of temptation; you knew beforehand that she would not be thereby troubled. Not that she felt naturally invulnerable. But she had confided her innocence to the guardianship of the Virgin Mary and St. Joseph. In the strength of their protection she never lost her peace of soul, even in presence of dangerous and unavoidable occasions.

We remember her fervent prayer to Our Lady of Victories on the eve of her departure for Italy. Not without reason had she feared the snares of Satan during this pilgrimage undertaken on behalf of her vocation. Not to speak of the museums and public places through which she passed without allowing her innocence to be ruffled by the slightest breath of evil, there were two occurrences which made her implore the special protection of the Queen of Heaven.

At Bologna, the pilgrims, on alighting from the train, found themselves surrounded by a crowd of students, whose boisterous demonstrations somewhat disquieted and annoyed them. One of these from amidst the crowd stared at Thérèse with effrontery for an instant, then seized hold of her, and in a moment lifted her across the track. But the saintly child, recommending herself to the Blessed Virgin, turned on him such a look that he went away dumbfounded with confusion.[10]

A more subtle temptation was later to come her way. A young man, one of the pilgrims, of perfect manners and education, showed her rather too marked attentions. She received his advances with the coldest reserve, finding this the surest means of checking the tendencies of her own nature so responsive to affection. When alone with Céline, she confided her trouble to her: "Oh, it is indeed time that Jesus took me away from the poisoned breath of the world. I feel that my heart would easily let itself be taken captive by affection, and where others have perished, I would perish too, for every creature is weak, myself in particular." Referring to this in her Autobiography, she writes: "I can claim no merit in not surrendering to the love of creatures since I was preserved only by the great mercy of God."[11]

She had placed her virginity under the protection of Mary and Joseph. She also made humility its guardian, taking at the same time the most assiduous precaution to preserve that great virtue. God rewarded her vigilance by keeping her free, as she herself testifies, from the slightest interior suggestion against chastity. She could discern, besides, with extraordinary wisdom the snares of the enemy, and even recognized the profit that could be derived from such a struggle by a soul living in simple abandonment to God. In this strain she wrote to a young girl in the world: "Pure hearts are often surrounded by thorns. . . . Then the lilies think that they have lost their whiteness; they fear that the thorns surrounding them have succeeded in marring the beauty of their corolla. . . . But lilies in the midst of thorns are beloved by Jesus. Happy those who have been found worthy to suffer temptation."[12]

With even scrupulous fidelity to the religious promises made to her Divine Spouse, Sœur Thérèse had also, through love of Him, sacrificed a dearer and more personal good than earthly possessions or even attachment to creatures. She gave up her own will. She realized that to love Jesus, "as He had never before been loved,"[13] she must dispossess herself for ever not only of every earthly thing but even of self.

On the testimony of her contemporaries in the cloister, Thérèse was from the first moment of her religious life a perfect model of obedience. "Never," declared one of these, "have I seen her in the slightest degree unfaithful to the rule. She was careful to obey in the very least details. When our Mother recommended certain things, she invariably followed these counsels to the letter. She left everything at the first sound of the bell, even if in the middle of a conversation however interesting. If engaged in sewing, she immediately laid her needle aside, not even finishing the stitch she had commenced."[14] Her sister Marie wished one day, while the bell was sounding, to finish writing down some thought that she had given her and which she was afraid of forgetting. Thérèse reproved her gently but frankly: "It would be far better to lose that and act with regularity. If we but knew all that regularity means."

The mistress of novices, Sœur Marie des Anges, has given another striking instance of her religious punctuality:

> One day in winter when, profiting by the authorization of custom, she had taken off thick woollen stockings, which were wet through, to let them dry at the fire during recreation, there came a message that the bell was ringing in the sacristy, of which she then had charge. Simply putting on her hempen sandals, which we call *alpargates*, she went through two cloisters without a thought of the risk she ran in thus exposing herself to the icy-cold blast. How many would have asked for a moment's delay? For her, however, God had spoken; she ran to the call of duty without thinking of the consequences.[15]

Such acts were but the outcome in practice of her theories on obedience. Has she not written in her *Histoire d'une*

Ame: "How happy are simple religious. The will of their superiors being their only guide, they are sure of never deceiving themselves. . . . But when they cease to consult this infallible guide, the soul strays immediately into arid ways where the waters of grace soon fail her."[16]

Nothing less than this firmness of principle would have enabled her to impose on herself the severe privations which the exact observance of religious obedience, in her opinion, demanded. Other facts, also attested to by her sister, show how rigorously she acted towards herself in order to fulfil the Master's command. "It is forbidden in the convent," says Sœur Marie du Sacré-Cœur,

> to read books or papers which are not for our own special use, even should it be only a few words. After a preached retreat, Sœur Thérèse de l'Enfant Jésus told me that she had accused herself of having looked at an illustrated sheet of a catalogue of novelties. And when I remarked that it was not forbidden to look at pictures, she replied, "That is true; but the Father has told me that it is more perfect to deprive oneself even of this. Yet that sight of the world's vanities did but raise my soul to God. Now, however, when I find any such prints, I no longer look at them."
>
> She told me that the fact of our Mother Prioress having given permission to Mère Agnès de Jésus to speak to her occasionally was for her the matter of very great sacrifice, for, not having received permission to reveal her own thoughts, she merely listened to the confidences of her whom she called "her little mother" without giving any of her own. And yet a word would have procured the necessary authorization. "But," she said, "we must not seek permissions which lessen the sacrifices of the religious life, for then it would become a merely natural existence without merit."

Critical circumstances and, more especially, painful doubts were to put to a still sharper test the obedience of Sœur Thérèse de l'Enfant Jésus. We are aware of the service rendered her by Père Alexis during a retreat, by his clear comprehension of her aspirations towards sanctity and his unhesitating pronouncement concerning God's designs in her regard. But, by a regrettable abuse of authority, Mère Marie de Gonzague forbade her, after the first interview, to go back again, as others did, for the purpose of speaking more at leisure on the affairs of her soul. This was a great trial for the Saint, but she suffered in silence.

Her chief object in asking to be kept in the novitiate beyond the ordinary time of probation and remaining there till the end was that she might better practise obedience. When we think that the novice-mistress was then Mère Marie de Gonzague, who joined this charge to the office of Prioress, we can have nothing but unreserved admiration for the young religious who thus chose to remain indefinitely subject even in the smallest details to the superior who had treated her with so little consideration.

Mère Marie de Gonzague had, moreover, made of her own accord a number of little regulations, which, through lapse of memory, she neglected after a short time to enforce, and which, once fallen into disuse, had become for the community a dead letter. In spite of this, Thérèse de l'Enfant Jésus continued to observe such rules until they were duly and expressly revoked.

This fidelity to forgotten or lapsed regulations sometimes cost her dear. She herself has told of the trouble caused by a certain avowal which she made each day in obedience to an order received. "Our mistress," she says,

> had commanded me, when I was a postulant, to tell her whenever I felt sick. This happened every day, and the command became for me a real torture. When the attack of pain came on, I would have preferred a hundred strokes of the lash to the obligation of making it known; nevertheless, I told it each time through obedience. Sœur Marie des Anges, who no longer remembered the order she had given, would say to me on these occasions: "My poor child, you will never have health sufficient to follow the rule; it is too severe for you." And she went for remedies for me to Mère Marie de Gonzague, who, astonished and dissatisfied on hearing of my daily reports, replied sharply: "This child is continually complaining. . . . If she cannot bear her

> pains and aches, her place is not amongst us." Notwithstanding all, I continued for a long time through pure obedience to confess this trouble at the risk of being sent away, until at last, the good God, taking pity on my weakness, permitted that I should be relieved of the obligation of speaking about it.[17]

Through obedience also, and contrary to every personal inclination, she wrote her *Histoire d'une Ame.* A formal command from her Prioress was required to decide her to do that which, if undertaken on her own initiative, would in her eyes have been opposed to humility. We can judge of her mind on the subject by her answer to a young nun who told her that she also intended to write an account of her vocation. "Beware of doing anything of the sort," she said.

> You cannot write it without permission, and I advise you not to seek that. As for me, I would not have wished to write anything about my life had I not received an express command, a command that I would not have sought. It is more humble to write nothing about self. The great graces of life, like that of vocation, cannot be forgotten. The memories of such graces will be of more worth to you if you confine them within your own mind than if you entrust them to paper.[18]

Following her Divine Master's example, the young Saint was to remain obedient unto death. During the last days of her life, when she was burning with fever, her sister Marie, in order to cool and refresh her a little, wanted to take away the sheet which covered her feet. Thérèse stopped her with these words: "I would indeed like it, but it is perhaps not permitted. Ask our Mother." She had thought even that she ought to keep the woolen coverlet, though its weight sorely oppressed her, because Mère Marie de Gonzague had once said, when speaking to the strong and healthy nuns, that it was a laudable practice to bear with this coverlet in the heat of summer.[19]

Invariably faithful from the moment of her profession to the strictest practice of poverty, chastity, and obedience, Sœur Thérèse de l'Enfant Jésus had thus held aloof from every creature calculated to hinder in the least degree her union with her Beloved. By this heroic struggle, she continually offered to her Divine Master a holocaust of love. The suffering, at times severe, entailed by these repeated efforts against temptation kept her in continual tribulation but very near to God, beneath His Divine regard, and close to His Heart. For this reason she submitted in joyful thankfulness to the Divine gift of sorrow. But the saving power of trial, the worth of adversity in steadying the soul on dangerous heights, does not entirely explain Thérèse's loving attraction for suffering nor the fervour with which she trod her path to Calvary unto the end.[20]

We know that she valued suffering lovingly accepted as a means of completing in herself and others the Passion of Christ. If for a moment we take this point of view, we shall understand the attraction for suffering which made the angelic Carmelite, ever smiling beneath her cross, the martyr of love recently extolled by Pius XI.[21]

Without doubt, the sacred Passion of Our Saviour possesses in itself unbounded efficacy. But this efficacy does not become perfect in Christians, does not produce its full effect until, participating in the Divine Passion by faith and the sacraments, they associate themselves with Christ's sufferings, in as far as they are able and God demands, by real imitation and effective compassion. "If a man has not suffered for Jesus and with Jesus," says Mgr. Gay, "he cannot be sure that he loves Jesus."[22]

Sœur Thérèse had probably meditated on these words of the holy Bishop, written especially for Carmelites. At all events, she showed clearly that the difficult virtues of patience in trials of faith, of boundless devotedness to all around her, of poverty, chastity, and obedience, were at once the condition and the result of that compassionate love which from childhood the fervent nun had promised to her suffering Saviour.[23]

As to this love itself, tender and strong, confiding and filial as it was, and for her the source of so many perfections, she gives us to understand that she obtained it above all in virtue of a special grace cherished and turned to profit from her earliest years by faithful co-operation.

She made progress, nevertheless, in this holy love and in her great charity towards her neighbour, more especially for "little souls" called to sanctify themselves in the daily round of ordinary life.

She proposed, in writing her autobiography, to delineate the method which had helped her in her progress onward, and which she has called "the little way of spiritual childhood."

Her exposition is by no means didactic, as we may well surmise, and its elements are found scattered through the *Histoire d'une Ame.* For this reason some profit may, perhaps, be derived from the perusal of the following effort to bring together these elements, these means of advancing in perfection which so quickly made Thérèse a saint of the highest order, means which, as she asserts, prove infallibly efficacious for every soul of good will.

12

Idea, Advantages, and Necessity of the "Little Way of Spiritual Childhood"

Before considering in its highest degree the love which was to consume the heart of Thérèse, it would seem that we should have completed the description of those virtues that sprang from it as from their principle.

Besides the faith of which, in spite of obscurities permitted by God, she gave such continual and such signal proofs, it would have been natural to note her invincible hope, her profound humility, her perfect abandonment into the hands of God.

It happens, however, that these virtues, completing as they do her spiritual endowment, form part of the ascetical method she has expounded in a manner that is altogether original. First of all, then, must be noted the place which humility, confidence in God, holy abandonment, zeal, and, above all, love itself, hold in this system. An exact knowledge of her spiritual doctrine, and the praise that Pope Benedict XV has given it, will show its high importance and even necessity. Following this theoretical examination, we shall study in the next chapter the practice in detail of these same virtues in the daily life of the Saint.

Not that the supernatural qualities already observed in Thérèse were strangers to her doctrine of perfection; but, excepting love, they were perhaps of lesser consequence thereto than those that are to occupy our attention at present.

From her very childhood, Thérèse had commenced to walk in this way. Only in 1895, however, did she begin to reveal its secret. In Chapter IX of the *Histoire d'une Ame* she has described it to her Mother Prioress thus:

> You know, Mother, that I have always longed to be a Saint. But, alas! I have always felt, when comparing myself with the Saints, that there exists between them and me the same difference as we see in nature between a mountain with its summit hidden in the clouds and the grain of sand trodden under the feet of passers-by.
>
> Instead of being discouraged, I said to myself: "The good God would not inspire unattainable desires; I may, then, in spite of my littleness, aspire to sanctity. I cannot make myself greater; I must bear with myself just as I am with all my imperfections. But I wish to seek a way to heaven, a new way, very short, very straight, a little path. We live in a century of inventions. The trouble of walking upstairs exists no longer; in the houses of the rich a lift replaces the stairs. I, too, would like to find a lift to raise me to Jesus, for I am too little to ascend the steep steps of perfection."
>
> Then I sought in the Holy Scriptures for some indication of this lift, the object of my desires, and I read these words from the mouth of Eternal Wisdom: "Whosoever is a *little one*, let him come to me."[1]
>
> I then drew near to God, realizing well that I had found what I sought. Still desiring to know how He would deal with *little ones*, I enquired further, and found this: "As one whom the mother caresseth, so will I comfort you; you shall be carried at the breasts, and upon the knees they shall caress you."[2]
>
> Ah, never have more tender and melodious words gladdened my soul. *Thine arms, O Jesus, form the lift which will raise me to heaven.* For this I have no need of becoming greater; on the contrary, I must remain little and become even smaller. O my God, Thou hast surpassed my hopes, and I will sing Thy mercies: "Thou hast taught me, O God, from my youth, and till now I have declared Thy wondrous works; and unto old age will I continue to declare them."[3]

Here in a few sentences we have the exposition of a spiritual doctrine which, after having made of a weak child a great saint, continues each day to waken in the humblest souls virtues worthy of angels'admiration.

In order, however, that they may prove a sure guide to those whom Thérèse wishes to lead, these lines call for brief commentary.

♦♦♦

And first, we note that nothing is more frequently and more expressly inculcated in Holy Scripture than the necessity of spiritual childhood. Let us add to the text quoted by Thérèse the clear and commanding words of the Master, "Amen, I say to you, unless you be converted, and become as little children, you shall not enter into the kingdom of heaven."[4]

Nothing could be clearer; in order to be saved, and with all the more reason, in order to arrive at eminent sanctity, we must become as little children, we must clothe ourselves spiritually with the virtues of childhood.

What is it, if not littleness and weakness and the lack of all things, which inclines the child to rely with all confidence and simplicity on the affection of his parents, to look to them for everything with perfect abandonment?

This state of want, this radical powerlessness to be self-sufficing are precisely the dispositions which give the child real dominion over the father's heart. Knowing by experience its parents' unbounded anxiety for its welfare, the little one seeks refuge instinctively in their arms, abandoning itself to them without fear. The smaller and weaker the father sees his child to be, and the more he notices its need of support, and its ready confidence, the more does he open his heart to that child. It is not merely momentary protection that this loving abandonment obtains. Paternal love grows at each new service which the child demands, just as the latter's affection expresses itself by new marks of tenderness at each succeeding act of kindness. Thus there takes place a sweet and touching interchange of love, founded originally on the weakness and insufficiency of the little one so tenderly cherished.

But if such be the history of a father's heart, what shall we say of the immeasurable devotedness of the mother towards her new-born babe, who, without her aid, must droop and die? Is it not she, above all, who becomes more and more attached to her child in proportion to its weakness? What can be a surer means of gaining her heart than to make her realize the immense needs of this frail little creature?

Let us now compare these observations with the teaching of Holy Scripture. God is a father, and the burning ardour of His love surpasses all human tenderness. His charity exceeds, moreover, that of the most devoted of mothers here below, since, on the testimony of His prophet, if even the impossible should happen, that a mother forget her infant, yet never need we fear such abandonment on His part.[5] It follows that the surest means of gaining His Heart is to remain or to become again a child, in His eyes, that is to say, to recognize our nothingness in His sight, to lay our poverty before Him, to make ourselves truly little in presence of His Majesty, confiding without fear in His sovereign goodness so that we may move Him to generosity towards us. We have here the initial lines of the way planned out by Sœur Thérèse de l'Enfant Jésus, and the secret which she proposed to reveal to "little souls."

This secret appears simple; it contains nothing which can inspire fear in the feeblest Christian heart. It is essential, however, to discern clearly the true signification of the actions enjoined by this method.

First, there is the recognition of our incapacity and poverty. But this can be recognized and at the same time hated, reviled. What is necessary is that we willingly proclaim our nothingness in regard to the greatness of the Almighty. In other words, the surest disposition to draw from the Father in heaven a kindly smile is *humility* of heart by which we really and truly love to see ourselves as we are, and look with joy into the depths of our lowliness.[6]

This disposition is, alas, comparatively rare, even amongst Christians. The greater number are, indeed, willing to admit their weakness, but only to a certain point. They credit themselves with real personal strength, on which they are content to rely while all goes well, only to fall into discouragement at the first serious obstacle they meet with. They have not understood that the child's strength lies in its very weakness, since God is inclined to help His creatures in proportion to their recognition and humble avowal of their natural helplessness.

To these Thérèse gives an unequivocal lesson when she writes: "In order to be raised to heaven in the arms of Jesus, I need not become greater; I must, on the contrary, remain little and even become smaller."[7] And again: "What pleases Jesus in my little soul is to see me love my littleness and poverty, to see the unquestioning hope I have in His mercy."[8] She goes farther, and says: "It is Jesus who has accomplished everything in me; I have done nothing but remain little and weak."[9]

Let us, however, note henceforward that the workings of Jesus in the soul do not dispense from personal effort. The little child who is helped, supported, saved by its father must repay these benefits by active and generous love as far as it is able. We shall speak later of this necessary co-operation.

A second characteristic trait of spiritual childhood is *poverty.* The child possesses nothing of its own; everything belongs to its parents. But is it not precisely this absolute want of all things which moves the father to provide for every necessity, especially if the child is insistent in drawing attention to the excess of its misery? We give to the little child who has nothing of its own precisely because it has nothing, because it realizes its poverty and pleads for pity. When this state of penury has ceased to exist through the child growing up and commencing to earn his own livelihood, the father, be he ever so affectionate, discontinues his bounty. "Even amongst the poor," observed Thérèse, "the little child is given what is necessary. But when it has grown up, the father is no longer inclined to continue his help, and says: 'Work now; you are able to support yourself.'" Well then, she added, "it is so that I may never hear such words that I have not wished to grow up, feeling incapable of gaining for myself life eternal, for I have never been able to do anything by myself alone. I have always therefore remained little, occupying myself solely in gathering flowers of love and sacrifice and offering them to the good God for His pleasure."[10]

The child, then, who wishes to obtain the help due to its tender years, must say to its father: "I am not able to do anything; be my strength. I have nothing; be my riches."

In the same way, the soul will gain everything by possessing nothing and by looking to God for all. She must, however, accustom herself to await the coming of each day for gifts thereof, asking nothing except what is needed at the present instant, because the grace required is, in God's designs, an actual grace to be given at the opportune moment.

To realize this we have but to meditate on Thérèse's example of supernatural indifference towards what the morrow may bring, as expressed in the following lines.

What matters it, my Lord, if the future sombre be?
To pray Thee for the morrow—ah no, not thus my way;
Preserve my heart unstained, protect me lovingly
Just for to-day.[11]

Moreover, the poor in spirit, when once in possession of God's gifts, be they spiritual or corporeal, will guard against assuming any proprietorship over them, for they belong always to God, who has simply lent them and is free to take them back as He wills. In this also Thérèse, especially towards the end of her life, will be found a perfect model for imitation. "Now," she wrote, "I have received the grace of being detached from the things of heart and spirit as well as from the goods of earth."[12]

Finally, one who chooses the "little way" must be resigned to remaining poor all her life. By this also she will imitate the dear saint who, while multiplying her acts of virtue, did not concern herself with storing up merits for eternity, but laboured for Jesus alone, giving over to Him all her good works to "purchase souls."

The following declarations of Sœur Thérèse de l'Enfant Jésus will help wonderfully in the difficult task of interior despoliation, the fruits of which she extols. "To love Jesus," she says,

> to be His victim of love, the more weak and miserable we are, the better disposed are we for the operations of this consuming and transforming love. . . . The sole desire of being a victim suffices; we must, however, be always willing to remain poor and weak. Herein lies the difficulty, for where are the truly poor in spirit to be found? "They must be sought for afar off," says the author of the *Imitation*. . . . He does not say that they must be sought for amongst the great, but afar off—that is to say, in lowliness, in nothingness. . . . Ah! let us remain far away from pomp; let us love our littleness, let us love to feel nothing. Then shall we be poor in spirit, and Jesus will come to seek us, be we ever so far away. He will transform us into flames of love.[13]

Besides humility of heart and the spirit of poverty, something more is required. *Confidence*, unbounded, unwavering confidence in the merciful goodness of the heavenly Father is the infallible means of inclining His Divine Heart to compassion and bounty. With St. John of the Cross Thérèse repeated from her heart: "From the good God we obtain all that we hope for."[14]

Besides, how can we refuse our confidence to that God who, having out of His gratuitous bounty created man, loved him even unto sacrifice on Calvary? How can we doubt the infinite mercy of Jesus, who has pardoned Magdalen, who opened paradise to the penitent thief, who prayed for His very executioners? To those who dwelt on the rigour of God's justice in order to excite fear, Sœur Thérèse would reply with assurance: "It is because He is just that God is also compassionate and full of tenderness, slow to punish and abounding in mercy, for He knows our frailty; He remembers that we are but dust."[15]

The chief practical conclusion from this doctrine is that a soul initiated into the "little way" must confide in the divine mercy regarding past faults, however grave and multiplied they may have been, that she must look to the same mercy for the pardon of her daily falls. Has not Sœur Thérèse said that "the fault thus cast with filial confidence into the furnace of love is immediately and wholly consumed."[16]

This confidence is also necessary in failure; the futility of human actions draws pity from the Divine Heart. It is equally required in darkness and aridity. The saint, who, towards the end of her life, experienced all these so poignantly, repeated in moments of direst distress: "I turn to God and to all the saints, and I thank them in spite of everything. I believe they wish to see how far my confidence will go."[17] She requires that the care of the future be left with God, and in justifying that demand, she shows what her own practice was in this matter: "The good God has always come to my assistance; He has led me by the hand from my tenderest years; I count upon Him. . . ."[18]

In fine, she wished that no bounds be set to our hopes and desires of attaining to holiness, supporting her words by reference to the merciful omnipotence of "Him who being Power and Holiness itself would have but to take a soul in His arms and raise it up to Him in order to clothe it with His infinite merits and make it holy."[19] And, asserting more definitely the efficacy of confidence even in arriving at the highest perfection, she does not hesitate to add: "If weak and imperfect souls like mine felt what I feel, not one of them would despair of reaching the summit of the mountain of love."[20]

The soul who has chosen the "little way" will endeavour above all to imitate the child in its ingenuous and warm affection for its parents. She will try, as Thérèse charmingly says, to "win Jesus by caresses," to lose no occasion of giving Him pleasure, to let slip no little sacrifice, act, or word which would serve to show our constant affection, not only to suffer but rejoice through love, to know how to smile for His sake always, in everything we do and suffer—such is the infallible way to obtain not only that we be regarded by Him with love, but that we be raised up in His paternal arms and pressed to His Heart.

Let it not be said that this love is inaccessible to a soul in its earthly exile. On the day of baptism it received the mysterious seed of Divine charity; its sole duty consists in tending and fostering that seed by personal and constant effort, helped on by Divine assistance.

It will be objected, perhaps, that love is "the crown of the spiritual edifice," that it would be illusion to commence where we should finish. Yes, perfection of love, it is true, should crown the edifice. But it is no less true that love should direct the whole construction. Let us begin through love, let us continue through love, and we shall see that no better worker than love can be found for the work of perfection. None other builds more quickly, none more solidly, more magnificently, or more beautifully, for love makes everything light and easy. To him that loves, as St. Augustine remarks, nothing costs; or if perchance something does cost in the doing, love rejoices thereat, and works with renewed ardour.[21]

We are in possession of Thérèse's secret of advancing surely on the way of perfection. But the heart of a saint, when consumed by this love which penetrates and envelops it with inextinguishable flames, is not satisfied with devoting itself to Jesus on Calvary, and in the Sacred Host. It longs to give more, to give unceasingly, to give until it covers, if that were possible, the distance separating its poor and feeble love from the Infinite.

But a point is reached where it feels itself held back by the limitations of its nature. If union is to become more intimate still, and more perfect, God must intervene, and, in His liberality, act directly on that soul. That such intervention can take place, and that the history of the Church holds eminent examples of such intervention, Thérèse could have no doubt, she who had so often meditated on the riches of the Blessed Virgin's soul, filled as it was from the moment of her creation with a marvellous plenitude of grace, she who had read with so much admiration and envy the account of the sudden transformation of the Apostles. Therefore, being unable to raise herself by her own strength to the most sweet and close intimacy with the Heart of Jesus, she had recourse in her weakness to the "Divine life."

She recalled the memories of her infancy; she saw herself as a little child vainly trying to climb unaided the stairs that led to her mother's room. She remembered how her mother came at her call, extended her arms, and carried her in a few seconds to that sanctuary where her caresses soon calmed and reassured her child. Her mother's arms had been her lift in reaching the first floor of her own home; the arms of Jesus, who is a thousand times more tender than any earthly mother, would carry her still more swiftly and surely to the happy resting-place amid the delights of pure love.

"Herein, we believe," says Père Martin,

> lies the chief originality of the "little way" of childhood, making it truly a "new way, very short and straight" to arrive at perfection. To place oneself in the hands of God, and in confidence, love, and abandonment, allow oneself to be carried by Him to the highest pinnacle of charity by means of perfect correspondence with His grace—such is the "little way." Thus it is God who does everything. As to the soul, it follows simply with docility the interior movements inspired by its Divine Bearer. It will rejoice simply in being carried in His all-powerful arms.
>
> Nevertheless, it is important to note that a soul which slumbers in indolent quietism cannot rejoice. The soul's rest in the arms of God does not exclude vigilance. "I sleep, but my heart watcheth,"[22] says the Spouse of the Canticles. "*I sleep*" shows abandonment, "*my heart watcheth*" portrays the soul's activity and correspondence with grace. Even in the most perfect state of abandonment, this grace of activity continues. It does not suffice to surrender oneself once for all to the Divine dispensation. As the latter is unceasingly active, so must the soul be constant in its co-operation.
>
> The above remark was necessary in order to exclude erroneous interpretation. But, with that reservation, we can say definitely that when a soul has once taken its place in the Divine "lift," the only thing required by its heavenly Father is its unreserved surrender to His love to be wholly consumed therein, giving itself unresistingly into the hands of Providence to be led as He wills.[23]

Such, then, as a whole, is the doctrine of perfection given by Sœur Thérèse de l'Enfant Jésus. Was this doctrine intended exclusively for her own use, or are its fruits reserved for certain chosen souls resolved to follow the seraphic Carmelite in her upward flight, or again to ingenuous souls inclined by nature towards the happy simplicity of childhood? In other words, is the way of spiritual childhood optional for Christians in general?

The question does not even arise for those who remember the Gospel's explicit invitation. What is capable of variation is the degree of love with which each soul will practise the virtues of the "little way"; all are not obliged, not even all the fervent, to make that offering to merciful Love which epitomizes Thérèse's relations with Jesus. But no Christian soul can be dispensed from practising these virtues which form an integral part of the "little way": humility, the spirit of poverty, confidence and filial love. To Thérèse de l'Enfant Jésus belong the incomparable merit, the everlasting glory of having, without endeavour to conceal difficulties, presented holiness in such an attractive light, of having shown it to be within the reach of every soul of goodwill, even to the lowliest and poorest.[24]

The praise with which the Soveriegn Pontiff, Benedict XV, has honoured this method is of itself sufficient testimony in its favour. At the risk of insisting perhaps too much on the views already given, let us quote in part at least those pages which express the most explicit and authoritative judgement that could be desired in favour of religious teaching.

> There is no one who, knowing anything about the life of "little Thérèse," would not unite his voice to the great chorus proclaiming this life to be wholly characterized by the merits of Spiritual Childhood. *There* lies the "secret of holiness," not only for the French, but for the faithful throughout the entire world. We have, then, reason to hope that the example of the new French heroine will serve to increase the number of perfect Christians, not only of her own nation, but amongst all the sons of the Catholic Church.
>
> To gain this end, a right understanding of *spiritual childhood* is necessary. But is not to-day's Decree,

exalting as it does a fervent disciple of Carmel who attained to the heroism of perfection by the practice of virtues that spring from *spiritual childhood*, is not this Decree itself destined to spread abroad a correct idea of what *spiritual childhood* means?

The harmony existing between the order of sense and that of spirit allows us to base the characteristics of *spiritual childhood* on the former. Observe a child just able to walk, who has not yet the use of speech. If molested by another of its own age or one stronger threaten it, or if it be frightened by some animal unexpectedly appearing, to whom does it run for safety, where does it seek refuge? In the arms of its mother, is it not? . . . Welcomed by her and pressed to her heart, all fears are set at rest, and heaving a sigh of which its little lungs seemed hardly capable, it regards courageously the object of recent alarm and trouble, and even incites it to fight, as though saying: "I have now a sure defender; safe in my mother's arms I abandon myself to her care, assured not only of being protected against enemy attacks, but also of being treated in the way best suited to advance my physical development." So, likewise, is *spiritual childhood* fostered by confidence in God and trustful abandonment into His hands.

It will be useful to consider the qualities of this *spiritual childhood* both as regards what it excludes and what it implies. Spiritual childhood excludes first the sentiment of pride in oneself, the presumption of expecting to attain by human means a supernatural end, and the deceptive fancy of being self-sufficient in the hour of danger and temptation. On the other hand, it supposes a lively faith in the existence of God, a practical acknowledgement of His power and mercy, confident recourse to Him who grants the grace to avoid all evil and obtain all good. Thus the qualities of this spiritual childhood are admirable, whether we consider their negative aspect or study them in their positive bearing, and we thereby understand why our Saviour Jesus Christ has laid it down as a *necessary* condition for gaining eternal life.

One day the Saviour took a little child from the crowd, and showing him to His disciples, He said:

"Amen I say to you, unless you be converted and become as little children, you shall not enter into the kingdom of heaven."[25] O eloquent lesson, which destroyed the error and ambition of those who, looking on the kingdom of heaven as an earthly empire, desired to occupy the first places, or sought to be the greatest there. *Quis, putas, major est in regno coelorum?* And as if to make it still more clear that pre-eminence in heaven will be the privilege of *spiritual childhood,* the Saviour continued in these terms: "*Whosoever therefore shall humble himself and become like to this little child, he shall be the greater in the kingdom of heaven.*" Another day certain mothers drew near and presented their children that He might touch them, and when the disciples would drive them away, Jesus said with indignation: "Suffer little children to come to Me and forbid them not; the kingdom of heaven is for such." And here as before He concluded: "Amen I say to you, whosoever shall not receive the kingdom of God as a little child shall not enter into it. *Quisquis non receperit regnum Dei velut parvulus, non intrabit in illud.*"[26]

It is important to notice the force of these divine words, for the Son of God did not deem it sufficient to affirm positively that the kingdom of heaven is for children—*Talium est enim regnum coelorum*—or that he who will become as a little child shall be the greater in heaven, but He explicitly threatens exclusion from heaven for those who will not become like unto children. Now, when a master expounds a lesson under several different forms, does he not wish to signify by this multiplicity that he has that lesson especially at heart? If he seeks so earnestly by this means to inculcate it, it is that he desires by one or other expression to make it the more clearly understood. We must then conclude that the Divine Master was particularly anxious that His disciples should see in *spiritual childhood* the *necessary* condition for obtaining life eternal.

Considering the insistence and force of this teaching, it would seem impossible to find a soul who would still neglect to follow the way of confidence and abandonment, all the more so, we repeat, since the divine words, not only in a general manner, but in express

> terms, declare this mode of life obligatory, even for those who have lost their first innocence. Some prefer to believe that the way of confidence and abandonment is reserved solely for ingenuous souls whom evil has not deprived of the grace of childhood. They do not conceive the possibility of *spiritual childhood* to those who have lost their first innocence. But do not the Divine Master's words, *Nisi conversi fueritis et efficiamini sicut parvuli,* indicate to them the necessity of change and of work? *Nisi conversi fueritis* points out the *change* which must be effected in Christ's disciples in order to *become* as little children *once more*. And who should *once more become* a child if not he who is so no longer? *Nisi efficiamini sicut parvuli* inculcate the *work,* for we know that a man must work to become and appear what he has never been, or what he is not at present. But since a man must necessarily have been a child at one time, the words *Nisi efficiamini sicut parvuli* inculcate the *obligation* of work in order to regain the gifts of childhood. Any such thought as that of reassuming the appearance and helplessness of early years would be ridiculous; but it is not contrary to reason to find in the words of the Gospel the precept addressed alike to men of advanced years to return to the *practice* of *spiritual childhood.*
>
> During the course of the centuries, this teaching was to find increased support in the example of those who arrived at heroic Christian perfection precisely by the exercise of these virtues. Holy Church has ever extolled these examples in order to make the Master's command better understood and more universally followed. To-day, again, she has no other end in view when she proclaims as heroic the virtues of Sœur Thérèse de l'Enfant Jésus.[27]

Impossible to improve upon this masterly exposition. After thus outlining the theory proposed by the dear saint, we must now study its realization in her own life. How has she herself practised the virtues she declares essential to the "little way"? How has she finally delivered herself up as a victim to Merciful Love, abandoning herself wholly to God's paternal providence? We shall review these briefly, before recalling the circumstances which marked the end of her mortal life.

13

The Virtues of the "Little Way" in Practice: Humility, Simplicity, Spiritual Poverty, Confidence—Thérèse's Consecration to Merciful Love, and Its Effect on Her Life

The "little way of childhood" is based on humility. Feeling herself weak and incapable of all good, seeing herself "unable," as she said, "to climb the rugged steps of perfection," the young saint threw herself into the arms of the good God and established there her dwelling.[1]

Let us consider some of the steps in her ascent, noting her principal supports.

Simplicity accompanies humility, of which it is the charm and the aroma. We shall see what an attractive grace this virtue gave to her least actions. We shall then give some new examples of that spiritual poverty and confidence in God which, wholly penetrated as they were by a love that approached ever nearer to perfect union, preceded Thérèse's consecration to "the Merciful Love of the Good God." In this consecration we cannot but recognize the surest means and the most striking manifestation of this supernatural union. Finally, we shall briefly note the principal forms of this effective love in the predestined soul who surrendered herself unreservedly to Divine Providence and desired to give without measure—namely abandonment and zeal for the glory and joy of her celestial Spouse.

These virtues of humility, detachment, confidence, and abandonment shone especially in the life of St. Thérèse de l'Enfant Jésus in the solitude of Carmel, and it is in the silent cloister that we shall now seek for their most characteristic manifestations. But it should be remembered that those virtues had also adorned her childhood, and had preserved the years of her youth from all taint of the worldly spirit.

The reader will have observed the numerous passages where Thérèse protests her littleness before God, her weakness and nothingness. But she proposed to draw down on herself, by other means than mere words, the eyes of her Heavenly Father, which naturally turn towards His little ones. Her love for what she called her lowliness, and her desire for humiliation had been remarked in the world; in Carmel she gave reiterated and daily proof of these same virtues, of which we shall pick out a few of the principal manifestations.

We know what she had to suffer from the state of humiliation to which Providence had reduced her father, and with what resignation of heart she declared this catastrophe to be the most precious sign of the Saviour's mercy. Other occasions of humiliation arose in her community life and became through her virtue motives of spiritual joy. Her fellow-worker in a duty assigned to her was an invalid who did not content herself with merely exercising Thérèse's patience by her eccentricities of character. The young nun had sometimes to endure her bitter reproaches. And this is how she received them. "One day," relates a novice,

> when I went to Sœur Thérèse de l'Enfant Jésus for advice, she came to me looking quite radiant. I asked her why she was so happy. She replied: "I have been with Sister X., and she told me everything that displeased her in me. She thinks, perhaps, that she has caused me pain; but no; on the contrary, she has given me pleasure. How I wish to meet her again, so as to greet her with a smile!" At that moment someone knocked at the door. It was the very Sister in question. Thérèse received her with sweet affability, just as if they had been exchanging compliments during the preceding hours.

To an old nun who expressed astonishment at seeing her, though only twenty, charged with the formation of the novices, and remarked disapprovingly that at her age she had perhaps more need of learning how to direct herself than of assuming the direction of others, the young saint replied with angelic sweetness: "Ah, Sister, you are indeed right; I am even far more imperfect than you imagine."

Humble and gentle under unmerited reproaches, she was much more so if it happened that, by inadvertence, she caused pain to one of her companions. "I have seen her," says Mère Agnès de Jésus, "ask pardon with touching humility of the Sisters to whom she believed she had caused pain. Addressing one of them during her last illness, she said with holy fervour: 'Oh, I sincerely ask your pardon. Pray for me.' And large teardrops rolled down her pale cheeks." This act of humility accomplished, she recovered all her serenity, and a few days before her death, she said to Mère Agnès: "I experience very great joy not only in knowing that I am considered imperfect, but above all in realizing how great is my misery, and in feeling that I have so much need of God's mercy at the moment of death."[2]

She fearlessly exposes in her conferences with the novices the depths to which a truly religious soul should abase itself in order to find its true place before God.

"To be humble," she said to a Sister placed under her direction, "we must joyfully consent to the commands of all. When a service is asked of you, or when you tend the sick and find any who are not of an agreeable disposition, you should consider yourself as a little slave whom everyone has the right to command."[3] And she took great care on her own part to fortify herself against self-esteem which could easily result from the manifestly high place she held in the opinion of those around her.

To the novices' words of flattery she remained indifferent. "These," she said, "mean nothing to me. I am in reality what the good God thinks I am. . . . You envy me. But do you not know that I am very poor? It is the good God who gives me all according as I need it." She expressed the same thought in the *Histoire d'une Ame:* "All creatures may turn towards the 'little flower,' admire her, heap praises upon her—all this is powerless to add a single atom of false joy to the true happiness she feels in her soul in realizing what she is in the eyes of God, a poor, insignificant little creature, nothing more."[4] And later she confirmed this opinion on hearing extolled the graces and favours she had received from the Almighty. "I think that I am the fruit, perhaps, of the desires of an unknown soul to whom I shall owe all the graces given me by the good God."[5]

Not that Sœur Thérèse de l'Enfant Jésus failed to recognize God's generosity towards her. Had she not freely written to Abbé Bellière: "Think not that humility prevents me from recognizing the gifts of God. I know that He has done great things in me, and I sing of them every day with joy."[6] But she understood that the gifts of God in her did not lessen her own weakness and insufficiency.

She thus became in the religious life ever more lowly in her own eyes, ever more desirous of oblivion and contempt. Her illness, in lessening her physical powers, was to furnish her with fresh occasions for humbling herself.

A Sister who had often experienced her kindness asked her one day to do some painting for her. Thérèse was already very weak and unable to accede to such a desire without extreme fatigue. Mère Agnès de Jésus, who was present, pointed out to the Sister that the invalid was consumed by fever, and that work requiring application would exhaust her. The nun insisted. A struggle then ensued in Thérèse's soul, and, in spite of herself, her face became slightly flushed from the inward strife. She felt that her sister had noticed her emotion. Was there not occasion for the little invalid to accuse herself of want of courage? That evening she addressed the following lines to Mère Agnès:

> Just now your child has shed sweet tears, tears of repentance, but still more of thankfulness and love. To-day, I have shown you my virtue, my treasures of patience, I who preach so well to others! I am glad you have seen my imperfection. . . . You did not chide me. . . . I deserved it nevertheless. But ever and always your gentleness has meant more to me than severe words; you are for me the symbol of Divine Mercy. Oh, my beloved Mother, I confess that I am far more happy

> through having been imperfect than if, sustained by grace, I had been a model of patience. It does me good to see that Jesus always is so gentle, so tender towards me. I feel I could in truth die of thankfulness and love.[7]

The nearer she approached the end, the more did she become penetrated with the sense of her unworthiness, even giving expression to outbursts of compunction which drew tears from those around.

One morning, when holy Communion was brought to her, she experienced at the moment of the *Confiteor* an extraordinary sentiment of humility. After her thanksgiving, she said to Mère Agnès de Jésus: "I saw Our Saviour about to give Himself to me, and this humble confession seemed so necessary! . . . I felt myself, like the publican, a great sinner. I thought the good God so merciful! When I felt the sacred Host on my lips, I shed tears. I believe those were tears of perfect contrition." And she added in earnest tones: "Ah, how impossible it is to arouse such sentiments in oneself! The Holy Spirit alone can produce them in the soul."[8]

But see what may be called the crowning point in a life of entire abnegation. Amongst those who had access to Thérèse in her last illness was a lay Sister who, having merely seen her perform punctually things which seemed so ordinary, found it difficult to understand that a high opinion could be entertained of her virtue. She offered some food one day to the dying Sister which would infallibly have brought on vomiting. The latter gently refused it, gave as her reason the danger of what might follow, and asked that she might be excused. The temporary infirmarian showed displeasure at this refusal, though so gentle and so fully justified, and she went so far as to say to some one afterwards: "I do not know why they talk so much of Sœur Thérèse de l'Enfant Jésus; she does nothing remarkable; one cannot even say that she is exactly a good religious."

When the dear saint was told of this remark, her face lit up with a smile. Shortly afterwards, she confided her happiness at being thus misunderstood to a Sister of solid virtue who had come to visit her. "To hear on my bed of death that I am not a good religious, what joy!"

Recalling the scene later, this Sister declared: "It is the most edifying souvenir that I have retained of the Servant of God."[9]

Thus she who had always sought the last place, who, while directing the novices of her community, had desired to remain to the end as one of themselves, who on every occasion had declared her nothingness, was to end, in the sacred joy of the humiliations of Calvary, her life which had been entirely hidden from the world, and for the greater part unknown by many of her companions in the cloister. Her weakness and her lowliness, accepted, desired and loved, had given her sure access to the "little way" which was so soon to lead her to the summit of pure love, towards which she advanced with a train of other virtues as well.

Her simplicity placed an aureole of exquisite charm even around those actions of hers which, closely examined, presented the character of austerity or heroism. "How simple it is to love Thee, my Saviour!" she writes. And this child, so near to our ordinary lives, found means almost from her infancy of investing with the highest supernatural value the humblest actions of earth, and of offering to Jesus the love of a saint from amidst her playthings—her doll, her bird-cage, her bowl of goldfish, her butterfly-net. Later on, it is in plying her needle, in sweeping the cloister, and washing rough clothing that she will adorn with sparkling jewels the nuptial robe destined for her by her Divine Spouse. Her chief instrument of penance was an austere rule practised silently at each moment of every day during the long months of nine years. Her favourite book, that book which led her into the most secret dwelling-place of the Holy of holies, was not a treatise of high mysticism, nor a dissertation on the different stages of contemplation; it was the *Imitation,* with its unction so accessible and so sweet to the humble of heart. But before all others came the Gospels in their divine simplicity, so that when there was question later on of setting down in the conventional phrases of asceticism the different phases of her interior life, the learned found not where to assign place therein to the "prayer of quiet," or the "spiritual nuptials." Everything in her life had been simple, natural, without noise, without learned terminology. What she had done is within the power of all, provided they remember always that—

> A lowly life, with small and tedious actions filled,
> Is precious toil, enjoining heart-filled love.[10]

Childlike simplicity, joined to the weakness of infancy, moves a father's heart. But he turns more lovingly still, as we know, towards his little child on reflecting that it has nothing of its own, that it can acquire nothing of itself, but looks to him for everything.

Sœur Thérèse was fully conscious of this, she who, a short time before her death, said to Mère Agnès de Jésus: "I have found great consolation in the thought that never in my spiritual life have I been able to pay back a single one of my debts to the good God, but that this meant for me real riches and strength; then I recalled the words of St. John of the Cross, and repeated with indescribable peace the same prayer: 'Oh, my God, I beseech Thee to pay all my debts for me.'"[11]

From whence did such assurance come? From her entire despoliation which she spoke of joyously as her greatest wealth, since it was to procure for her the treasures of the Heart of Jesus.

"Nothing remains in my hands," she said. "Everything I get is for the Church and souls."[12] On this, then, she founded her undying hope.

Wishing that others might appreciate them too, she extolled the advantages spiritual poverty had gained for her. She endeavoured to fortify her novices against dejection at the sight of their own deficiencies. To one of them in particular she said: "You are quite little; remember that. And one who is quite little has no need of 'beautiful thoughts.'"

One day when she had told her sister of a pious thought which to the latter seemed original and of deep signification, Céline expressed regret that such thoughts did not come to her. "The good God," replied Thérèse, "well knows the beautiful thoughts and ingenious ideas which we would like to have."

"Yes," said Céline, "but you feel very tenderly towards the good God, whereas I do not. Yet I so much wish it. Perhaps my desire will supply for it."

"Certainly it will, especially if you accept the humiliation of this deficiency, if you even go so far as to rejoice in it. That will give more pleasure to Jesus than if you had never been wanting in tenderness. Say: 'My God, I thank Thee that I have not a single tender feeling, and I rejoice to see them in others.'"

The parable of the labourers who had worked but one hour in the vineyard, and whom the master of the household rewarded equally with the others, charmed Thérèse. "You see," she said, "that if we abandon ourselves, if we place our confidence in the good God, exerting our own feeble efforts and placing all hope in His mercy, we shall be rewarded and paid as much as the greatest saints."[13]

Happy in seeing herself despoiled for the Church and souls even of her most precious spiritual treasures, the dear saint rejoiced with greater reason at finding herself deprived of all sensible sweetness in her relations with her Divine Master. Thérèse understood that he loves God purely who has sacrificed the too personal satisfaction of feeling that love. Love does not consist in sensible feeling, but in self-forgetfulness. Listen to Thérèse's words: "*My consolation is to have no consolation on earth.*"[14]

> She will walk henceforth in the bleak night. She will suffer a veritable martyrdom of body and soul. Made naturally for love, her extreme tenderness of heart and the delicacy of her feelings seem to call for torrents of Divine tenderness. Yet she will have naught to sustain her but cold, bare, and clouded faith. . . . "To suffering," she says, "I have become accustomed to respond with a smile." She tastes no longer the least pleasure, but she is fixed in happiness.[15]

The joyous acceptance of insufficiency supposes in the poor in spirit an absolute confidence in Him who is able by a single act to enrich them. It would be useless to multiply the declarations by which our Saint has affirmed her trustful faith in Divine assistance. We will merely add some further characteristic details, with purpose to show this confidence in its active manifestation, confidence which she had at all times practised before preaching.

She felt assured that God would always bless her efforts if she on her part neglected no duty. During her father's illness, she showed a calmness and spiritual contentment which caused those around her to wonder. She wrote at the time to Céline: "Life is but a dream. Soon we shall awaken, and what joy that will be! The greater our sufferings are, the brighter will be our glory with God."

Discouragement never got any hold over her. The frailty she felt in herself, the terrible aridity of soul which threatened to sap her energy were met by only more assiduous practice of her difficult duties.

Persuaded that we should never be afraid of desiring or asking too much, she said with conviction: "We must say to the good God, 'I know well I shall never be worthy of that for which I hope, but I stretch out my hands to Thee like a little beggar, and I am confident that Thou wilt grant all I ask, because Thou art so good.'"[16]

When she did not, apparently at least, obtain anything after long and fervent prayer, she would thank Our Saviour and the saints for having exercised her patience for her greater good.

The Communion of saints was for her a powerful motive of hope. On this subject she one day unfolded to her sister Céline a theory based on solid ascetical authority which may be a source of great encouragement in the struggle for perfection. Sœur Geneviève de la Sainte-Face found in Thérèse's virtues an incentive to salutary emulation. Once, in the course of conversation, she naïvely said to her: "What I envy you are your works of zeal. I wish I could compose beautiful poetry like yours which would make God loved. . . ."

"Ah," replied the saint,

> we should not be anxious about such things. No, we should not grieve over our powerlessness, but apply ourselves solely to love. . . . If, however, we do feel too

> much distressed on account of this poverty in ourselves, let us offer to the good God the works of others. That it is possible to get them accepted in this way is a benefit that comes from the Communion of saints. Tauler has said: "If I love the good that is in my neighbour as well as he loves it himself, this good belongs to me as well as to him. By this communion, I can be enriched with all the perfection which is in heaven and on earth, in the angels and in all who love God." You see, you will do as much as I, and even more, when, with the desire to do the good you see me or others do, you accomplish through love the humblest action, when, for example, you overcome your repugnance and render a slight service.[17]

She committed to God the care of her health as well as the interests of her soul. "The good God sees all," she said. "I abandon myself to Him. He knows well how to inspire our Mother to see that I am looked after should it be necessary."[18]

She wished to see this confidence also in the hearts of her novices. One of these met with strong opposition in the community when the time came for her admission to profession. At the moment when everything seemed hopeless, Thérèse asked her: "Are you confident of succeeding in spite of all?"

"Yes, I am convinced that I shall obtain this grace, and nothing can shake my confidence."

Then in a tone of conviction, Thérèse said: "Hold fast your confidence. It is impossible for the good God not to respond to it, for He ever measures His gifts by our hope in Him. Nevertheless, I admit that if I had seen you waver, I would have felt doubtful myself, as, from the human point of view, all hope is lost."

The novice was admitted and became a fervent religious.

In order to appreciate the merit of such acts, we should remember in the midst of what darkness they were often produced. Sœur Thérèse de l'Enfant Jésus had to undergo, as we know, a terrible temptation against faith, and consequently against hope, a temptation lasting not less than eighteen months. Her soul, at that time, passed through a crisis, during which heaven seemed closed to her, leaving her in profound darkness. But it was then especially that she multiplied her acts of confidence and abandonment to God. "I saw her at this period of her life," writes R. P. Godefrey Madelaine. "Judging from the exterior, no one could guess the pain that was within. I asked her how she was able thus to hide the trial she was undergoing. 'I try,' she said, 'not to let others suffer on account of my pain. It is known only to God, to our Mother Prioress, and to the confessor of the convent.'"[19]

Moreover, it was in the midst of this temptation regarding particularly the existence of heaven that Thérèse expressed most ardently the hope and desire of eternal happiness. She was already seriously ill when she learned that the doctor who attended the community had said regarding her: "Out of a hundred persons attacked as she is, perhaps two at most might have a chance of recovery." Addressing one of her sisters, Thérèse gaily remarked: "What a misfortune if I were going to be one of those two!"

"Then you are not afraid of death?"

"On the contrary, it frightens me greatly when I see it represented in pictures as a spectre. But death is not a spectre. To have an idea of death, I need only recall the answer in my catechism. 'Death is the separation of soul and body.' Well, I do not fear a separation which will reunite me for ever to the good God."[20]

Thus spoke this soul, though tortured by the bitterest agony of doubt regarding the reality of the future towards which she soared with all the strength of her love and faith.

The dear saint knew besides that neither hope, even heroic hope, nor spiritual poverty, nor simplicity, nor humility could, without love, win the Heart of the Divine Spouse. Thus every act of virtue performed by her was impregnated and, as it were, embalmed with love.

Thérèse de l'Enfant Jésus has then not only taught and preached her "little way"; she has first travelled every step of it herself. She has consequently struggled through all its rough places like the humblest of "little souls." She walked the more securely therein, and invites others to follow her with all the more conviction since according to her own avowal, this way was pointed out expressly to her by the Divine Master Himself. "It is Jesus alone," she affirms, "who has instructed me. No book, no theologian taught me; yet I feel in the depths of my heart that I am in the right."

This upward march meant each day new progress in Divine union. By "strewing before Jesus the flowers of little sacrifices," that is to say, by renunciation through humility and detachment, and by manifesting to her heavenly Father that filial confidence which rendered her love more and more tender, the young maiden arrived at a rare degree of intimacy with Jesus. But was not the Spouse on whom she lavished her affections the Jesus of Bethlehem, of Nazareth and of Golgotha? And must she not raise herself up, even to the Cross, to receive His loving embrace? How, then, could she worthily love a God who for man's redemption became a slave and poor, was born in a stable, lived in a workman's shop and died on a gibbet, without giving her body, her soul, and her life for Him, for His honour, the extension of His Kingdom, and for those souls for whose sake He had delivered Himself to the executioners?

In the measure in which Thérèse's love for Jesus increased, this Jesus who had delivered Himself for her and to whom she had consecrated her life, she felt growing within her the thirst for devotedness, the desire of sacrifice, the need of union between the little flame that burned within her and the consuming fire of the Divine Heart, which the most glorious dreams of immolation could not express nor satisfy.

Then it was that she wrote these lines in the *Histoire d'une Ame,* lines said to have been written in her blood, and which, since the *Ego libentissime impendam* of St. Paul, constitute perhaps the most Divinely impassioned apostolic cry that has ever come from human lips.

> To be Thy spouse, O Jesus, to be a Carmelite, to be, by my union with Thee, the mother of souls, all this should satisfy me. Nevertheless I find within me other

vocations. I find the vocation of soldier, of priest, of apostle, of doctor, and of martyr. . . . I long to accomplish all that is most heroic; I feel within me the courage of a Crusader; gladly would I die on the battle-field in defence of the Church.

The priestly vocation! . . . With what love, O Jesus, would I bear Thee in my hands, when my words had brought Thee down from heaven. With what love would I give Thee to souls. But, alas, while desiring to be a priest, I admire and envy the humility of St. Francis of Assisi, and I feel the call to imitate him in his refusal of the sublime dignity of the priesthood. How, then, can these contrary desires be reconciled? . . .

I would enlighten souls as did the prophets and doctors of the Church. I would travel the earth, O my beloved, to preach Thy Holy Name, and plant Thy Cross in heathen lands. But one mission would not satisfy me. I would wish to proclaim Thy Gospel at the same time in all parts of the world, even in the most remote of its islands. I would desire to be a missionary, and that not only for a few years, but from the very creation of the world until the very end of time.

Above all, I long to be a martyr. Martyrdom! That was the dream of my youth. This dream has grown in my little Carmelite cell. But here, again, is folly, for I desire not one kind of suffering only; I will not be satisfied with less than all. Like Thee, my adored Spouse, I would be scourged and crucified. . . . I would be flayed like St. Bartholomew, plunged into boiling oil like St. John; like St. Ignatius of Antioch, I would be ground by the teeth of wild beasts, thus to become a bread worthy of God. With St. Agnes and St. Cecilia, I would offer my neck to the sword, and, like Joan of Arc, murmur the name of Jesus as I burned at the stake.

When my thoughts turn to the frightful torments which will be the lot of Christians in the days of Antichrist, my heart leaps with emotion, and I wish that they were reserved for me. Open, O my Jesus, Thy Book of Life wherein are recorded all the deeds of the saints. How I long to have accomplished those same deeds for Thee!

> What wilt Thou reply to all these follies? Is there on earth a soul weaker, more powerless than mine? Yet, by reason of that very weakness Thou hast been pleased to grant all my childish desires, and to-day Thou wilt fulfil other longings, greater than the universe. . . .

Anxious to find out the secret of these aspirations, which could not have existed without some object, since God Himself had inspired them, Thérèse had recourse to the Epistles of St. Paul. She there noticed the following invitation: "Be zealous for the better gifts. And I shew unto you yet a more excellent way."[21]

And this way, more excellent, according to the Apostle, than the apostolate, or than martyrdom itself, is no other than love. Henceforth, Thérèse could find some repose. She understood that love performs the heart's functions in the mystical body of the Church, that consequently it alone vivifies the members, that, "if love were extinct, apostles would no longer preach the Gospel, nor martyrs shed their blood." She saw clearly too that "love comprises in itself every vocation, that love is all, extending over all time, including every place, because it is eternal."

Then in an outburst of rapture, the young maiden cries out with seraphic ardour: "O Jesus, my Love, I have at length discovered my vocation. My vocation *is love*. Yes, I have found my place in the bosom of the Church, and this place Thou, O my God, hast given me. In the heart of the Church, my mother, *I shall be love*. . . . Thus I shall be all. Thus will my dream be realized."[22]

What must have been the burning charity in the heart of a simple creature which could enable it to embrace the entire world in its devotedness, urging it to accomplish at the same time the office of priesthood, the labours of doctors, the immolation of martyrs? Human love alone could never prove sufficient; the love of God Himself was required, elevating to Him, penetrating, assimilating and making godlike the love of His child; this and this alone could work such marvels. To attain to that charity, that sublime dream inspired by God, Thérèse had need again of a "lift." This indispensable lift, required to raise finite love beyond its natural limits and unite it to the Divine, was supplied by Jesus Himself, her "Divine Eagle" who carried her on His own wings.

This union of two loves in a transforming and deifying furnace is principally and properly God's work. But, with the help of Divine grace, it is also the work of the creature who submits herself willingly to those furnace-flames in order that she may be consumed.

This Act, so elevated and holy, so meritorious and fruitful, was pronounced by Thérèse de l'Enfant Jésus on the feast of the Holy Trinity, June 9, 1895. She called it her *"Act of oblation as victim of holocaust to the Merciful Love of the Good God."*

It sprang spontaneously from her soul during holy Mass.

"O my Divine Master," she thought,

> shall Thy Justice alone receive victims of holocaust? Has not Thy merciful Love itself need of them? Everywhere it is ignored, rejected. . . . The hearts Thou dost desire to fill with Thy love turn to creatures, seeing their happiness in the miserable affection of an hour, instead of throwing themselves into Thine arms, and accepting the sweet consuming fire of Thine infinite love.
>
> O my God, is Thy rejected love to remain in Thy Heart? I think that if Thou shouldst find souls offering themselves as *victims of holocausts to Thy Love,* Thou wouldst consume them rapidly, Thou wouldst be happy in not having to hold back the flames of infinite tenderness which are pent up in Thee.
>
> If Thy Justice, so far as it is confined to earth, is pleased to avenge itself on voluntary victims, how much more does Thy merciful Love desire to inflame souls since *Thy mercy reacheth to the clouds.*
>
> *O Jesus, may I be that happy victim! Consume Thy little victim by the fire of Divine Love.*

Without reserve, following the generous leading of her heart, the dear saint surrendered herself. But reflecting on the new and far-reaching import of such an oblation, she wished through obedience to submit it to her Mother

Prioress for consent before binding herself irrevocably, and even before defining that offering in words. Mère Agnès de Jésus was then prioress, and Thérèse came to her at the end of the thanksgiving, her face aglow with heavenly fervour. Mère Agnès gave her the desired authorization, without however appearing to attach special importance to the matter. The saint then expressed her burning aspirations in a definite formula, the last lines of which seem to echo a seraphic hymn. This done, she desired that her offering might be revised and approved by a theologian.

We give this act of oblation, as found after her death in a copy of the Holy Gospels which she carried night and day near her heart:

> O my God, Most Blessed Trinity, I desire to love Thee and to make Thee loved, to labour for the glory of Holy Church by saving souls on earth and by delivering those who suffer in Purgatory. I desire to accomplish Thy Will perfectly and to attain to the degree of glory which Thou hast prepared for me in Thy Kingdom; in a word, I long to be a saint, but I know that I am powerless, and I implore Thee, O my God, to be Thyself my sanctity.
>
> Since Thou hast so loved me as to give me Thine only Son to be my Saviour and my Spouse, the infinite treasures of His merits are mine; to Thee I offer them with joy, beseeching Thee to behold me only through the eyes of Jesus and in His Heart burning with love.
>
> Again, I offer Thee all the merits of the saints, in heaven and on earth, their acts of love and those of the holy angels; finally, I offer Thee, O Blessed Trinity, the love and the merits of the holy Virgin, my most dear Mother; to her I entrust my oblation, begging her to present it to Thee.
>
> Her Divine Son, my well-beloved Spouse, during the days of His life on earth, told us: "*If you ask the Father anything in My Name, He will give it to you.*"[23] I am then certain that Thou wilt hearken to my desires. My God, I know it; the more Thou willest to give, the more dost Thou make us desire.
>
> Immense are the desires that I feel within my heart, and with confidence I call upon Thee to come and take

possession of my soul. I cannot receive Thee in Holy Communion as often as I would; but, Lord, art Thou not Almighty? Remain in me as in the Tabernacle; never leave Thy little victim.

I long to console Thee for the ingratitude of the wicked, and I pray Thee to take from me the power to displease Thee. If through frailty I sometimes fall, may Thy Divine glance purify my soul immediately, consuming every imperfection, as fire transforms all things into itself.

I thank Thee, O my God, for all the graces Thou hast showered on me, in particular for having made me pass through the crucible of suffering. With joy shall I behold Thee on the last day bearing Thy sceptre the Cross. Since Thou hast deigned to give me for my portion this most precious cross, I have hope of resembling Thee in heaven, and of seeing the sacred stigmata of Thy passion shine in my glorified body.

After exile on earth, I hope to enjoy possession of Thee in the eternal Fatherland; but I have no wish to amass merits for heaven; I will work for Thy love alone, my sole aim being to give Thee pleasure, to console Thy Sacred Heart, and to save souls who will love Thee for ever.

At the close of life's day, I shall appear before Thee with empty hands, for I ask not, Lord, that Thou wouldst count my works. . . . *All our justice is tarnished in Thy sight*; I therefore desire to be clothed with Thine own Justice, and to receive from Thy love the eternal possession of Thyself. I crave no other throne, no other crown but Thee, O my Beloved.

In Thy sight time is nothing; *one day is as a thousand years*.[24] Thou canst in an instant prepare me to appear before Thee.

That my life may be one act of perfect love, I offer myself as a Victim of Holocaust to Thy Merciful Love, imploring Thee to consume me unceasingly, and to let the floodtide of infinite tenderness, pent up in Thee, flow into my soul, that so I may become a very martyr of Thy love, O my God.

May this martyrdom, having first prepared me to appear before Thee, break life's thread at last, and may my soul take its flight unhindered to the eternal embrace of Thy merciful Love.

I desire, O my Beloved, at every heart-beat, to renew this oblation an infinite number of times, *till the shadows fade away*,[25] and I can tell Thee my love eternally face to face. . . .

Marie-Françoise-Thérèse de-l'Enfant Jésus et de la Sainte Face
Rel. Carm. Ind.[26]

This long formula was presented for examination to R. P. Lemonnier of the Missionaries of La Délivrande who had come to preach a retreat at the Carmel. He considered it orthodox, and suggested no modification except the change of one adjective.[27]

Two of the requests expressed in this prayer, with regard to the obtaining of the stigmata in heaven, and the conserving of Our Saviour's presence in the intervals between her Communions, appeared to him, it is true, rather daring; but he realized that the loving confidence of the saintly child led her to act with what may be called audacity towards her heavenly Spouse, and for that reason, he did not curtail them in any way. Besides Thérèse kept this consecration secret except from two novices of whose generosity she felt assured; but she accustomed herself to recite the above Act very frequently, so that it became the authentic expression of her habitual dispositions. She was to renew that oblation until her last hour.

What is exactly the signification of this Act? It is an offering of self to God's Merciful Love, but an offering made by the creature in order to draw down to her this merciful Love. If, then, the oblation is accepted, its first effect will be to draw from the Divine Heart torrents of love to set that soul aflame. She will also become the object of the Master's sweetest mercies, since the Almighty's charity towards His feeble creature implies abundant indulgence and pardon. The soul will be consumed, not by material fire, but by the symbolic flame of Divine Love, with which, by her union with the Heart of Jesus, she is henceforth surrounded and penetrated.

Thérèse speaks of martyrdom; she meant, however, not strictly the martyrdom of physical suffering but of love. This latter is effected by the floods of infinite tenderness which submerge the soul, so that it cannot, without groaning beneath the weight, endure their Divine force. But can we not imagine what ineffable sweetness must temper the rigours of such a martyrdom, and how, if it is good to live through this suffering, it is better to die by the same sweet martyrdom?

True it is, as we have shown previously, that suffering is the inseparable companion of love; but the trial will be proportioned to the supernatural energy with which the grace of the Well-beloved will have previously fortified the soul, and the act of oblation to Merciful Love will not bring as its necessary consequence, exceptional sufferings.

R. P. Martin sums up the salutary and happy results of this consecration in a few lines, the theological depth and precision of which the reader will appreciate.

> The essential and by far the most desirable result of martyrdom by love is to make the soul live in the continual exercise of charity, or according to the saint's own words, "in an act of perfect love."
>
> Now, when love so takes possession of the soul, it becomes master of all her faculties and animates all her acts. Consequently, all her actions, even the most indifferent, are stamped with the Divine seal of love, and their value in the eyes of God becomes immense.
>
> This is not all. Divine Love cannot suffer the presence, or even the trace of sin in the soul where it reigns supreme. Undoubtedly, the oblation to Merciful Love does not give impeccability nor prevent absolutely every fall. A little victim may still be guilty of infidelities. But the love which penetrates and surrounds her *renews her*, so to speak, *at each moment, and ceases not to consume her, destroying thus in her everything which could displease Jesus.*[28]

Thérèse, one day, had said to God, as we may remember: "I fear but one thing; it is to keep my own will. Take that, for I choose everything that Thou willest." Herein was holy abandonment, the distinctive characteristic of spiritual childhood. If she resolved to practise it in this degree from the very beginning of her career, what will be its perfection now that she has surrendered herself by formal and definite engagement to follow all the leadings of Divine Love?

She will accustom herself more than ever "to look into the eyes of the good God," to find out what will please Him, and to accomplish it without delay. Amid the desolation and darkness that surround her, especially after her consecration to Merciful Love, she will repeat with her charming smile which reflects the peace of her soul: "If my Jesus appears to forget me, well, He is free to do so, since I am no longer mine but His. He will tire more quickly of making me wait than I of waiting for Him."[29]

And when, in the throes of cruel agony, she shall hear those sympathetic words: "It is frightful what you are suffering." "No," she will reply, "it is not frightful; could a little victim of love consider frightful what her Spouse sends her?"[30]

Love is essentially active. When that high degree in the union which transforms the soul is attained, which was the privilege of Thérèse, it will inevitably manifest itself in an all-consuming zeal. Her apostolic ardour shines through every page of the *Histoire*. We notice especially that her zeal for the sanctification of priests, which had been the great preoccupation of her religious life, grew more intense after her act of oblation and became a flame which was never to be extinguished, even beyond the tomb.

We have here, then, some of the admirable results of a sublime act of oblation, crowning a life of hidden sacrifice. But are not these heights inaccessible for the generality of souls? Let us repeat that, in spite of certain aspects or rather, certain expressions which alarm superficial minds, the "little way of spiritual childhood" is open to every soul of goodwill, and easy in proportion as that soul is little in its own esteem. This is, as we have seen, the teaching of Benedict XV; it is, moreover, the formal opinion of Pius XI, according to whom "spiritual childhood is a way which, without giving to everyone assurance of reaching the heights to which God has led Thérèse, is not only possible, but easy for all."[31]

The supernatural benefits of this blessed state of childhood may be gained during the course of a long life without any of those sensible phenomena by which God sometimes manifests the presence of pure love. But it is not always thus in the lives of certain saints who have attained to more than ordinary heights of perfection.

We remember the javelin plunged by an angel in the heart of the great Teresa of Avila. A short time after her oblation, the humble nun of Lisieux was to receive in her turn a mystic touch from the Hand of God as a prelude to the breaking of life's chain. We give her own words regarding the mystery of this Divine visitation of her heart by fire.

"Some days after my offering to Merciful Love," she said "I was commencing in the choir the Way of the Cross, when I suddenly felt myself wounded with a dart of fire so ardent that I thought I should die. I know not how to explain the transport; no comparison could make known the intensity of that flame. It seemed to me that an invisible power plunged me wholly in fire. Oh, what fire! what sweetness!"[32]

Mère Agnès de Jésus asked her if this extraordinary phenomenon was the first that she had experienced in her life. She replied candidly:

> My Mother, I have had transports of love several times, once in particular during the novitiate when I remained for a whole week far indeed from this earth. I cannot explain it; I acted, as it seemed, with a body not my own; for me there seemed to be a veil thrown over every earthly thing. But I was not burned by a real flame; I could endure those delights without expectation of seeing my bonds riven asunder by their force; whereas, on the day of which I now speak, a minute, a second more, and my soul must have parted from the body. . . . Alas! I found myself still on earth, and aridity returned immediately to my soul.[33]

Each day, the dear saint besought her Beloved that her martyrdom of love, "having prepared her to appear before Him, might break life's thread at last." The Hand of God had drawn back His flaming javelin, but the wound was unto death.

14

Beginning of Her Illness— The *Histoire d'une Ame*—The "Novissima Verba"—End of Exile—Funeral Ceremonies

Sœur Thérèse de L'enfant Jésus believed readily in the mysterious messages which God sometimes sends by means of dreams.[1] It would then delight her that, by this way at least, her Divine Spouse should send a ray of joy into the dark night which now ordinarily enveloped her. This joy was hers in the spring of 1896.

"On the 10th of May," she writes,

> in a dream at the first light of dawn, I thought I was walking in a gallery with our Mother alone. Suddenly, without knowing how they entered, I perceived three Carmelites; they wore their white mantles and their large veils, and I knew they came from heaven. "Oh, how happy would I be," thought I, "to see the face of one of these Carmelites." As if my desire had been heard, the tallest of the saints came towards me, and I fell on my knees. O joy! she raised her veil and covered me with it. I at once recognized the Venerable Anne of Jesus, Foundress of Carmel in France.[2]
>
> Her face was beautiful with a beauty not of this earth; no rays came therefrom, and yet, notwithstanding the thick veil that covered us, I could discern her face illumined by a marvellously delicate light which it appeared to produce of itself.
>
> The saint tenderly caressed me, and seeing myself so loved, I found courage to speak to her: "O Mother," I said, "I beseech you, tell me if God will leave me long on earth. Will He come soon for me?" She answered

> with a gracious smile: "Yes, soon . . . soon. . . . I promise you." "Mother," I added, "tell me if the good God requires nothing more of me than my poor little acts and my desires. Is He satisfied with me?"
>
> At this moment, the Venerable Mother's face shone with a far brighter radiance, and her expression appeared to me incomparably more tender as she replied: "God desires nothing more from you; He is satisfied, well satisfied. . . ." And laying her hands on my head, she caressed me so fondly that it would be impossible to tell my joy. My heart was filled with gladness, and then I thought of my sisters, and wished to ask some graces for them. . . . Alas! at that moment, I awoke.[3]

This dream confirmed the presentiment which the little saint ever had of dying young.[4] The hour was in truth approaching when Divine Love, having already wounded her with the fiery dart, was about to consume the holocaust.

A month previously, on April 3, 1896, during the night between Holy Thursday and Good Friday, according to her own poetic expression, she had heard, "as it were, a far-off murmur announcing to her the coming of the Spouse." In 1897, she related the happening herself.

> At the time of Lent, last year, I felt stronger than ever before, and this feeling of strength, notwithstanding the fast which I observed in all its strictness, continued until Easter-tide. But, at the very first hour of Good Friday, Jesus gave me the hope that I would soon go to join Him in His beautiful heaven. Oh, how sweet this memory is to me! Not having obtained permission on the Thursday evening to remain at the sepulchre all night, I went to our cell at midnight. No sooner did my head rest on the pillow, than I felt a burning stream rise to my lips; I believed that I was going to die, and my heart was thrilled with joy. However, as I had just extinguished our little lamp, I mortified my curiosity until morning and slept peacefully. At five, when the signal for rising was given, I reflected immediately that there were glad tidings awaiting me, and, going to the window, my suspicions were verified by finding our handkerchief all

> blood-stained. Oh, my Mother, with what hope my soul was filled. I was intimately persuaded that my Beloved, on this the anniversary of His death, let me hear the first call, as a distant and sweet murmur which announced His blessed coming.
>
> With great fervour I assisted at Prime, and afterwards at Chapter. I then hastened to kneel beside you, Mother, and confide to you my joy. I did not feel the slightest fatigue or suffering, and so I easily obtained permission to finish Lent as I had begun. Thus, on Good Friday, I shared in all the austerities of Carmel without any mitigation. Ah, never before had these observances appeared so sweet to me. . . . I was in transports of joy at the thought of going to heaven.
>
> At the close of that happy day, I again went to our cell with a glad heart and was peacefully going to sleep when my good Jesus gave me, as on the preceding night, the same sign that the time of my entrance into eternal life was drawing near. I enjoyed such unclouded living faith, that the thought of heaven was my greatest happiness.[5]

Two years previously, Thérèse had providentially been asked to write those memoirs which by their wonderful influence were to perpetuate for the greater good of souls the examples of her holy life.

One winter evening in December, 1894, Mère Agnès de Jésus then Prioress, Sœur Marie du Sacré-Cœur, and our little saint were, during recreation, gathered around the fire in the community-room, the only place where the nuns had permission to warm themselves. The presence of the Prioress gave them an opportunity of speaking for a few moments on their reminiscences of the old days. Thérèse, who still retained her charming childlike simplicity of speech, began to tell some incidents of her early years. Her words brought a flood of happy memories to these souls who were ever ready to attribute all to God with loving gratitude. Sœur Marie du Sacré-Cœur afterwards took the Mother Prioress aside, and said: "It is really a pity, that although Sœur Thérèse writes verses for one or other of the Sisters, she writes nothing that will preserve to us the memories of her childhood. Our little sister is an angel who will not long remain on earth, and we shall be sorry later on to have lost these details which mean so much for us."

Mère Agnès de Jésus hesitated for some weeks, but finally directed Thérèse to write for her feast day an account of the principal events of her childhood. The latter began the work at the opening of the year 1895. She gave to it only rare leisure moments, for her duties in the sacristy encroached very often on her free time. Nevertheless, on January 20, 1896, she was ready. On going to the choir for evening Prayer, she approached the Mother Prioress, and kneeling, gave her the manuscript, written without erasure on poor paper that a servant would have disdained to use.

Mère Agnès acknowledged it by a simple inclination of the head, laid it down on her stall, and did not even examine it until months afterwards when, relieved of the office of Prioress, she had a little more time at her own disposal. During this long period Thérèse de l'Enfant Jésus never once suffered any anxiety as to the fate of her work, and when her "little mother" one day said that she had not read it, did not appear astonished, nor in the least disturbed, thus showing the perfection of her detachment.

When reading the manuscript, Mère Agnès de Jésus was carried back by every line and seemed to live again in those bygone years, filled as they had been, in spite of passing trial, with such pure and peaceful happiness. Still more did she admire the marvels of grace wrought by God in her sister's soul from the very dawn of reason. Hence, she formed some idea of the good that could be accomplished by these pages later on, and began to wish that Thérèse would complete the account of her life in religion which was but outlined in what had already been written. But, being no longer Superior, she could not command her to continue her life-story then comprised in the first eight chapters of the *Histoire d'une Ame.*

Seeing Sœur Thérèse attacked by a malady which was rapidly consuming her, she finally persuaded Mère Marie de Gonzague, then Prioress, to make the young saint write something of her life in the cloister. The resulting manuscript furnished the matter of Chapters IX and X of the future *Histoire.* Some supplementary pages, written by Thérèse during her retreat of 1896 on her "little doctrine," as she called it, were addressed by her to Sœur Marie du Sacré-Cœur. These were later on to form the eleventh chapter of the same work.

On August 1, 1897, Mère Agnès de Jésus thought it well to tell Thérèse that she intended to have the manuscript read later in the community, and afterwards even to publish it; she, however, expressed her fear that certain Sisters would be opposed to this design. The saint replied simply and without hesitation: "My Mother, after my death, my manuscript should not be spoken of to anyone until it is published. If you do otherwise, or if you delay the publication, the demon will set many snares for you in order to hinder God's good work . . . *a work that is very important. . . .*"

Her counsel was followed, as will be seen later. Having obtained the *Imprimatur* of Mgr Hugonin on March 8, 1898, the *Histoire d'une Ame* appeared during the October following. A few weeks later, by reason of newly-arisen circumstances, its publication would have been impossible.

One day, Mère Agnès de Jésus begged Thérèse to revise a passage of the manuscript that seemed to her incomplete. Entering the infirmary shortly afterwards, she saw that her eyes were wet with tears. "You are crying?" she said to her. Thérèse, with an indefinable expression, replied: "It is indeed the manifestation of my soul. . . . Yes, these pages will do a great deal of good. Through them God's gentleness and sweetness will become better known. . . ." And she added in an inspired tone: "Ah, I know it, everyone will love me. . . ." It is impossible, considering what has since taken place, to deny the saint's gift of prophecy, manifested also on several other occasions.

In these striking and unforeseen circumstances, then, did St. Thérèse de l'Enfant Jésus, already weakened by the austerities of the rule, wasted by consumption, distracted at every moment by a thousand interruptions, compose these soul-stirring pages which aroused such universal sentiments of admiration. We know the opinion of Pius

XI on "this marvellous book, the freshness and grace of which are so natural."[6] On the day he canonized its author, he wished to set forth one of the reasons for that august act. "The book on her own life written by Sœur Thérèse de l'Enfant Jésus in the limpid beauty of her mother-tongue, in order to make known her way of spiritual childhood, is not only in the hands of all, but its sweetness penetrates the hearts of men most estranged from Christian perfection. Numbers of them have been converted by reading it, and are now firmly established in the charity of Christ."[7]

Apart from this approbation of the Head of the Church, attesting the high ascetical value of the book, competent judges do not hesitate to praise its literary worth. A scholar of undoubted literary taste, the abbé Henri Bremond, has paid a tribute worthy of remark to the young saint. For the *Légende d'Argent* that he so much desired, and in which he wished that nothing but the best and most beautiful should find place, he would ask for some of Thérèse's narratives and also some extracts from her letters which "are of an incomparable freshness, grace, and charity."[8]

But above and beyond the opinion of literary men, there is the testimony of millions of readers differing in language and country, who are every day being instructed and impressed, encouraged to follow the path of duty and sacrifice, led into the secret of intimate love of Jesus, by the 400,000 copies of the *Histoire d'une Ame* now in circulation.

On this Good Friday, 1896, which had brought to Thérèse a pledge of her fast-approaching departure for heaven, the Prioress in charge was the recently re-elected Mère Marie de Gonzague. Deceived by Sœur Thérèse's energy, she did not at first think that the hæmorrhage was serious. She allowed her to follow all the austere practices of the rule without alleviation, and even to spend the interval of the long Offices of Good Friday in cleaning the convent windows. It was then that one of the novices, finding her pale as death and almost fainting under the exertion of this laborious task added to the fatigue which resulted from the fast on bread and water, offered, but without success, to replace her.

The delicate tenderness of her fraternal love made the invalid careful to conceal the state of her health from her three sisters. They noticed her pallor, but, seeing her follow all the exercises of Holy Week and faithful as ever to every observance, they suspected nothing. Some weeks later, however, they found themselves listening to the dry persistent cough that nothing could alleviate, and began to realize that a deeply-rooted malady was secretly undermining her strength. The Mother Prioress herself grew uneasy about her at last, and relieved her of the duties of the sacristy.

Dr. de Cornière, who usually attended the community, and Dr. La Néele, a relative by marriage of the invalid, had not up to that time noticed anything to cause alarm. Nevertheless, in order to prevent the possible recurrence of hæmorrhage, they subjected her to a course of painful treatment; massage, blistering, cupping, cauterizing, etc. Ever smiling, and with gentle words of gratitude, the little sufferer endured these remedies, at that time more painful than the malady itself.

A strengthening régime banished the cough for a few months; her dream of quickly going to heaven seemed for the moment not about to be realized. She wrote to one of the novices: "Sickness is truly too slow a conductor; I rely on love alone."

This alleviation brought back to her for an instant the hope of at last acceding to the wishes of the Carmelites of Hanoi who were again asking for her. She could not, of course, dream of going there unless the malady were completely cured. To obtain this favour, she commenced in November, 1896, a novena to Venerable Théophane Vénard. Scarcely was the novena finished, when a grave relapse clearly manifested God's holy will. This time, intense and continuous fever, joined to persistent difficulties of digestion, rapidly sapped her remaining strength. Nevertheless, Mère Marie de Gonzague, having grown accustomed to see the saint bear up valiantly under suffering, allowed her to follow all the community exercises. Thus, before she was finally sent to the infirmary, the heroic child could be seen, whenever she had to go to her cell unaided, stop at each step to take breath, reaching the cell at last in so exhausted a state that she would take an hour to undress. There on her hard and narrow pallet, wrapped in two poor blankets, she would await, nearly always in feverish unrest, the return of day and work renewed.

All through the winter, her strength gradually declined. Dr. de Cornière, so long hopeful, did not now conceal his anxiety. "I shall not be able to cure her," he said sadly; "besides, this soul is not made for earth."

Towards the end of Lent, 1897, very alarming symptoms declared themselves. Though with little hope of curing the implacable malady, the doctor, bent on trying every means, continued his severe remedies, especially more and more frequent applications of the cauterizing needle. After each of these courses of treatment, Thérèse had to remain very quiet for some hours. One day, when lying in her cell during recreation in order to allay the pain of this cruel cauterization, she heard a Sister in the kitchen speak about her thus: "Sœur Thérèse de l'Enfant Jésus will soon die, and in truth, I ask myself what can our Mother say of her after her death?[9] She will be embarrassed, for this little Sister, amiable though she is, has surely done nothing worth recounting." The infirmarian, who had heard all this, said to Thérèse: "If you had set any value on the opinion of creatures, you would be indeed disappointed today!"

"The opinion of creatures! Ah, happily the good God has always given me the grace of being absolutely indifferent to it."

Between Thérèse and the Sister who tended her a conversation took place which revealed to the latter certain facts till then unknown to the community.

"It is said," observed the infirmarian, "that you have never suffered very much."

The saint smilingly pointed to a glass containing some liquid of a beautiful bright red colour. "Do you see that little glass?" she said. "One would believe that it contained a delicious liqueur; in reality, I take nothing more bitter. Well, that is an image of my life. To the eyes of others, it has always appeared in radiant hues. To them it seemed that I drank a delicious cordial, when instead it was but bitterness. I say bitterness, and still my life has not in reality been bitter, for I have known how to turn every bitterness into joy and sweetness."

"You are suffering greatly at this moment, are you not?"

"Yes. But then, I have so much desired it."[10]

She suffered more especially from constantly recurring temptations against faith which, although she overcame them, prevented her from enjoying fully the thought of her near approaching deliverance.

The few months that yet remained to her were filled with a double suffering, moral and physical, of which we shall try to show various phases. Perhaps the reader will be astonished that such severe trials should fall to the lot of one so innocent. But it must be remembered that the dear saint had wished to suffer, to suffer intensely even till the end, in order that she might bring help to priests, further the interests of the Church, and save souls.

From April 6, 1897, Mère Agnès de Jésus, foreseeing that her angelic "little Thérèse" would soon leave them for heaven, began to write down in a note-book what most struck her as they talked together during the daily visits. Thérèse at first felt troubled at her doing so, but yielded to her sister's wish rather than deprive her of this last consolation. Mère Agnès de Jésus was thus able to form a collection of pious reflections, of observations showing a delicately clear discernment, of fervent aspirations, and sighs of resignation and of hope which would form the best *Vade Mecum* for sufferers of every age. We shall borrow from these pages passages which best show the thoughts that preoccupied the saint during the last months of her life. Her favourite themes seem to have been the worth of the "little way of spiritual childhood," the advantage of conformity with God's will, the privileges and favours of the Blessed Virgin, the example of simplicity given by the holy Family, and the wonderful benefits we derive from the communion of Saints.

Towards the end of the month of Mary, she enjoyed a few days of sweet peace, and even of tranquil joy. "They say that I shall be afraid of death," she said. "That may well happen; if they could but know how little confidence I have in myself. . . . But I wish to enjoy the dispositions that the good God now gives to me. It will be time enough to suffer the contrary when it comes."

During the first fortnight of June, another relapse was the only response to a novena made for her by the entire community. "I am resigned to live or die," she said. "I wish what the good God wills; whatever He does, that do I love."

Her calmness came, it is true, from a source little known to worldlings. Mère Agnès de Jésus, on entering her cell one evening, said to her: "Why are you so joyful today?" "Because I have had this morning two little trials, and very painful they were. . . . Nothing gives me little joys so much as little trials."

She looked on death not only as a liberator, but even as a friend. "I know I am going to die soon, but when will it be? Oh, it comes not. I am like a child to whom a cake is continually being promised; it is shown him from afar, and then, when he draws near to take it, the hand that offers it is withdrawn. But I am wholly abandoned to the will of the good God."

She desired that her very death should benefit the dear missions that she had always so generously helped. "You must not," she said, "let people give wreaths to place around my coffin, as was the case with our good Mother Geneviève. But ask them to use the money in rescuing poor little negroes from slavery. Tell them that they will please me by so doing."

In every Carmel, the infirmary is a comfortable apartment in comparison with the cells, so the nuns wished to transfer Thérèse thereto, but she gently persuaded them to wait awhile. "I prefer," she said, "to remain in our cell than to go to the infirmary, because here my cough cannot be heard, and I disturb nobody. Besides, when I am too well looked after, I have no happiness."

She trained herself, moreover, to be courageous in face of suffering. "I have so often been told," she said, "that I am courageous, and it is so far from being true, that I said to myself: 'After all, everybody must not be led astray in this manner.' And I set myself to acquire courage by the aid of grace. . . . I have no fear of the final combat, nor of the sufferings which sickness brings, however great they may be. The good God has helped me and led me by the hand from my infancy. I count on Him; I feel assured that He will continue to help me to the very end. My sufferings may indeed be extreme, but I am sure that He will never abandon me."[11]

She needed this energy, not only in her violent attacks of suffering, but also when, in spite of her weakness, she went out to the garden to seek a little relief in the spring sunshine.

She had been recommended to take a little exercise for a quarter of an hour every day. One afternoon, a Sister, seeing her walk with great difficulty, said to her: "It would be better for you to rest. In your present condition, walking cannot be of any benefit; you are more fatigued by it; that is all."

"It is true," said the little saint, "but do you know what gives me strength? . . . Well, *I walk for a missionary.* I reflect that in a distant land, one of them is perhaps worn out by apostolic labour, and to lessen his fatigue I offer mine to the good God."

One evening, the community met for the purpose of singing a hymn in one of those little sanctuaries named in Carmel "hermitages." The invalid, then greatly weakened by her malady, dragged herself painfully to the spot, and, once there, was forced to sit down immediately. One of her companions, who did not yet realize the gravity of Thérèse's condition, gave her a sign to rise like the others to sing the hymn. The humble child obeyed instantly, and in spite of her exhaustion, remained standing till the end.

During her hours of solitude she worked without intermission. Paintings on silk, pretty miniatures, pious emblems succeeded one another from her still deft fingers, whether for use in the sacristy or the consolation or pleasure of her Sisters. She did not forget the novices, whom she could rarely see now, but to whom she occasionally sent a word of encouragement or even of reproof.

Her weakness increased from day to day, and intense pains in her side made her realize the progress of the destructive disease. Persuaded that the end was not far off, on June 4, she took advantage of the presence of her three sisters in her cell to bid them farewell. She was radiant that evening, as if transfigured, and seemed to suffer no longer. "O my little sisters," she said,

> how happy I am! I see that I am soon to die: I feel sure of it now. Be not astonished if I do not appear to you after my death, or if you see nothing extraordinary that would make my happiness known to you. Remember that it is my "little way" to desire nothing of that kind. You know well what I have so often said about the good God, the angels, and the saints:
>
> That my desire does not lie
> In seeing them with earthly eye.
>
> —I would wish, however, to have an easy death in order to console you. But do not feel disturbed if I suffer greatly and if, as I have said, you cannot see in me any signs of happiness at the moment of my death. . . . Our Saviour was truly a Victim of love, and see how great was His agony.

The dear saint seemed to see by light from on high the martyrdom reserved for her by the Almighty before her entrance into eternal happiness. But the thought of being able to serve souls made her accept all, even suffering in the life beyond if necessary. "I do not know," she said, "whether I shall go to Purgatory; but if I do, I shall not regret having done nothing to avoid it; I shall never repent of having worked for the one purpose of saving souls. How glad I was to learn that our Mother St. Teresa was of the same mind."[12]

A period of calm succeeded this alarming crisis, and "little Thérèse" profited by it to go out to the garden and there offer her pale brow to the sun's caressing rays which were calling forth the flower-blossoms. On June 7 she was returning, with the assistance of Mère Agnès de Jésus, when she noticed a little white hen sheltering her brood of chickens under her wings. The sight brought tears to her eyes.

Her sister asked the reason. "I cannot tell you now," Thérèse answered; "it has touched me so deeply; let us go in." On entering her cell, she turned towards her "little mother" with a heavenly expression of countenance. "I thought of Our Saviour," she said, "and of the charming example He chose to make us believe in the tenderness of His love. He has done this for me all my life; He has entirely hidden me under His wings. If I have shed tears, they were tears of thankfulness and love. I could not contain the feelings with which my heart overflowed."

Thérèse, as we know, sometimes spoke of the future with prophetic insight. One day, Sœur Marie du Sacré-Cœur said to her: "What a sorrow it will be for us when you die!"

"Oh, no," she replied joyously, "you will see; there will be as it were a shower of roses."

Thus, by an act of His goodness, did the Divine Spouse dispel at times the darkness which oppressed the soul of His gentle victim. But these moments of joy were only as lightning-flashes between the thunder clouds.

On July 4, a fresh hæmorrhage aroused the greatest anxiety. The saint, believing herself to be on the verge of death, said simply to her sisters: "I have read a beautiful passage in the *Reflections on the Imitation.* Our Saviour in the Garden of Olives enjoyed all the bliss of the Trinity, and yet His agony was none the less cruel. It is a mystery; but I assure you that I comprehend in some degree its meaning from what I now feel."

After a still graver attack, she said to Mère Agnès de Jésus: "I am going soon to see the good God."

"Are you afraid of death, now that you see it so near?"

"Ah, I fear it less and less."

In allusion to a passage in the Gospel, she often called Jesus the "Divine Thief" who comes with suddenness to steal souls. "Are you afraid of the 'Thief'?" her sister continued. "He is now at the door."

"No, He is not at the door; He has come in. But what is this you ask me, little mother? Am I afraid of the 'Thief'? How could I fear one whom I love so much? These words: 'Although He should kill me, yet will I trust in Him,' have delighted me from my childhood. But I have taken long to gain this degree of abandonment. Now I have reached it. The good God has taken me and placed me there."

This admirable serenity was astonishing in one whose last hour was apparently so near. Fearing that fresh hæmorrhages would carry her away suddenly, it was thought best to take her to the infirmary. It was July 8. On leaving her poor cell, the silent witness of so many prayers, mortifications and hidden pain, Thérèse de l'Enfant Jésus felt her heart deeply moved. She said to Mère Agnès de Jésus: "When I am in heaven, you must bear in mind that a great part of my happiness was won in this little cell, for," she added, with a deep longing gaze towards heaven, "I have suffered greatly here; I would have liked to die here."

On a table beside her bed had been placed the miraculous statue of the Blessed Virgin whose smile had once cured her. She looked at it lovingly on entering the infirmary. "What do you see?" asked her sister Marie, who had before witnessed her ecstasy.

"Never has it appeared so beautiful to me; but today it is the statue; *before, as you well know, it was not the statue.*"[13]

During the days that followed, in spite of the continual imminence of death, she wished to remember nothing except her great mission, the saving of souls. She could no longer talk with the novices regularly for their edification; still less could she give them the example of her strict observance. But there was, at this time, at the Grand Seminary of Bayeux, a student about to set out for the novitiate of the White Fathers. This young student had been adopted by her as spiritual brother, and now, facing the difficulties of the life before him, he sought for encouragement, light, and consolation from her sufferings, sacrifices, and, if possible, from her parting counsels.

There was also in the heart of the Far East, as yet so impenetrable to the doctrines of salvation, a priest who, amid hostile surroundings, daily risked his life in Chinese villages to win souls to the Saviour.

Thérèse's merits were acquired in part at least by the work of these foreign missions. She wished still, up to the very end, to fan the flame that she had enkindled in the hearts of these apostles, and she resumed her correspondence first of all with the abbé Bellière. Nothing could be more touching than these three letters written on a bed of agony and addressed to a seminarist who aspired to martyrdom.

She commenced on July 26 by telling him of her approaching death.

> Perhaps when you receive these few lines, I shall be no longer on earth but in the midst of eternal delights. I do not know the future; yet, I can say with certainty that the Spouse is at the door. A miracle would be required to keep me in exile, and I think that Jesus would not work a useless miracle. Oh, my brother, how happy I am to die. Yes, I am happy, not at being delivered from suffering here below, for, on the contrary, suffering united to love is the only thing which appears to me desirable in this valley of tears. But I am glad to die because I feel that such is God's will, and because in heaven, far more than here, I shall be helpful to the souls dear to me, especially yours. . . .
>
> When my brother sets out for Africa, I shall follow him not only in thought and in prayer. I shall be always with him, and his faith will know well how to discern the presence of a little sister that Jesus has given him to be his helper not only during two short years, but till the end of his life.
>
> These promises may perhaps appear fanciful to you; but you must begin to realize that the good God has always treated me like a spoiled child.[14]

The very day before she addressed these lines to the Abbé Bellière, she had, in conversation with her sisters, given utterance to the following never-to-be-forgotten words.

"You will look down upon us from heaven," they said.

"No," she replied, "I will come down."

And again: "One hope alone makes my heart throb; it is the thought of the love I shall receive and that I shall be able to give. I think of all the good that I want to do after death, to have little children baptized, to help priests, missionaries, the whole Church. . . ."

To anyone doubting the efficacy of these desires, it would be sufficient to tell of the marvels obtained in our own day through Thérèse's intercession, by numerous apostles in foreign mission fields.

Let us revert to the assistance given by the saint from the very brink of the grave to Abbé Bellière. The poor missionary aspirant had been greatly upset on learning of the rapidly approaching end of her upon whom he had counted for help during long years to come. She set herself first of all to console him, but did not stop at this work of common charity. Her desire was to lead him swiftly to sanctity by the way in which she herself had succeeded so well, her "little way" of spiritual childhood.

> I feel that we are destined to go to heaven by the same way, the way of suffering joined to love. When I have reached the end, I will teach you how you must steer over the tempestuous sea of the world with the abandonment and love of a child who knows that his father cherishes him and will not leave him alone in the hour of danger.
>
> Oh, how I long to make you understand the tenderness of the Heart of Jesus and the return He expects from you. Your last letter made my heart thrill with joy. I understood to what a degree your soul is akin to mine, since it is called to raise itself to God by *the lift of love,* not to climb the rude and steep ascent of fear. I am not astonished that familiarity with Jesus seems difficult to you; we cannot attain to that in a day; but of this I am sure, that I shall help you far more to walk in this delightful way when I am delivered from mortal bonds, so that soon you will say with St. Augustine: "Love is the force which carries me along."[15]

On the feast of Our Lady of Mount Carmel, the little invalid received Holy Communion amidst touching circumstances. A young priest celebrated his first Mass in the convent chapel. Along the cloisters strewn with wild flowers and rose petals he carried the sacred Host to the Infirmary which was prepared like a sanctuary. Before the Body of Christ was placed on Thérèse's lips, Sœur Marie de l'Eucharistie sang in a melodious voice the following strophe composed by the young saint:

> To die of love, 'tis martyrdom divine
> For which my spirit thirsteth day and night;
> O Cherubim, attune your harps with mine,
> Full soon from exile shall my soul take flight.
>
> . . . . .
>
> O Jesus grant my dream, my one desire,
> Of love to die.

On the following day, Thérèse made to Mère Agnès de Jésus another prophetic confidence. It was this announcement, now become celebrated, since it is every day being splendidly realized throughout the world:

> I feel that my mission is soon to begin, my mission to make the good God loved as I love Him, to give to souls my little way. If the good God grants my desires, my heaven will be spent upon earth until the end of the world. Yes, I WILL SPEND MY HEAVEN IN DOING GOOD UPON EARTH. It is not impossible, since from the very midst of the beatific vision the angels are watching over us.
>
> I shall not be able to rest until the end of the world. But when the Angel shall have said, "Time is no more," then I shall rest. I can then enjoy repose, for the number of the elect will be complete and all will have entered into eternal bliss.

"By what way," her sister asked, "do you wish to lead souls?"

"By the way of spiritual childhood, Mother, the way of confidence and self-surrender. I wish to show them the little way that has so perfectly succeeded with me, to tell them that there is but one thing to do here below, to strew before Jesus the flowers of little sacrifices, to win Him by caresses. It is thus I have won Him, and it is for this that I shall be so well received."[16]

These considerations presuppose a spirit free from all discouragement. Profiting by a short respite from severe pain, Thérèse hastened to write letters of farewell to her relatives who, of course, could not visit her in the infirmary. She had first of all written to her sister Léonie on July 17. Listen to her last counsels to one whom, she had largely contributed to establish in fervour.

> I am so glad to be able to write to you once more. Some days ago, I thought that I should never again have that consolation on earth; but the good God seems to will that my exile should continue a little longer. I am not disturbed at this, for I do not wish to enter heaven a minute sooner by my own will. The only happiness on earth is to make it our study always to take delight in the part that Jesus assigns to us. Yours is indeed beautiful, my dear little sister. If you wish to be a saint, that will be easy for you, because in your heart the world is nothing to you. Like us then, you can occupy yourself with the one thing necessary, that is to say, give yourself with devotedness to the external occupations, with sole intention of pleasing Jesus and of uniting yourself more intimately with Him.
>
> You wish that I should pray to the Sacred Heart for you when I am in heaven. You may feel sure that I will not forget your commissions, nor to ask for everything that you need in order to become a saint. Farewell, my dear little sister. I would that the thought of my entrance into heaven might fill you with gladness since I shall then be able to love you still more.[17]

With this charming simplicity did Thérèse take leave of her elder sisters. But was it really farewell? Was it not rather an invitation to an early rendezvous in a land where parting is unknown?

Thérèse next addressed to her uncle a most touching letter,[18] if we are to judge by the reply of M. Guérin on July 25, 1897.

"My dear little angel," wrote her uncle,

> your letter has given us surprise and indescribable joy; it brought tears to my eyes. Of what nature were

those tears? I cannot say. Many different feelings were responsible for them; pride in my adopted daughter; admiration of such great courage and such great love of God; also, for I cannot hide it from you, my dear child, sorrow which human nature must suffer, at a separation which to it appears eternal. Faith and reason protest. We submit to their arguments, but they are powerless to prevent our sighs, our sorrow. . . . You were your good mother's precious pearl, last in coming, your venerated father's "little queen," and you are the most beautiful jewel in this crown of lilies which encircles me and gives me a foretaste of the perfection of heaven. However great the grief which at certain moments besets and oppresses me, never has the thought come of seeking to keep you from the arms of the Spouse who is calling you. . . . It is said that the swan, though silent during its whole life, breaks into a sublime song as death approaches. Your letter, my dearest one, is, without doubt, your last song for us. The pious thoughts that it has inspired will teach us perhaps to feel a little of that flame of divine love which consumes you and to which you desire to be more intimately united.

Little privileged soul, you who have seen the burning bush from your tender childhood, and have been fascinated by its brightness, you have now drawn so near to it that soon you will find yourself in its very heart.

Farewell, my beloved child, precious pearl confided to me by your good mother. The memory of your virtues and your innocence shall be ever with me, and I hope that your prayers will bring me the grace of being one day reunited to all my own in the eternal dwellingplace.

He who has perhaps some small claim to be called your second father embraces you with deep affection.

I. Guérin.[19]

This letter, the last sweet breath that came to her from that dear sanctuary which had sheltered her infant joys, moved Thérèse's heart to gladness and to sadness too; but, having paid a final tribute of tenderness to her earthly relatives, she continued to consecrate entirely to the interests of the apostolate her last few days of respite from suffering. Her farewell to Père Roulland in his difficult mission amidst obdurate and savage tribes was another cry of hope: "I announce to you with gladness my fast approaching entrance into the city of joy. What attracts me in the fatherland of heaven is the hope of at last loving God as I have so longed to love Him, and the thought that I shall be able to make Him loved by a multitude of souls who will praise Him for ever."[20]

For the Abbé Bellière her solicitude was almost maternal. This young man was, as we know, a fervent missionary aspirant; but the remembrance of certain failings, exaggerated no doubt by his humility, caused him to hesitate before entering on the way of entire abandonment shown him by Thérèse. She urged him, then with an insistence redoubled by the thought of her approaching death, towards confidence in God's merciful love: "Is not Jesus your sole treasure? As He is in heaven, your heart should dwell there only. This sweet Saviour has long ago forgotten your infidelities; to Him your desires for perfection alone are present to rejoice His Heart. Remain no longer at His feet, I pray you; obey the first impulse which drives you to His arms; there is your place, and I affirm more definitely than after your former letters that it is forbidden you to go to heaven by a road other than that taken by your little sister."[21]

This message bears the date of July 13. It was as a last look given towards earthly scenes, towards happenings under far-off skies. The eyes of the young saint were now to be supernaturally closed to the earth.[22]

Hæmorrhages of more serious nature than ever took place during the last days of July, so that it was thought wise to administer the last sacraments. She prepared for these with particular fervour. Before the Extreme Unction, she asked pardon of all the community in such touching words that the Sisters shed tears. Then radiant with smiles, she said: "The door of my dark prison is half open. I am in great joy, especially since our Father Superior has told me that my soul today resembles that of a little child after baptism."

She then received Holy Viaticum. Scarcely had she finished her thanksgiving, when several of the nuns came to speak to her. She said afterwards to Mère Agnès de Jésus: "How disturbed I have been during my thanksgiving. . . . But I reflected that when Our Saviour retired into the desert, the people followed Him, and He did not send them away. I wished to imitate Him in receiving my Sisters well."

It was expected then that Sœur Thérèse's pure soul would detach itself from mortal coils without effort. So sweet a death would have been a privilege, but would not have sufficiently satisfied the ardour to suffer for souls which was to consume that predestined child till the very end. In reality, a martyrdom of two long months was commencing for her. And, more terrible still than these physical torments, the moral agony of Gethsemani too was near.

For several days the infirmarian remarked the signs of cruel anguish on Sœur Thérèse's countenance, while she insistently repeated: "Oh, how necessary it is to pray for the agonizing. If people did but know!"

One night, she begged the Sister who was tending her to sprinkle Holy Water on the bed, saying:

> The demon is near me; I do not see him, but I feel his presence. He torments me; he holds me with a hand of iron, preventing me from getting the slightest relief; he increases my pain in order to lead me to despair. . . . And I cannot pray. I can only look at the Blessed Virgin and say "Jesus." How necessary is that prayer at Compline: "*Procul recedant somnia, et noctium phantasmata!* (Deliver us from the phantoms of the night)." I experience something mysterious; I do not suffer for myself but for another soul . . . and the demon is displeased.

Deeply impressed, the infirmarian lit a blessed candle, and the spirit of darkness fled, to return no more.[23]

It was one of the temptations experienced at times by those who have made special effort to oppose Satan's power on earth. Thérèse came out victorious from this hand-to-hand struggle with the infernal foe; but the consoling light which would make God's nearness felt continued to evade her. To those around, this was not apparent. Thus, one day, when she seemed to find joy in gazing through the half-open window at a radiant summer sky, a Sister said to her: "Soon you will be up there, beyond that blue sky; with what love you gaze at it." The young saint smiled sweetly, and said afterwards to Mère Agnès de Jésus: "The Sisters do not know what I suffer. As I looked at the blue firmament, my only thoughts were of its material beauty; the other—heaven—becomes more and more closed to me."

We know what she thought about the worth of Holy Communion. We have seen her, during the preceding winter, drag herself painfully from her cell to the chapel, no matter what the cost, to receive the Divine nourishment. This consolation was now withheld. From August 17, vomiting became so frequent that it was impossible to afford her the happiness of this union with Jesus. That was the most cruel trial of all. "But I reflect," she says, "on the words of St. Ignatius of Antioch. I, also, must be ground by suffering, in order to become the wheat of God."[24]

From this time onwards, the suffocating oppression she suffered was alarming. Sœur Geneviève de la Sainte-Face had been appointed assistant infirmarian, and thus had the consolation of attending on Thérèse. She slept in an adjoining cell, and hardly left the bedside except during the hours for office, when Mère Agnès de Jésus came to take her place. After a day of painful suffocations, Thérèse asked the Blessed Virgin that her cough might cease so that her infirmarian might snatch a little sleep. But she added: "If you do not hear me, I shall love you still more."[25]

At each visit, the doctor expressed to the Mother Prioress his admiration: "Ah, if you knew what she is enduring," he said. "Never have I seen such suffering borne with that expression of supernatural joy. She is an angel."

Seeing her reduced to extreme weakness, he ordered her some strengthening medicine; but she was under no illusion as to its efficacy. . . . "I am convinced," she said, "of the uselessness of remedies as regards curing me; but I have arranged with the good God that He will turn them to profit for the poor missionaries who have neither the time nor the means to look after themselves."

Certain remedies, instead of relieving her, increased her sufferings. But when the pain was too intense, the divine Saviour sent at times a ray of joy to his agonized little spouse. "One evening," she relates,

> during the *Great silence*, before I had been transferred from the cell to the infirmary, the infirmarian came to put a hot-water bottle at my feet and tincture of iodine on my chest. I was racked by fever; burning thirst consumed me. While undergoing these remedies, I could not help complaining to Our Saviour: "My Jesus," I said, "Thou seest that I am burning with fever, and they bring me yet more heat, more fire. Ah, if I had instead a half-glass of water, how much more relieved I should be. . . . O my God, Thy little child is consumed with thirst. But she is happy nevertheless to have this opportunity of doing without what is necessary, so that she may the better resemble Thee and save souls."
>
> Soon, the infirmarian left me, and I thought I should not see her again until morning, but to my great surprise she returned after a few moments bringing a refreshing drink. "I have just this moment thought," she said, "that you might be thirsty. I will bring you this cooling drink every evening." I looked at her dumbfounded, and when once more alone, my tears flowed freely. Oh, how good Our Saviour is! How easy it is to touch His Heart![26]

A few rays of spiritual consolation, too, pierced at intervals the dense clouds that surrounded her. For an instant, the Saviour would unveil to His beloved one the splendour of the privileges He had heaped upon her, and, without any loss of humility, she declared quite simply the magnificance of His liberality towards her. One day, they brought her a sheaf of wheat, those beautiful ears of wheat that she had formerly loved to see waving in the corn-fields of Normandy amid the wild poppies and the cornflowers. She took an ear so laden with grain that it bent on its stem, and said to the Mother Prioress: "My mother, this is an image of my soul. The good God has laden me with graces for myself and others." That was a recognition of the supernatural benefits conferred on her. But she immediately added: "Ah, I desire always to bow down, like this beautiful ear of corn, under the abundance of Heaven's gifts, recognizing that they all come from above."[27]

Without lessening the weight of her cross, the Saviour provided oftentimes unexpected helps so that she might bear it without faltering. On September 6, a relic was received at the Carmel, of Blessed Théophane Vénard, the martyr missionary whose type of sanctity had always appealed strongly to Thérèse. She had several times, but in vain, expressed the desire to possess a relic of this servant of God; then seeing that her prayer remained unanswered, she said no more about it. She now welcomed with delight the long-coveted relic, recalling why she had specially loved this "little saint whose life had been quite ordinary"; and as he had "great affection for his family" she sought to imitate him to the end in copying "as a farewell souvenir" for her sisters some passages from the last letters of the martyr "which," as she said, "expressed her own thoughts, and manifested her own soul fully."

But these fleeting moments of happiness were ever as lightning flashes in her continually clouded sky. On August 28, the invalid, pointing from a window to a dark corner of the garden, said to Mère Agnès de Jésus: "Do you see that dark place down there beside the chestnut trees where you can distinguish nothing? . . . As regards both soul and body, I am in a place like that. What darkness! Yet I am in peace there."[28]

Even in the midst of this darkness, she had a supernatural intuition of her sisters' suffering, though they tried to conceal it from her. Once, when one of them had passed moments of agony at the thought of the inevitable and fast approaching separation from Thérèse, and on entering the infirmary immediately afterwards, had taken care to hide every trace of her grief, she was much surprised to hear Thérèse say to her in serious and sorrowful accents: "You should not mourn like those who have not hope."

God, too, allowed her to experience some natural apprehensions regarding the mystery of death. "I am afraid," she said on September 11, "that I have had fear of death; but I have not had fear of what will follow after my death. . . . I only said to myself: 'What is this mysterious separation of soul and body?' It is the first time I have experienced that feeling; but I immediately abandoned myself to the good God." And she added: "Please give me the Crucifix that I may kiss it after my act of contrition in order to gain the plenary indulgence for the souls in purgatory. I now give them nothing of more worth than that."

To kiss her Crucifix, that little Crucifix with its Figure worn by her caresses, was one of the saint's principal manifestations of love; at times, too, she added other marks of devotion.

On September 14, a rose was brought to her. Taking its petals, she tenderly touched with each one the wounds of her dying Saviour. Surely she must have recalled to mind lines which she had formerly addressed to Jesus:

> In unpetalling the spring-time rose for Thee,
> I would to wipe away Thy tears.

Some of the petals fell from her bed on to the floor, and she said to her sisters: "Gather up these petals; do not lose one of them; later on, they will enable you to give pleasure. . . ." No doubt, she foresaw the marvels which God would work by means of these lowly relics;[29] but her humility prevented her from speaking more explicitly.

With surprising calmness, she confided her interior dispositions to her "little mother." "I am like a little child; I have no thought except simple consent to everything God wills, suffering what He sends me from moment to moment, without being preoccupied about the future. I only rejoice in death inasmuch as it is the expression of God's will for me. I do not desire death more than life. Following natural choice, I prefer death; but if I had the choice, I would choose nothing; what the good God does, that do I love."[30]

Even in her very darkest hours of trouble, nothing could shake her confidence. "O my God," she cries out, "how good Thou art to Thy little victim of Merciful Love! Even now, when Thou dost join exterior suffering to trials of soul, I cannot say: 'The anguish of death hath encompassed me,' but I cry out in thankfulness: 'I have gone down into the valley of the shadow of death; yet I fear no evil, because Thou, my Saviour, art with me.'"[31]

At the height of her most severe attacks, she contented herself with murmuring gently: "O my God, have pity on me; Thou who art so good." Sometimes when breath was failing her, she moaned at each painful respiration: "I suffer! I suffer!" But she said one day to the faithful watcher at her side: "Each time that I shall say: 'I suffer,' reply, 'So much the better,' for that is what I wish to say to complete my thought; I have not always the strength to say it."

In order to encourage her, or perhaps because he expected that death would come more rapidly, the doctor told her that she would have no suffering at the last. When the end of September brought such intensified pain, she said to her sisters: "I was told that I would have no agony! . . . But after all, I am very willing to have it."

"What if you were given a choice?"

"I would choose nothing."[32]

But it was little for this passionate lover of Jesus to resign herself to His divine will. On the eve of their blessed meeting, she gave in a special way evidence of her ardour towards the Beloved, now so near. On one of her last nights on earth, Sœur Geneviève de la Sainte-Face, entering the infirmary, found her with hands joined and eyes raised to heaven.

"What are you doing thus?" she said. "You should try to get a little sleep."

"I cannot sleep; I am praying then."

"And what are you saying to Jesus?"

"I say nothing to Him; I love Him."[33]

At another time, her sister found her with the crucifix in her hand and passing her fingers lovingly over the wounded brow and mangled limbs of her Saviour.

"What are you doing?" she asked.

"I am taking out the nails, and raising from His brow the crown of thorns."

One day, when the three sisters were together, Sœur Marie du Sacré-Cœur and Sœur Geneviève de la Sainte-Face expressed the hope that her last look might be given to her "little mother," Agnès de Jésus. "No," declared Thérèse, "that would be too human. If the good God leaves me free, my last farewell shall be to my Prioress, Mère Marie de Gonzague." We can realize how great the abnegation and spirit of faith required for such a wish.

To add to her trials, Sœur Thérèse was deprived for some time of visits from the chaplain, who was kept away by a grave illness. Canon Faucon came to supply for him, and to this worthy priest the dying nun made her last confession. He entered the infirmary feeling as though it were a sanctuary. Seeing her so beautiful,[34] and as if transfigured in the midst of her sufferings, he was seized with profound veneration. Filled with emotion, he said to Mère Agnès de Jésus before leaving: "What an angel! She is confirmed in grace." One of his friends, Père Granger, a missionary of La Délivrande, had told him to ask the prayers of the little saint for two very great favours. After her confession, Thérèse humbly and simply promised to make the desired intercession. Before long, Pére Granger's petitions were fully granted.[35]

The dying saint wished to the very end to declare her thoughts on the privileges of "little souls." Five days before her death, Mére Agnès de Jésus related to her a conversation that had taken place during recreation on the responsibility of those who die after a long life spent in charge of souls. "*Those who are little,*" said Thérèse,

> *will be judged with extreme gentleness. . . .*[36] And it is quite possible to remain little even when charged with the heaviest responsibilities, and that, during a very long life. If I were to die at eighty, and had held responsible charges in several monasteries, I feel sure that at my death I would be as *little* as I am today. It is written that *at the end, the Lord will arise to save the meek and humble of the earth.*[37] It is not said to "judge," but to "save."

Thus with a soul overflowing with supernatural hope, in spite of the trials of her faith, she went on her way to the Father of mercies.

But He wished to set another jewel in her eternal crown. On September 24, the anniversary of her veiling, Mère Agnès de Jésus had asked that Mass might be celebrated for her benefit. Thérèse thanked her gratefully. Seeing that she continued to suffer, her sister said sadly: "Alas! you have got no relief."

"Was it then for relief from my sufferings that you had Mass offered?"

"It was for your good."

"My good . . . that, without doubt, is to suffer."[38]

In truth, her sufferings continually increased. From September 25, she was so weak that she could no longer make the least movement unaided. The sound of voices even in low tones near her bed became a torment to her. In the burning heat of fever, and with the terrible sense of suffocation, she could not articulate a word without cruel pain. Nevertheless, Heaven still sent her in her agony an occasional ray of sunshine. One of her last joys was the sight of a little robin that came through the open window and flitted about her bed.

The evening before her death, at about nine o'clock, a sound of fluttering wings was heard in the garden, and a turtle-dove—they knew not whence it came—alighted on the window-sill, and there stayed long, softly cooing. Thérèse and her sister Geneviéve de la Sainte-Face then recalled to mind the words of the Canticle: "The song of the turtle is heard in our land. . . . Arise, my love, my dove, and come, for winter is now past."[39] Yes, the call of the Spouse was very near.

From early morning of September 29, a distressing rattle in the throat seemed to announce the end. Towards midday, the dying nun said to the Prioress: "Mother, is this the death-agony? . . . How am I to prepare for death? . . ." The Office of St. Michael the archangel was read to her in French and also the prayers for the dying. The doctor came for his usual visit. On his departure, Thérèse asked Mère Marie de Gonzague:

"Is it today, Mother?"

"Yes," answered the Prioress.

"The good God," added her sisters, "is joyous today because He is going to receive you into heaven."

"And I too!" she cried. "Oh, if I should die immediately, what a happiness!"

Some hours later, a fresh attack succeeded this short period of calm. "I am utterly exhausted—can do no more," she sighed. "Ah, pray for me. If you but knew!"

After matins, she joined her hands, and with a sweet and plaintive voice said: "Yes, my God! yes, yes! I accept all willingly."

Contrary to the opinion of those around her, Thérèse de l'Enfant Jésus was to pass another night of agony here below, but the morrow, Thursday, September 30, brought the dawn of that happy day, that *Dies natalis* for which she had so ardently longed. That morning, her sufferings appeared inexpressible. Casting a look on the miraculous statue of the Blessed Virgin which was facing her bed, she joined her hands and said: "Oh, I have prayed to her so fervently; but it is pure agony without any measure of consolation."

All day, fever, more burning than ever, consumed the gentle victim. "Ah," she sighed, "if this is the agony, what then is death?" Then, addressing the Mother Prioress, "Oh, my Mother, I assure you that the chalice is full to the brim." And in a fresh outburst of abandonment, she cried out: "Yes, my God, do whatever Thou willest, but have pity on me."

Turning then to her sisters, she said: "My little sisters, pray for me," adding as if in recognition of fresh pain: "My God, Thou who art so good; oh yes, Thou art good, I know it. . . ."

Towards three o'clock, she put her arms in the form of a cross, and Mère Marie de Gonzague placed on her knees an image of Our Lady of Mount Carmel. She gazed at it for a moment and said: "Oh, my Mother, present me to the Blessed Virgin without delay. Prepare me to die well."

The Prioress reminded her that, as she had always understood and practised humility, she could count on receiving mercy. Thérèse thought for a moment, and then, as if to encourage herself, said: "Yes, I have never sought anything but the truth. Yes, I have understood humility of heart. . . ."

She added: "All that I have written of my desire for suffering, all is most true." Then in tones of conviction: "*I do not repent,*" she said, "*of having surrendered myself to love.*"

Meanwhile, her torments became more and more acute. The innocent victim who had so often offered herself for the salvation of sinners, was moved to sigh in astonishment: "I would never have believed that it was possible to suffer so much, never, never! I cannot explain it except by the ardent desire I have had of saving souls."

Towards five o'clock, Mère Agnès de Jésus, who was alone with her, noticed a sudden change in her countenance. This time, it was indeed the death agony. A hurried summons of the bell called the community to the infirmary. The little saint had a smile for each of the Sisters. Then she became absorbed in the comtemplation of her Crucifix.

For two hours, the terrible death-rattle tore her chest. She trembled in every limb, and the sweat of death was so profuse that soon the bed-covering and mattress were saturated. To cool the burning fever that so cruelly parched her lips, Sœur Geneviève refreshed them with a small particle of ice. A look of infinite tenderness, and a smile of heavenly sweetness rewarded the "little companion of her childhood" for this last act of fraternal charity.

Towards seven o'clock, as her condition had not grown worse, the Mother Prioress dismissed the community. Turning towards her, the dying saint murmured: "Has the agony not yet come, Mother? Am I not going to die?"

"Yes, my child, this is the agony; but the good God wishes perhaps to prolong it for a few hours. . . ."

"Well then, let it be so. Oh, I would not wish to suffer less." Then fixing her gaze on the Crucifix: "Oh," she murmured, "I LOVE HIM! MY GOD, I . . . LOVE . . . THEE. . . ."

These were her last words. All at once, she sank down on the bed, her head leaning to the right in the attitude of those virgin martyrs who submitted themselves to the sword of the executioner, or rather in the attitude of abandonment with which a victim awaits from conquering Love the flaming arrow for which she longs. But, to the great surprise of all, she suddenly raised herself up as if called by some mysterious voice, opened her eyes, which beamed with heavenly peace and indescribable joy, and gazed fixedly at a point a little above the statue of the Blessed Virgin which stood facing her bed. Her countenance which, a moment before had been distorted with agony, regained its lily whiteness. The features expressed joyful wonder as if at sight of unsuspected marvels and, at the same time, the powerlessness of her mortal nature to bear up under the repeated attacks of victorious Love. After some moments of silent contemplation,[40] her head fell back and she expired in this seraphic ecstasy. It was September 30, 1897, at about 7.20 p.m. Her age was then twenty-four years and nine months.

Scarcely had she drawn her last breath, when a reflection of celestial happiness illumed her countenance. Clothed in her religious habit, a crown of white roses on her head, and a palm branch in her hand,[41] they laid her first on the paillasse from her own cell, brought down to the infirmary for this purpose. It was here that the nuns came to offer the first homage of regret and veneration to her who for more than nine years had been the model and the joy of their community.

According to the custom of Carmel, deceased nuns are laid out with face uncovered near the grille of the choir before the day of burial. The public then saw for the last time, and now through the cloister bars, the "little Queen" whose charming modesty they had formerly so much admired. The sight drew crowds to the Carmel who came to pray near the saint and to pass in their rosaries, medals, and crucifixes so that these might touch the remains. Even before leaving her convent for the little enclosure recently acquired by the Carmelites in the cemetery of Lisieux,

Thérèse wished to give the first wonderful sign of her undying charity.

We remember the lay-sister who had so harshly treated her on account of her arrangement of wreaths around Mère Geneviève's coffin. This lay-sister suffered from cerebral anæmia. In sorrow for her former injustice to Thérèse, and vividly impressed by the exemplary death of the angelic young nun, she approached the remains, and kissing the saint's feet, leant her forehead upon them for some moments and felt herself suddenly cured. Other members of the community too noticed the perfume of lilies and violets in places where no flower ever grew. This was no doubt the sweet-scented "shower" in its commencement. But the hour of separation had come. The coffin-lid hid for ever from her community that countenance so long the mirror of angelic beauty, and on Monday, October 4, the Church solemnly invoked the Seraphim and martyrs to lead their little sister near to the throne of God.

A goodly number of priests had gathered in the chapel around her who had so fervently prayed for priestly souls. Nevertheless, the funeral procession of the poor Carmelite to the cemetery was small and unassuming as befitted a humble nun long separated from the world.

A deep grave had been dug in a corner of the enclosed space reserved to the Carmelites. Without further ceremony than that of the liturgical prayers and blessings, the virginal body was lowered into the grave and was quickly covered beneath the clay. The few mourners withdrew, convinced that the little Sister's earthly rôle was over. But, a few days later, a wooden cross was erected at the head of the grave. In addition to the name of Sœur Thérèse de l'Enfant Jésus, it bore these mysterious words: "JE VEUX PASSER MON CIEL A FAIRE DU BIEN SUR LA TERRE."[42] This announcement, which was so promptly realized, was to make of this lowly mound crowned with lilies and roses a shrine of supplication and thanksgiving almost unparalleled in the whole world.

15

First Phases of Her Glorification— Continuous "Rain of Roses"— Sœur Thérèse de l'Enfant Jésus Raised to the Altar

"I feel that my mission is about to begin, my mission to make the good God loved as I love Him." Deeply impressed by this solemn promise of Thérèse, her Sisters in religion sought from the moment of her departure to heaven for its verification. On whom would she bestow her first favours? Her powerful and persevering intercession was expected first of all for her dear Carmel of Lisieux. This hope was realized in the fullest measure. We know that the fervour of the monastery, solid for the most part and truly worthy of praise, had been at times affected by the unequable temperament of Mère Marie de Gonzague, a fact which explains the trials inflicted on Sœur Thérèse by two or three Sisters who were unconscious of her high virtue. The circumstances of her holy death enlightened all minds, so that the most prejudiced of the nuns reproached themselves for their rash judgments, and highly praised the admirable patience of her whom they had misunderstood. The Prioress herself had been profoundly moved when witness of the saint's last agony, and during the months that followed Thérèse's departure from their midst, her character became noticeably more equable and gentle, her charity more stable under the influence of an ever growing humility, and the now cherished memory of Thérèse filled her with gratitude and veneration. She received a signal grace, known to herself alone, when before a portrait of the "little Queen" as a child upon her mother's knee. She could never afterwards look at this picture without tears, and once when thus weeping, she said to Sœur Geneviève de la Sainte-Face: "I alone can know what I owe her. Oh, what she said to me! . . . but so tenderly."[1]

Led by these dispositions, she accomplished an act of vast significance for the saint's glorification and her spiritual influence on souls. After the death of each nun, the Prioress sends, as we know, a notice on the deceased to every monastery of their Order. Mère Marie de Gonzague adopted the idea suggested to her, of having the *Histoire d'une Ame* printed and sent as the biographical notice of Sœur Thérèse to at the Carmels. The book appeared in October, 1898.[2]

From the first there was an outburst of astonishment; the book was read, and from different parts of France came enthusiastic expressions of admiration. From the monasteries, where it was read with avidity, it was lent to friends. Then, demands for copies poured into the convent at Lisieux. It was the beginning of a circulation which undoubtedly no other spiritual work has had for more than a century.

But the book was to gain something better than a wonderful circulation. Amongst the young girls from Brittany to the Pyrenees who read the *Histoire d'une Ame*, many felt themselves penetrated with the sweet perfume exhaled from its every page, and became fired with the desire to be united by fraternal bonds to the "little Flower" of Carmel. From different French provinces at first, then from Ireland, Portugal, Italy, Constantinople, and the Argentine Republic, postulants came to Lisieux. It was impossible to receive all these in the monastery of Sœur Thérèse. A large number had to be directed to other convents, where they did honour to the little saint who seemed to have called them. Those who were retained in the Carmel of Lisieux were, for the most part, to bring forth in a few years new flowers of sancity.

Three of the latter deserve special mention: Rev. Mère Marie-Ange de l'Enfant Jésus, who for a period of eighteen months held the office of Prioress, Mère Isabelle du

Sacré-Cœur and Mère Thérèse de l'Eucharistie, each of whom held the office of Sub-Prioress at the time of her death.

The first of these three was of Breton origin. Her rather egoistic character, joined it is true to genuine greatness of soul, had developed in her a leaning towards vanity and an inordinate desire for a worldly life. For those whom she disdainfully styled the "good Sisters" she had nothing but aversion and pity. She read the *Histoire d'une Ame.* It was as a flood of light in the darkness where her conscience groped its way. A little later, she knocked at the convent door at Lisieux, as "Sœur Thérèse's conquest."

From the first, she applied herself to copy, as far as in her lay, the model that had attracted her to this holy place. Her generosity in sacrifice, her constancy in pain, and her anxiety to attain at all costs to intimacy with the Divine Lover of souls were noticed with especial edification.[3]

Her sterling qualities caused her, though very young, to be proposed as Prioress. Her admiration for the saint had long inspired her with the desire to see that life of virtue sanctioned by the solemn decision of the Church. Now that she held the office of Prioress, she used every means to secure this happy result, and had the joy, in 1908, of persuading Mgr. Lemonnier, the newly elected Bishop of Bayeux, to lend his assistance. Unfortunately, she, like her heavenly friend, had contracted consumption, which was to bring her to the grave. She spent seven years in the cloister before going to join Thérèse in heaven. Before her death, she had said: "I will spend my heaven in helping 'my little Thérèse.'"[4]

Of no less refined intellect or brilliant imagination, Mère Isabelle du Sacré-Cœur also showed, first by her virtues and afterwards by her writings, the profound influence exercised on her by Thérèse's autobiography. Entering at once and whole-heartedly into the "little way," she passed on through its different stages quickly enough to taste very soon the incomparable sweetness of divine union. Coming from a family of good social standing, she had, as she said, willingly renounced all worldly advantages for the love of Jesus, and she added:

> In leaving all, with all have I been blest;
> The hundred-fold e'en here doth He bestow;
> He gave the rose when thorns were my request,
> I live at heaven's threshold here below.[5]

With rare delicacy she cultivated the flower of poetry which Thérèse had made to spring up in such beauty in the garden of Carmel. She became so conversant with the secrets of French metre, that she undertook to outline the "little way" in charming rhythm, and to compose another work of still greater merit on the *Douceur divine.*[6]

She was appointed mistress of novices, and we can judge from some remarkable fragments left us of her instructions with what fidelity she continued in the footsteps of her predecessor. She died on July 31, 1914, at the age of thirty-three, having been sub-prioress for some time previously.

Her successor in this office was a young nun who in the world had been the Countess de la Tour-d'Auvergne. Scarcely was she initiated into the ways of Carmel, when Sœur Thérèse de l'Eucharistie, the name she bore in religion, determined, in order to acquire humility "to be the little slave of all without letting this appear." Before each sacrifice, she put to herself the question: "How would our little Thérèse have acted?" Then, immediately, she felt ready to accept anything and hastened to accomplish the task before her.[7]

It was at this time that a priest giving a retreat at the convent said to the Prioress: "Mother, it is easy to see that a saint has lived in your Carmel." And in truth, through these young Sisters, penetrated with her spirit, imitating her in every detail of their lives and even in the circumstances of their deaths, Sœur Thérèse taught, edified, and sanctified still the house she had loved so well. A shower of graces descended on the monastery that sheltered those dearest to her here below.

Thérèse de l'Enfant Jésus had promised to help priests. Numerous, assuredly, were they who had received spiritual assistance from her during her short life. Was it not for them, that they might grow in perfection, fervour, and love, that she became a Carmelite? But her work here below had been only in its commencement.

Priests have been and still are those whom the dear saint favours most. "Pray to her," said Benedict XV to one of them; "it is her vocation to teach priests how to love Jesus Christ." Examples could be given of eminent ecclesiastics who placed no faith in Thérèse, considering her as a nun of charming qualities no doubt, but nothing more. She has so well succeeded in winning these over, that they are now her most ardent disciples. Nor was she content until she had led them to enter seriously upon her little way, the way of holy abandonment and heroic charity. It would be impossible to enumerate these whom she has visited, consoled, and strengthened in hours of weakness and agony, whom she has inspired with the joy of sacrifice, with supernatural happiness in bearing the cross for Jesus. Many have declared by word and writing that to her they owe the wonderful success of an apostolate previously most disheartening and barren of results.

A single incident will serve to show how the saint won over a priestly soul. It is taken from the writings of R. P. Flamérion of the Society of Jesus (he died in 1925), who received every year the confidences of hundreds of ecclesiastics at the house of retreat in Clamart.

"A priest, whose director I was," he writes,

> held a high position in one of the most important secondary schools in Paris. He was in no way predisposed towards devotion to Thérèse de l'Enfant Jésus; quite the contrary. At least, so I thought, with the result that, notwithstanding my own devotion to the saint, I would not venture to speak of her to him lest I should receive but a sarcastic smile in return. One day, a colleague said to him: "You ought to read the Life of a Carmelite, Sœur Thérèse de l'Enfant Jésus. You are a psychologist; you would find it an interesting study."

> My penitent was persuaded; he asked for the most complete Life, and spent a whole day in reading the work from cover to cover; he was completely won over.
>
> This priest was a great lover of the poor. In co-operation with a charitable lady, he had looked after an unfortunate poor woman who had been given up by the doctors, and whose death would leave two young orphans alone in the world and completely without support. For several weeks, the poor dying woman was in despair at the thought of her children's future, and bitterly rebelled against Providence.
>
> Realizing the peril to this soul, her benefactor suddenly thought of Sœur Thérèse, and commenced a novena to obtain her intercession. The charitable lady did the same without informing the priest of the fact. A complete change in the dispositions of the dying woman resulted; she became fully resigned, and expired with eyes fixed on a picture of the Blessed Virgin, while her two children stood beside her saying the rosary for her until the last moment. The priest, whose altered sentiments had led to this conversion, sent to Lisieux a detailed account of the double wonder.[8]

Another remarkable example of her influence was to follow. It was one of her own directors, he who had so earnestly exhorted her to confidence; the saint resolved to lead him now to the practice of her "little way." The apostle of holy abandonment, R. P. Pichon, wrote in 1909 to Sr. Geneviève de la Sainte-Face: "Yes, God wills to glorify His humble little spouse. After that, how can we refrain from endeavour to become as little children? It is for that end I labour now, at 66 years."[9]

Prodigal in spiritual favours to diocesan priests, Thérèse was still more generous towards missionaries, those dear missionaries whose apostolic work she had regarded with so much envy and exalted in such pathetic accents.

She had announced the intention of beginning her conquests immediately after her death, and while all the time watching over her dear Carmel, of visiting first of all the missions. From the year 1898, the *Annals of the Propagation of the Faith* record results which the missionaries describe as hitherto unknown and unhoped for. In numerous villages, the natives came of their own accord to receive instruction and baptism. Unacquainted as yet with Sœur Thérèse de l'Enfant Jésus, the greater number of these priests, isolated in the heart of savage countries, attributed these signal graces to a particular intervention of the Holy Spirit in favour of their flocks.

After encouraging in numerous ways the apostolate of Père Roulland, Sœur Thérèse willed to extend her protection to his confrères of the Foreign Missions. "I can testify," says her spiritual brother, "that in our missions in Japan, China, and the Indies, not only is confidence in the holiness and powerful intercession of Sœur Thérèse widespread, but she exercises very remarkable influence in converting souls and advancing them in virtue. In Japan, in particular, many Trappistine nuns declare that they owe their vocation to the influence of Sœur Thérèse de l'Enfant Jésus, whose Life they had read."[10]

The African territory where P. Bellière laboured seems also to have benefited by Sœur Thérèse's most fruitful apostolate. A single instance will give an idea of the marvels she wrought especially in favour of a mission directed by the White Fathers. One of these wrote in December, 1910:

> In almost all the dwellings of our Christians, and in all our Catechism schools, I have had placed a picture of the young saint. Everybody asked who is this little "bikira" (virgin). I assembled my catechists and gave them a résumé of Sœur Thérèse's life, adding that she must have great influence with God. I then gave her picture to each one, and recommended them to ask through her intercession the conversion of the entire country. They did so. From that day onward, the pagans came to catechism, not in small numbers but in compact crowds, so that, on Sundays, the mission enclosure was packed with people. . . . Note too that a great number of these poor natives came from villages which I had never visited, and which had hitherto been, if not hostile, at least completely indifferent to the missionaries.[11]

All the facts narrated refer to the spiritual order. Without refusing her efficacious compassion to physical suffering, the saint had willed to commence by healing souls. But she knew that bodily cures, more evident to the eyes of the multitude, would equally serve God's cause by strengthening confidence in His mercy and by increasing the number of prayers addressed to His servant. She had already relieved or cured many infirmities during the years immediately following her entrance into heaven. But it was again for a future priest that she reserved one of her first great miracles, one of the two that were brought forward for her beatification.

Since her fame had gone beyond the limits of her convent, recreations at the Grand Seminary of Bayeux were often passed in discussion on the merits and marvels of the young nun of Lisieux. Certain amongst the seminarists considered her piety fanciful or unattainable, while others spoke in glowing words of the *Histoire d'une Ame*, and quoted the miracles already performed by "little Thérèse." Noticeable amongst the latter was a young cleric, M. l'abbé Anne, a native of Lisieux. His health previously had always been good, but towards the month of June, 1904, it began to fail. Two years later, on August 23, 1906, he collapsed after an attack of hæmorrhage, which plainly indicated consumption far advanced. On examination, the doctors found immediately the symptoms of this dread disease in its most advanced stage; there were large cavities already in the lungs, burning fever had set in, with an utter aversion to food of any kind. No hope remained; death within a few days seemed inevitable. However, a novena to Sœur Thérèse was begun. A relic of the saint was hung around the neck of the dying cleric. But the ruthless malady continued its destructive work. One evening, the nursing Sister, convinced that he would pass away during the night, exhorted him to make the sacrifice of his life generously. But the abbé did not wish to die. He felt that Sœur Thérèse was near him, that she protected him, and warded off his death, so that she might give him back to his family and to the Church. Hardly had the Sister spoken her charitable words of advice, when he seized the relic of the saintly Carmelite, pressed it to his heart, and in an out-burst of irresistible confidence, mentally offered up this prayer: "Little Thérèse, you are in heaven; of that I feel sure. I am on earth where there is good to be done. You *must* cure me." This appeal made silently but with an intensity of hope had scarcely been formulated, when the dying man sat upright in his bed. The suffocating struggle for breath had ceased; the pain and the ravaging fever were gone. He wanted to get up instantly; he was cured. The hastily summoned doctors declared that the dying man was now in perfect health. Instead of thc lungs which were consumed and destroyed, new lungs had suddenly been formed, and now normal respiration gave fresh vigour to the whole system. The worn appearance of the abbé was the only indication of his recent illness, and even this quickly disappeared with a few days of regular nourishment. It was a veritable resurrection.

M. l'abbé Anne is today chaplain to the public hospital of Lisieux, where he attends to the spiritual needs of eight hundred patients. He is in the prime of life, and seems blessed with perfect health. "Little Thérèse" did not do things by halves. Not content with curing him, she has blessed him with strength of constitution above the ordinary. Impossible to present a more remarkable case to the ecclesiastical judges charged with the pronouncement of a decision on divine intervention.

We have next to record how, through the same intervention, a bishop was restored to health. Well known is the admirable work of Mgr. Augouard who contributed so largely to the extension, not only of the kingdom of the gospel, but also of French influence in the vast regions of central Africa. The labours of this Vicar Apostolic of Ubanghi were perilously near their end when, in 1910, he was attacked very severely by rheumatism of a type which threatened to render him permanently helpless. We have his own account of the manner in which he was restored to the full possession of those active powers that he was still to use for many years in the service of the Church.

Brazzaville, *November* 10, 1912.

. . . Two years ago, I was confined to my room for three months by very painful rheumatism which caused me great suffering. During this time, I had an opportunity of reading the Life of little Sœur Thérèse, and was deeply edified. One evening, when the sufferings had increased, I besought the dear Carmelite to ask God for my cure or my death, for I had no wish to remain a burden on my mission. Having reflected during the night, I withdrew this petition, and said to the little Sister: "Let me suffer, since such is the will of God. I ask nothing now for myself, but save Fr. . . . (naming one of my missionaries) from death." The missionary in question had been attacked by the fatal sleeping sickness which has claimed so many victims in the Congo. He was sent back to France, where he was examined at the Pasteur Institute, and was pronounced entirely *free from any microbe*. He returned to the Congo, and never again gave any cause for anxiety on the score of health, although he had had for two years previously symptoms of the dread disease.

To crown all, I myself, who no longer asked anything personal, was *cured the day after I had withdrawn my petition*.

In thanksgiving for this double cure, I made a pilgrimage to the little saint's tomb at Lisieux.

Thus am I happy to join my voice to those of my venerable colleagues in the Episcopate asking the Holy Father to introduce as soon as possible the Cause of this dear Carmelite who has already accomplished such wonders.

Prosper Augouard
Bishop of Upper French Congo[12]

At the time this letter was written, the number of cures and other temporal favours obtained by Thérèse for her clients in different parts of the world were already past counting.[13]

The diocesan authority of Bayeux, moved by these happenings, undertook a canonical inquiry. Mgr. Lemonnier received from the Sacred Congregation of Rites, on February

10, 1910, authorization to commence the Process of Beatification by examination of Sœur Thérèse's writings.

It was the first stage towards the supreme glorification. The "little Queen" seems to have waited for this before showing to the eyes of the whole world with incomparable splendour her power with God.

In the beginning of the year 1910, the writer of these lines was in the company of a group of Sulpician priests at Issy, when a venerable prelate, Mgr. de Teil, who had recently been appointed vice-postulator of the Cause, spoke of a young Carmelite of Lisieux who had died a few years previously and was attracting the attention of the public by the fame of wonders obtained through her intercession.[14]

For instance, she had just conferred a signal favour on the Carmel of Gallipoli in the south of Italy by putting in the empty coffer bank-notes sufficient to pay off a pressing debt.[15]

This was the first time that the Vicar-general of Meaux had heard the name of Thérèse Martin mentioned since the pilgrimage of 1888, when he had been so near her, and had almost met her at the feet of the Sovereign Pontiff, Leo XIII. Listening with amazement to the story of Gallipoli, he little thought that, when fifteen years later he would be called upon to relate her wonderful life, it would have become impossible for him to make a catalogue of her miracles, so numerous would they be.

Soon it became impossible for Mgr. de Teil himself to note all the miraculous interventions attributed to the wonderworker. Fortunately, these accounts have been carefully collected and recorded with fraternal solicitude at the Carmel of Lisieux. It was the "rain of roses" predicted by Thérèse, rain growing every day more and more beneficent and sweet, and by degrees extending its refreshing showers to all parts of the world.

The nuns of Lisieux conceived the idea of putting together in volumes a great number of letters relating conversions, cures, and other favours which were now arriving in hundreds. Thus were these volumes composed which in the space of fifteen years have comprised no less than 3,000 pages of close type. Yet this written account presents but a small fraction of her miracles.[16] Throughout the pages of these seven volumes, we are brought face to face with the most poignant human misery, and we see everywhere the gentle hand of the saint carrying the saving power of Jesus to all, like the Master long ago in Galilee, "*sanans omnem languorem et omnem infirmitatem.*"[17]

Her help extends to every rank of society, but she appears to have a special regard for the poor and humble, the sick and the abandoned, above all for little children. Thousands of unfortunate people who have received her assistance could repeat the touching words of a poor woman who had come to the saint's grave to make known her distress: "Oh, with what gentleness she spoke to me! I have now no fear of anything."[18]

Apart from the alleviation of bodily suffering, these miracles usually bring sweet and strengthening interior peace; they pour into the heart a perfume as from paradise, and engender a longing for the kingdom of God; they envelop the soul with a penetrating fragrance and leave it immersed in celestial love. "To love, to be loved, and to return to earth to make Love loved," was the part to which Thérèse aspired and the rôle which in reality she now fills.

She exercises it all the more effectively because this cure of bodily and moral wounds is but the negative element of her mission. She instructs, she sanctifies, she leads souls upwards in thousands to the summits of the spiritual life by the interior help she gives, especially through the reading of the *Histoire d'une Ame.*

We shall readily agree that the circulation of this book alone is one of her grandest miracles, when we realize that from 1898 to 1925, 410,000 copies of the complete edition have been sold, without mentioning the two million copies of the abridged Life summarized from the original work.[19]

Added to this unprecedented success of the French original is that of its thirty-five translations into different languages which have found their way into every corner of the world during the last fifteen years. Such a result, obtained as it was without advertisement, seems to denote supernatural intervention. Consider furthermore that this book, written by bits and scraps, at odd moments snatched whenever possible, written, too, without any effort at literary style, yet possesses an irresistible charm which leads people to re-read it in many cases six or seven times and more, producing in the soul an ever increasing detachment from passing things, a clearer understanding of divine realities and a further advance in divine love.

The principal fruits of grace obtained by the reading of the book in France, Spain, and Italy are enumerated in the several volumes of the *Shower of Roses;* we can but refer the reader to these. We shall merely note some of the wonders wrought in Protestant lands.

A former United Free Church minister of Lochranza in Arran wrote from Edinburgh on April 23, 1911, to the Mother Prioress of the Carmel of Lisieux:

> It is now more than a year since I became acquainted with the autobiography of Sœur Thérèse de l'Enfant Jésus in its English translation. I opened it at random, and was immediately struck by the beauty and originality of the thoughts. I found that the work of a genius as well as a theologian had fallen into my hands, the work of a poet too of the first order. . . . I felt as one to whom the invisible world is suddenly revealed, and I said to myself: "Thérèse is here in this room"; her image came repeatedly before my mind; she refused to leave me, and I seemed to hear her say: "See how Catholic saints love Jesus Christ. Listen to me; choose my little way, for it is a sure way, the only true way." I then commenced to invoke her aid with a joy I shall not attempt to describe. One day, she said suddenly to me: "Why do you ask me to pray for you if you do not wish to know and to invoke the Blessed Virgin?" I realized immediately how illogical it was to invoke Thérèse and yet neglect the Mother of God. The light had come; I turned forthwith to the Blessed Virgin. The promptness of her response astonished me. All at once, my soul was filled with impassioned love hitherto unknown, a love which has gone on increasing and is now an abyss.[20]

Rev. Alexander Grant was baptized on April 20, 1911, at Edinburgh, by a Jesuit Father. He was the first member of the Free Church of Scotland to enter the Catholic Church. His position having become difficult in his own country, he came to France with his wife who was also a convert. As a mark of their gratitude, they came to live at Alençon in the house where the saint had been born, there to welcome the numerous pilgrims who visit it through devotion. Mr. Grant died a holy death on July 19, 1917.

In a remarkable letter the Anglican minister of Stantonbury, the Rev. Newmann Guest, expresses the greatest hope for the reunion of all England under the one pastor through the power of Thérèse: "I believe," he wrote even before the canonization,

> that one day the East (which is partly Catholic) and the West (Protestant) of England will again be joined in real unity. For the attainment of this end, I count on the influence of the autobiography of the "Little Flower" of Jesus, this young soul who will soon, let us hope, be canonized by the Church of Rome.
>
> If we Anglicans and Roman Catholics could unite in the same prayer, and if a novena for our reunion through the intercession of Sœur Thérèse de l'Enfant Jésus were begun, I have no doubt this happy result would come suddenly, as came the conversion of three thousand Israelites on the day of Pentecost. I say again: Cease your controversy and pray.[21]

If the Protestants of the United Kingdom were so much struck by Thérèse, what shall we say of English Catholics? The "Little Flower" exercised over them an influence that manifested itself from time to time in practical efforts to improve social conditions.

A rich factory-owner in Liverpool who employed over a hundred workers of both sexes acknowledged that before he came to know of St. Thérèse de l'Enfant Jésus he never gave a thought to ameliorating the condition of his employees. He read the *Histoire d'une Ame*, and became a new man. Not content with distributing copies to each of the workers, and having the picture of the saint put up in his workshops, he gave an annual holiday of eight days to every one in his employment during which they received their usual wages. He organized little social gatherings to bring some rays of joy into their dull and monotonous lives; he sent many of them to make retreats, "for," said he, "it is eternal happiness above all which I wish to procure for these poor people." He advanced with steady strides in the "little way"; he had learned the lesson of love.[22]

In America, the same confidence, the same enthusiasm is continually shown in act. Examples might be given of Catholic dioceses in Canada where "little Thérèse" is perhaps more popular than in France itself. Large cities in the United States send up to her supplications and appeals each day more numerous. In the immense Protestant hospitals there that shelter so much human misery, doctors and nurses vie with one another in invoking the saint. When a doctor has come to the end of his scientific resources, he says to his patient: "Pray to the 'Little Flower,'" and the nurses bring round from bed to bed pictures and souvenirs of Thérèse.

The British colonies, especially India and Australia, rival the mother country in this devotion. From Sydney and Ceylon, as from New York and Philadelphia, requests pour into Lisieux for relics, biographies, and pictures.

South America followed the lead of Spain, where from the first the *Histoire d'une Ame* was eagerly read. Italy breathed with delight the perfume of this lily of purity; Austria boasted of having obtained several grand miracles; even Germany, in spite of its early indifference towards this saint who had lived on the other side of the Rhine, was compelled to recognize her protection, and its Catholic population invoke her with growing fervour. From all these countries requests for prayers reached Lisieux simultaneously with accounts of miracles wrought in the distant missions of the Congo, Nyanza, and the Far East.

It would be impossible to number the wonders, the cures, conversions and apparitions with which the "little Queen" has blessed every land. Nor does she tire of bestowing her favours. "She is called, and she comes. White, radiant and smiling, she manifests herself to the raptured eyes of innocent children or to old soldiers who long to wash out with their tears the stains of a lifetime. Through closed doors and windows she passes, bringing her wondrous gifts of roses. She is invoked, and a mysterious and most sweet perfume fills the air."[23]

Facts like these inspired more and more confidence of success in the Cause that had been undertaken. In August, 1910, the first session of the Informative Process took place at Bayeux. This Process which treated of the life and virtues of the servant of God was terminated in December, 1911. In the following year (on December 10, 1912), the Sacred Congregation of Rites issued the decree of approbation of Thérèse's writings, and less than two years later, on June 10, 1914, the Sovereign Pontiff Pius X signed the decree for the introduction of her Cause. Close at hand, alas, was the terrible war, which was to throw the world into confusion, and the saintly Pope, as though he had a presentiment of the future, hastened to put the little saint on the way to liturgical honours before the horror of the carnage foreseen caused him to die of grief.

In spite of the anguish that tore the hearts of the people at this tragic time, one felt that the rôle of the young virgin messenger of joy was to increase. Already in Normandy her official glorification had begun. On September 6, 1910, her body had been exhumed in the presence of Mgr. Lemonnier. To insure the preservation of the precious relics, they were placed in another coffin and in a cemented vault at a short distance from the first grave.

The virginal body, it is true, had not remained intact after its thirteen years' sojourn deep in the earth. As Thérèse had foretold, nothing was found of her but her bones. The thick material of the habit in which she was buried had become quite thin and perishable. In her remains, as in her life itself, nothing extraordinary appeared; but the bones exhaled a sweet perfume (noticed by several witnesses); the very earth that had touched the coffin remained for months impregnated with heavenly fragrance. This was but the prelude of other wonders.

From the day that war was declared, Thérèse de l'Enfant Jésus left her place in heaven and entered the field side by side with the "poilus"[24] of France. In the mud of the trenches, on the plains of death, near the bed of agony, she was to remain with them, faithful to the end. Thus did her name become speedily known in the camps at the front and in the barracks at the rear. With the quickened perception of realities which comes in hours of extreme peril, the poor soldiers realized the miraculous influence of this beneficent mediatrix endowed with heavenly grace, and they invoked her with intense fervour. Moreover, they realized in their simple and upright hearts the necessity, in order to "win the war," of a virtue which Thérèse had practised even to heroism, namely constancy in doing and suffering all in the spirit of duty. Thus was she their model as well as their protectress.

Henceforth, she became, like St. Michael and St. Joan of Arc, one of the invisible captains of the army in the field. And it was to her that the most confiding and intimate prayers were addressed. "True, we have Joan of Arc," wrote a soldier daily faced with death, "but the little Sister is nearer to us."

The faith of these brave men was manifested in naïve and transparently sincere expressions. "I am in despair," writes a member of the Air Force, "I have lost the little saint's relic." A soldier of the line wrote to his mother: "The moment I received the relic of St. Thérèse, I was filled with great joy; now I have no longer any fear." What could be more touching than this simple prayer of an artilleryman: "Sœur Thérèse de l'Enfant Jésus, protect me, take the place of mother who is there no longer."[25]

Artillery officers gave their battery the name of the Carmelite saint; air pilots named their machines "*Avion Soeur-Thérèse*"; entire regiments were consecrated to her. Nor was it merely the simple and illiterate who thus invoked her whom they called their "second angel guardian" or their "war godmother." The story is told of a sub-lieutenant, infected by the philosophy of the German school, and professing atheism, who died a holy death after he had consented to wear a relic of Sœur Thérèse. Officers of high rank, like General Duplessis, made a vow to go on a pilgrimage to her tomb if their lives were spared, and when peace was restored, loudly proclaimed the efficacy of her assistance.[26]

The power of the "little Queen" was manifested with a clearness that forced recognition from even the most incredulous. After a few months of warfare, the number of bullets rendered harmless by coming in contact with a relic, a medal, a picture, even a booklet concerning Sœur Thérèse had gone beyond count. Many of these "bucklers" were sent to the Carmel of Lisieux, and on most of them can be seen the mark of the bullet which had been thus stopped in its course, turned aside, or flattened.

Anyone who has followed the history of the war will readily class amongst the heroes the air-pilot Bourjade, that fearless attacker of the German aircraft who, more fortunate than his rival Guynemer, was at the end able to hail victory for France. It is well known that this great soldier was none other than a humble Missionary of the Sacred Heart from Issoudun who was afterwards to consecrate his last years and give his life to the service of the inhabitants of New Guinea. But what is not so generally known is that his magnificent success was due to supernatural protection. Fortunately, he noted down in the course of his campaigns the favours he received, under the form of letters of thanksgiving addressed to his dear little saint. These letters have lately been published.[27] Some of the many interventions attributed by this aviator to Sœur Thérèse date from the time when Père Bourjade, as a foot-soldier, went on scout duty through the barbed-wire entanglements up to the very entrenchments of the enemy. "How often," he says, "when obliged to advance under the hail of shells that fell on every side, have I under thy protection, Sœur Thérèse, come through all without a scratch."

Later, Thérèse protected on numberless occasions amidst the dangers of aerial warfare Père Bourjade's machine, which carried as its emblem a picture of the saint; in recognition of this heavenly assistance rendered with maternal solicitude the missionary felt bound to express his gratitude in fresh outbursts of thanksgiving. "Oh, Sœur Thérèse," he exclaims, "how can I ever thank you? How many times have you snatched me from death! I shall only know in heaven. What I do know is that on more than ten occasions, I have had hair-breadth escapes of fatal accidents. . . . In thus protecting me you have brought me decorations too. In these, alas, lies great danger of vainglory and self-esteem. Therefore, dear little Thérèse, do not forget that *it is your fault if I am decorated*; help me, then, always to combat this new danger which I feel very near me."

Père Bourjade was a missionary, so it is not astonishing that he was an object of Thérèse's predilection. But no one was excluded from her loving protection. Amongst the soldiers to whom she deigned to appear radiant and smiling in the midst of the carnage were to be found lukewarm Catholics who had started for the front without approaching the sacrament of penance, contenting themselves by accepting a picture or relic of "the little Sister."[28]

Though belonging to France, like St. Joan of Arc, Sœur Thérèse did not refuse her pity to those who invoked her even from the ranks of the enemy. A Bavarian prisoner who had lost both legs was on the point of death. The French chaplain recommended him to have recourse to the "saint of Lisieux," and the dying man, having spent a whole night in prayer, saw her descend towards him. From that time onward, his wounds healed in an astonishing manner. He was snatched from the jaws of death, and went away repeating: "Oh, how I will make known this French saint in my own country."

The gratitude of our soldiers manifested itself in a striking manner. A good number of them pleaded the cause of their "little Sister" with the Holy See. She had obtained laurels and decorations for them; they asked in return the halo of the blessed for her.

These few facts, gathered amongst hundreds of others, give but a most inadequate idea of Thérèse's miraculous intervention on behalf of the soldiers in the Great War. To gain a fuller notion of them, it would be necessary to see the thousands of letters and photographs sent by the "poilus" from the front, of her who had been an ever tender, ever watchful mother to them. It is in the Carmel chapel, within those walls covered with crosses of the Legion of honour and other decorations, together with epaulettes and swords sent as ex-votos from the trenches, that one can realize how much the little saint meant to our troops, and how, by her constant encouragement in face of supreme danger, she contributed immeasureably to the final victory.

To fully appreciate also the numberless and marvellous favours obtained through her intercession for her clients in every land and of every social condition, we should see the marble memorial tablets that are erected in certain cloisters of the convent. In the chapel itself, as we know, the walls are literally covered over with plaques that proclaim in letters of gold the manifold recognition of her miracles.

Such manifestations of heavenly power made the process of Beatification easy while helping also to hasten its happy conclusion. The cause had been introduced and the apostolic process was being pursued at Bayeux, when a new miracle of the first order, bearing the marks of undeniable authenticity, further confirmed the favourable opinion of the ecclesiastical judges. A religious of the Congregation of the Daughters of the Cross, Sœur Louise de Saint-Germain, had from 1912 suffered from a dangerous ulcer in the stomach which caused frequent hæmorrhage. This Sister belonged to the provincial convent of Ustarritz (Basses-Pyrénées). She had, on two different occasions, tried to resume her duties as teacher in a Spanish convent to which she was attached; but each time, violent hæmorrhages had forced her to abandon her work. In spite of all this, she continued to hope in Sœur Thérèse who had favoured her with heavenly perfumes in the midst of her greatest sufferings. At the beginning of 1915, she had become so weak that it was thought advisable to administer the last sacraments. Abandoning all hope of being cured, she had ceased to pray for that favour, and now besought her heavenly advocate for nothing but the grace to die well. Let us hear her own account of Thérèse's decisive intervention to restore her to health.

"In the beginning of September, 1916," she says,

> a Sister who happened to be in the convent at the time induced me to renew my petitions to the dear saint. Yielding to her wishes, I joined sacrifice to prayer with redoubled confidence. What was my astonishment when, on the night of September 10, Sœur Thérèse de l'Enfant Jésus came herself to me and said: "Be generous; you will soon be cured; I promise it." She then disappeared. In the morning, the three Sisters who were sleeping in the infirmary were greatly surprised to find rose-petals of different colours scattered around my bed. They were the heralds of my cure. But there were yet a few days of waiting, during which I suffered a real martyrdom and was reduced to the last extremity. It was only on the evening of September 21 that, after a most violent attack, I suddenly and very unexpectedly fell asleep to awake on the following morning completely cured. Instead of suffering, I experienced a feeling of general well-being and was very hungry. I rose joyously and asked permission to assist at Mass. My good Mother-Superior prudently obliged me to go back to bed, where I was served with a plentiful breakfast. My complete cure was soon apparent, and I was enabled to resume my regular duties. I have from that time enjoyed perfect health, and I cherish feelings of profound gratitude towards Sœur Thérèse de l'Enfant Jésus which I would like to make known to all.[29]

This miracle attested by the formal certificates of renowned doctors was selected, together with the cure of the abbé Anne, as that on which to found the papal Decree attesting the reality of Thérèse's miracles.

The first Decree, signed on August 14, had affirmed that the Servant of God had practised virtue to an heroic degree. We have already noted in our chapter on the "Little Way of Spiritual Childhood" the admirable Discourse given by Pope Benedict XV on that occasion. The soul of the saintly Pontiff, naturally inclined to the doctrine of humility and confiding abandonment, poured forth from his heart, as we may remember, a masterly and enlightened résumé of Thérèse's method which he authoritatively pronounced *"the secret of holiness."*

The Decree of Approbation of her miracles was given on February 11, 1923. His Holiness Pius XI borrowed from Manzoni, for whose jubilee preparations were then being made, a beautiful comparison to exalt the little saint's humility. "God it is," says the poet, "who has created the pine-tree that braves the storm and the willow that bends in the hand, the fir-tree that resists the winter, and the poplar that fears not the floods. He also it is who has brought into being the flower that displays the magnificence of its colouring for Him alone, that exhales towards heaven its perfume, and in silence fades and dies." To this the Holy Father adds: "This silent flower, these petals of resplendent hue, this perfume which fills the air, this beauty that displays itself only for the eyes of God, is not this the little Thérèse de l'Enfant Jésus?"[30]

Some weeks later, on the occasion of the Decree *de tuto*, announcing that the final steps towards the Beatification of so fruitful a wonder-worker might in all certainty be taken, the Sovereign Pontiff, when about solemnly to place the "little Queen" in the ranks of the Beatified, spoke the touching address already mentioned, in which he exalted this time Thérèse's charity and called her "the true flower of love come from heaven to earth to astonish heaven and earth."[31]

Before the public glorification of the humble child of Lisieux and the signal homage reserved for her by the Holy See, a ceremony was necessary, a ceremony which was to offer to the people of her native France, and more especially to those who had known her from her early years, an unforgettable spectacle.

On August 9 and 10, 1917, the remains of the Servant of God had been exhumed a second time, and for the first time officially identified. Before the Beatification, these venerated remains had to be translated to the Carmel and identified again with more solemn ceremony. The translation was fixed for March 26, 1923. At no period perhaps in its history, not for centuries at all events, had Lisieux witnessed so great a celebration. On that morning, fifty thousand pilgrims arrived in the town. With repeated *Aves*, they awaited the opening of the cemetery, where, under the direction of the Bishop and the civil authorities, the work of exhuming the precious coffin was proceeding. By a special permission, a poor woman who had come from Angers obtained entrance to the graveside. She carried in her arms her little god-daughter who was suffering from spinal disease and unable to move a limb. Already the grave had been opened and most of the earth removed, but some yet remained. The god-mother leant over and laying the suffering child on this earthly bed so nearly in contact with the sacred relics, commenced to pray fervently. After a few moments, the poor half-paralysed little one sat straight up; the child who for months had been unable to walk, came unaided from the glorious tomb where she had recovered strength and activity. That was not all. Scarcely had the slabs placed over the coffin been loosened, than a distinct perfume of roses came from the tomb, reaching the workmen and the other bystanders who proclaimed with admiration the reality of the phenomenon.

When the legal formalities had been completed, the coffin was placed on a carriage richly adorned with white drapery embroidered with silver thread, and the "little Queen," escorted by more than two hundred priests and all the communities of the town, by twenty Catholic delegations, by a group of officers from every rank, including even a guard of honour from the American Legion with drawn swords, and a multitude of people from every province in France, set out, this time in triumph, on the road to her convent. Before the departure from the cemetery, nature which for twenty-five years had decorated her grave with the wild flowers she had loved so well, seemed desirous of paying a last tribute of homage to Thérèse. "The sun shines in radiant magnificence just above the horizon, lighting up the beautiful valley of the Orbiquet that encircles with so much charm the cemetery of Lisieux. All is light and loveliness in this springtime scene, and around the glorified remains of the angelic saint the brightest sunbeams play and form an aureole."[32]

At last the procession set out; "little Thérèse" departed for ever, making this, her last journey, in all the splendour of an apotheosis. The immense cortège, extending over two kilometres, formed an imposing sight, so grave and recollected. Not a hymn, no sound of trumpet nor joyous bells broke the stillness; the laws of the Church forbade any manifestation resembling religious cult until Rome had given its official decision. But the murmured decades of the rosary alternated unceasingly with the recitation of psalms from the common of virgins. It is not surprising, then, that in answer to this great united prayer, a new host of miracles should come from the hands of the beloved saint. One was the cure of a badly wounded soldier who for fifteen months had lost the use of his legs and who recovered suddenly as the carriage bearing the precious relics passed by. Another, that of a lady from Paris suffering from a serious malady of the stomach and unable to take food without acute pain. She returned joyously from Lisieux, completely cured. A third was the case of a blind girl whose eyes were opened to behold with rapture the holy relics arrive at the threshold of the Carmel.

What a difference between the isolation of the lowly hearse which on October 4, 1897, bore the unknown Carmelite to the grave and this triumphal chariot that, twenty-six years later, brought back to her convent the glorious virgin amidst the fervent exultation of devoted thousands. *Exultabunt Domino ossa humiliata.*[33] Never perhaps was the Divine promise so magnificently fulfilled.

Heralded by the first rich notes of the new organ, the coffin, covered with cloth of gold, was brought into the chapel where little Thérèse Martin had so often knelt in prayer before her entrance into Carmel.

After the second canonical recognition, her glorified relics were divided, the Postulator of the Cause, Rev. Father Rodrigo of St. Francis of Paula, delegate of the Sovereign Pontiff, taking such portion of them as he was to bring to Rome. The more important relics were placed in the base of the rich shrine prepared for them. The rest were enclosed in the tinted marble figure representing Thérèse in her last sleep.

This first triumph was but the prelude of others which the supreme authority of the Church held in store for the "little flower" of Lisieux. On April 29, 1923, Thérèse's beatitude in the glory of Heaven was proclaimed by the Head of the Church. In the splendidly decorated Basilica of the Vatican were assembled forty-five archbishops and bishops, all the ambassadors to the Holy See headed by the specially delegated French ambassador, together with the prelates and dignitaries from the various religious Orders and an immense concourse of the faithful.

When all had taken their places according to hierarchical order, the function commenced with the reading of the pontifical Brief. This Brief, after having extolled, with the Apocalypse, the prerogatives of virginity, set forth briefly Thérèse's life and her "little way of spiritual childhood," noted her extraordinary power of intercession, and in conclusion conferred on her the honours of Beatification with the privileges which belong to it—namely, public exposition of her relics, Mass and Office for the diocese of Bayeux as well as for the churches and convents of the Carmelite Order.

Holy Church had spoken; little Thérèse Martin had become Blessed Thérèse de l'Enfant Jésus. Mgr. Lemmonier, Bishop of Bayeux, in a voice trembling with emotion, intoned the *Te Deum*, and suddenly a blaze of light filled the immense nave. In one second, all the chandeliers were ablaze; the "Glory of Bernini," in the centre of which was the picture of Thérèse, gleamed in the shining of a thousand lights, and the new Beata was seen in the midst of a wonderful radiance.

The painting represented Thérèse with arms extended in ecstasy, gently rising heavenwards, borne on the clouds, while two angels with their eyes fixed upon her, unrolled scrolls bearing the words, "Way of Childhood," and, "I will spend my heaven in doing good upon earth."

The vast congregation trembled with enthusiasm. Certain it is, that were it not for the reverence due to the holy place, loud acclamation would have hailed the newly Beatified.

The hour had come for solemn celebration of the Mass, the Mass composed in honour of the dear saint. To the Bishop of Bayeux was reserved the privilege of being celebrant. With sweet emotion, the hundreds of priests who formed the choir repeated in union with the fervent prelate, "Lord, who hast said 'Unless you become as little children you shall not enter the kingdom of heaven.' Grant us, we beseech Thee, that we may follow Blessed Thérèse in the way of humility and simplicity of heart so faithfully that we merit to share her eternal reward."[34]

The morning ceremony was ended. As the crowd filed slowly out from the great building, magistrates and soldiers with eyes dimmed by emotion mingled with the throng of monks and nuns. Words of joyful enthusiasm were heard on all sides, as those of an old officer who had been through the war and had come hundreds of miles to do honour to his "little sister of the trenches" and went away exclaiming with genuine fervour: "Ah, what a great day; how happy I am!" Towards evening, His Holiness Pius XI went to St. Peter's for the first time on the occasion of a beatification, Thérèse being his first Beata. He was escorted thither by an immense cortège of Swiss Guards, Noble Guards, Chamberlains, Prelates and Cardinals who surrounded the *Sedia gestatoria*. The Holy Father descended from the *Sedia* and kneeling like the humblest of the faithful, prayed silently to her whom he had just declared Blessed. With countenance expressive of supplication and homage he raised his eyes towards the "Gloria." There he beheld her smiling, the humble child whom his infallible word had just exalted, she, the untiring strewer of roses whom he has chosen for "his patron and counsellor." Could she remain indifferent to this homage from the Head of the Church who was pleased to recognize in her the radiant "Star" of his pontificate? No. In the silence of the Vatican she had already given him proof of her mysterious help. "She has in truth thrown light on questions that I was unable to solve," declared the Holy

Father. He even added in confidence: "These days I feel quite near me the presence of Blessed Thérèse."[5]

Here then we have the "little maiden of Lisieux" crowned with the aureole. The Catholic nations which had one and all received from the cherished saint favours beyond number and had been blessed by multiplied miracles felt bound to vie with one another in celebrating her entrance into glory. During the remainder of 1923, there was a succession of solemn celebrations in her honour in the old cathedrals and convents of Europe as well as in the younger churches of the New World. The spectacle was as touching as it was magnificent, for the fervent prayers of faithful clients obtained unhoped-for favours.

"It is a torrent of roses that I shall now shower down," Thérèse had said. And these wondrous roses from heaven, cures, conversions, protection against every ill of soul and body, descended on grateful multitudes in the measure in which earthly roses made Thérèse's sanctuaries beautiful here below and proclaimed her power and munificence.

The most renowned orators lent their voices in order to express the grateful thanks of these multitudes to her who wearied not of bestowing help, consolation and blessings. Amongst these eloquent panegyrics of Blessed Thérèse one delivered by R. P. Perroy in the cathedral of Lyons deserves special mention. The eminent orator feared, seemingly, that the sight of so many roses strewn in the streets and churches would give the people an incorrect idea of Thérèse's sanctity and prove harmful to their devotion. For this reason he vigorously attacked the false notion which might occupy certain minds.

> Little Thérèse de l'Enfant Jésus, let me defend you against those who represent you as walking at your ease in a fragrant rose garden. I want to tell the world that your soul was above all virile; I wish to tell them that you could take your place between Joan of Arc and Margaret Mary. I desire to make known that your combats against self were the combats of God. I would declare you heroic amongst heroines because you have chosen the way most contrary to nature, the way of little ones.

> I desire to say, that if every knee on earth bends before you, if your name has become the most renowned in the world, it is not alone because you bring roses but because, with the Crucified for whom your flowers have exhaled their fragrance, you have been obedient even unto the Cross.[36]

But how they longed at the Carmel of Lisieux to venerate beneath her glorious halo her whom humility had kept so hidden during nine years within the austere convent walls. Friends outside liked to think of the sisters of the new Beata behind the sombre grilles kneeling in solemn liturgical prayer before her whom they had formed and trained in divine love.

To meet the requirements of the faithful in view of the approaching splendid ceremonies, the Carmel chapel had been enlarged. All was ready for the triduum of the 28th, 29th and 30th May, when Cardinal Vico, Ponent of the Cause and Papal Legate, arrived at Lisieux.

Yet, this triduum had to be of a somewhat informal character as the restricted dimensions of the Carmel sanctuary would not allow of the more elaborate celebrations which took place later in Lisieux and in which a great number of bishops took part. Nevertheless, the presence of the Papal Legate, together with the Primate of Normandy and the Bishops of Troyes and Évreux drew to the town a fervent throng, including several princes of royal blood and official representatives of numerous Catholic nations.

The preacher on this occasion was the Rev. Père Martin, superior of the Diocesan Missionaries of Vendée, whose learned and devotional treatise on the elements of *The Little Way of Spiritual Childhood* had gained universal esteem. Again he embarked on his favourite subject, this time with such power of persuasion that he inspired eminent personages present with the desire of being numbered among the "little souls" so favoured by Jesus.

After three days of solemn celebration, the precious relics enclosed in the beautiful silver-gilt reliquary presented by Brazil were borne in procession through the poorest lanes as well as the principal streets of the town. Then the solemn benediction given in the cathedral by the Roman cardinal was, for the moment, the farewell of this prince of the Church to the humble nun whom, by his active and benevolent zeal, he had caused to be so quickly inscribed amongst the Beatified.

The Carmel had with recollected devotion offered homage and congratulation to its gentle Beata. The people of Lisieux who had so often seen "little Thérèse" pass through their streets, and had as often remarked her modesty and candour, wished in turn to celebrate the memory of the saintly child. This time, the purple of three cardinals, Bourne, Primate of England, Dougherty, Archbishop of Philadelphia, and Touchet, Bishop of Orleans, was to throw its reflection on the golden reliquary, while a crown of fifteen bishops and mitred abbots formed an aureole around the relics of the Beatified. On the morning of August 6, the entire town was in festal array. Girandoles and festoons decorated every house-front, and the grimacing carved figures of the old pointed gables were hidden beneath sweet-scented flower garlands. Each church in the town was to have its own Pontifical Office in presence of the venerated relics of her who in former days had so often lingered to pray before their altars. The reliquary surrounded with lilies and white roses was to penetrate into every corner of Lisieux on this great occasion.

One of the most touching incidents of the triumphal procession was the visit of "little Thérèse" to her old convent school. Under the shade of the lime-trees where she had played as a child, the *Magnificat* was chanted by her former teachers as the golden reliquary halted for a moment before the statue where Thérèse Martin on the day of her first Communion had pronounced her act of consecration to Mary. She came now to thank her dear Benedictines for the example and counsels that had helped her forward on her way towards the glory of the elect.

The 8th of August, the last day of the Triduum, was the "crowning splendour." The Pontifical Mass was celebrated that morning at the cathedral by Cardinal Bourne. Late in the day after Vespers, Cardinal Touchet was to preach the panegyric. "What shall this eagle say of the dove?" murmured one of the bishops. The eagle began by capturing with a glance the attention of the six thousand people who thronged the vast church. He then winged his flight towards the dazzling heights where he was wont to soar.

The Bishop of Orleans had come to pay a debt of gratitude to Blessed Thérèse. Was it not she who, in answer to the Prelate's prayer, when the Process for the canonization of Joan of Arc was about to be interrupted, had caused Pius X to revoke his decision, thus hastening the supreme exaltation of *La Pucelle*? The Cardinal dwelt on her wonderful power of intercession with God, and showed that this power was derived from her incomparable love—ardent, generous, unwearied love—which drew the Almighty towards the humble child of His Heart, and won for her the sweetest intimacy of Divine love. He then went on to speak of her rôle of consolatrix amongst the soldiers in the Great War. Suddenly addressing himself directly to the two Cardinal visitors, he called upon them to proclaim to their people at home that France had a horror of these hecatombs, that her one aspiration was for peace, a peace which would respect her rights. . . . This unexpected and touching finale was received with prolonged applause.

After the liturgical ceremony, another procession, the most majestic of all, formed in the open space before the cathedral. It would seem as if the little saint in her flower-laden car, more gracious than ever in her solemn magnificence, was making a royal visit of courtesy and benevolence to her delighted fellow citizens. Around the golden reliquary crosiers and mitres gleamed in the summer sun. There, too, shone and glistened the gold on many a military uniform, while French and foreign flags floated in the air or, fluttering, touched caressingly like angels' wings those who stood beneath. But hidden from the eyes of all were the celestial roses which the little sower scattered untiringly along the way.

Amongst the hundred thousand in the procession at Lisieux that day were many victims of disease, many who were weighed down by sorrow. To a number of these came the grace of consolation or of bodily or spiritual healing as the precious relics passed by.

Now, the roses that adorned the streets and public places have disappeared. The garlands are gone. But those days of triumph had their influence throughout France. By uniting at Lisieux with the same spiritual purpose and in one and the same devotion the most distinguished and highly qualified representatives of the allied nations, they had done more, perhaps, to consolidate international friendship than by long diplomatic conferences.

Was the "little Queen" to rest content now beneath her glorious laurels? To do so would be contrary to her designs. As long as there are tears to dry here below, as long as there are burdens to lighten or wounds to heal, she will "come down" according to her generous promise to apply to the wounds of poor humanity the balm that heals. On the very day of her beatification, thirty new miracles were recorded.

Scarcely had the honour of public cult been conferred on her than Sœur Thérèse de l'Enfant Jésus, so generous ever in helping priests, came to the aid of two princes of the Church who were suffering from severe and dangerous maladies, Cardinal Granito Pignatelli di Belmonte, bishop of Albano, and Cardinal Tosi, archbishop of Milan. Through her intercession, both were restored to health in a marvellous manner.

Considering these miraculous happenings and others each day more numerous, an assistant-general of an important congregation thus expressed his conviction: "The glory of Thérèse steadily increases. . . . But it is still far from reaching its full height. This little saint will yet accomplish marvels to which those we now see are but a prelude. In the kingdom of heaven this child holds the palm of victory, and she will manifest her power."

The religious had prophesied aright. Shortly afterwards, new miracles of the first order were brought forward for examination by the Sacred Congregation of Rites. Amongst the numerous cures then obtained through the intercession of Blessed Thérèse, two were specially singled out for the Process of Canonization, that of a young Belgian girl, Marie Pellemans, and of a religious of a Congregation called *Chieppine* at Parma, Gabrielle Trimusi. Both were suffering from grave tubercular disease, and through the invocation of Blessed Thérèse, each obtained a complete cure.

According as her miracles grew in number and frequency, the faith and devotion of the people towards the wonder-worker became in itself a marvel.

The reports of unanimous veneration, coming successively from every continent, were to Rome as the expression of an international plebiscite demanding that the Holy Father should officially sanction Thérèse's right to the confidence of Christendom. This unanimous voice of the people, together with the evidence of miracles, brought Pius XI to an immediate decision. The canonical statutes appointing a long delay between beatification and canonization should yield, he said, to the supplication of the Catholic world. Twenty-eight years after her death, and but two years after her beatification, while yet her four elder sisters were living in the sanctity of the cloister, the "little Queen" of Alençon, the "little flower" of Les Buissonnets, the Angel of the Carmel of Lisieux, the untiring "Strewer of Roses," the providential helper of the outcast poor and of the suffering, was, to the indescribable joy of the universe, to become ST. THÉRÈSE DE L'ENFANT JÉSUS.

The 17th of May, 1925, saw the triumph of the humble nun in Rome's magnificent Basilica of St. Peter, that earthly reflection of heavenly splendour. In good time, ambassadors from the principal Catholic nations, and the chevaliers of the Papal Orders in full dress uniform, took their places in the tribunes to pay homage to this well-beloved of the celestial Spouse.

Soon the eager eyes of the vast congregation beheld the approach of the Papal procession, the largest and most distinguished perhaps that had passed beneath the cupola of Michelangelo for centuries. To-day, thirty-four cardinals, over two hundred archbishops and bishops, innumerable prelates and thousands of religious walked before the Pontifical *Sedia*, while behind came the college of apostolic protonotaries. The first groups in the procession had filed past when universal and prolonged acclamation hailed the appearance of a splendid banner bearing a painting of Blessed Thérèse.

Beneath his jewelled mitre, the countenance of Pius XI was radiant with joy: was not the unprecedented triumph of her whom he has proclaimed *Star* of his pontificate, *Advocate* of his dearest causes, second *Angel guardian* of his life, was not her triumph also his own?

Slowly, beneath the brilliance of electric garlands that decorated marble wall and golden ceiling with roses of light, hailed with enthusiasm by the unanimous voice of 50,000 faithful, the Pontiff was borne to the splendid throne erected in the apse, in front of St. Peter's Chair. The cardinals, patriarchs, primates, archbishops, bishops and abbots then came forward to offer their obedience, ratifying beforehand by this public act of homage to the supreme Head of the Church the decision he was about to give.

The moment had come to declare solemnly to the Universal Church the entrance of "little Thérèse" into the glory of the thrice holy God. The customary formula of postulation was read, and the invocations to the Holy Spirit repeated. Then came the solemn words of the Secretary of Briefs: "Arise; Peter is about to speak by the mouth of Pius." Tense silence held captive that immense assembly. Seated on the chair of Peter, Pius XI, crowned with the pontifical mitre, his face radiant with celestial joy, pronounced the formula which was to send heavenwards a fervent *Hosanna* from the Universal Church:

> In honour of the Holy Trinity and each of the Divine Persons, for the exaltation of the Catholic faith and the progress of Christian religion, by the authority of Our Lord Jesus Christ, of the holy Apostles Peter and Paul and Our own, having carefully deliberated and frequently implored help from God, having taken counsel with Our venerable brothers, the Cardinals of the holy Roman Church, the Patriarchs, Archbishops, and Bishops present in the city, We declare Blessed Thérèse de l'Enfant Jésus to be a Saint, We define that such she is, We inscribe her in the catalogue of saints,

> and We decide that each year, on the day of her birth (in heaven), that is September 30, her memory shall be, ought to be devoutly commemorated by the Universal Church. In the name of the Father and of the Son and of the Holy Ghost, Amen.

The infallible teacher has spoken. Immediately from the cupola burst forth the exultant flourish of the silver trumpets like a *vivat* from heaven. The bells of St. Peter's pealed, and with their deep notes were mingled the joyous tones of every bell in the Eternal City; the acclamations of the multitude swelled into one great thunder of applause wherein could be distinguished many a voice broken by sobs of emotion. But it remained to the Pope to lead the final chorus of joy. He intoned the *Te Deum*, and accompanied by the Schola of the Basilica, continued it to the end. Then he chanted, for the first time, the prayer proper to St. Thérèse de l'Enfant Jésus.

Now came the splendour of the Papal Mass with its accustomed ritual, and an atmosphere of supernatural joy seemed to invest each action with a penetrating sweetness. After the Gospel, the Holy Father, in the course of a striking address, spoke in exalted praise, as his predecessor had done, of the "little way of spiritual childhood." "We conceive the hope to-day," he said,

> of seeing arise within the souls of Christ's faithful a holy eagerness to acquire this *evangelical childhood*, which consists in thinking and acting under the influence of virtue as a child feels and acts naturally. Just as little children whose vision is not obscured by any shadow of sin, who are free from every prompting of passion, enjoy peaceful possession of their innocence, and, unacquainted with malice or dissimulation, speak and act in accordance with what they truly think, and reveal their real selves to others, so did Thérèse appear more angelic than human, endowed as she was with child-like simplicity in the practice of virtue and righteousness. . . .

The great liturgical acts succeeded each other in their majestic order, while the sweet and solemnly impressive symphony from the trumpets of the Palatine Guard served to increase devotion. Finally, amid the joyous acclamations of the entire congregation, the Sovereign Pontiff, crowned with the tiara, returned through the vast nave, continually giving his blessing right and left to all as he passed.

Of the hundreds of thousands who had come to Rome for this glorious day, only 50,000 were able to enter the basilica. The remainder stood outside in the square of St. Peter's, awaiting their turn to pay their first tribute of devotion to the new Saint. As a quite exceptional concession in their favour, the Holy Father ordered that the church with its splendid illuminations should remain open all the day, and that the solemn Vespers of St. Thérèse de l'Enfant Jésus should be chanted by the Chapter of St. Peter's.

That night, the pilgrims, as well as the Roman people themselves, witnessed a spectacle that had never been revived since 1870. The gigantic cupola, the basilica facade, and even the double colonnade of St. Peter's square were illumined by thousands of torches which marked out their architecture in lines of light throwing the reflection afar, even over the distant waters of the Tiber. The crowds of pilgrims that surged around the Vatican feasted their eyes on the fairy-like scene. Many amongst them had, no doubt, read the *Histoire d'une Ame*, and recalled Thérèse's striking words: "God's glory; that is my only ambition; mine I abandon to Him" and witnessing the quite unique triumph of the humble Carmelite, they would ask themselves what glory must not the Almighty have in store for His elect in the splendour of heaven.

Rome had exalted "little Thérèse" with incomparable éclat. The Catholic world now owed her a testimony of devotion worthy of her new title. It would be impossible to describe the magnificence of the solemnities with which every capital in Europe and the New World hailed the new saint; even villages the most obscure did their part. But Lisieux, naturally, should surpass all in honouring its illustrious child. We shall endeavour to give a short account of these celebrations in that little town of Normandy.

We can well imagine that, behind the grille of the Carmel, the 17th of May was not spent in the usual unvaried round of ordinary days in the cloister. In the presence of two presiding bishops, solemn high Mass had been celebrated, commencing at the very moment when the Sovereign Pontiff approached the Altar in St. Peter's; and when Pius XI was proclaiming the supreme exaltation of Thérèse, Rev. Père Martin, whose efforts that glorious moment crowned, was commenting with impressive words on the Pontifical formula. That evening, another panegyric was preached by the same devoted apostle of St. Thérèse, and the illumination of the little cupola of the Carmel appeared as a distant reflection of the flaming torches on the dome of St. Peter's.

This, however, was but the private homage of the Carmel of Lisieux to its beloved saint. It was fitting that in every corner of that town where her youthful days were passed in innocence, in every dwelling where her childlike virtue had exhaled its fragrance, another visit of her glorified relics should manifest to the ever-increasing throng of pilgrims the fidelity of God who has promised to exalt the humble. It was fitting, above all, that the Convent where she had prayed, suffered, and loved unto death should be from henceforth singled out as one of the holy places sanctioned by the Church for the veneration of the faithful. The Bishop of Bayeux resolved, therefore, to commemorate the great event of the 17th of May by a novena of solemn functions from the 4th to the 12th of July, during which would be consecrated the renovated and enlarged chapel whose little sanctuary, now extended, had witnessed Thérèse's reception of the religious habit. More numerous than in August, 1923, came bishops and prelates, leading with them multitudes of pilgrims eager to witness the approaching solemnities and devotional celebrations.

After the consecration of the chapel, by which Mgr. Lemonnier opened the series of novena celebrations, Pontifical High Mass was celebrated each morning and an instruction given by Père Martin, ever untiring in his study of the different aspects of the saint's life and teaching. On Sunday July 12, an immense procession of the relics filed through the streets, permitting the dear saint to visit thus once more Les Buissonnets, the Benedictines, and the Cathedral before returning to her Carmel shrine.

These celebrations had as yet, however, satisfied the devotion of only the more intimate friends of the saint. It was but right, therefore, that Lisieux should provide solemnities on a grander scale for those who had been unable to go to Rome, solemnities that would bear the character of public homage to the child who was already "loved throughout the whole world."[37]

The supreme glorification, then, of the "Little Flower" in her own native land was fixed for September 30, 1925. On that day, His Eminence Cardinal Vico, sent as the Pope's Legate for the second time, was to place in the hand of the recumbent marble figure, representing Thérèse in her last sleep, the precious golden rose presented and blessed by the Holy Father for that purpose. A double *triduum* had been announced in preparation for this great day, and throngs of pilgrims, headed by their respective bishops, flocked to Lisieux from every quarter of the globe.

This time, the reliquary of the triumphant little saint was to visit in succession the different churches where she had so often knelt in adoration, communicated, offered her sufferings and her life for the glory of her Well-beloved. Pontifical Masses were then celebrated in presence of the venerated relics at Saint-Jacques, at Saint-Désir, at the Cathedral of Saint-Pierre and at the Carmel. Present at each were numerous Prelates, and the music, vocal and instrumental, liturgical and exceptionally beautiful, was rendered with masterly perfection. It was fitting, too, that these days of rejoicing should be made the occasion of eloquent panegyrics on the saint. But what orator could for several days in succession maintain a height of eloquence in keeping with the subject? Père Martin once again undertook to extol her with whose life and teaching he was so familiar, and his prolonged contact with the mind of Thérèse, his close study of her virtues inspired him with a loftiness of thought and fervour of language greater than he had ever before attained.

Père Martin preached in the chapel of the Carmel. The congregations in the other churches of the town were addressed successively by Abbé Thellier of Poncheville, an eloquent and convincing exponent of every holy cause, Canon Barette of Brussels, eager to make known in detail by simple and precise language the miraculous cure of Mlle Pellemans, and that inspiring and apostolic preacher, Mgr. du Bois de la Villerabel, Archbishop of Rouen.

The afternoon of September 30 was to be the crowning of these magnificent celebrations in honour of the new saint. From early morning, pilgrims of every nation moved shoulder to shoulder through the gaily decorated and flower-strewn streets of the ancient town. At the Carmelite chapel, a few hundred privileged persons had been present at the Pontifical Office, celebrated with all the solemnity of a Roman function by Cardinal Vico. Afterwards, they had watched with tender emotion the placing of the golden rose in the hand of Thérèse.

The procession that formed and marched through the streets a few hours later was the most distinguished and splendid, and, at the same time, the most devotional, recollected and edifying that Normandy had witnessed since the middle ages. Along the flag-bedecked streets, beneath the many triumphal arches, more than thirty bishops from the old world and the new, an Oriental Patriarch, and three Cardinals followed the saint's relics. The reliquary, carried by Carmelite Fathers and surrounded by a guard *d'élite* of officers, was escorted, we may say, by a whole nation. Forty national flags floated proudly over that procession manifesting the spirit of forty different peoples.

Nor was it the splendour alone of the sight that made an impression upon the mind. There was also food for reflection—how this town, formerly somewhat indifferent in spiritual matters, and perhaps a little too much given to pleasure, had become a mystical garden refreshed by the divine dew of tears. Yes, many were the tears shed in Lisieux on that September 30. As the reliquary moved slowly onward beneath a shower of roses, numbers of men, with heads bared beneath the burning sun, dried tear-dimmed eyes, undeterred by human respect.

The procession wended its way to the wonderful public garden, that ancient property of the bishops of Lisieux, of which the little town is justly proud. On the terrace at the end of this garden had been erected an immense altar, in front of which the ecclesiastical dignitaries ranged themselves in order.

The entire procession then filed into the vast *parterre* before the altar. The spectacle presented was one of incomparable grandeur. The rich velvety lawn, with flower-beds like rubies set in the pale emerald of the sward, the brilliantly coloured banners, the splendour of the sacred vestments sparkling with gold; on the terrace above, near the altar, the purple of the Cardinals contrasting with the violet robes of Bishops and Prelates; giant trees, with their wealth of autumn-tinted leaves throwing flickering shadows over the whole; such was the splendid court, such the surroundings of the "little Queen" on that September 30, a scene which even the fairest dreams of her childhood had never foreshadowed.

Before this illustrious and immense audience Père Martin once more spoke of the saint. In eloquent words, he outlined the life-picture of her whose soul floated unseen over the throng. Then, thousands of strong manly voices wakened the echoes with the affirmations of the *Credo.* Time had retraced its steps for an instant to the middle ages when the words of St. Bernard inspired an enthusiastic multitude to ransom the Holy Places.

That night, at the moment when, twenty-eight years before, the soul of Thérèse had taken its flight to God in an ecstasy of love, the brilliantly illuminated town enveloped the monastery chapel as with a circle of fire, while the little dome, with its bright cross surmounted by a shining star, recalled vividly the memory of the "dear Star" of Pius XI.

As they passed by the brightly lighted facades, the older inhabitants spoke to one another about the unexpected fame which the Carmel shed over their town. Even those who in their hearts placed love of the homeland first, felt a thrill of pride and joy. They well knew that, although the splendour of this night might pale and pass away, the glory of Lisieux would never more grow dim.

Appendix A

Unpublished Letters of St. Thérèse de l'Enfant Jésus to the Guérin Family

Fragments

These letters were not sent to the author in time to be used in the body of the work. They shall contribute to the interest of the text in the next edition. As the unpublished letters of the saint are comparatively rare, we thought it well to insert in this edition the following excerpts, feeling that they will certainly be appreciated by our readers.

They are published with the consent of Mme La Néele, *née* Jeanne Guérin, who has handed them over to the Carmel of Lisieux.

To Her Cousin, Jeanne Guérin

July, 1887

My dear little Jeanne,

I suspect that you are not sorry to hear no longer my sermons on death, and to escape from my eyes "which fascinated you."[1]

I have to announce to you the death of eight of my little silkworms; I have now only four. Céline has given them so much care in my absence, that she has succeeded . . . in making them almost all die of vexation or apoplexy. I greatly fear that the remaining four are attacked with the germ of their brothers' malady, and will follow them to the grave. . . .

It seems quite strange to find myself at Les Buissonnets once more. I was really surprised this morning to see Céline at my side. . . .

To Mme Guérin

Rome
November 14, 1887

My dearest Auntie,

If you but knew how happy your little niece would be if she could be near to greet you on your feast-day. But since this happiness is denied her, she desires at least that a word from her heart should travel over the mountains in her stead. Poor little word! How insufficient it will be to reveal to my dear aunt all the affection I have for her. . . .

I do not know how I shall speak to the Pope; indeed, if the good God did not guide me in everything, I know not what I should do. But I have such great confidence in Him that He cannot abandon me; I place all in His hands.

We do not yet know on what day the audience will be. It appears that, when giving a public audience, the Holy Father passes along in front of the faithful; I do not think he stops. In spite of all, I am determined to speak to him.

To Mme Guérin

The Carmel
August 23, 1888

My dear Aunt,

We heard yesterday evening of the death of Monsieur X. . . . I find, dear Aunt, that in moments of great sadness, we must turn our eyes to heaven instead of weeping. All the saints rejoice because Our Saviour has now one more added to His elect; a new sun adds its radiance to the halls of heaven; all there are enraptured, and they wonder that we can call death that which is really the beginning of life; they consider us to be in a narrow tomb. . . . When we think of the death of the just, we cannot but envy his lot: for him exile is no more; God alone exists for him now. . . .

Oh, dear aunt, how many things your little niece would wish to say to you. Her heart has so long pondered on them! This morning, she is quite absorbed in the thought of the death of saints. . . .

To Mme Guérin

November 18, 1888
My dear Aunt,

This morning, after Communion, I earnestly prayed Jesus to shower His joys upon you. Alas, it is not joy He has sent for some time past; it is the Cross, the Cross alone He has given us to rest on. . . .[2] Oh, if no one else were to suffer but myself, that would be of little consequence; but I know how greatly our trial affects you also. I would wish, on your feast-day, to relieve you of all sadness, to take upon myself all your grief. This request I have just now made to Him whose Heart beats in unison with mine. . . . I then felt that suffering is the best that He can give us, and that He gives it only to His chosen friends. . . .

To Mme Guérin

December 28, 1888
My dear Aunt,

I want to be the first to wish you a happy New Year for 1889. When I think that your little niece will soon be nine months in the Carmel, I cannot get over my astonishment. How quickly life passes; already I am sixteen years on earth. Soon we shall be re-united in heaven. I love these words of the Psalmist: *A thousand years are in the eyes of the Lord but as yesterday which is already gone.* What rapidity! Oh, I want to work well while the day of life still shines, for afterwards *will come the night when I shall be unable to* do anything. Pray for your little niece, dear aunt, that she may not abuse the graces showered on her by God in the little valley of the Carmel.

To Mme Guérin, whom the saint is thanking for the wreath sent for her reception of the habit.

January 2, 1889

. . . Your little niece is filled with joy. . . . How good you are to her. It is indeed too much; how shall I thank you? . . . But a mother can read the heart of her child. I will not then be uneasy, for I feel sure that you will guess how grateful I feel.

The lilies are delightful; one would say that they had just been plucked. How good of my little cousins to send them to me. It will be a great joy for me, the day of my reception, to think that it is they who have adorned me to go to my divine Fiancé. These flowers will speak for them to Jesus who, I am sure, will shower His graces on them and on you also, dearest auntie.

Our mother thinks the wreath very beautiful. Never have I seen flowers that pleased me so much; lilies are so pure. I would that my soul were all adorned with them when going to Jesus, for to have them in my hair is not sufficient; it is the heart that Jesus always regards. . . . Pray that your little niece may be as well adorned interiorly as she is exteriorly.

To M. and Mme Guérin

December 30, 1889

My dear Uncle and Aunt,

Your Benjamin wishes you, in her turn, a happy new year. As each day has its last hour, so each year sees the arrival of its last evening. In looking back over the year that is gone, I feel bound to thank the good God, for if His Hand has held out to us the chalice of bitterness,[3] His Divine Heart has sustained us in our trial. What has He in store for us during the year that is now to begin? . . . It is not given to me to penetrate this mystery; but I beg God to reward a hundred-fold my dear relatives for all their goodness to us.

The first day of the year contains for me a host of memories. Once again, I see papa showering his caresses upon us. . . . He was so good! . . . But why speak of these memories? This dear father has received the recompense of his virtues. God has sent him a trial that is worthy of him. . . .

To Mme Guérin

November 17, 1890

How many memories does not November 19 hold for me! . . . For long beforehand, I looked forward to it with joy, because it was the feast-day of my beloved auntie. Now, with the passing of the years, the little birds have grown, they have spread their wings, and have flown from the dear nest of their youth. But in growing, the heart of your little niece has also increased in affection for you; now, more than ever before, does it realize all that it owes to you. . . . I have but one means of paying my debt; poor indeed myself, but having for Spouse a very rich and powerful King, I charge Him to bestow bountifully on my dear aunt the treasures of His love, thus repaying her for all the maternal care with which she surrounded my early years. . . .

To Mme Guérin

August 10, 1893

. . . O dear aunt, every line that you have written has revealed your heart to me; it is a heart as tender as that of the tenderest of mothers. That of your little Thérèse is the heart of a child filled with love and gratitude. . . . I cannot tell you the happiness I feel in realizing that my beloved father is in your midst,[4] surrounded with tenderness and care. God has done for him what He did for His servant Job; having humiliated Him, he now showers favours upon him, and it is through you that all these blessings and all this affection are given. . . .

To Mme la Néele[5]

October 22, 1893

My dear Jeanne,

I have delayed very long in thanking you for all your kindness. . . . Our mother St. Teresa was of so grateful a disposition, that, as she was wont to say pleasantly, "her heart could be won with a sardine." What would she have said, had she known Francis[6] and Jeanne? . . .

Our holy Mother also had a sister named Jeanne, and I have been greatly impressed in reading her Life to see with what tenderness she watched over her little nephews. And so, without forgetting the good St. Anne, I turn to St. Teresa to obtain through her intercession that I also may be an aunt. I do not doubt that she will hear me, by sending my dear little Jeanne a holy family that will give great saints to the Church. . . . The long delay does not discourage me, for I know that Rome requires a long time in order to make saints. . . .

To Mme Guérin

November 17, 1893

How sweet it is to your little Thérèse to offer you her good wishes for your feast each year. Nevertheless, I have nothing new to say to you: you have long known how much I love you.

In affirming this again, dear auntie, I have no fear of wearying you, and I shall tell you the reason why. When I am before the Tabernacle, I can say nothing to Our Saviour but this: "My God, Thou knowest that I love Thee." And I know that Jesus is not wearied by my prayer; knowing the powerlessness of His little spouse, He is satisfied with her good will. I also know well that the good God has infused into the hearts of mothers something of the love with which His own Heart overflows. And she whom I now address has received that maternal love in so large a measure that I cannot have any fear of being misunderstood. . . .

Besides, my powerlessness cannot endure for ever; in the eternal Fatherland, I shall be able to say to my dearest auntie many things that human language cannot convey.

To M. and Mme Guérin

December 29, 1893

My dear Uncle and Aunt,

I have but a few minutes in which to offer you my wishes for a happy new year. I would, if such were possible, that this new year should bring you nothing but consolations. But, alas! the good God, who knows the reward in store for His friends, often wills that they should win His treasures by sacrifice. Our Mother, St. Teresa, smiling, spoke these words to Our Saviour, words that contain so much truth: "My God, I do not wonder that Thou hast so few friends, so badly dost Thou treat them!" Nevertheless, in the very midst of the trials He sends, God is full of tenderness. My dear father's illness is to me an evident proof of it. This cross was the greatest I could imagine; but having allowed us to taste the bitterness, Our Saviour has willed to sweeten by the hands of our dear ones the chalice of grief He had sent, and which I expected to drink to the dregs. . . .

O dear uncle and auntie, if you knew how affectionate and grateful is the heart of your little Thérèse.

The hour for matins has come; pardon this wandering letter, and such scribbling . . . ; consider only the heart of your child.

To Mme Guérin

July 16, 1896

My dear Aunt,

I would have wished to forestall you, but now there remains for me only the sweet and pleasant duty of thanking you for the charming letter I have received. How good you are to think of your little Thérèse. I assure you that she in turn is not ungrateful.

I would like to tell you something new, but although I rack my brains, I can find nothing to speak of save affection for my dear ones . . . and this, far from being new, is as old as myself. . . .

You ask me, dear aunt, to give you news of my health as I would to my mother. That is what I am going to do; but if I tell you that I am in wonderfully good health, you will hardly believe me; so I will let the doctor who examined me yesterday speak. He declared that "I looked well. . . ."

This *declaration* has not deterred me from thinking that I shall soon be allowed "to go and join the little angels in heaven," not as a result of my state of health, but by reason of another *declaration* made by the Abbé Lechêne today in the chapel of our Carmel. Having shown us the illustrious origin of our holy Order, and compared us to the prophet Elias in strife against the priests of Baal, he *declared* that a "period similar to that of Achab's persecution was about to begin." It seemed to us as though we were already hastening to martyrdom. . . . What happiness, dear auntie, if all our family were to enter heaven on the same day. I seem to see you smile. . . . Perhaps you think that this honour is not in store for us. One thing is certain; all of us together, or one after another, shall one day leave this exile for the Fatherland, and then we shall rejoice over all those things that receive heaven as the prize. . . .[7]

To Mme Guérin

November 16, 1896

My dear Aunt,

Your little niece is sad at the thought of confiding to a lifeless pen the care of telling you the feelings of her heart. . . . Perhaps you will say to me: "But, my little Thérèse, would you express those feelings more easily by spoken words?" My dearest auntie, I am forced to admit it as true that I cannot find expressions to satisfy the sentiments of my heart.

The poet who ventured to say:

> Thoughts well conceived find utterance clear,
> For words to clothe them readily appear.

certainly did not feel what I feel in the depths of my soul. . . . Happily I have the learned Father Faber to console me. He well understood that "earthly words and phrases are incapable of expressing the thoughts of the heart, and that full hearts are those most shut up within themselves."

My dear aunt, I am wearying you with my quotations, all the more so as the letters of my four sisters are there to contradict what I have said. . . . If you do not believe me now, you will be forced to admit one day when we shall all be re-united in heaven, that the last and least of your nieces was not so in affection and gratitude, that she was the last and least only in age and wisdom.

I ask you, my dear aunt, to beseech the good God that I may grow in wisdom like the Infant Jesus; I am not doing so, I assure you, although I shall soon be nine years in the house of the Lord. . . . I should be already well advanced in the ways of perfection, but I am yet only at the bottom of the ladder. That does not discourage me; I am as merry as the grasshopper. Like her, I sing always, hoping, at the end of my life, to share the riches of my sisters who are far more generous than the ant.

Ah, I have indeed been born under a lucky star, and my heart is profoundly stirred with gratitude towards the good God who has given me relatives such as are no longer to be found on earth.

Since, dear auntie, I am a *poor* grasshopper who has nothing but her songs (and she cannot now sing except in her heart, for there is little melody in her voice), I shall sing my best song on your feast-day, and I shall try to do so in such touching accents that all the saints, pitying my misery, will give me treasures of graces which I shall be happy to offer you. They will be so abundant that my heart shall have nothing further to desire, which, I assure you, auntie, is saying a good deal, as my desires are great.

Pardon me, dear aunt, for saying to you so many things that have neither rhyme nor reason, and believe that I love you with all my heart.

To M. and Mme Guérin

July 16, 1897

My dear Uncle and Aunt,[8]

I am very happy to prove to you that your little Thérèse has not yet left this exile, for I know that you will be pleased. But I think, my dear ones, that your joy will be greater still when instead of reading a few lines written by my trembling hand, you will feel my soul near yours.

Ah, I am certain that the good God will allow me to shower His graces bountifully upon you, on my little cousin Jeanne and her dear Francis; I shall choose the most beautiful cherub in heaven and ask God to give it to them. If I am not heard, my little cousin may rejoice in the thought that in heaven the Lord will give her the joy of seeing herself the *mother of many children*, as the Holy Ghost has promised when he sang by the mouth of the Prophet-King the words that I have just written. These children will be the souls whom her cheerfully accepted sacrifice will have brought forth to the life of grace.

I wished, dear uncle and aunt, to speak to you in detail of my Communion this morning which you made so impressive or rather so triumphant by your flowers. I will let my dear little sister, Marie de l'Eucharistie,[9] tell you the details, contenting myself with saying that before my Communion, she sang a little couplet I had composed for this morning. When Jesus had entered my heart, she sang another couplet from *Vivre d'amour*:

To die of love, O martyrdom most sweet.

I cannot tell you how beautiful and clear her voice was; . . . in order to please me, she had promised not to weep; my hopes were indeed surpassed. The good Jesus must have perfectly understood and approved what I expected from Him, and all is just as I wished. . . .

My sisters have, I know, told you of my joyousness. True I am like a lark except when the fever attacks me; happily, it only comes at night, when larks sleep with heads hidden beneath their wings. I would not be as lighthearted as I am if the good God had not shown me that the only joy on earth is in the accomplishment of His will.

Adieu, my dear ones; only in heaven shall I tell you of all my affection for you; my pencil cannot convey it now.[10]

Letter of Soeur Thérèse de l'Enfant Jésus to Mère Saint-Placide, her former School-Directress.[11]

My Dear Mistress,

I am indeed touched by your kindly attention. I have received with pleasure your dear circular for the Children of Mary. Certainly I shall not fail to assist in spirit at this grand fête. For was it not in that blessed chapel that the Holy Virgin deigned to adopt me for her child on the beautiful day of my first Communion, and on that of my reception into the congregation of the Children of Mary?

I could not forget, dear Mother, how good you were to me at these great epochs in my life, and I cannot doubt that the signal grace of my religious vocation was implanted that happy day when, surrounded by my good teachers, I consecrated myself to Mary at the foot of her altar, specially choosing her for my mother, after having received Jesus that morning for the first time. I love to think that she did not then consider my unworthiness, and that, in her wonderful goodness, she deigned to consider the virtues of the dear teachers who had with so much care prepared my heart to receive her Divine Son. I love to think that, for this reason also, she has deigned to make me more completely her child in doing me the favour of leading me to Carmel.

I think, dear Mother, that you have heard all about my beloved father's illness. For some days, I feared that God would take him from me; but Jesus, in His kindness to me, for the moment has restored him to health, for my reception.

I was counting, every day, on writing to tell you of my reception at the Chapter; but being in constant expectation of hearing what date Monseigneur would fix for the ceremony I waited.

I hope, dear Mother, that you have not taken this delay for indifference. Oh, no; my heart is always the same, and I believe that, since my entrance into Carmel, it has become more tender and loving. And so, I think often of all my kind teachers, and I love to mention them by name to the good Jesus during the precious hours that I spend at His Feet. I venture to ask you, dear Mother, to be my interpreter, in remembering me to them, in particular to the Mother Prioress for whom I retain most filial and grateful affection. Do not forget either to remember me to my good companions whose little sister in Mary I shall always remain.

Good-bye, dear Mother. I hope you will not forget in your prayers her who is and will always be your grateful child.

Soeur Thérèse de l'Enfant Jésus
Post. Carm. Ind.

Appendix B

Documentary Evidence

I

Record of the Baptism of St. Thérèse de l'Enfant Jésus

Extract from the Register at Notre-Dame, Alençon[1]

On Saturday, the fourth of January, eighteen hundred and seventy-three, has been baptized by us the undersigned, Marie-Françoise-Thérèse, born on the second, of January of the legitimate marriage of Louis-Joseph-Aloys-Stanislas Martin and Zélie-Marie Guérin, both of this parish (rue St-Blaise, 36). The godfather has been Paul-Albert Boul, and the godmother Marie-Louise Martin, sister of the child. These, together with the child's father, have signed their names with us. Marie Martin, Paul-Albert Boul, Louis Martin, P. Boul, F. Boul, Pauline Martin, Léonie Martin, Léontine Boul, Louise Marais.[2]

L. Dumaine
Vicaire de N.-D.

II

Record of the Marriage of Captain Pierre-François Martin and Marie-Anne-Fanie Boureau (Paternal Grand-Parents of St. Thérèse de l'Enfant Jésus)

Extract from the Register of the Parish of Saint-Martin d'Ainay, Lyons

On the seventh of April, eighteen hundred and eighteen, after one duly made publication of banns (dispensation from the other two having been obtained) without having found any impediment or opposition whatever to the consent of the respective parties, the civil formalities required by the mayoralty of Lyons having been complied with on the——,[3] I, the undersigned, have solemnized the marriage of M. Pierre-François Martin, legitimate son of the late John Martin and Marie-Anne Bohard of Athis, captain on active service of the 42nd regiment of the line, residing at Lyons, bridegroom, on the one part.

And Miss Marie-Anne-Françoise[4] Boureau, legitimate daughter of M. Nicolas Boureau and Marie Ney,[5] with whom she lived at Lyons, rue Vaubecourt, bride, on the other part.—The witnesses were M. the Count de Labesse, colonel of the Legion of the Loire-Inférieure, M. Averin[6] battalion commandant in the same Legion, M. Moyat, major of that Legion, M. Larue and M. Gourd, who with other relatives and friends have affixed their signatures with mine.

Signed: Bourganel, *Vicaire*

This copy of 23 April, 1926, is conformable to the original.

P. Vignon
Curé d'Ainay

III

Record of the Marriage of Isidore Guérin and Louise Macé (Maternal Grand-Parents of the Saint)

Extract from the Register of the Parish of Pré-en-Pail (Mayenne)

On the sixteenth of September, eighteen hundred and twenty-eight, after the publication of the banns of future Marriage between Isidore Guérin, gendarme, eldest and legitimate son of the late Pierre Guérin and of Marguerite-Elizabeth Dupont, of the parish of St. Denis, diocese of Séez, bridegroom, and Louise-Jeanne Massé,[7] eldest and legitimate daughter of the late Louis Massé, and of Marie Lemarchand, of this parish, bride, fully announced at the principal Mass here and in the parish of St. Denis on three consecutive Sundays, without any impediment having been brought to our knowledge, we, the undersigned priest, vicar of this parish, have received in this church the mutual consent to matrimony of the above-named parties, and have given them the Nuptial Blessing according to rites prescribed by holy Church. Witnesses present: Théodore

Guérin, brother of the bridegroom, Jacques Chénevière, brother-in-law of the bridegroom, Isidore Besnard-St-Marc, cousin of the bridegroom, Louis Massé, brother of the bride, Joseph-Victor Besniard, friend of bride and bridegroom and several others.

Signed: Aoury, *prêtre vic*

This copy of 19 June, 1926, is conformable to the original.

M. J. Menu
Curé-doyen de Pré-en-Pail

IV

Record of the Baptism of Zélie-Marie Guérin (Mother of St. Thérèse de l'Enfant Jésus)

Extract from the Baptismal Register of the Parish of Saint-Denis-s.-Sarthon (Orne).

To-day, the twenty-fourth of December, eighteen hundred and thirty-one, has been baptized by us, the undersigned *vicaire*, Azélie[8]-Marie, born yesterday of the legitimate marriage of Isidore Guérin, gendarme, and Louise Massey. The godfather, François-Michel Septier, Brigadier gendarme, and the godmother, Marie Berrier, cousin of the child, have together with the father signed their names with ours.

Signed: F. Hubert, *vicaire*
Marie Berrier, Septier, Guérin

This copy, taken at St. Denis-s-Sarthon, on the second of July, 1915, is conformable to the original.

P. Germain-Beaupré
Curé de St. Denis

V

Record of the Marriage of Louis Martin and Zélie Guérin (Parents of St. Thérèse de l'Enfant Jésus)

Extract from the Register of Notre Dame d'Alençon

On Tuesday, the thirteenth of July, eighteen hundred and fifty-eight, after publication in the churches of Notre-Dame and Montsort of the banns of the future marriage between Louis Martin, watchmaker, living in Alençon, parish of Montsort, eldest son of Pierre-François Martin, retired captain, knight of St. Louis, and Marie-Anne-Fanny[9] Boureau.

And Zélie-Marie Guérin, manufacturer of *Point d'Alençon*, living in this parish of Notre-Dame, eldest daughter of Isidore Guérin and Louise-Jeanne Macé.

No impediment or opposition having been found—dispensation from the other two publications of banns having been obtained—and the civil formalities gone through, after the ceremony of betrothal, we, dean of Saint-Leonard, with delegation from M. l'abbé Jamot, *Curé-Archiprêtre* of Notre-Dame, having received their mutual consent to matrimony, and having given them nuptial blessing,[10] in presence of their relations and friends who have signed their names with ours.

Louis Martin, Azélie[11] Guérin, F. Martin, Guérin, F. P. Martin, Louise Guérin, A. Leriche, Lefort, Tessier, I. Guérin.

F. Hurel
Curé-Doyen de St-Léon

Certified copy conformable to the original, 17 July, 1922.
A. Bogage
Curé-Archip. de Notre-Dame

VI

Military Service of Captain Martin (Grandfather of St. Thérèse de l'Enfant Jésus)

Enlisted in the 65th regiment of Infantry (made 61st in 1814) on the 26 August 1799; became corporal on 22 December 1800, sergeant on 7 March 1804, sub-lieutenant on 14 April 1813, lieutenant 25 October 1813, captain (provisional) 27 June 1815, commission ratified 21 August 1816, ranking from the 1st January preceding.

Passed in 1816 into the departmental Legion of the Loire-Inférieure in 1821 to the 19th regiment of Light Infantry, and in 1828 was placed on the military staff at

Strasbourg from which position he retired on the 12 December 1830.

Campaigns

1779–1801	Army of the Rhine
1803	Belle-Ile en Mer
1804–1805	Sous Brest
1806	Army of Nord
1807	Prussia and Poland
1814	Army of Nord and campaign in France
1815	Royal army in Morbihan
1823–1824	Spain.

Decorated with the royal and military Order of St. Louis on August 20, 1824.

VII

Military Service of Captain Boureau (Great-Grandfather of the Saint)

Notes on His Family

The maternal grandfather of M. Martin, Jean-Nicolas Boureau, was also a worthy soldier. At seventeen years of age, he enlisted in 1791 as a sergeant in the army of Nord, and was promoted to the rank of sub-lieutenant in the following year. At twenty, he obtained the rank of captain, and served in the army of the Côtes de Brest. Having in 1796 resigned on the score of health, he resumed service in the Grand Army in 1812. On the 19 August 1813, he was taken as a prisoner of war by the Prussians in Silesia; his son Jean-Prosper, aged 12½ years, who with him was also held prisoner, died there on the 21 September of the same year. In 1816–1817, he served in the royal army at Lyons with Captain Martin. On receiving his discharge in 1817, he returned home.

Twice during his military career, he was the victim of hateful accusations which led to his discharge, but which are refuted by the highest attestations from civil and military authorities in his papers.

Amongst these numerous testimonies of praise, we find that of the Marquis of Averin, peer of France, and of

M. Degrandmaison (de Grandmaison) chaplain to the royal and catholic army of Vendée. The parish priest of Ainay (his own parish in Lyons) also attests that "M. Nicolas-Jean Boureau, captain, living in this parish, *rue Vaubecourt n°* 4, with his wife and two daughters, led a life dictated by the principles of honour, wisdom and religion, and that this respectable family have merited the esteem and admiration of the inhabitants of this town for their virtue."

His elder daughter Sophie married Staff-Colonel de Lacauve,[12] who was Governor of Pampelune and St. Sebastien in 1823–1824. His second daughter Fanie married Captain Martin. His grandson, Charles-Henri de Lacauve, officer of the Legion of Honour, served also in France. He retired with the rank of major, and died at Versailles on the 20 May, 1899.

Notes

Foreword to the New Edition

1. In the original edition the author references *Shower of Roses* published by the Carmel of Lisieux (1912) and *Thèrése de l'Enfant Jesus: Meditation on the Grandeur of Spiritual Childhood,* by Louis Theolier (1923).

Introduction

1. Expression of Pius XI in his address to the pilgrims of Bayeux.
2. *Story of a Soul.*
3. Agnes of Jesus, born Pauline Martin.

1. Ancestral Origin

1. For the paternal ancestors of the saint see the booklet *Athis-de-l'Orne and Blessed Thérèse de l'Enfant Jésus,* by M. l'Abbé Madeline of Athis-de-l'Orne (Klers-de-l'Orne, Imprimerie Catholique).

2. The Appendix at the end of this book contains information regarding the particulars of Captain Martin's military service, and copies of a certain number of documentary records (certificates of baptism and marriage) concerning the ancestors of the saint.

3. M. Louis Martin, father of Thérèse, had one brother Pierre, early destined for the navy, but he was lost in a shipwreck while still young. He had also an elder sister, Marie, who married, but died in her twenty-sixth year, 1846. Two sisters were born after him: Françoise—in English, Fanny—who, after her marriage, died in 1853, aged twenty-seven; and Sophie, the godchild and favourite sister of Louis, who died at the age of nine years.

4. The following is a copy of the register of baptism: "In the year One thousand eight hundred and twenty-three on the twenty-eighth of October, has been baptized by me, priest, undersigned, Louis-Joseph-Aloys-Stanislas Martin, born the twenty-third of the month of August last, legitimate son of sieur Pierre-François Martin, Captain in the Nineteenth Light Infantry, and of dame Marie-Anne-Fanny Boureau his wife, living at No. 3, rue Servandoni. He had for god-father Léonce de Lamothe, and for godmother Ernestine Beyssac who have signed with me

Jn-Ant. Martegoute, priest, de licentia parochi.
Léonce de Lamothe;
Ernestine Beyssac, Jules Guibre.
Fanie Martin, née Boureau.
Copy conformable to the original:

Jaure, Curé de Sainte-Eulalie."

Followed by the attestation of Mgr. d'Aviau.

5. This decoration was conferred on him by Charles X, August 20, 1824.

6. It was, however, at Strasbourg, where he was on the staff, that his discharge was definitely granted him in 1830.

7. Unpublished letter in family archives. The letter written by his father to Louis on this occasion exhibits even more clearly the same Christian spirit. We give it as a novel and unique example of the type of family correspondence in Normandy at that period:

> May God be for ever glorified and loved above all things!
>
> My dear Son,
>
> On behalf of your sisters Fanny and Sophie and all the family, I wish you a happy feast, in honour of your blessed patron, who is also my own as a Knight of Saint Louis, and to whom I have and will ever have devotion. The bouquet which we are sending is a gift from your sister and godchild, Sophie. We should like to offer you in person our heartiest wishes, and clink glasses in sprinkling the bouquet; but let us make this sacrifice, since it is the will of the Master.
>
> We are, thank God, enjoying good health. I hope you also are equally blessed. In conclusion, my dear Louis, I give you with all my heart the kiss of friendship for myself and all the family.

8. "This is my resting-place for ever and ever," Ps. 131:14.

9. See *Histoire d'une Ame*: Introduction.

10. Below is a résumé of the military service of M. Isidore Guérin, maternal grandparent of Thérèse Martin. Born at Saint Martin I' Aiguillon (Orne) July 6, 1789, he entered the army on June 6, 1809, and went through his first military training at Wagram. Some months later he was in the Oudinot Division. He remained there after the defeat of Vittoria until the battle of Toulouse, and on the fall of the Empire returned home. He entered the foot *gendarmerie,* October 1, 1816, and passed into the mounted *gendarmerie,* June 1, 1823. He served first in the Compagnie de la Vendée; then, from February 23, 1827, in the Compagnie de 1'Orne (2nd Legion) at Saint Denis sur-Sarthon (Orne). On September 10, 1844, he left the service finally to retire to Alençon, where he died September 3, 1868. (Taken from the Archives of the Guérin family and the Archives of the Ministry of War.)

11. The "point d'Alençon" is manufactured from hand-spun and twisted linen thread, exceptionally fine and consequently very costly. These laces are composed of pieces measuring from twenty to thirty centimetres joined together by imperceptible stitches. At Alençon the industry was started under the administration of Colbert about 1664, that Minister having brought from Venice thirty skilled workers with this object in view.

12. Apostolic Process of Beatification and Canonization—Deposition of Rev., Mère Agnès de Jésus.

13. Unpublished letter of Mme Martin to her daughters Marie and Pauline, January 17, 1875: Archives of the Carmel of Lisieux.

14. Isa. v 8.

15. Unpublished letter to her sister-in-law, September 28, 1872.

16. Unpublished letter of January 1, 1863. Some of the above lines contain an allusion to the supernatural counsel which she received on December 8, 1851, to undertake the manufacture of point d'Alençon.

17. Unpublished letter to her brother, March 28, 1864.

18. Unpublished letter, April 23, 1865.

19. Little Hélène died of consumption February 22, 1870, at the age of five.

20. Unpublished letter.

21. Ibid.

22. *Ibid.*

23. Unpublished letter to her brother and her sister-in-law, January 1869.

24. An allusion to the prayers of the Martin family to obtain from God a "little missionary," or at least a son who would do great things for the extension of God's kingdom on earth.

25. Unpublished letter of February 23, 1870.

26. Unpublished letter, October 17, 1871.

27. Unpublished letter, October 28, 1868.

28. He remained in the rue du Pont-Neuf, however, until July of the following year.

29. *Histoire d'une Ame*: Introduction, p. xxxi.

30. One day, as Mme Martin was singing, she seemed to hear the child singing also. It was a happy augury. The soul which was about to make its entrance into the world was truly *une äme chantante.*

31. Some readers may consider the details regarding the ancestors of Thérèse too diffuse. In fact, had this work conformed to the canons of an ordinary biography it would have been necessary to abridge. But the desire of Catholic readers to learn every detail connected with the life of this new saint seems to show that they would be glad to enter as far as possible into that family circle so worthy of her.

2. Early Infancy of "Little Thérèse"

1. The stained glass windows of Notre-Dame are admirably executed. They form two series. One depicts scenes from the life of the Blessed Virgin; the other scenes from the Old Testament. Between the two series is a window showing the tree of Jesse. All are in good preservation.

2. A slab to commemorate the baptism of Thérèse Martin has recently been put up in this chapel. A statue of the saint with a richly ornamented altar has also been erected there. A new window depicting the baptism of Thérèse has replaced the old one described above.

3. Abbé Dumaine was as learned as he was wise. He has left an important work on local history entitled *Tinchebray et sa région au bocage normand.*

4. Unpublished letter to her sister-in-law, March, 1873.

5. Unpublished letter.

6. *Ibid.*

7. Unpublished letter to her sister-in-law, April 13, 1873.

8. Unpublished letter.

9. A servant in the Martin family.

10. Unpublished letter to Pauline, May 5, 1873.

11. Unpublished letter.

12. *Ibid.*

13. Unpublished letter to her brother and her sister-in-law, January 11, 1874.

14. Unpublished letter to her sister-in-law, June 1, 1874.

15. Unpublished letter to her daughters Marie and Pauline, November 1, 1873.

16. Letter to her daughters Marie and Pauline, June 25, 1874.

17. Unpublished letter.

18. Unpublished letter to Marie and Pauline at the Visitation Convent.

19. Unpublished letter to her sister-in-law.

20. Unpublished letter to her sister-in-law, March 14, 1875.

21. Unpublished letter to her brother and her sister-in-law, April 29, 1875.

22. Letter of Mme Martin to her daughter Pauline, December 5, 1875.

23. Unpublished letter to her sister-in-law, December 23, 1875.

24. Unpublished letter to Pauline, March 22, 1877.

25. Unpublished note of Sœur Marie du Sacré-Cœur (Marie), of the Carmel of Lisieux.

26. Unpublished letter to Pauline, December 5, 1875.

27. Unpublished letter: Family Archives.

28. Céline was, in fact, of a delicate constitution. Unpublished letter of November, 1875.

29. Unpublished letter to her daughter Pauline, December 5, 1875.

30. Unpublished letter to Pauline, January 16, 1876.

3. Growing Virtue of Thérèse

1. *Histoire d'une Ame,* ch. i, p. 8.

2. This statue had been presented to M. Martin before his marriage by a pious lady in Alençon, who was called "the saint."

3. This happened before the birth of Thérèse.

4. Unpublished letter of Mme Martin.

5. *Histoire d'une Ame,* ch. i, p. 8.

6. Unpublished letter.

7. Letter of Mme Martin to her daughter Pauline, October 29, 1876.

8. *Ibid.*, May 10, 1877.
9. Unpublished letter, March 4, 1877.
10. Unpublished letter to Pauline, March 4, 1877.
11. *Histoire d'une Ame*, ch. i, p. 11.
12. Unpublished letter to Pauline, May 21, 1876.
13. *Histoire d'une Ame*, ch. i, p. 11.
14. *Ibid.*, p. 12.
15. Unpublished letter to Pauline, October 8, 1876.
16. Letter to Pauline, November 8, 1876, reproduced in part in *Histoire d'une Ame*, ch. i, p. 14.
17. *Histoire d'une Ame*, ch. i, p. 14.
18. Letter of Mme Martin, quoted in the *Histoire d'une Ame*, ch. i, p. 9.
19. She liked the open-air exercise of the swing, but this taste seems to have been an exception.
20. Henry Thédenat, *Quelques vers*, p. 19: Paris, Jouve.
21. The statue thus honoured was that before which Mme Martin had already obtained an extraordinary favour, and which was afterwards to become lifelike and smile on Thérèse.
22. Unpublished letter.
23. Unpublished letter of Mme Martin to Pauline, October, 1876.
24. Letter to Pauline, May 14, 1876.
25. *Histoire d'une Amc*, ch. i, p. 10.
26. Letter to Pauline, February 13, 1877.
27. Letter of Mme Martin to Pauline, May 21, 1876.
28. See unpublished letter of May 14, 1876: Archives of the Martin family.
29. Mme Martin alludes to this in one of her letters.
30. *Histoire d'une Ame*, ch. i, p. 16.
31. *Cf.* R. P. Carbonel, *Histoire de Sainte Thérèse de l'Enfant Jésus pour les enfants* (Eng. trans., *Little Thérèse*, Burns, Oates and Washbourne).
32. *Histoire d'une Ame*, ch. i, p. 15.
33. Cited by Mme Martin in an unpublished letter to her brother, February 26, 1877.
34. Unpublished letter to her sister-in-law, January 28, 1877.
35. *Ibid.*, May 10, 1877.
36. Unpublished letter, May 13, 1877.
37. Unpublished letter to her sister-in-law, May 29, 1877.
38. *Ibid.*, June 24, 1877.
39. Unpublished letter to Pauline, June 25, 1877.
40. *Ibid.*
41. Unpublished letter to her sister-in-law, July 8, 1877.
42. *Ibid.*, July 15, 1877.
43. *Histoire d'une Ame*, ch. ii, p. 19.
44. Unpublished letter of August 9, 1877.
45. Unpublished letter to her brother, August 16, 1877.
46. *Histoire d'une Ame*, ch. ii, p. 20.

47. Mme Martin's daughters, now nuns, remember still the expression of unearthly serenity on her countenance.

48. Thérèse in thus acting was unknowingly directed by a prophetic action of her dying mother, who, seeing Pauline by the bedside, had taken her hand with respect and kissed it. She seemed, by this action, to entrust her with the office of mother, which she was to fulfill during her whole life.

49. M. Martin himself was buried at Lisieux in 1894, and M. Guérin, in order to re-unite all together in the one grave, had the remains of Mme Martin, of her little deceased children, and of the two grandparents, M. Guérin and Mme Martin, brought from Alençon to the cemetery of Lisieux.

50. The house was then as we see it today: red brick, mouldings, cornices, and carved wood, as shown by a painting done at that time. The only change made later was to clear a space to the right and provide an additional exit for the convenience of pilgrims.

4. Lisieux

1. She was a relation of Thomas-Jean Monsaint, one time parish priest of Orbec-en-Auge, afterwards of Saint Roch, Paris, who was massacred at the Abbey on September 2, 1792. *Cf.* Joseph Grente, *Les Martyrs de Septembre* 1792 *à Paris.*

2. *Histoire d'une Ame,* ch. ii, p. 22.

3. Unpublished letter.

4. It is to this room that crowds of pilgrims come today, to see in a gallery fronted with glass—formerly Léonie's tiny room—the little saint's bed, the different objects that were formerly hers, and even the toys with which she amused herself.

5. Pauline's firmness was ever tempered by gentle affection, as can be seen from the following incident:

One day Thérèse returned hot and tired from a long walk and much talking. "O Pauline," she cried, "if you only knew how thirsty I am!" Finding this a suitable opportunity to drive home certain lessons, the elder sister suggested a sacrifice. "Will you deprive yourself of a drink in order to save a sinner?" "Yes, Pauline," said the little one with a deep sigh. Evidently the sacrifice was great. Seeing, however, that it had been accepted, Pauline, who suffered more than her little sister from the imposed mortification, decided to bring her a refreshing drink.

But should Thérèse accept this and abandon the sinner to perdition? Pauline hastened to reassure her by explaining that, after having had the merit of sacrifice, she was also to have that of obedience, thereby gaining a further chance of assisting some soul in distress. *Cf.* R. P. Carbonel, *op. cit.*

6. *Histoire d'une Ame,* ch. ii, p. 24.

7. *Ibid.,* p. 25.

8. These words ran as follows: "My God, I give Thee my heart; may it please Thee to accept it, so that no creature can take possession of it but Thou alone, my good Jesus!"

9. *Histoire d'une Ame*, ch. ii, p. 26.

10. *Ibid.*, ch. ii, p. 30.

11. *Ibid.*, ch. ix, p. 129.

12. *Ibid.*, ch. ii, p. 28.

13. The same impression was produced at Lisieux. A lady, a friend of the family, said one day to Thérèse's sisters: "How do you account for that child's angelic expression? One sees other children with features as well formed, but she has heaven in her eyes."

14. *Histoire d'une Ame*, ch. ii, p. 35.

15. The above unpublished fragment is unsigned, but there are grounds for attributing it to M. Martin: *Archives of the Carmel of Lisieux.*

16. Private notes: Archives of the Carmel of Lisieux.

17. *Histoire d'une Ame*, ch. ii, p. 32.

5. The Benedictine Convent

1. *Deposition for the Apostolic process*, p. 126. The fact that Thérèse called her former state "feebleness" and the change wrought in her on December 25, 1886, "conversion" must be attributed to her humility, for Céline shows above that, even during this period, her virtue never failed.

2. From a manuscript notice on the Abbey of Notre-Dame-du-Pré.

3. She gave her evidence in the Process of Beatification under the name of Sr. Joséphine de la Croix.

4. *Process of the Ordinary*, p. 136.

5. *Histoire d'une Ame*, ch. iii, p. 37.

6. *Cf.* manuscript notice on the Abbey of Notre-Dame-du-Pré.

7. Manuscript notice on the Abbey of Notre-Dame-du-Pré.

8. *Histoire d'une Ame*, ch. iii, p. 42.

9. *Deposition at the Process of the Ordinary*, p. 130.

10. *Cf. Deposition of Sœur Marie du Sacré-Cœur (Marie) at the Process of the Ordinary.*

11. *Histoire d'une Ame*, ch. iii, p. 48.

12. Thérèse's fears, which were sometimes so great as to obscure in her memory the reality of the heavenly vision, could only be the effect of divine permission with the object of keeping her humble. Besides, the account which she gave of her cure has been confirmed in every detail by that of her sister Marie. The following is her deposition on this subject at the Process of the Ordinary:

"The most terrible crisis in Thérèse's illness was that which she has described in her *Life*. I believed that she was about to succumb. It was then that, with my sisters, I threw myself on my knees at the feet of the holy Virgin. Three times I repeated the same prayer. At the third repetition I saw Thérèse gaze fixedly at the statue of the Blessed Virgin. Her countenance became radiant like one in ecstasy. She confided to me that she had seen the Blessed Virgin herself. This vision lasted four or five minutes, then she looked tenderly at me. From this time onward no trace of her malady was apparent. On the following day she resumed her ordinary mode of life." *Summarium* of 1919, p. 416.

The statue which became animated before Thérèse is that mentioned earlier in the book, which had been for a long time previously in the possession of the Martin family. It is a copy of Bouchardon's model, which had been executed in silver for the Church of Saint-Sulpice, Paris, and which disappeared during the Revolution. The venerated statue of the Blessed Virgin now stands over the Saint's tomb in a side chapel of the Carmel of Lisieux called "the Chapel of the Shrine," where rest her holy remains.

13. *Histoire d'une Ame*, ch. iv, p. 58. The concluding words of this paragraph explain what would at first sight be misleading as regards the meaning of "fusion." Thérèse is evidently speaking of intimacy in its highest degree, which nevertheless leaves intact the duality existing between the weakness of the creature and the "Divine strength."

14. *Histoire d'une Ame*, ch. iv, p. 59.

15. *Deposition of Sœur Françoise-Thérèse (Léonie) religious of the Visitation, at the Process of the Ordinary*, p. 132.

16. *Histoire d'une Ame*, ch. iv, p. 61.

17. *Deposition of Sœur Geneviève de la Sainte-Foie at the Process of the Ordinary*, p. 123.

18. *Histoire d'une Ame*, ch. iv, p. 63.

19. *Ibid.*, ch. iv, p. 64.

20. *Cf. Deposition of Sœur Josephine de la Croix, a Benedictine nun, at the Process of the Ordinary*, p. 141.

21. *Cf.* "La Mission providentielle de la Bienhereuse Thérèse de l'Enfant Jésus," an article published in *La Croix* of November, 1913, by M. l'Abbé Lepetit, professor of the Seminary of Caen.

22. *Histoire d'une Ame*, ch. iv, p. 67.

23. *Ibid.*, p. 66.

24. Affectionate titles which M. Martin loved to give to his daughters.

25. Unpublished letter of August 30, 1885.

26. Unpublished letter of September 27, 1885.

27. Unpublished letter of October 6, 1885.

28. *Histoire d'une Ame*, ch. iv, p. 68.

29. *Cf. Deposition of Sœur Saint-Jean l'Evangéliste at the Process of the Ordinary*, p. 154. It was this older companion who, once wishing to tease Thérèse by pretending to suspect her sincerity, drew this reply from the grieved and astonished little one: "Marie, I never tell a lie."

30. We shall give later the letter which she wrote soon after entering the Carmel to Mother Sainte-Placide, her old Directress at the convent. See Appendix A.

31. *Histoire d'une Ame*, ch. v, p. 75.

32. *Cf. Histoire d'une Ame.* Poem: "What I have Loved."

6. Vocation to Carmel

1. *Histoire d'une Ame*, ch. v, p. 75.

2. *Ibid.*, ch. v, p. 75.

3. *Deposition of Sœur Françoise-Thérèse of the Visitation, at the Apostolic Process.*

4. *Deposition of Sœur Joséphine-de-la-Croix, O.S.B., at the Apostolic Process*, p. 140.

5. *Histoire d'une Ame*, ch. v, p. 87.

6. *Deposition of Sœur Geneviève de la Sainte-Face at the Apostolic Process*, p. 369.

7. *Histoire d'une Ame*, ch. v, p. 76.

8. *La Croix*, 1 September, 1887.

9. *Histoire d'une Ame*, ch. v, pp. 76–77.

10. *Deposition at the Process of the Ordinary*, p. 204. During Thérèse's journey to Rome, a pilgrim lent her annals of missionary nuns. After having accepted them with enthusiasm, she gave them to her sister saying: "I will not read them, for I have too ardent a desire to consecrate myself to works of zeal, and I wish to be hidden in a cloister so as to *give myself* more completely to the good God."—*The Spirit of Saint Thérèse de l' Enfant Jésus.*

11. Cant. viii 1.

12. *Histoire d'une Ame*, ch. v, p. 78.

13. *Ibid.*, ch. v, p. 81.

14. This scene has been reproduced by a skilful artist who has erected in this very place in the garden of Les Buissonnets a beautiful group in white marble.

15. The Carmelite Constitutions did not fix an age limit for the entrance of postulants; at that time they merely directed that profession must not be made before completion of the seventeenth year.

16. *Deposition of Rev. Mère Agnès de Jésus at the Apostolic Process*, p. 161.

17. See the *Vie de l'Abbé J. M. Reverony, Vicaire-Générale de Bayeux.* (Anonymous.) La Chapelle Montligeon, 1900.

18. *Histoire d'une Ame*, ch. v, pp. 89–91.

19. *Imit.*, b. iii, ch. xxiv, 3.

20. *Histoire d'une Ame*, ch. vi, p. 95.

21. *Ibid.*, ch. vi, p. 97.

22. *Ibid.*

23. *Ibid.*, ch. vi, p. 97.

24. *Ibid.*, ch. vi, p. 98.

25. Thérèse Martin, on arriving at Venice, was brought to the Hotel della Luna, where the author of this book, a member of the same pilgrimage, also stayed. Without knowing her, he probably passed her often in the corridors or on the stairs.

26. She, however, confided later to one of her sisters that the embalmed body of the saint was for her a not very attractive sight.

27. This hotel, situated in the Via Capo le Case, still exists, and a memorial tablet, bearing a representation of the saint (in relief), was set up there on May 17, 1925, the date of her canonization.

28. *Histoire d'une Ame*, ch. vi, p. 102.

29. The reproduction of Maderna's statue had not, at this time, been placed there.

30. *Histoire d'une Ame*, ch. vi, p. 103.

31. She makes exception for the Basilica of the Holy Cross of Jerusalem, where she enjoyed a privilege which she gladly acknowledges.

32. *Histoire d'une Ame*, ch. vi, p. 110.

33. The writer of these lines was introduced by Mgr. Germain as the author of a Manual on Thomistic Philosophy, and the Pope of the Encyclical *Æterni Patris* deigned to address to him the most encouraging congratulations.

34. *Histoire d'une Ame*, ch. vi, p. 109.

35. *Ibid.*, ch. vi, p. 111.

7. The Carmel of Lisieux

1. On this early period of its beginnings see *The Foundation of the Carmel of Lisieux, and its Foundress, Rev. Mère Geneviève de Sainte-Thérèse*, Central Office, Lisieux.

2. Léonie had returned home after a trial of the religious life in the Novitiate of the Poor Clares, which her delicate health made it impossible for her to continue.

3. *Histoire d'une Ame*, ch. vii, p. 116.

4. "I witnessed the departure of my little sister for the Carmel," declares Léonie, "and I was particularly struck by her strength of soul. She alone was calm. . . . I told her to reflect well before entering religion, adding that my experience had shown me that the life demands many sacrifices and should not be lightly undertaken. The reply she gave me and the expression of her countenance showed that she was ready for every sacrifice, that she would accept all with joy." *Deposition of Sœur Françoise-Thérèse at the Process of the Ordinary*, p. 211.

5. *Histoire d'une Ame*, ch. vii, p. 116.

6. *Deposition of Mère Agnès de Jésus at the Apostolic Process*, p. 162.

7. Deposition of Mère Marie des Anges at the Apostolic Process, p. 184. The deposition of Mère Agnès de Jésus on this subject is more explicit still. "At her entrance," she declares, "the Sisters, aware of her youthfulness, expected to see a child. Her presence, however, inspired them with respect; they admired her dignified yet modest bearing and her air of deep resolve. One of them, Sœur Saint-Jean de la Croix, who had been opposed to the entrance of so young a postulant, said to me some time afterwards: 'I thought that you would soon be sorry for all you had done to give us your little sister.' I said to myself, 'They will both be disappointed.' How deceived I was. Sœur Thérèse de l'Enfant Jésus

is extraordinary; she is an example to us in everything." *Summarium of 1914*, p. 679 (2831).

8. The motto of Carmel is "*Zelo zelatus sum pro Domino Deo Exercitum.*"

9. She was born at Caen, in 1834.

10. *Histoire d'une Ame*, ch. vii, p. 117.

11. One time Prior of the Premonstratensian Abbey of Mondaye (Calvados), and vice-provincial of his order in France, afterwards Abbot of Saint-Michel de Frigolet.

12. *Deposition of R. P. Godefroy Madelaine at the Apostolic Process*, p. 739.

13. She was a daughter of the de Chaumontel family, one of the oldest and most deeply Christian in Calvados, which had as its device: "*Douceur et discrétion.*" She died in 1924, aged seventy-nine years.

14. *Deposition at the Apostolic Process*, p. 215.

15. *Deposition at the Process of the Ordinary*, p. 665.

16. See the biography of *La Révérende Mère Geneviève de Saint-Thérèse*, p. 88. One day, for example, when M. Martin was in a condition which was most painful to the hearts of his daughters, Mère Geneviève, then an invalid, sent for Thérèse and her sisters, and calmed their fears by repeating to them a word which Our Saviour had said to her, and which was verified on the following day. *Ibid.*, p. 89.

17. "Several confessors and preachers of retreats," declares Mère Agnès de Jésus "succeeded in frightening her or paralysing her ardent desires. 'Father, I want to become a saint,' she said one day to R. P. Blino; 'I want to love the good God as much as St. Teresa did.' 'What pride and presumption!' he replied. 'Confine yourself to the correction of your faults; see that you offend the good God no more, make each day some little progress, and moderate your rash desires.' 'But, Father, I do not think that these desires can be called rash, since our Saviour has said, "Be ye perfect, as your heavenly Father is perfect. . . ."' But the priest was not convinced." *Summarium* of 1919, p. 248 (605).

18. In 1915, four years before his death, he had already given 1,015 Retreats.

19. *Histoire d'une Ame*, ch. vii, p. 119. The following are a few lines of the deposition made later by R. P. Pichon at the Process of Beatification: "It was easy to direct that child; the Holy Spirit led her, and I do not think that I ever had, either then or later on, to warn her against illusion. . . .

"What struck me during that retreat were the spiritual trials through which God made her pass. I had then a very strong impression that the good God willed to make her a great saint." *Summarium* of 1919 (362 and 364).

20. *Testimony of Sœur Geneviève de la Sainte-Face at the Apostolic Process*, p. 330.

21. *Testimony at the Apostolic Process*, p. 702.

22. Unpublished notes.

23. More particularly those of the latter.

24. *Histoire d'une Ame*, ch. vii, p. 146.

25. Letter published at the end of the *Histoire d'une Ame*, p. 370.

26. *Deposition of Mère Agnès de Jésus at the Process of the Ordinary*, p. 570. These acts of self-abnegation which unenlightened worldlings may judge with severity have been called "magnificent" by R. P. Auriault, S.J., one of the most authoritative witnesses who gave evidence on the Saint's doctrine at the Process of Beatification.

27. Letter of May 8, 1888, published at the end of the *Histoire d'une Ame*, p. 315.

28. This delay has been attributed to the opposition of M. Delatröette, who did not cease to put forward the extreme youthfulness of the postulant.

29. Letter published at the end of the *Histoire d'une Ame*, p. 342.

30. *Histoire d'une Ame*, ch. vii, p. 124.

31. A statue of the Child Jesus which stood then, as now, in the cloister, and of which Sœur Thérèse had the charge.

32. *Histoire d'une Ame*, ch. vii, p. 124.

33. Victor Hugo, *A. Villequier*.

34. *Histoire d'une Ame*, ch. vii, p. 126.

35. St. John of the Cross.

36. Letter of January, 1889.

37. Letter of February 28, 1889.

38. *Histoire d'une Ame*, ch. vii, p. 127.

39. *Ibid.*, ch. vii, p. 127.

40. *Ibid.*, ch. x, p. 193.

41. We shall give later in a special chapter the principal manifestations of these virtues which for Thérèse formed part of the "Little Way of Spiritual Childhood."

42. Regulations or Points of Observance taken from those which the first Spanish Nuns had introduced into France, p. 35.

8. Profession

1. Appendix to the *Histoire d'une Ame—Letters*, p. 344.

2. *Letters*, p. 352.

3. *Histoire d'une Ame*, ch. viii, p. 134.

4. This Vigil, customary in Carmel on the eve of profession, is continued till midnight, the sisters surrounding the bride elect.

5. Is. lxvi 12.

6. Philip. iv 7.

7. *Histoire d'une Ame*, ch. viii, p. 134.

8. *Letters*, p. 325.

9. *Ibid.*, p. 324.

10. Cf. *Summarium* of 1919, p. 549 (1517).

11. The Sovereign Pontiff, Benedict XV, has thrown full light on the fitness of the title Thérèse bore in religion. "By Divine ordinance," he says,

she was placed under the patronage of the Child Jesus who was pleased to recognize in this manner the solicitude she had already shown to honour the virtues of His childhood. But may we not say also that this title was for the fervent Carmelite a stimulus to entire abandonment to her Saviour? The Infant of Bethlehem revealed Himself to her as He lay in the arms of His Mother, docile and willing to allow Himself to be carried from Bethlehem to Egypt and from Egypt to Nazareth. Thérèse, in her turn, placed herself in the arms of the holy Carmelite rule, allowing herself to be guided in everything by religious obedience. The Divine Worker of Nazareth showed Himself always occupied with the work which His adopted father gave Him to do, always submissive to commands vested for Him with the authority of His Heavenly Father. Following His example, Thérèse carried out with eagerness every command of the Prioress and the novicemistress. She did all this in the most perfect manner without complaint or remark of any sort, having no longer, as it would seem, any will of her own. This perfect imitation of the virtues of the Saviour's childhood was so striking in the young Carmelite, that, if the name "of the Child Jesus" had not been providentially given her, the companions of her religious life would have bestowed it upon her. (*Discourse of His Holiness Pope Benedict XV, on the occasion of the Decree regarding heroicity of virtues,* August 14, 1921)

12. She often repeated the following prayer composed by herself: "O little Infant Jesus, my only treasure, I abandon myself to Thy Divine good pleasure. I desire no other joy than that of making Thee smile. Infuse into my soul Thy grace and the virtues of Thy childhood so that, on the day of my birth in heaven, the angels and saints may recognize me as Thy little spouse, Thérèse de l'Enfant Jésus." *Summarium* of 1919, p. 338, 871.

13. *Summarium* of 1919, p. 549, § 1521.

14. It was by her inspiration from beyond the tomb that her sister Céline painted from the Holy Shroud of Turin the striking picture of the Holy Face now known all the world over.

15. This incident gave her the idea of writing her version of the invitation sent out for the recent marriage. The following lines are worthy of note as bringing home to novices the inferiority of earthly unions compared to the honour of being the spouse of Jesus.

The Almighty God, Creator of heaven and earth, Sovereign Ruler of the world, and the ever glorious Virgin Mary, Queen of the celestial Court, desire to announce to you the spiritual nuptials of their august Son, Jesus, King of kings and Lord of lords, with little Thérèse Martin, now Queen and Princess of kingdoms given her as dowry by her Divine Spouse, namely the Childhood of Jesus and His Passion, from which come her noble titles "*Of the Child Jesus and of the Holy Face.*"

You could not be invited to the nuptial feast, which was celebrated on Mount Carmel on the 8 September, 1890—the Celestial Court alone being admitted—but you are requested to be present at the home-coming, which will take place to-morrow, the day of Eternity, when Jesus, the Son of God, will come in the clouds of heaven in all the glory of His majesty to judge the living and the dead.

> The hour being yet uncertain, you are invited to hold yourselves in readiness, and to watch. (*Histoire d'une Ame*, p. 135)

16. *Summarium* of 1919, p. 409, § 1035.

17. *Histoire d'une Ame*, ch. viii, p. 138.

18. *Summarium* of 1919, p. 559, § 1544.

19. On July 13, 1897, Sœur Thérèse de l'Enfant Jésus, then an invalid in the infirmary, stated exactly to Mère Agnès de Jésus the different offices she had fulfilled. "On my entrance," she said,

> I was put in the linen-room with Mother Sub-Prioress (Sœur Marie des Anges). I had also a staircase and dormitory to sweep. It was at this period that I went every evening at half-past four to weed the garden, a thing which displeased our Mother.
>
> After my reception, I was sent to the refectory until I was eighteen. I had charge of the sweeping, and of putting the water and beer on the tables. After the Forty Hours celebration, in 1891, I was assigned to the Sacristy. From the end of June in the following year, I was for two months without any office. It was during this time that I painted the fresco around the tabernacle in the oratory, and was third in the portress' office. At the end of those two months, I was appointed portress, and still to continue painting. In these two duties I was employed until the elections of 1896, after which I returned to the Sacristy. During this latter period, I fell ill, and it was then that I asked to be allowed to help Sister X with the mending.

Although she omits to mention it, the Saint had also, when refectorian, the duty of distributing the bread to the community.

20. She had been hastily laid out by the few sisters who were still able to attend the sick.

21. *Histoire d'une Ame*, ch. viii, p. 140.

22. Her hymn "Vivre d'Amour" was an exception. It was composed in its entirety at the one time, during her hour's adoration before the Blessed Sacrament. (See the *Summarium* of 1919, p. 599, § 1732.)

23. *Poésies de la Bienheureuse Thérèse de l'Enfant Jésus*, Preface, pp. vii and ix.

24. *Ibid.*, Preface, pp. vii and ix.

25. An attractive little book entitled *La Nielle des blés, ou Mission de sainte Thérèse de l'Enfant Jésus auprès des pécheurs*, expounds in several allegorical scenes the Saint's predilection for this "sister of tares" which symbolized in her eyes the souls of sinners. The book can be had from the Central Office of St. Thérèse de l'Enfant Jésus at Lisieux.

26. Letter of April 25, 1893.

27. Letter of August 13, 1892.

28. Sixteenth Letter (undated).

29. Céline had already made this vow privately before she entered the convent.

30. *Cf. Summarium* of 1919, p. 400, § 1013.

31. Letter of August 19, 1894.

9. Interior Life at the Carmel

1. Letter to Marie Guérin, 1894.

2. Letter to Céline, July 6, 1893.

3. *Cf.* I Cor. xiii.

4. Cited in *The Spirit of St. Thérèse de l'Enfant Jésus according to Her Writings and the Testimony of Eye-Witnesses*, p. 21. We have frequently, in writing this and the following chapters, consulted this excellent work composed from the most reliable sources.

5. *Histoire d'une Ame*, ch. ix, p. 174.

6. *Ibid.*, ch. ix, p. 161.

7. Letter to Mère Agnès de Jésus, February, 1884.

8. *Adimpleo ea quae desunt passionum Christi in carne mea* (Col. i 24).

9. *Sine sanguinis effusione non fit remissio* (Heb. ix 22).

10. *Cf. Summarium* of 1919, p. 623, § 1822.

11. *Ibid.*, p. 203, § 702.

12. *Ibid.*, p. 715, § 2166.

13. *Ibid.*, p. 509, § 1368.

14. *Ibid.*, p. 624, §§ 1828–1829.

15. The Carmel of Hanoi had been founded by that of Saigon, which was itself founded from Lisieux.

16. Letter to Mère Agnès de Jésus, January, 1889.

17. Hymn entitled: *Why I love thee, Mary.* She had expressed the same thought in that other hymn *Vivre d' Amour*:

> To live Love's life means gifts unceasingly—
> No thought of recompense below—
> Unreckoning I give, urged by the certainty
> That lovers' hearts no paltry counting know.

18. *Summarium* of 1919, p. 577, § 1627.

19. *Histoire d'une Ame*, chap. ix, p. 160.

20. Poem entitled: *My Arms.*

21. *Histoire d'une Ame*, chap. xi, p. 218.

22. *Spirit of St Thérèse de l'Enfant Jésus*, p. 43.

23. *Summarium* of 1919, p. 512, § 1578.

24. Letter to Mère Agnès de Jésus, January, 1889.

25. Cited in *The Spirit of St. Thérèse de l'Enfant Jésus*, p. 49.

26. Deposition of Sœur Geneviève de la Sainte Face, *Summarium* of 1919, p. 334, § 852.

27. *Summarium* of 1919, p. 496, §§ 1339 and 1341.

28. *Ibid.*, p. 577, § 1626.

29. We shall refer later on to her loving obedience towards superiors, whom she considered as the lieutenants of God.

30. *Cf. Summarium* of 1919, p. 563, § 1556.

31. *Histoire d'une Ame*, ch. v, p. 80.

32. *Summarium* of 1919, p. 490, § 1397.

33. *Ibid.*, p. 490, § 1328.

10. Charity of St. Thérèse

1. *Summarium* of 1919, p. 497, § 1342.
2. *Ibid.*, p. 604, § 1754.
3. *Ibid.*, p. 498, § 1345.
4. It must be said in the interest of truth that, on Thérèse's part, the intimacy proceeded solely from compassionate charity towards this Sister who was by no means gifted.
5. Ps. xxxiii 6.
6. Ps. cxi 4.
7. Prov. xviii 19. Extract from *l'Histoire d'une Ame*, ch. x, p. 180.
8. *Summarium* of 1919, p. 565, § 1562.
9. *Ibid.*, p. 501, § 1348.
10. *Histoire d'une Ame*, ch. x, p. 195.
11. Beads sometimes used for counting acts of virtue.
12. *Summarium* of 1919, p. 373, § 951.
13. *Histoire d'une Ame*, ch. x, p. 183.
14. *Ibid.*
15. Book III, ch. v, 5, 7.
16. *Summarium* of 1919, p. 381, § 972.
17. *Conseils et Souvenirs* (Appendix to the *Histoire d'une Ame*), p. 298.
18. Cited in *l'Esprit de Ste Thérèse de l'Enfant Jésus*, p. 98.
19. *Ibid.*, p. 99.
20. *Conseils et Souvenirs*, p. 298.
21. *Histoire d'une Ame*, ch. x, p. 184.
22. She wished the truth for the novices under her charge but still more for herself. She was particularly glad when some postulant or novice addressed a reproach to her. She saw in it a salutary corrective to the praise which came from others.

"At times," she writes,

> I long to hear some other thing than praise; my soul tires of food too sweet. Then Jesus provides that a wholesome little salad shall be served to me, highly spiced and with plenty of vinegar; nothing is wanting except oil, but its absence adds a new savour. This salad is presented to me by the novices just when I least expect it. God withdraws the veil which hides my imperfections from them, and my dear little Sisters, seeing the reality, no longer find me quite to their taste. With a simplicity that charms me, they tell me of the struggles I cost them, and what, in me, they find displeasing. In fine, they are as unrestrained as if it were question of some one else, for they know that by so acting they give me great pleasure.
>
> It is indeed more than a pleasure, it is a delicious feast which fills my soul with joy. How can anything so displeasing to nature give such happiness? Without the experience, I could not believe it possible.
>
> One day, when I had an ardent desire for humiliation, a young postulant happened so fully to satisfy my longing that the thought of Semei reproaching David came to mind, and to myself I repeated with

> the holy king: "Yes, it is indeed the Lord who has bidden him to say all these things" (*Cf.* II Reg. xvi, 10).
>
> Thus does the good God take care of me. He cannot always offer me the strength-giving bread of exterior humiliation; but from time to time He permits me to eat the *crumbs that fall from the table of the children.* Oh, how great is His mercy! (*Histoire d'une Ame*, ch. x, p. 190)

23. *Conseils et Souvenirs*, p. 267.
24. A stitch of sewing.
25. *Conseils et Souvenirs*, p. 275.
26. *Ibid.*, p. 280.
27. *Ibid.*, p. 280.
28. *Ibid.*, p. 284.
29. Cited in the *l'Esprit de Ste Thérèse de l'Enfant Jésus*, p. 92.
30. *Conseils et Souvenirs*, p. 291.
31. *Ibid.*, p. 298.
32. Appendix to the *Histoire d'une Ame*, p. 596: After a minute examination of the several photographic negatives preserved in the archives of the Lisieux Carmel, the Ecclesiastical Tribunal set up by Mgr. Lemonnier to pronounce on the exactitude of these photographs of Sœur Thérèse de l'Enfant Jésus, formulated in 1915 the following decision:

> The portrait *en buste*, the frontispiece of the large edition of the *Histoire d'une Ame*, presents the best idea of the expression of St. Thérèse de l'Enfant Jésus, by a most conscientious and very carefully studied synthesis of the different photographs of the saint.

33. Père Roulland was not the first missionary, in the order of time, who was given as spiritual brother to Thérèse. His correspondence with her was less frequent, but no less edifying than that of R. P. Belliére who was the first recommended to her prayers. We shall have to speak of him more at length later on. For this reason, we give first place to the facts relating to R. P. Roulland.
34. Letter of November 1, 1896.
35. *Summarium* of 1919, p. 617, § 1918.
36. Letters of July 30, 1896, and of March 19, 1897.
37. *Summarium* of 1919, p. 648, § 1920.
38. Letter of July 14, 1897.
39. Letter of August 14, 1897.
40. Père Roulland spent twelve years in China, and was then recalled to the Foreign Missions' Seminary to take up the office of Procurator to the Society. He has lately been sent with some companions to Dormans (Marne) to serve the "Souvenir" chapel built in memory of the battle of the Marne.
41. Abbé Belliére had lost his mother a few days after his birth, but he always gave his aunt, Mme Barthelemy, the title of "mother," in affectionate recognition of the care he had received from her.
42. Letter cited in the Appendix to *l'Histoire d'une Ame*, p. 364.
43. *Ibid.*, p. 365.

44. Partly unpublished letter, February 24, 1897.
45. *Ibid.*, June 21, 1897.
46. Letter, June 21, 1897.
47. *Summarium* of 1919, p. 562, § 1553.
48. 1 Cor. xiii 13.
49. Discourse of His Holiness Pope Pius XI on the occasion of the promulgation of the Decree "De Tuto," March 19, 1925.
50. *Sine dolore, non vivitur in amore. Imit.*, L. iii, ch. v.

11. Suffering's Rôle in the Providence of God

1. *Life and the Christian Virtues*, t. II, p. 312.
2. Letter to Sœur Agnès de Jésus, 1887.
3. *l'Esprit de Sainte Thérèse de l'Enfant Jésus*, p. 107.
4. *Ibid.*, p. 108.
5. *Histoire d'une Ame*, ch. ii, p. 21.
6. Letter of July 14, 1889.
7. *Histoire d'une Ame*, ch. xii, p. 233.
8. *Cf. Summarium* of 1919, p. 402, § 1018.
9. *Ibid.*, p. 394, § 1001.
10. *Ibid.*, p. 398, § 1007.
11. *Ibid.*, p. 632, §§ 1869, 1870.
12. *Ibid.*, p. 400, § 1013.
13. Her wish was expressed in these heroic words.
14. *Cf. Summarium* of 1919, p. 480, § 1297.
15. *Ibid.*, p. 678, § 2042.
16. *Ibid.*, p. 698, § 2043.
17. *Ibid.*, p. 518, § 1393.
18. *Ibid.*, p. 724, § 1393.
19. *Ibid.*, p. 588, § 1677.
20. Corporal suffering was not, besides, her principal means of renunciation and redemption. She even considered that certain authors, in their lives of saints, have insisted too much on their extraordinary penances as the proof and the almost indispensable character of sanctity. "This is a cause of trouble to souls," she says. "Many imagine that to please God they must give themselves over absolutely to exaggerated practices of mortification. Then the demon deceives them, and leads them into certain dangerous illusions such as preoccupation about self, pride, etc."

One day during the last year of her life, while walking in the garden at recreation time, Thérèse broached this subject to Mère Agnès de Jésus, and said:

> I have been struck by a passage in the life of Blessed Henry Suso concerning bodily penances. He had practised frightful penances, which had ruined his health, when an angel appeared and told him to desist, adding: "You have till now fought only like an ordinary soldier; I am going to make you a knight." And he made the Saint understand the superiority of spiritual combat over mortifications of the flesh. "Well,

> Mother," concluded Sœur Thérèse, "the good God has not willed that I should fight like a common soldier; I received at once a knight's armour, and I set out to war against myself in the spiritual domain by renunciation and little hidden sacrifices. I have found peace and humility in this obscure combat where nature has no place."

21. Discourse on the occasion of the promulgation of the Decree *di Tute* (towards the end).

22. *De la vie et des vertues chrétiennes*, t. ii, p. 327.

23. To this explanation of Thérèse's attraction for suffering, one of the authors who has written best concerning her has added others of equal importance. "Love," he says,

> carries within it the germ of suffering, and ordinarily this germ develops with it. It is impossible to love God ardently without suffering. It is very painful, first of all, to see Him so little loved and so greatly offended. It is a sorrow, moreover, to be unable to love Him ourselves as we desire. We suffer from the narrowness and incapacity of our hearts, which do not suffice to contain the floods of tenderness that come from the Heart of God in almost overwhelming torrents.
>
> There is another reason, too, why every soul that loves Jesus ardently, also loves suffering, and accepts sorrow with joy. It is because she finds in every cross that comes, an efficacious means of "purchasing souls for Him." To love Jesus does not satisfy her devotion; she wishes at all costs to gain other souls that will love Him eternally. She wishes to save sinners for Him. But sinners are not saved except by the application to them of the Saviour's infinite merits. Only grace can convert them, and grace, the fruit of the bloody sacrifice of Calvary, often reaches their souls by a mysterious channel formed and maintained by those voluntary immolations by which pure souls prolong the sacrifice of the Cross in the mystical body of Christ. Those whom Christ has redeemed by His death are saved by suffering.
>
> For all these reasons, then, is suffering the inseparable companion of love. (G. Martin, *La "petite voie" d'enfance spirituelle*, pp. 79–80)

12. The "Little Way of Spiritual Childhood"

1. Prov. IX 4.

2. Isaias lxvi 13.

3. *Cf.* Ps. lxx 18. *Histoire d'une Ame*, ch. ix, pp. 153–154.

4. Matt. xviii 3.

5. Isaias xliii 25.

6. Sœur Thérèse has herself explained what she understands by this littleness so pleasing to God. "To be little," she says, "means not to attribute to self the virtues that one practices, believing oneself capable of anything; it means recognizing that the good God places this treasure of virtue in the hand of His little child to be used by him when he has need of it; but always it is God's treasure. In fine, it means not being discouraged about our faults, for children fall often, but are too small to do themselves much harm." Cited in the *Summarium* of 1919, p. 260.

7. *Histoire d'une Ame*, ch. ix, p. 154.

8. Sixth letter to Sœur Marie du Sacré-Cœur.

9. *Spirit of St. Thérèse de l'Enfant Jésus.* She has expressed the same thought in the *Histoire d'une Ame:* "Because I was little and weak, Jesus gently stooped down to me, and instructed me in the secrets of His love" (p. 81).

10. *Conseils et Souvenirs.*

11. *My Song of To-day.*

12. *Histoire d'une Ame,* ch. x.

13. Sixth letter to Sœur Marie du Sacré-Cœur.

14. *Histoire d'une Ame,* ch. xii, p. 246.

15. Sixth letter to the missionaries.

16. Fifth letter to the missionaries.

17. *Histoire d'une Ame,* ch. xii, p. 236.

18. *Ibid.,* p. 237.

19. *Ibid.,* ch. iv, p. 55.

20. *Ibid.,* ch. xi, p. 209.

21. G. Martin, *La "petite voie" d'enfance spirituelle,* p. 53.

22. Cant., v. 2.

23. G. Martin, *op. cit., cf.* p. 69. The theory of "the little way" of spiritual childhood that we have just given has been taken in part from this excellent work, the best undoubtedly that has been written up to the present on the ascetical doctrine of St. Thérèse de l'Enfant Jésus.

24. St. Thérèse de l'Enfant Jésus has had the singular privilege of presenting holiness under its truly Evangelical aspect, in divesting it of all the complications with which the human mind had, in the course of centuries, enveloped it. Referring to this, a learned theologian has lately said: "St. Thérèse de l'Enfant Jésus has cleared the way to heaven." And an eminent prince of the Church: "What I admire in this little saint is her charming simplicity. She has excluded mathematics from our relations with God."

25. Matt. xviii 3.

26. Mark x 15.

27. Discourse of His Holiness Pope Benedict XV on the occasion of Promulgation of the Decree regarding the heroicity of her virtues, August 14, 1921.

His Holiness Pius XI was later to speak with no less praise of the "little way" in his homily at the canonization ceremony on May 17, 1925.

> We to-day conceive the hope of seeing spring up in the souls of Christ's faithful a holy eagerness to acquire this *evangelical childhood,* which consists in feeling and acting under the empire of virtue as a child feels and acts in the natural order.
>
> If this way of spiritual childhood became general, who does not see how easily that reform of human society would take place which we set before us in the early days of our Pontificate and in promulgating this solemn Jubilee?

We offer, then, as our own this prayer of the new saint, Thérèse de l'Enfant Jésus, with which she terminates her precious Autobiography: "O Jesus, we beseech Thee to cast Thy divine eyes upon a great number of little souls, and to choose out of this world a legion of little victims worthy of Thy love."

13. The Virtues of the "Little Way" in Practice

1. *Histoire d'une Ame*, ch. ix, p. 154.
2. *Summarium* of 1919, p. 309, § 758.
3. *Ibid.*, p. 413, § 1043.
4. Ch. ix, p. 152.
5. *Summarium* of 1919, p. 412, § 1042.
6. Unpublished letter of April 25, 1897.
7. *Summarium* of 1919, p. 309, § 759.
8. *Ibid.*, p. 310, § 760.
9. *Ibid.*, p. 573, § 1610.
10. Verlaine.
11. *Summarium* of 1919, p. 265, § 630.
12. Conversation with Céline, July 12, 1897.
13. *Summarium* of 1919, p. 610, §§ 1773, 1774.
14. *Histoire d'une Ame*, ch. xi, p. 208.
15. Louis Théolier, *Thérèse de l'Enfant Jésus: Meditation on the Grandeur of Spiritual Childhood*, Religious Studies (May 5, 1923).
16. *Summarium* of 1919, pp. 594–595, §§ 1708–1713.
17. *Ibid.*, p. 594, § 1706.
18. *Ibid.*, p. 493, § 1333.
19. *Ibid.*, p. 528, § 1424.
20. *Summarium* of 1919, p. 596, § 1716.
21. I Cor. xii 31.
22. *Histoire d'une Ame*, ch. xi, p. 213 and the following.
23. John xvi, 23.
24. *Cf.* Ps. lxxxix 4.
25. *Cf.* Cant, iv 6.
26. *Summarium* of 1919, p. 552, § 1526.
27. The saint had originally written "*Infinite* are the desires that I feel within my heart." This word seemed, in her opinion, best to express the vehemence of her aspirations. On the advice of R. P. Lemonnier, she substituted the adjective "*Immense*," which is theologically more exact.
28. *La "pelite voie" d'enfance spiritual*, p. 84.
29. *Summarium* of 1919, p. 260, 630.
30. *Histoire d'une Ame*, ch. xii, p. 247.
31. *Discourse for the Approbation of Miracles*, February 11, 1923.
32. The very day she received this grace, the saint confided it to Mère Agnès de Jésus, then Prioress. The latter did not appear to pay any special attention to her communication, and Thérèse did not revert to it again. She did not even mention it in her manuscript, she kept absolute silence

on the subject. Only on July 7, 1897, did Mère Agnès de Jésus question her anew on the occurrence and obtain her reply as quoted above.

She humbly added: "I then understand what the saints have said concerning those states which they experienced so often. As for me, I have had the experience but once, and that for an instant only; I then fell back immediately into my habitual aridity."

33. *Histoire d'une Ame*, ch. xii, p. 228.

14. Beginning of Her Illness

1. Was it not in a dream that St. Joseph received the command to fly into Egypt in order to shelter the Divine Infant and His Mother from the fury of Herod, and do we not find in Holy Scripture many instances of the same kind?

2. This great religious had been one of the companions of St. Teresa of Avila. Having been brought to France by Père de Bérulle, she established there St. Teresa's reform of the Order, and died in the odour of sanctity in 1621. Pope Leo XIII signed the decree for the introduction of her Cause of Beatification.

Sœur Thérèse de l'Enfant Jésus avows that, before this dream, her thoughts rarely turned on the Venerable Mother who so long ago had gone from our world.

3. *Histoire d'une Ame*, ch. xii, p. 211.

4. "From my childhood, I had a strong presentiment that I should die young. The good God has always made me desire what He willed to give me."—*Thérèse's words as recorded by Rev. Mère Agnès de Jésus during the saint's last illness* (*Summarium* of 1919, p. 889, § 2574).

5. *Histoire d'une Ame*, ch. ix, pp. 156, etc.

6. Letter of Cardinal Vico, May 14, 1923.

7. Extract from the brief read by the Secretary of Briefs to the Princes of the Church during the canonization ceremony.

8. The above appreciation is quoted by M. A. des Rotours in *La Bienheureuse Thérèse de l'Enfant Jésus*, p. 150. M. Bremond's study of Thérèse to which this author refers appeared in *l'Inquiétude religieuse*, 2nd series, 1909.

9. In France, on the decease of each Carmelite, the Mother Prioress sends to all the monasteries of the Order a biographical notice, oftentimes of some length, on the deceased nun.

10. According to *Histoire d'une Ame*, ch. xii, p. 235, etc.

11. These words as well as the preceding quotations are to be found in the *Summarium* of 1919, p. 868, etc.

12. *Summarium* of 1919, pp. 874–875.

13. Citations from the *Summarium* of 1919, beginning with p. 874; also from *Histoire d'une Ame*, ch. xii.

14. Partly unpublished letter.

15. Letter published in part in the *Histoire d'une Ame*, p. 370.

16. *Summarium* of 1919, p. 893, § 2585.

17. *Ibid.*, p. 951, § 2780.

18. See this letter in the Appendix.

19. *Summarium* of 1919, p. 961.

20. *Ibid.*, p. 756, § 2294.

21. Letter published in part in the *Histoire d'une Ame*, p. 371.

22. On August 14, it is true, she again addressed a letter to the Abbé Bellière to emphasize some words in her preceding counsels.

23. Nevertheless, keen anguish was the little saint's portion until the end. *Histoire d'une Ame*, ch. xii, p. 239.

24. *Summarium* of 1919, p. 913, § 2651.

25. *Ibid.*, p. 916.

26. *Histoire d'une Ame*, ch. xii, p. 250.

27. According to the *Histoire d'une Ame*, ch. xii, p. 244.

28. *Summarium* of 1919, p. 925.

29. In September, 1910, one of these petals cured of cancer on the tongue an old man named Ferdinand Aubry, a dependent of the Little Sisters of the Poor in Lisieux.

30. *Summarium* of 1919, p. 865, § 2488.

31. *Ibid.*, p. 865, § 2488.

32. *Ibid.*, p. 928.

33. *Ibid.*, p. 843, § 2427.

34. On this day, by reason of her extreme weakness and terrible difficulty in breathing, the veil which the Carmelites always keep lowered in such cases was raised.

35. *Summarium* of 1919, p. 854, § 2458.

36. *Cf.* Sap. vi 7.

37. *Cf.* Ps. lxxv 10.

38. *Summarium* of 1919, p. 929.

39. *Cf.* Cant. ii 12.

40. Her companions say, "For a space sufficient to recite a *Credo*."

41. This palm was found intact in the coffin thirteen years later at the time of her first exhumation (1910).

42. "I will spend my heaven in doing good upon earth."

15. First Phases of Her Glorification

1. *Summarium* of 1919, p. 994, § 2854.

2. It was Mère Agnès de Jésus who, following the counsel given her by the saint, induced Mère Marie de Gonzague to have the *Histoire d'une Ame* printed. The Prioress got the manuscript revised by Rme Père Godefroy Madelaine, then Prior of the Premonstratensians of Mondaye. This religious presented it to Mgr Hugonin for his *Imprimatur*, and drew up the letter of approbation.

Mère Marie de Gonzague died on December 17, 1904, in sentiments of the most profound humility.

3. The little saint's inspiration will be recognized in the following verses taken from a prayer where Mère Marie-Ange gives in poetic language the history of her vocation:

With twenty summers past, the world's ways I knew;
Alas! how disenchanted was my heart;
Did nectar pure and fresh as waves my soul renew?
No, nought but burning poison was my part.

. . . .

A thousand blessings on thee, little queen,
For thou hast brought me to this cloister blest;
Beyond the world's every prize I love this scene
Of striving, where *in song* I wish to die at last.

4. She had previously explained these words by saying that she would spend her heaven working in the interest of the Saint's cause. She died on November 11, 1909.

5. *Mère Isabelle du Sacré-Cœur*, p. 24. Work published by the Carmel.

6. On this subject she composed a poem of between five and six hundred verses.

7. Her life has been sketched in a little pamphlet entitled *Mère Thérèse de l'Eucharistie* (Carmel of Lisieux).

8. *Summarium* of 1919, p. 752, § 2289.

9. *Ibid.*, p. 1032, § 2928.

Père Pichon had asked of God through the intercession of His "little Thérèse," that he might celebrate Holy Mass to the last day of his life, and he died just when going to the Altar, November 15, 1919, in his seventy-seventh year.

Desiring to belong to the "Legion of Victims of Merciful Love" he had made the saint's act of oblation.

10. *Summarium* of 1919, p. 1022, § 2504.

11. *Ibid.*, p. 989, § 2844.

12. Cited in the *Shower of Roses* for the year 1912, p. 107.

13. Amongst the first hundreds of cures reported by lay persons may be mentioned that of Mme Debossu of Marnes-le-Coquette (Seine-et-Oise) who was suffering from a fibrous tumour in her left side, and from peritonitis. She recovered her health suddenly in September, 1901, on the last day of a novena.

Another, worthy of note is the cure of a Jesuit lay-brother in Cracow suffering from a serious malady of the liver. This miracle took place in March, 1906.

Two years later, on May 26, 1908, the instantaneous cure was announced of a little blind child of four years to whom the saint appeared.

We recommend to our readers who desire fuller details of the saint's influence at this period the volumes entitled *Showers of Roses*, published by the Carmel of Lisieux.

14. Mgr. de Teil had become acquainted with the Carmel of Lisieux in the lifetime of the saint, when he gave a very interesting discourse

there on the venerable Carmelites of Compiègne, and insistently asked whether the nuns had not heard accounts of miracles obtained through their intercession. On coming away from the parlour, Sœur Thérèse de l'Enfant Jésus made the following remark: "How touching is the zeal of this postulator! How glad one would be to have miracles to make known to him!"

In the beginning of the year 1909, he was appointed by Mgr. Lemonnier and the Carmel to forward the Cause of the Servant of God. After labouring for this end during thirteen years, with indefatigable ardour and prudence, he died at Paris on May 20, 1922, holding in his hand the picture of Sœur Thérèse de l'Enfant Jésus.

15. For further details of this striking and important miracle, see *Shower of Roses* (extract from vols. i and ii, p. 110).

16. These volumes are on sale at the Central Office of Lisieux. The first recorded facts go back to the year 1902. Vol. vii, which has just appeared, records the miracles obtained through the saint's intercession during the interval between her Beatification and Canonization.

17. Matt. iv 23.

18. Cited by Abbé Fernessolle: *La Bienheureuse Thérèse de l'Enfant Jésus*, p. 84.

19. Apart from the circulation of the *Histoire*, the enormous number of 30,388,000 pictures and 17,507,000 relic-sachets and relic-pictures have been distributed within the same period.

20. *Shower of Roses*, extract from Volumes I and II, p. 118.

21. Extract from a letter addressed to *The Universe* (London).

22. See *Shower of Roses*, t. IV, Preface, p. 8.

23. Louis Théolier. To this appreciation it will not be out of place to add the following lines written in a very worldly publication, *Le Journal*, by a man little inclined to credulity in supernatural matters, Maurice de Waleffe:

> What was there extraordinary about the saint of Lisieux? Her short and uneventful life was that of a lily which opens at morn and silently fades at eve.
>
> What has she done? Very little. She has written a book, or rather she has committed to paper some intimate confidences which the Carmel put together in a volume published after her death under the title of the *Histoire d'une Ame.* And this soul has been found so beautiful, so gentle, so adorable, that the world has fallen on its knees. The book was immediately translated into every language. Millions of the faithful have wept on reading it. It is not even necessary to be a believer to realize that you are in the presence of one who has attained to the very summit of moral perfection, and who is of so rare a beauty and nobility of soul as to bring tears to the eyes. I do not hide the fact that coming to Lisieux as a sceptic, I read this book, and I in my turn was thrilled with tender admiration. Here we have the real miracle. There are souls so powerful that they literally create that which they desire. We cannot come near them without being carried along by the force of their wings.

Thus the ardent dream of a child has triumphed over the dull realities of earth. "I will spend my heaven in doing good upon earth," she repeated in her agony. Whether we believe this or treat it sceptically, we cannot deny that these ex-votos, these gifts, these pilgrimages, mean . . . authentic cures of suffering, or other help received. The holocaust of the little martyr has not then been an illusion. And who knows but that the supreme secret of peace of heart, sought with pride of intellect by religions and philosophies, may be found in her doctrine of love for God and men "as a little child would love them"!

France has just given to the world the purest soul that has lived since St Francis of Assisi (quoted in the *Annales de sainte Thérèse de Lisieux* of July 1, 1925).

24. A name given to French soldiers.

25. See *Interventions de Sœur Thérèse de l'Enfant Jésus pendant la guerre*, Preface.

26. *Ibid.*, p. 188.

27. In the journal *La Croix* of February 19 and 21, 1925.

28. For example, Auguste Cousinard who has sent an account to the Carmel of an apparition with which he was favoured. *Interventions*, etc., p. 3.

29. Cited in the *Journal des Pèlerins*, etc., of October 5 to 18, 1924.

30. Discourse of His Holiness Pope Pius XI on the occasion of the Approbation of her miracles, February 11, 1923. He had described Sœur Thérèse on the same day as an "exquisitely fine miniature of perfect holiness." He called her, besides, "his dear star," a "miracle of virtues and a prodigy of miracles."

31. Discourse of His Holiness Pius XI on the promulgation of the Decree *de tuto*, March 19, 1923.

32. *La Bienheureuse Thérèse de l'Enfant Jésus: sa béatification*, p. 71. *Album of the Fêtes*, published by the Carmel of Lisieux.

33. Psalm 1 19.

34. Prayer from the Mass of Blessed Thérèse.

35. *La Bienheureuse Thérèse de l'Enfant Jésus: sa béatification*, p. 110.

36. Cited in *La Bienheureuse Thérèse de l'Enfant Jésus: sa béatification*, p. 140.

37. Expression of H. H. Pius XI.

Appendix A: Unpublished Letters

1. She had come back from a holiday in Trouville with the Guérin family.

2. The Saint here alludes to the first attack of her father's illness.

3. Her father's sad illness.

4. At the *château de la Musse.*

5. Her cousin Jeanne Guérin, who had married Dr. la Néele.

6. Dr. la Néele.

7. The saint herself underlined the repetitions penned in the above letter.

8. This letter was written in pencil.

9. Her cousin Marie Guérin.

10. To this letter M. Guérin wrote the reply quoted on pages 318–319.

11. This letter was written in reply to a circular sent by the nun to all the Children of Mary amongst her past pupils announcing to them the fête of the twenty-fifth anniversary of the Association's commencement.

Appendix B: Documentary Evidence

1. Copied from the autograph of the original record.

2. The servant who carried the child.

3. On April 4, 1818 (the space for the date is left blank in the original, but it is given in the State records).

4. Read Fanie instead of Françoise.

5. Read Nay.

6. As several proper names are illegible on the parish register, reference had to be made to the civil records.

7. The correct spelling of this name is Macé.

8. Usually called Zélie.

9. Read Fanie.

10. The marriage was celebrated at midnight without any parade. Only the members of the family living at Alençon and the witnesses were present. The civil formalities had been gone through on the evening of July 12.

11. Mme Martin, in this case, used the form *Azélie*, as is shown by the official document. All her letters are signed *Zélie.*

12. Knight of the Orders of St. Louis and St. Ferdinand of Spain.

Index

A

B

C

N

P

R

S

V

W

August Pierre Laveille (1856–1928), the vicar-general of Mieux, was commissioned by the Mother Prioress of the Carmel of Lisieux, St. Thérèse's biological sister Pauline, to write the official biography of the Little Flower. Msgr. Laveille also wrote several other popular biographies, including those of Belgian Cardinal Désiré Mercier and St. Louis de Montfort.

Michael Fitzsimons, O.M.I.,was appointed provincial of the Oblate Anglo-Irish Province of the Missionary Oblates of Mary Immaculate in June 1951. He translated August Pierre Laveille's work on St. Thérèse of Lisieux into English in 1928.

Susan Muto, executive director of the Epiphany Association, is a renowned speaker, author, teacher, and dean of the Epiphany Academy of Formative Spirituality.

Founded in 1865, Ave Maria Press, a ministry of the Congregation of Holy Cross, is a Catholic publishing company that serves the spiritual and formative needs of the Church and its schools, institutions, and ministers; Christian individuals and families; and others seeking spiritual nourishment.

For a complete listing of titles from

Ave Maria Press

Sorin Books

Forest of Peace

Christian Classics

visit www.avemariapress.com